CRIME, RISK AND INSECURITY

Just what is the 'fear of crime' and how does it impact upon the lives of the citizens of late modern societies? These are topical questions in an era when politicians compete to diagnose and respond to our worries, when newspapers are sold on the hook of our anxieties and when fortunes are made promoting the latest security technology for the home and the high street. How can the social sciences contribute to this part of the self-understanding of our times?

This book presents new empirical and conceptual work on the questions of fear, anxiety, risk and trust – both as problems of everyday living and as key themes in the culture and politics of contemporary western societies. The volume includes contributions from distinguished social researchers from Britain, the United States, Germany and Italy and will be of interest to academics and students in the areas of criminology and sociology.

Tim Hope and **Richard Sparks** are both Professors in Criminology at the Department of Criminology, Keele University.

CRIME, RISK AND INSECURITY

Law and order in everyday life and political discourse

*Edited by Tim Hope
and Richard Sparks*

London and New York

First published 2000
by Routledge
11 New Fetter Lane, London EC4P 4EE

Simultaneously published in the USA and Canada
by Routledge
29 West 35th Street, New York, NY 10001

Routledge is an imprint of the Taylor & Francis Group

Typeset in Baskerville by Taylor & Francis Books Ltd
Printed and bound in Great Britain by Clays Ltd, St Ives plc

British Library Cataloguing in Publication Data
A catalogue record for this book is available from the British Library

Library of Congress Cataloging in Publication Data
Crime, risk and insecurity: law and order in everyday life and political discourse /
edited by Tim Hope and Richard Sparks.
p. cm.
Includes bibliographical references and index.
1. Fear of crime. 2. Security (Psychology) 3. Victims of crimes. I. Sparks, Richard,
1961– II. Hope, Tim.
HV6250.25 .C747 2000
362.88–dc21
00–042473

ISBN 0–415–24343–2 (hbk)
ISBN 0–415–24344–0 (pbk)

CONTENTS

CONTENTS

ILLUSTRATIONS

Tables

Figures

CONTRIBUTORS

Jessica Allen was formerly a researcher at the London School of Economics and is at present a researcher and evaluator at the American Museum of Natural History, New York.

Uwe Ewald works in the Berlin Criminological Research Centre (*Kriminologische Forschungsstelle Berlin*), affiliated to Humboldt University.

Evi Girling is Lecturer in Criminology, Keele University.

Wendy Hollway is Professor of Psychology, The Open University.

Tim Hope is Professor of Criminology, Keele University, and was formerly Director of the ESRC Crime and Social Order Research Programme.

Tony Jefferson is Professor of Criminology, Keele University.

Sonia Livingstone is Professor of Social Psychology, London School of Economics.

Ian Loader is Senior Lecturer in Criminology, Keele University.

Dario Melossi is Professor in the Faculty of Law, University of Bologna and Visiting Professor in Community Safety, Keele University.

Robert Reiner is Professor of Law, London School of Economics.

Theodore Sasson is Associate Professor in the Department of Sociology, Middlebury College, Vermont, USA.

Rossella Selmini is a public servant working for the *Regione Emilia-Romagna*, where she is responsible for research and documentation on the *Citta Sicure* project. She also teaches criminology in the Faculty of Law, University of Bologna.

Richard Sparks is Professor of Criminology, Keele University.

Elizabeth Stanko is Professor of Sociology, Royal Holloway and Bedford New College, University of London, and Director of the ESRC Violence Research Programme.

Kevin Stenson is Professor of Criminology in the Faculty of Applied Social Studies and Humanities, Buckinghamshire Chilterns University College, and Director of the Social Policy Research Group.

Sandra Walklate is Professor of Sociology at Manchester Metropolitan University.

Lucia Zedner is Reader in Criminal Justice, University of Oxford and Fellow in Law, Corpus Christi College Oxford. She is a member of the Oxford Centre for Criminological Research.

ACKNOWLEDGEMENTS

Several of the essays in this volume originated in research projects supported by the Economic and Social Research Council (ESRC) under its Crime and Social Order Research Programme. Tim Hope was Director of the Programme, and the papers here by Walklate, Jefferson and Hollway, Loader *et al.*, Reiner *et al.* and Zedner all report work conducted under its auspices. Richard Sparks received further support under the ESRC's Risk and Human Behaviour Research Programme and this was instrumental in the development of the conceptual framework outlined in his paper. The Crime and Social Order Programme also provided financial support for a small symposium held at Lincoln College, Oxford, in January 1998 at which early drafts of several of the papers included here were presented.

INTRODUCTION

Risk, insecurity and the politics of law and order

Tim Hope and Richard Sparks

The risks that crime poses to the security and well-being of citizens, and responses to crime-risk by states, firms, individuals and social movements, are among the most salient and contentious topics in the cultural and political life of late modern societies. 'Crime' connotes, *inter alia*, harm, violation and loss; menace, mistrust and fear; blame, punishment, exclusion and censure. (It should at the same time not be forgotten that 'it' may signify *inter alia* excitement, thrill, escape, bravery, self-assertion, aspiration, opportunity and membership.) As Giddens notes in another but not altogether unrelated context, what is 'out there' in the form of the changing landscape of risks is also 'in here' in the shape of our inventories of worries, anxieties, resentments and defences. Like the practices in which we engage to insulate ourselves from it, or to secure ourselves against loss and harm, crime is necessarily both materiality and meaning.

The essays in this volume gather in a particular corner of the contemporary crime perplex, but a crucial one. They are concerned to explore questions of risk, insecurity and fear of crime in both their personal and political dimensions as these arise now in late modern 'western' societies. As we know from our nightly television broadcasts and blaring headlines, not to mention the white-knuckle rides of our popular entertainment, fears and worries about crime, disorder and the safety of streets, transport systems and homes seem pervasive. Once the dispassionate domain of academics and government researchers, the 'fear of crime' has become a currency of political competition and a cultural preoccupation. In many countries – even if perhaps first and maybe still most flagrantly in the United States – leading politicians and media commentators struggle for attention, and outbid each other to channel, diagnose and react to these currents of concern.

How should the social sciences respond to these conditions? As the 'fear of crime' and citizens' demands for order have become traded commodities in the marketplace of political discourse, and security hardware and services have come to form the basis of an ever-burgeoning industry, so some conventional styles of analysis and research have lost some of their critical purchase. Neither existing debates surrounding the minute interpretation of survey data nor the radical scepticism of the notion of 'moral panic' seem adequate on their own to

1

penetrate these thickets of political rhetoric and cultural representation or to comprehend the texture of lived experience in these fretful times. What does it mean, under the conditions that now prevail, to be a citizen, a parent, a home-owner, a consumer, a tenant, a victim (or for that matter a suspect, a prisoner, a 'youth', a 'vagrant', an 'asylum-seeker')? And in what kinds of practices of punishment, policing and protection are we being enlisted to participate or passively to support? And how differently do we experience these invitations depending on where we live and who (socially, economically, ethnically) we are? Such topical questions pose novel challenges to the sociological imagination. Which conceptual vocabularies can help us find our bearings here? At the same time how do we develop programmes for empirical enquiry and for intervention that are responsive to context, place and circumstance? Each of the papers in this volume, though they differ in method of enquiry and in substantive focus, seeks to rise to these challenges.

This volume therefore draws together research on the concrete, particular and everyday experiences of anxiety about crime and disorder (the troubled life-world of late modernity) and the exploration of their relations with the emergent forms of criminal justice politics and practice and other contemporary mecha-nisms of security. Such connections are sketched or implied (or less helpfully *assumed*) in diverse contemporary writings. For example, Beck's (1992) or Giddens's (1991) versions of the social theory of risk impute to late modern citi-zens an array of concerns and worries and suggest a permanently unfulfilled quest for security. They point, moreover, to the development of a variety of tech-niques and forms of expertise for the calculation, prediction and management of risk. Yet adequate links to crime and punishment are rarely made in this litera-ture. When Giddens does make such a connection – in the context of his more overtly political writings (Giddens 1998) – it is roundly to endorse one currently popular and rather common-place account of the impact of crime on urban communities, in a way that stands dubiously close to the 'zero tolerance' model of policing (Kelling and Coles 1996; see Stenson, this volume).

Among major contemporary social theorists of risk it is Bauman who has latterly come to address these issues in a sustained and direct fashion (Bauman 1997, 1998, 2000). This encounter takes Bauman in a quite different direction from Giddens's terse certainties. His concerns are instead with the location of anxieties about crime and punishment among the various 'icebergs' that menace our trust in political authorities and our faith in the future, with the standing temptation on politicians to lay claim to muscular solutions, and with the readi-ness of contemporary states (and their commercial contractors) to provide ever larger reservoirs of carceral containment for the at once most menacing and most excluded factions of their populations. These themes in Bauman's later work chime productively with the more specialist and empirically substantive work of criminologists and other investigators on the dynamics of what Wacquant has called 'advanced marginality' (Wacquant 1999a; see also Young 1999) and on the often incendiary political potential of the penal question

2

(Simon and Feeley 1995; Garland 1996). Yet such arguments from generic features of late modernity too often flatten out differences of history and local contingency, or treat the most drastic case (principally the drive towards mass incarceration in the United States) as if it were inherently indicative or premonitory of developments elsewhere. We need, therefore, at this point in the discussion to remind ourselves of the workaday virtues of empirical inquiry and sensitivity to difference. Each of the contributions in this book has something to report *from somewhere*. Their common feature is a concern to explore *in situ* the relations between people's fears, feelings and dispositions towards crime and punishment and the shifting political cultures in which they reside.

Meanwhile, in another part of the theoretical wood, the growing body of work inspired by Foucault's late writings on 'governmentality' points to the inventiveness of our time in generating diverse 'strategies' and new technical knowledges which position us within networks of security and frameworks of regulation, guiding and facilitating the 'conduct of conduct' (Foucault 1991; Garland 1997). Some of the more characteristic socio-technical innovations of recent decades (developments in insurance, credit-rating, the camera surveillance of shopping areas, roads, car parks, airports and other quasi-public spaces) are anatomised in this post-Foucauldian literature (Lianos 2000; Jones 2000). The changing modes of risk management affect not only the tasks and functions of 'traditional' agencies of the state such as police (Ericson and Haggerty 1997) and the penal system (Simon 1993; Kemshall 1998). They also portend new ways of sharing out the provision of security between state agents, commercial organisations and individual consumers. Arguably, what goes less well explored in this perspective are the passions and anxieties which *motivate* us in our pursuit of security but which may not be sated merely by the provision of a certain level of comfort and convenience, nor even by reductions in measurable risks. The 'society of security' (Castel 1991) turns out in many ways to be endemically and perhaps necessarily quite insecure (Ericson and Haggerty 1997).

Yet the implications of this rather unsurprising discovery either for the quality and character of quotidian experience and social relations or for the appeal of certain forms of political rhetoric are more often gestured at than explored. Nevertheless, some authors influenced by this style of thinking have lately begun to address more directly the relations that may obtain between the infrastructure and technique of prevention and control, the moral and emotive charge carried by experiences of victimisation, fear and threat in community life and the positions assumed by states in matters of blaming and punishing (Garland 2001). Thus, for O'Malley the innovations that states and commercial actors so frequently try out in the arenas of risk management and security are *'moral inventions'* (O'Malley 1992: emphasis added). For Rose (2000: 335–6) these developments entail new forms of 'ethical subjectivity', with fatal consequences for the condemnation and sequestration of those who fail to demonstrate the required competence, prudence and self-restraint.

The convulsive penal politics of our times (and their close kin in arenas such as the politics of immigration and asylum) perhaps appear in sharper relief once we grasp that these controversies stand at a nodal point of connection between our intense and frequently unsettling experiences of inhabiting a restless, mobile and sometimes outrightly menacing world and the fateful decisions of states, corporations and other macro-actors. It is to this extent unsurprising that social scientists of various theoretical and political shades (by no means all of whom self-define as criminologists – see e.g. Bauman 2000; Wacquant 1999b) should be drawn increasingly to this meeting point.

In the face of these perplexities this book revisits C. Wright Mills's (1959) long-standing challenge to the social sciences of understanding the relations between private troubles and public issues. In so doing we take it that Mills was, and remains, correct in insisting that it is here that the sociological imagination finds some of its most fruitful and demanding applications. At the same time it is clear that the relations between the private trouble and the public issue have shifted in more profound ways than even that prescient thinker could have anticipated. The range of outlooks and experiences that are commonly called 'fear of crime' occupy just this ever more confused boundary. On one side 'fear' reaches down into the unilluminated corners of the inner life. On the other 'it' extends out into the public domains of culture and political communication, and into the routinisation of practices of safety in housing, transport, shopping, leisure. The organisation of this book reflects the view that responses to crime stand on the cusp between the intimate and the institutional regions of social life: it is in this sense, as Uwe Ewald puts it (this volume) a 'hinge concept'. This collection of essays therefore both presents new research on crime, insecurity and anxiety and explores their connections with some emergent forms of criminal justice politics that seem particularly topical and characteristic.

Private troubles: risk, crime and everyday life

With these concerns in view the essays in Part I present recent work on fear, anxiety and other public responses to crime, deploying concepts and methods that supersede many of the stale polarisations that have come to dominate that terrain. Rather, the purpose of this part of the book is to explore the *in situ* meanings of public insecurities about crime in the everyday worlds of contemporary western societies. As Betsy Stanko argues in her opening contribution, much of the received wisdom about the phenomenon of public insecurity has derived from a peculiarly American political discourse that took shape in the 1960s at a time of social transformation and cultural turmoil. Latterly, though, the elements of this discourse – especially the notion of 'fear of crime' – have migrated internationally, becoming a political invocation both for the framing of a popular politics of law and order and as a counterpoint for activist concerns about the forms of domination which find their expression through everyday violence. In contrast to many off-the-peg applications of the notion of 'fear', the contributions here draw not only from the contemporary conditions and cultures of societies other than the United States – namely Britain (Jefferson and Hollway, Walklate, Loader *et al.*, Reiner *et al.*) and, in Part II, Germany (Zedner, Ewald) and Italy (Melossi and Selmini) – but also from the everyday life-worlds and private responses of individuals within these societies. Together, they call for a severe reconsideration of the concept of 'fear of crime' and the development of a more nuanced and contextual approach to understanding the meanings associated with individuals' perceptions of the threats of criminal victimisation.

The contributions seek to locate people's apprehensive feelings about crime within a dialectic: on the one hand, such feelings may reflect the outcome of people's subjective adjustments and life-strategies in the face of risk and uncertainty in their everyday lives (Jefferson and Hollway, Walklate). The character of such experiences – and the way that these relate to individual identity and lifestyle – may be shaped by individuals' social positions (Stanko, Walklate); their 'internal' personal senses of security (Jefferson and Hollway); their sense of trust in and reliance upon their neighbours and upon 'the authorities'; and the images and messages from entertainment and popular culture around which they orientate their perceptions (Reiner *et al.*). These influences shape the way in which individuals think about, talk about and respond to crime victimisation. In turn, these feelings become a part of the way people adjust to and cope with the world around them (Jefferson and Hollway, Walklate, Stanko).

On the other hand, feelings of insecurity about crime are also expressions of the wider social and cultural transformations within which individuals are located. Just as the 'fear of crime' discourse originated in the politics of change in 1960s America and became interpreted in social movements for civil and social rights (Stanko), so contemporary insecurity about crime arises out of the way individuals experience and respond to the social and cultural transformations of the present. 'Fear of crime' thus intersects with the larger consequences of modernity, and finds its lived social meaning among people's senses of change and decay, optimism and foreboding in the neighbourhoods, towns, cities and wider political communities in which they live and move. Sometimes the question of fear seems chronically enmeshed with the dynamics of de-traditionalisation and an accompanying sense of disruption of formerly settled moral and customary orders. At such times issues of crime, disorder and punishment appear inevitably to assume a nostalgic and conservative, and not uncommonly a politically reactionary, tone. They lend themselves to being read through a commonplace narrative of decline, of lost community and authority. We find ourselves caught in ambivalence between a world of experimentation, novelty and possibility and a recurring allegation of decadence and 'desubordination' (Reiner *et al.*).

At the same time it is the peculiar responsibility of the social sciences to qualify and stratify such generic stories – to note, for example, the materially distinct and diverging places of crime among the lived experiences and defensive strategies of more affluent (Loader *et al.*, Hope) and of poorer communities within such transformations (Walklate, Jefferson and Hollway). So, for example,

Tim Hope seeks to uncover the implications of individual citizens' security practices as these have developed in one country, namely Britain. Hope asks a number of theoretically informed questions about the nature of the security of private property as a 'good' and about the social distribution of such security. Examining the differential take-up of voluntary crime-prevention activity (especially participation in 'neighbourhood watch' schemes) Hope opens up discussion about whether access to security is now best considered as a purely private good (an extension of property rights), a public one (an extension of a nominally universal public service, namely policing) or as an intermediate form (a 'club good' contingent upon membership). To consider the security of private property in this light opens analysis to themes from social and political theory, in particular the model of 'complex equality' outlined by Michael Walzer.

In sum, the focus of this part of the book is on the place of the apprehension of crime risk among the 'private troubles' that people contend with in the ordinary settings of their lives. Nevertheless, the experience and expression of private troubles is unintelligible without reference to the larger worlds of economic, cultural and political change that people perforce also inhabit, and our struggles to adjust to, or change, such circumstances. As such, this part of the book offers perspectives in which 'public issues' – the various discourses of the politics and order – may be grounded and assessed.

Public issues: the new politics of order

The essays in Part II draw out the implications of these new sociologies of fear and anxiety for the character of specific forms of criminal justice politics and practice now evident in advanced liberal societies. The essays consider related developments in Europe and North America in each of three topical and contested fields. These are, respectively, the discourse and practices of 'community safety' and 'security' (Melossi and Selmini, Zedner, Ewald); the vocabulary of 'zero tolerance' in policing and local government (Stenson); and the mixed discourses of retributive severity and risk management now visible in the formation of penal policy, especially in North America (Sparks; Sasson).

The notion of risk is a recurrent preoccupation in many of the essays in this collection as it is throughout much current social and political thought. Here we consider it as a motif that connects the two parts of this volume – that is, as a theme that simultaneously inhabits both 'everyday life' *and* political discourse. In introducing Part II Richard Sparks takes up this theme in relation to the mixed and tangled sources that provide for the shifting directions of penal politics in western countries at the century's turn. For Sparks the sightings noted in these essays and elsewhere in this period indicate a heightened politicisation of all decisions touching public safety, but especially the sentencing and release of prisoners. Although 'risk' is increasingly a key term – and the exposure of the public to risk via 'incompetent' or 'misguided' sentencing or release decisions always potentially a source of scandal – neither Sparks nor, later, Theodore Sasson detects the wholesale displacement of an 'old' penology by a 'new' one. Rather, there are a series of curious hybrids, whose common context is an intense attention to the process of punishment and to politicians' increasingly extravagant claims to be able to buttress social order through the incarceration of offenders. These conditions pose challenges for empirical enquiry, for theoretical development and for attempts at intervention designed to restrain the 'penal temptation' (Wacquant 1999b) to which all late modern societies appear to be in some degree exposed. One such challenge is that of promoting more supple movement between the larger claims of recent social theory (the image of 'risk society', the arguments about globalisation, the intimations of penal post-modernity) and investigation of the particular economic, cultural and political conditions that prevail in given times and places.

Dario Melossi and Rossella Selmini argue that the shifting thematisations of fear, safety and prevention in Italian politics, and the primacy accorded at different times to particular targets and priorities, can be related to determinate periods in the recent histories of state and civil society in that country. In particular, the recent shift towards the assertion of regional and municipal competencies in matters of public safety entails a competition for legitimacy and a reallocation of authority to levels of government below that of the 'sovereign' nation-state. At the same time a re-focusing of attention on to 'micro-criminality' (and the shocks to the self-image of national homogeneity posed by immigration) suggests a transfer of concern away from offences that directly threaten the central state (corruption, political subversion) and towards a more characteristically late modern preoccupation with safety and low-level public disorder.

Uwe Ewald similarly addresses the location of crime, and fear of crime, in processes of social and political change – this time with special reference to societies in transition such as the former East Germany. In Ewald's view, fear of crime has a magnified significance in light of the upheavals, aspirations, shocks and disappointments that people experience in such transitional conditions. The dissolution of borders, both political and psychic, and the reduced sense of power and control that many citizens of the former East Germany experience engender a generalised sense of insecurity and make crime a metaphor for apprehension and dismay in a more than usually potent way. Yet even so, in Ewald's view, crime and its fearful apprehension also plays a socially 'productive' role in articulating citizens' adaptations to modernisation. Ironically, it is the resilience and solidarities of the former East Germans – learned under the previous regime – which may enable them to overcome their anxieties about crime and modernity, perhaps in ways that are unavailable to Western Germans, brought up on the individualistic success-goals of the post-war era.

Lucia Zedner also draws upon perspectives from Germany (in this case arising from a comparative study, conducted with Nicola Lacey, on discourses of crime and community in Britain and Germany) in her reflections on some contemporary meanings of 'security'. 'Security', in Zedner's view, may connote such various topics as national defence, crime control and the personal sense of well-being, safety and bodily integrity. How do these diverse connotations differ between places and political cultures? And how do they influence our conceptions of what public interventions or privately provided innovations we will accept as legitimate, or consume as desirable? In examining certain salient differences between British and German practices, preferences and vocabularies on these dimensions, Zedner illustrates the need for a culturally and institutionally differentiated approach to the analysis of risk and demands for security in different late modern societies.

Kevin Stenson investigates a term recently much in vogue in both North America and Britain (and latterly throughout much of Europe), namely 'zero tolerance' as a theme in policing and local government. Upon what constructions of danger and threats to public order is the notion of zero tolerance predicated? And in what practices of surveillance, order-maintenance and coercion does it issue? It is a practice that mingles the promise of increased public safety with the intrinsic satisfactions of tough action against internal enemies. Stenson similarly locates the appeal of 'zero tolerance' within the apparently pervasive reach of a characteristic bundle of anxieties. But he also emphasises its continuity with prior practices. However novel the slogan, 'zero tolerance' in most of its guises also depends on nostalgia for former times when hierarchies of authority and obedience were said to be more settled. Stenson thus weaves together an account of zero tolerance as a governmental *savoir* with an examination of its role as statecraft and its sponsorship by certain charismatic individuals embarking upon political bids for glory.

Finally, the essay by Theodore Sasson considers the political and cultural context of recent sentencing controversies, in explaining the renewed reliance upon incarceration evident in Massachusetts. Extending his earlier research into the 'meaning frames' at work in lay 'crime talk', Sasson now turns his attention to the 'crime talk' of policy elites in Massachusetts where a formerly somewhat (by US standards) parsimonious use of imprisonment has recently been displaced by an ambitious prison-building programme. Sasson seeks to disentangle the respective roles of systematic risk-management, of judicial reasoning and of populist punitiveness in animating this reversal.

Conclusion

While these essays are diverse in scope – and no attempt is made to impose a spurious unanimity upon them – they share a number of emphases in common. These include the awareness, outlined above, that 'fear' straddles and subverts the antique public–private boundary. There is, second, a commitment to forms of enquiry that are grounded, exploratory and theoretically curious. Arguably, a third common orientation is a less mentalistic view of fear than has generally prevailed in the research literature to date. Rather, these essays consider fear and anxiety as topics in talk, as prompts to action (for example in the routinisation of precautionary conduct), as themes in political discourse and as contexts of policy formation. Such approaches set a course for 'fear of crime' research which is very different either from an old objectivism on the one hand (how much fear do individuals have? what causes them to have it?) or from vapid generalities about the 'social construction' of fear on the other. Instead they treat these topics as woven into the lived culture and ordinary practice of situated actors, who are members of distinct linguistic and political communities. This alone renders 'fear' socially and politically intriguing; the language of concern about crime is caught up in the varying terms of debates about change, stability and crisis; about state authority and legitimacy and about blame and remedy. In this sense 'fear' is a crucial, but still underexplored, question of comparative politics.

The differential positioning of 'risk', 'danger', 'fear' and 'safety' in the politics of contemporary societies encodes not simply some linear and inevitable drift towards 'risk society', but rather also continues to bear the marks of disparate language communities and political cultures. It is by no means self-evident that terms such as 'community safety' either carry the same meanings or issue in the same practices in North America as in Britain or again in the diverse nations of Europe. The evidence here from the United States, Britain, Germany and Italy is that a certain broadly similar universe of discourse overlays some marked substantive and contextual differences. At a minimum, the question of whether 'safety' is pursued in defensive and exclusionary or in more solidaristic modes depends crucially both on the institutions and political cultures of the 'communities' in question and on the nature of the threats and dangers that they envision. This renders the issue complex, because it raises questions about the very translatability of various terms (crime, prevention, community) that criminology commonly treats as having fixed and settled referents. On the other hand it is a more politically hopeful outlook than many others, because the open-textured nature of these terms means that they can be inflected within more diverse and creative projects for the futures of social control than is generally acknowledged.

But 'fear' is also at issue in ways *internal* to particular communities. Even if fear will never map neatly on to measurable risks of victimisation (and it won't), it too is subject to unequal distribution. It impinges upon the lives of citizens with greatly varying intensity; and those citizens in turn enjoy very different access to resources (of economic or of social 'capital') to act to alleviate or resolve their concerns. For example, Tim Hope is not primarily concerned in his essay in this volume with the general societal impact of fear of crime discourse on the character of political debate and electoral competition. Rather (and this is a move expressly anticipated by Stanko and other feminists), he is concerned with exposure to risk (and its converse access to safety) as *distributional* issues; and who says distribution says politics. Even when we move beyond the mere exposure of the often bogus posturings of the politicians and their demagogic exploitations of our anxieties, these questions obdurately remain. Who gains safety and who is left unsecured? To whose account is our safety laid? Is it possible for us to live free from fear? And in what kind of habitat?

References

Bauman, Z. (1997) *Postmodernity and its Discontents*, Cambridge: Polity Press.
——(1998) *Globalisation: The Human Consequences*, Cambridge: Polity Press.
——(2000) 'Social issues of law and order', in D. Garland and R. Sparks (eds) *Criminology and Social Theory*, Oxford: Oxford University Press.
Beck, U. (1992) *Risk Society*, London: Sage.
Castel, R. (1991) 'From dangerousness to risk', in G. Burchell, C. Gordon and P. Miller (eds) *The Foucault Effect*, London: Harvester Wheatsheaf.
Ericson, R.V. and Haggerty, K. (1997) *Policing the Risk Society*, Toronto: University of Toronto Press.
Foucault, M. (1991) 'On governmentality', in G. Burchell, C. Gordon and P. Miller (eds) *The Foucault Effect*, London: Harvester Wheatsheaf.
Garland, D. (1996) 'The limits of the sovereign state', *British Journal of Criminology*, 36(4): 445–71.
——(1997) '"Governmentality" and the problem of crime: Foucault, criminology, sociology', *Theoretical Criminology*, 1(2): 173–214.
——(2001) *The Culture of Control*, Chicago: University of Chicago Press.
Giddens, A. (1991) *Modernity and Self-Identity*, Cambridge: Polity Press.
——(1998) *The Third Way*, Cambridge: Polity Press.
Jones, R. (2000) 'Digital rule: punishment, control and technology', *Punishment and Society*, 2(1): 5–22.
Kelling, G. and Coles, C. (1996) *Fixing Broken Windows*, New York: The Free Press.
Kemshall, H. (1998) *Risk in Probation Practice*, Aldershot: Ashgate.
Lianos, M. (2000) 'Dangerization and the end of deviance', in D. Garland and R. Sparks (eds) *Criminology and Social Theory*, Oxford: Oxford University Press.
Mills, C.W. (1959) *The Sociological Imagination*, New York: Oxford University Press.
O'Malley, P. (1992) 'Risk, power and crime prevention', *Economy and Society*, 21(3): 252–75.
Rose, N. (2000) 'Government and control', in D. Garland and R. Sparks (eds) *Criminology and Social Theory*, Oxford: Oxford University Press.
Simon, J. (1993) *Poor Discipline*, Chicago: University of Chicago Press.
Simon, J. and Feeley, M. (1995) 'True crime: the new penology and public discourse on crime', in T. Blomberg and S. Cohen (eds) *Punishment and Social Control*, New York: Aldine de Gruyter.
Wacquant, L. (1999a) 'Urban marginality in the coming millennium', *Urban Studies*, 36(10): 1639–47.
——(1999b) *Les Prisons de la Misère*, Paris: Editions Liber/Raisons d'Agir.
Young, J. (1999) *The Exclusive Society*, London: Sage.

Part I

PRIVATE TROUBLES
Risk, crime and everyday life

1

VICTIMS R US

The life history of 'fear of crime' and the politicisation of violence

Elizabeth A. Stanko

For most people, crime is no longer an aberration or an expected, abnormal event. Instead, the threat of crime has become a routine part of modern consciousness, an everyday risk to be assessed and managed in much the same way that we deal with road traffic.

(Garland 1996: 2)

Also typical is the swerving away from the central target that requires systematic change, and instead, focusing in on the individual affected. The ultimate effect is always to distract attention from the basic causes and to leave the primary social injustice untouched. And, most telling, the proposed remedy for the problem is, of course, to work on the victim himself.

(Ryan 1976: 24)

The purpose of this chapter is to reflect on the origins of the concept 'fear of crime'. Created through the developments in the crime survey, fear of crime has become the dominant popular tool in conceptualising vulnerability, assessing risk to victimisation and measuring anxiety about the possibility of encountering violence. A review of the origins of this concept reminds the reader how structural contexts about citizens' worry about safety and everyday life are consigned to the background of political discourses about law and order. As the criminological genre of the crime survey took the foreground of scientific inquiry, I argue, commentary about structural inequalities – that underpin people's day-to-day existence as well as contributing much to people's fear of crime – grew silent, only to be replaced by warnings about the danger of generic violence to generic, individual victims. We are told to minimise danger from crime, as Ryan suggests above, by mustering our own individual resources for self-protection.

Ironically, the crime survey has become one of the tools for groups campaigning for civil rights. Indeed, surveys highlighting high rates of fear and violence against women or sexual minorities, for example, have been vehicles for demonstrating structural inequalities experienced by some groups. This chapter

13

explores these tensions hidden in the origins and uses of the concept of fear of crime. The crime survey, as the main tool that documents victimisation, fails to engage in any dynamic way with the commentary on collective harm of particularised forms of discrimination manifest by targeted victimisation. Rather than remind us of the special collective impact of criminal harm, the crime survey, I suggest, transforms any socially excluded citizen into a generic potential crime victim, muting the special impact of social exclusion by ignoring the shared anxiety of being targeted for criminal harm because of who one is. Consigned to the background – rarely explicit in law and order discourse – is the politics of social inequalities. In the foreground is law and order discourse wrapped around concern for criminal violent victimisation and citizens' confidence in the police. These continue to overshadow the social relations of difference that often contribute to people's perceptions and experiences of unsafety. In short, there are contradictions in the way politics is borne out in the use of the concept of fear of crime.

A methodology for the generic victim: the birth and growth of the crime survey

During the early 1960s, concern for the victim of violent crime focused around the creation of mechanisms for state compensation to victims of violent crime (Miers 1978). In the United States, the death of J.F. Kennedy in 1963 and the heated, often extremely tense struggles around civil rights set the scene for the national anxiety about disorder. Barry Goldwater – although he lost the 1964 election – pushed law and order into the spotlight of his presidential campaign. Some twenty US inner-city 'ghettos' flared into riots in the summers of 1964, 1965 and 1966. Findings of the McCone Commission (1966), set up to analyse the cause of widespread unrest in US cities, and a UCLA study exploring the Watts riot of 1965 in particular, summarised by the President's Commission on Law Enforcement and the Administration of Justice, made explicit a link between civil rights and fear of crime. Emphasised was the UCLA survey which found

> the riot had a 'purpose ... hostility, resentment, revenge' ... The implication is evident that many Negroes [sic] believe that if only the white community realised what the ghetto was like and how its residents felt, the ghetto would not be permitted to exist.
>
> (President's Commission on Law Enforcement
> and the Administration of Justice 1967: 121–2).

In other words, if we *really* knew about how the structural conditions of poverty, fed by racial exclusion, fostered victimisation and its fear, we would find a way of tackling the causes of crime.

Connecting racial dissent with crime victimisation, and wider anxiety about

14

crime with institutionalised racism, was an explicit theme of this landmark report on the state of law, crime and justice in the USA. The President's Commission clearly located people's dread about crime within anxieties about race. To what extent the research arm of criminology, launched by the President's Commission through the newly created Law Enforcement Assistance Administration (see Quinney 1974), made any inroads into restoring the legitimacy of US legal order to local Afro-American communities today remains to be seen. The President's Commission, though, served as a cornerstone for bringing research about day-to-day criminal justice into the foreground of policy debates (see Feeley and Simon 1994).

It is, I feel, important to be reminded of this context within which the analytic mainstay of victimisation – the crime survey – was spawned. What is interesting to me, as a reader of this earlier material now, is the primacy and seriousness with which the Commission connected the unhappiness of those excluded by race from the American dream. Stated the Commission: 'anger, violence, despair and cynicism prevail in the Negro ghettos of America and these conditions contribute both to everyday crime and to protest riots' (President's Commission on Law Enforcement and the Administration of Justice 1967: 116).

Upheaval in Afro-American communities in the mid-1960s was explicitly linked by the Commission to experiences of racist treatment by the majority, white society. So too was black fear of crime. Anxiety of white Americans, moreover, was also linked to their fear of crime and to white Americans' fear that crime is committed by black people (Skogan 1995).

The President's Commission built upon this concern through its commissioned surveys that asked people directly about their experiences of crime. Identified as crucial to the development of better services and attention to the 'plight' of the victim of crime, the US President's Commission on Law Enforcement and the Administration of Justice (1967) set an agenda for the inquiry into victims of crime that was to change research on crime dramatically. An instrument of social science and for rational policy-making, the crime survey provides an opportunity to gain a wider picture of crime by allowing the public to give their own account of criminal harm and express anxiety about its potential.

At the time of the hearings of the President's Commission (the late 1960s), police statistics comprised the core of knowledge about crime, which were, admittedly, a poor reflection of what really happened to people. Speculation about the kinds of people who inhabited police files as victims led to the development of theories of culpability (Wolfgang 1958). Victims' behaviour (as recorded by the police) was scrutinised for any contribution to offenders' actions. The foundation for this speculation was laid through the theorising of the 'founding' fathers of victimology, who were lawyers by trade and concerned about the way offenders' crime could be characterised by the defence (Schafer 1968). The crime survey, it was felt, held a key to public policy about crime because it analysed victims' own experiences of crime unfiltered by the actions of the police. (The police were, of course, under scrutiny by these inquiries.

15

Criticism was well founded about the racist manner of policing 'ghettos'. The police's contribution to the urban riots of the 1960s was indeed acknowledged by the President's Commission reports.)

Through the discovery of what is still called 'the dark figure of crime', crime survey respondents specified those incidents which, if known to police, would be considered to be crime. These early surveys also exposed the police's own bureaucratic processes which filtered what the public reported as crime away from its books: not all incidents that came to police attention were treated as crime. This continues to be a consistent observation of crime surveys today (Maguire 1994). Today, national and international surveys, neighbourhood, campus or special topics crime surveys abound. The prominence of the crime survey within criminological policy-making is now well established. If a problem of crime is to be taken 'seriously', it seems that a crime survey is one of the major devices used to demonstrate the pervasiveness of an issue and to advocate for sympathetic treatment of newly identified 'victims'. The virtual dominance of crime surveys in providing the data for debate and discussion about a wide range of topics, from the people's confidence in the criminal justice system to the relationship between offenders and victims, has homogenised international debates about comparative crime (van Dijk *et al.* 1990). These debates are about *crime* and not the social contexts of inequalities that exist in different nations and jurisdictions.

The prime advantage of the crime survey, we are told, is that it estimates the impact of criminal victimisation by asking individuals themselves. In some ways, the crime survey has become the 'voice' of the people rather than a bureaucratic statistical exercise controlled by criminal justice agents. Jock Young has even suggested that 'the victimisation study, in the sense that it attempts to encompass all the victims in the community, is more democratic in its brief, however imperfect it may be in its accomplishment' (1988: 169).

But in many ways the social tensions that gave rise to the creation of the crime survey initially – that of white American anxiety about personal safety within a climate of racialised frustration – have been forgotten in the rush to embrace the democratic possibilities of the crime survey. Anxiety about the ability of the state to protect citizens from criminal victimisation began (and continues) to bubble over into the daily conversation. But the language of concern inevitably turns to the plight of victims of crime, especially of personal crime and usually of violent crime. Citizens' risks to crime merged with various civil rights claims about discrimination – to women, minorities, the disabled, sexual minorities and others. Commentary about structural inequalities or the wider climates of social disadvantage, though, became submerged to the discourses of 'victim'.

Undifferentiated fears and generic victims

We could now say that the crime survey has become the key tool for criminologists of all persuasions to explore the impact of crime from the perspective of its recipients. While the crime survey continues to have its critics, those of us who wish to say anything about victims and victimisation must, it seems, find some way of accounting for the problem. This general approach used by survey researchers is the following. Identify households systematically across an area (whether it is national, regional or neighbourhood-based). Select members of those households to answer a number of questions about a wide range of questions on experiences of crime (actual or attempts). At the same time, ask people about their concern or fear about crime and about precautionary behaviour aimed to minimise exposure to crime. Note the impact of such avoidance and/or actual experience. Include information on the lifestyle and living circumstances of those interviewed.

No doubt, the crime surveys serve to illustrate graphically how little crime comes to the attention of the police. The centrality of crime surveys, in measuring the kinds of crime victims encounter and their subsequent needs, fears and expectations, have drawn our attention to these annual findings – we wonder whether crime is up, down or just the same. Although victim surveys offer criminologists a wider picture of crime and victimisation, there are still a number of limitations to this method of 'counting victims' (see, most recently, Maguire 1999). For instance, people fail to recall or choose not to report crime to the researchers; questions may be misinterpreted, or not be specific enough to elicit the appropriate information (Young 1988). These limitations, Maguire suggests, are as much directed to the survey's methodological as well as its analytic deficiencies. While there is always a long list of caveats accompanying the publication of any crime survey results, the findings are analysed as 'truer' reflections of the incidence of crime. As we now know, individuals who report encounters with a variety of criminal events to survey researchers are most likely to manage these potentially criminal circumstances without the aid of law, with one notable exception. Thefts of and from cars are usually reported to the police. Other forms of crime, especially personal violence, are more likely to be kept away from police attention.

Maguire's (1994) recent analysis of the impact of crime surveys on the picture of crime suggests we have indeed experienced a massive shift in our thinking, influenced by the dominance of the victim survey in measuring crime. Maguire's analogy, using Rumpelstiltskin as a slumbering criminologist waking after a thirty-five-year sleep, is instructive: making sense of crime and victimisation has undergone a sea change, with victim surveys providing the new template, leading to a process of re-defining the victim of crime. Maguire summarises the overall finding of the crime survey as 'the bad news is that there is a lot more crime than we thought, the good news is that most of it is petty' (Maguire 1994: 264).

Over the years, the following general observations about victimisation have been gleaned from these surveys:

- most crimes are not reported to the police;
- motor vehicle crime is the most often reported crime (probably because of the primacy of the needs of the insurer);

- non-whites are more likely to be victims of crime than whites;
- males have higher rates of victimisation than females;
- persons under 25 have higher rates of victimisation than older persons;
- most victims are victimised by offenders of the same race;
- most victims are victimised by men;
- people who live in inner cities have higher victimisation rates than those living in rural or suburban areas;
- a minority of individuals account for a significant proportion of all incidents reported to crime surveys.

(Farrell 1992; Hope 1995; Farrell *et al.* 1995)

A composite picture of a victim began to emerge: he is young, single, unemployed, socially active outside the home, probably drinks and shares many characteristics with the young man who is his assailant. Rates of victimisation are reported for neighbourhoods, cities, countries, or special constituent groups (for instance, in England and Wales, black, Asian and white are used as 'racial' groupings) that paint a picture of an 'at-risk' population. Levels of victimisation are compared – over time, among various locales, among constituent groups and even among countries. Researchers explore the variations of risk of victimisation according to the lifestyle of the victim and speculate about why victimisation concentrates within specific categories of victim. My interest here is not to detail these analyses, but to remind us how crime surveys create the categories of 'victim' and 'non-victim', who might be justifiably 'fearful' or 'not fearful' of crime. When analysing fear of crime, researchers have searched for some way of explaining the curious counter-intuitive finding that those who fear crime most are least likely to be its recorded victims.

Lifestyle, victimisation and fear of crime

The late Michael Hindelang and his colleagues Michael Gottfredson and James Garofalo (1978), in *Victims of Personal Crime*, presented the first empirical exploration of risk of victimisation based on crime survey data. Hindelang *et al.*'s usage of the term 'lifestyle' includes a holistic assessment of routine activities, such as 'working outside the home, going to school, or keeping house, as well as typical leisure time pursuits' (Hindelang 1978: 244). Because 'differential lifestyles imply different probabilities that individuals will be in particular places, at particular times, under particular circumstances, interacting with particular kinds of persons' (1978: 245), lifestyle affects the probability of victimisation. So, as all the evidence from crime surveys in the USA, UK and around the world suggests that criminal victimisation is not distributed randomly across time and space, the academic debate turned to analyses of who was at greater risk to victimisation. These authors provided the groundwork to explore the convergence of opportunity, willing offenders and the absence of guardians for the categories of victims and non-victims.

Lifestyle, though, holds many clues about people's characters. Indeed, many (including the professional discretionary decisions of criminal justice agents themselves) draw upon lifestyle to make judgements about people's credibility and trustworthiness. Perhaps inadvertently, this analysis casts *victims* into categories of blameworthy and blameless victims, depending on their lifestyles. Governments and others talk about helping innocent, undeserving victims of crime. Great Britain's Criminal Injuries Compensation Scheme, for instance, states explicitly that it provides resources for compensation to 'blameless victims of crimes of violence'. Crime surveys note instances of victimisation, and do not make 'judgements' about which victims might be deserving and undeserving. Factors associated with exposure to situations with high risk of personal criminal victimisation are also those associated with judgements about who deserves to be at risk to victimisation, and who deserves to be considered an 'innocent' victim of crime.

So what are the lessons gleaned from crime surveys about risk to victimisation? Hindelang *et al.* (1978) observed that the 'propensity to precipitate' victimisation is not uniformly distributed among the population. Young single men – those most likely to be offenders – have the highest risk of personal victimisation. In general, young men consistently report to the same crime surveys that they feel safe walking alone on the street after dark. The crime survey data suggest that the risk of encountering victimisation rests on the following propositions:

1   The probability of suffering a personal victimisation is directly related to the amount of time that a person spends in public places (e.g. on the street, in parks, etc.) and particularly in public places at night.
2   The probability of being in public places, particularly at night, varies as a function of lifestyle.
3   Social contacts and interactions occur disproportionately among individuals who share similar lifestyles.
4   An individual's chances of personal victimisation are dependent upon the extent to which the individual shares demographic characteristics with offenders.
5   The proportion of time that an individual spends among non-family members varies as a function of lifestyle.
6   The probability of personal victimisation, particularly personal theft, increases as a function of the proportion of time that an individual spends among non-family members.
7   Variations in lifestyle are associated with variations in the ability of individuals to isolate themselves from persons with offender characteristics.
8   Variations in lifestyle are associated with variations in the convenience, the desirability and the vincibility of the person as a target for personal victimisation.

(see Hindelang *et al.* 1978: 250–66)

In its first report, the British Crime Survey (BCS) likened the chances of falling a victim to crime to encountering other mishaps, such as having accidents in the

19

home or car crashes. Risk of confronting a crime was associated with a personal encounter to a criminal event. The authors summarised risk as a 'statistical' average, and suggested that the generic individual could expect to encounter:

- a robbery once every five centuries (not attempts);
- an assault resulting in injury (even if slight) once every century;
- a family car to be stolen or taken by joyriders once every sixty years;
- a burglary in the home once every forty years.

(Hough and Mayhew 1983: 15)

Moreover, the role the so-called victim plays in generating crime, an active debate in the infancy of victimology at the time (see Schafer 1968), was not lost to crime survey researchers. The speculation of the early victimologists is very much a part of the theorising that arises from victim survey research. Sparks *et al.* (1977) proposed:

> But it has increasingly come to be realised that the 'victim' (in a legal sense) of a criminal act may in fact play an important part in the causation of that act, in a number of ways. He may be a willing participant in the crime; or he may consciously or unconsciously incite or provoke it; at a minimum he may be placed (or may place himself) specifically at risk.
>
> (1977: 10)

No longer, it was hoped, are we to look at the victim through the caricature of vulnerability and blamelessness, epitomised as the elderly, frail female attacked by heartless thugs. Victim survey findings all concurred: regardless of jurisdiction, nation or neighbourhood, property crimes – thefts, thefts from or of cars, burglaries and other types of acquisitive crime – not violent crime, make up the bulk of documented victimisation. Indeed, the British decision to conduct victimisation surveys, beginning in 1981, was made in the hope that the findings would 'act as an antidote to public misperceptions about crime', 'demonstrate the comparatively low risks of *serious* crime, and puncture the inaccurate stereotypes of crime victims' (Hough and Mayhew 1988: 157, emphasis in original). Perhaps the intention of the crime survey was to widen the distinction between blamelessness and blameworthiness. Michael Gottfredson, in his analysis of the dimensions of victim risk from the first BCS (1982), assures us that serious criminal victimisation is rare – as long as we are thinking about the generic victim. He concludes that

> It seems likely that at least some of the concern about crime and victimisation among the public is caused by uncertainty – uncertainty about one's chances of falling victims, uncertainty about when and

where it is likely to happen, and uncertainty about how it would be dealt with if it did happen.

(1984: 30)

This uncertainty of encountering violent crime – regardless of its proportion in the overall findings (26 per cent of reported victimisation in the latest US crime survey; 17 per cent (including simple assault) in the 1992 BCS) took centre stage in the debate about the concept 'fear of crime' in the 1980s. The debate was led by trying to theorise about the so-called 'paradox of fear'. This paradox is best summarised thus: those who fear crime least are most likely to experience its impact directly. Those who do fear crime do so through a wider under-standing of what it means to be vulnerable to violence and intimidation, and assess this possibility in a way that results in changes to everyday, routine behaviour. Studies show that avoidance of victimisation varies among different populations of people (Madriz 1997; Stanko 1990). Women and the elderly, for instance, are most likely to restrict their everyday lives so as to avoid potential encounters with violence (Gordon and Riger 1988; Gardner 1995). During the 1980s, the debate about fear of crime sought to offer various explanations for this paradox between fear and risk to crime (see Hale 1996 for a summary). While the crime surveys sought to put violent crime in perspective ('there's a lot of crime but most of it is petty'), in many respects challenges to the findings about fear of crime kept the spotlight firmly on violent crime. It did so by widening the understanding of the nature and the impact of violent crime to include assessments of threat and intimidation as contributing to feelings of unsafety.

Creating victims' fears: we are all (and only) afraid of crime

The voices of excluded groups emphasised the imagined and the experiences of danger because of who they are. Feminists, for instance, began by exploring why women's fear might be different to that of men's. What the research questioned was the use of the generic victim – ungendered, unsexed, not raced – in any speculation about risk to crime and its fear. Some critics, for instance, tried to argue that crime survey data failed to capture adequate information about violence between known others, especially physical and sexual assault of women (Stanko 1985, 1988). Others sought to conduct surveys themselves and to high-light the experiences of violence of those specially targeted because of hatred or exclusion (Fitzgerald and Hale 1996; Mason and Palmer 1996). In many ways, these critics widened our understanding about fear of violence.

Conceptualising 'threat' and 'intimidation' outside a legal definition of crim-inal behaviour brought controversy to the debates about fear of crime. Such inclusion challenges the criminological genre of the crime survey, placing the concerns of citizens within a web of wider social equality. As crime surveys developed, they became a popular device in relocating the concept of fear of crime within political discourse of citizenship. A right to walk the streets unhindered or unthreatened became one of a central argument of those who feel disenfranchised by contemporary society. While feminist surveys did reveal higher levels of actual physical and sexual violence against women than government-sponsored surveys, these also showed that the majority of women experienced threat and intimidation from men and that this threat changes their behaviour. The inclusion of questions about sexual harassment (as well as racist harassment or harassment of those not straight, for example) extended the way crime surveys demonstrated the impact of inequality on personal safety. It has also been shown that changing the language of crime surveys alters the way people are willing to report experiences of intimidation, threat and violence (Percy and Mayhew 1998). But intimidation and threat also reveals that people name *their* experienced and imagined social context as fear-producing.

Intimidation and threat, as a recent social audit of violence in the UK shows (Stanko 1998), is far more pervasive than physical and sexual assault. But such intimidation is interpreted by and through the crime survey genre. These groups, associated with the context of being a social person with a complex social identity, extend risk, which is associated within the surveys with lifestyle. But such textures of people's lives are rarely acknowledged within the crime survey genre. The criminal justice system, not wider social hierarchies, is typically cast as an envisioned solution to criminal harm. The slogan 'Domestic violence is a crime', for instance, illustrates how one campaign on behalf of the treatment of women's complaints about the violence of known men merged its strategies with those of law and order. Not all domestic violence, though, includes legally defined criminal behaviour. Women's experiences of domestic violence are far wider than existing legal categories, and demonstrate persistent patterns and structures of individual men's misogyny. Neither the structural features of women's inequality nor individual men's use of this inequality as a backdrop for their violent and abusive behaviour are adequately described as harm to women within a criminological framework.

However, what became a criminological problem was the fear of crime experienced by those supposedly less victimised. Fear of crime, when it became 'a problem in its own right', became a conundrum for the generic categories of 'women' and 'the elderly' initially. During the 1980s, fear of crime acquired the power of a discourse, one that captured recognition by politicians that citizens felt unprotected by the state. Other groups, namely women's advocates, minority campaign groups, children's rights and homophile organisations, harnessed the political message of the fear of crime for their own campaigning purposes. The crime survey was adapted by feminist researchers, for instance, and has demonstrated high rates of violence against women. Even crime survey data, when analysed explicitly to explore differences among different racial groups in terms of fear and experiences of crime, illustrated that differences exist in fear and experiences of crime among racial groups (Fitzgerald and Hale 1996). Most recently, homophile organisations have used crime surveys to capture gay people's experiences of homophobic violence (Mason and Palmer 1996). In the quest for demanding more equitable treatment as citizens, groups have used crime surveys as tools to demonstrate their differential relationship to safety and security in wider society (Stanko and Curry 1997).

Crime surveys provide a methodological tool to fuse the discourses of law and order to anxieties about personal safety. Such welding, as noted above, has attempted to make people understand what it is really like to be a woman, a racial minority, non-straight, and so forth. Unease about personal safety is supposed to expose the blight of racialised fear of crime, as well as embedded fears borne from social exclusion – such as gender and sexual orientation. To some extent, over the past thirty years the use of the concept of fear of crime, I suggest, has become a proxy term for social disadvantage. Its special power as a concept is in wrapping its discursive arm simultaneously around both discourses, law and order and social exclusion. (Ironically, in some ways, this has kept it closer to its original usage by the President's Commission.) Today, for instance, campaigners for non-whites, women, gay men and lesbians, or others who feel marginalised by democratic heterogeneity, claim that both anxiety about and higher levels of criminal victimisation are symptomatic of their group's social ostracism. Higher levels of anxiety of certain groups about criminal victimisation serve as evidence of social discrimination. Better police protection for their group as citizens, as well as for those who fall victim to targeted criminal violence, has become one prominent demand of government by various campaign groups.

In summary, victim surveys provide huge quantities of data. As a methodological tool, they also provide a 'democratic' voice of those groups who wish to paint a picture about the reality of differential access to personal security. But there are still difficulties in making analytic distinctions between those who report violence and those who do not. While the categories 'victim'/'non-victim' are somewhat flawed, as they are founded on the information interviewees themselves provide to researchers, nonetheless all citizens (or groups of citizens), advocates argue, fall into a potentially 'at-risk' category. Such risk includes worry about social disadvantage, named as 'fear of crime'. Crime surveys also ask whether people are concerned about the potential of being a victim in the future and whether such concern has any impact on their feeling of well-being. Hale (1996), in his useful summary of the literature on fear of crime, notes that there is 'considerable theoretical confusion' concerning the concept 'fear of crime', what it means and how it is measured. It is worth quoting Hale's analysis of this confusion:

> Indeed it is arguable that many of the debates concerning the ratio-
> nality of fear are due, at least in part, to this lack of clarity and a failure
> in many cases to distinguish between risk evaluation, worry and fear.
> The confusion has a long and distinguished history. More broadly, is

fear of crime simply measuring fear of crime, or perhaps in addition, some other attribute which might be better characterised as 'insecurity with modern living', 'quality of life', 'perception of disorder' or 'urban unease'?

(1996: 84)

More recently, Hale observes, there has been debate about how to interpret the fear of crime as indicative of social discrimination. Not all of us fear crime and particular forms of crime in the same manner. 'Fear of crime', as conceptual shorthand for citizen anxiety about personal safety, has led to narrowness in its usage in popular culture. Moreover, its popular form is bounded and framed by criminological concerns about crime and incivility, as if these phenomena are somehow untouched by historical context and political discourses. Why, we might ask, did analyses of fear of crime spark a debate at about the rationality or irrationality of such anxiety? Why did the paradox of fear – those who fear crime's potential rather than manage its actuality – take a central role in the debates about law and order? Perhaps we need to be reminded about the concept's original, clear grounding in a wider context of racial turmoil in the USA during the 1960s and 1970s. Now any fear of crime debate largely takes place as if a wider context of social turmoil can be held in abeyance for the purposes of theoretical discussion. For three decades now, the concept of fear has been largely dis-located from its foundation, a foundation that recognised the damage from the denial of civil rights and the lack of access to what democracies promise as a 'level playing field' in access to legitimate social resources. In the next section, I argue that failure to engage with this entanglement led to the creation of the generic victim, an artefact of the actuarial separation of victims from non-victims. Held in abeyance, rarely addressed directly, is the presumption that there are adequate ways to separate blameworthy and blameless victims. Conceptualising risk of victimisation keeps this distinction alive.

Risk of victimisation: Victims R Us

The adoption of the crime survey to capture the extent of violence to women, or violence against black people, the disabled, and the non-straight, has grown more widespread throughout the past two decades. The question 'What is the risk of victimisation because of social inequality?' became entwined with the use of the crime survey. The concept of fear of crime turned into a device to calculate the actuarial risk to violent victimisation for different people in different social contexts. The debate about the impact of the fear of crime, rather than leading to a wider understanding of how social differences articulate the fragmentation of inequalities, instead homogenised criminological debate through its framework of the generic 'blameless' victim. It may then come as no surprise that the resulting information about 'risk' has not led to social policy that challenges victimisation and assuages fear in any collective way. While we certainly have a number of official pronouncements condemning racism or homophobia (though not many condemning misogyny), the conditions of social inequalities prevail. Moreover, the underside of the dualism – blameworthiness and blame-lessness in characterising victims – continues to influence the practice of decision-making in the criminal justice system. Crime surveys may contribute to our understanding of the space between certain and uncertain risks of crime, but not its persistent link to social inequalities.

Sparks *et al.* (1977) note, as did others later, that one significant association does emerge between self-reporting of violent crime and reporting of violent victimisation. Risk of victimisation increases the closer one is to being an offender. But this likelihood raises the possibility that the so-called victim is not a 'true' – that is blameless – victim. These researchers note:

> First, the victim may act in such a way as to precipitate – or at least strongly encourage – the behaviour of the offender;
> Second, even if the victim does not take anything which could be called an active part in the crime, he may nonetheless offer a specially great opportunity or inducement to its commission;
> Third, it may be that certain persons – by virtue of their appearance or behaviour, or their place in a social system – are more likely than others to be victims of criminal behaviour, even though they themselves do not act in any way such as to bring this about.
>
> (1977: 98–9)

In many respects, crime surveys turned policy-makers and criminologists to consider the features of actuarial risk to becoming a victim of crime. While examining the common features of aggregates of populations, the seeds of concern for how individuals within aggregates may be at risk inevitably crept into the discourses and debates about criminal victimisation. The drafters of legislation granting compensation to victims of violent crime, for example, were well aware that as individuals some may have unwittingly or wittingly contributed to their own demise (Miers 1978). As noted earlier, provision exists in victim compensation legislation to exclude 'undeserving' victims. Although personal characteristics of offending are 'most highly predictive of suffering any personal victimisation' (1978: 106), having a criminal record excludes eligibility for compensation under the victims of violent crime compensation legislation.

The state's responsibility for reassuring and advising good citizens about how to avoid crime led it to advise citizens to monitor their lives and their lifestyles. Instead, what intervenes in this process of claiming special status as crime victims and as fearful citizens is what Garland (1996) describes as the 'crimi-nology of the self'. The onus of avoiding crime and minimising fear now falls squarely on the shoulders of individual victims, as Ryan's commentary foreshad-owed. To alleviate victimisation and its fear, these days individuals have to be on guard by and for themselves. Individual prudent behaviour, rather than the collective claim to equal rights, is how citizens are advised to avoid the fear of and experiences of criminal violence. O'Malley's (1992) analysis of the theoretical underpinnings of approaches to crime prevention notes the strength of private prudentialism in governmental crime reduction strategies devised in the late 1980s and early 1990s. Influenced by Foucault's conception of disciplinary power, O'Malley shows how the avoidance of victimisation is neatly transformed as a problem of the individual management of risk. Crime prevention advice implores us to reduce our possibilities of encountering crime. We should not be surprised when speculation about the lifestyles of 'victims' becomes the first port of call in any explanation of victimisation, for researchers wished to know whether and how victims might 'differ' from non-victims. Information collected by the surveys emphasised the riskiness of certain public spaces for some kinds of victims. Going to work, travelling on public transport, drinking in public places, walking in one's neighbourhood, and so forth, are explored for their association with being at risk to crime. The resulting advice on avoidance of crime is generic advice, aimed at the average person with an average lifestyle. But the analysis of multiple victimisation and the aggregate disadvantage – termed 'victimisation flux' by Hope (1995) – questions the ability of those most heavily affected by victimisation to alter their lifestyle. Such analyses point to wider structural disadvantages (including the serial targeting of particular individuals by particularly motivated offenders such as domestic batterers) that influence targeted criminal behaviour.

Risk to crime has become conceptualised as an individual problem, and its fear labelled as rational or irrational in the context of individuals' individual circumstances. Fear of crime, I argue here, reminded by my reading of the original discussions of its conceptual birth, recognises the impact of *societal* anxiety on many different kinds of people. If risk is to be assessed in light of uncertainty, then the uncertainty lies *not* in the alteration of individual lifestyles but in wider social structures. Today we live in an age fraught with uncertainty: global finance, natural and produced hazards of contemporary life (from nuclear explosions to the dumping of toxic waste), decreasing public domestic expenditure (to name only a few) all contribute to greater insecurities about everyday life (for detailed discussions of modernity, see Giddens 1984; Beck 1992). Risk, according to Mary Douglas, 'admirably serves the forensic needs of the new global culture' (1992: 22). Cultures need a common 'forensic vocabulary' with which to conceptualise danger. Crime provides one of the contemporary vocabularies for modern risk. The term 'risk' now substitutes for shorthand to describe potential threat. A risky investment is one in which one's money might be lost; a risky neighbourhood is one in which crime lurks; a risky cure is one in which recovery cannot be guaranteed. And within today's culture of consumption and choice, faulty choices mean loss. Speaking of potential risk means speaking of uncertainty. Adjusting uncertainty is approached as a problem of individual prudence, not collective disadvantage.

Yet, while the authors of crime surveys may be correctly locating so-called crime risks among the perils of other potentially damaging situations which dramatically impact people's lives, there is little discussion about the concept of security, the resultant state which theoretically exists outside risk itself. It seems to me that the contemporary debates, born at the juncture of late modernity (Giddens 1984), fail to take into account an embodied context of uncertainty that itself is so embedded in social inequalities. Herein lies a major tension in the debates about victimisation and risk. I suggest that the main problem, at least when thinking about victimisation, is guaranteeing safety. What use is the information about victimisation risks without a discussion about the possibility of safety? As the debate turns to discussions of risk avoidance, and especially that avoidance which can be orchestrated by individuals themselves, there is a failure to engage with the wider debate about unsafety arising from structural disadvantages. The accumulated criminological knowledge about risk of victimisation, generated from countless local, national and international crime surveys, has failed to assuage people's fears and anxieties about crime.

Some concluding remarks

Criminological knowledge about risk of victimisation has in fact led to maintaining sophisticated mechanisms for 'blaming the victim' for encountering crime (Ryan 1976; Elias 1986, 1993). As criminological 'experts', crime survey researchers have paid great attention to the dimensions of risk to crime, but have failed, I suggest, to pay attention to detail of the conceptualisation of what we might mean by risk itself. This has led to a deepening of the assessments about blameworthy and blameless victims. We have created techniques founded on supposedly scientific inquiry to separate the true victim from the person undeserving of the title 'victim'. The crime survey has allowed us to change the portrayal of crime, dominated by offender-based information and painted through the use of police-generated statistics. We now agree that child abuse, racist violence, violence against women, and most property crime affects more people than those who come to police attention. Moreover, many of these are repeatedly affected. Detailed analysis of 'who' these people are reveals a very complicated picture and complex understanding of why and how such labels are used (see Jefferson and Hollway, Walklate, this volume).

What prompted the suspicion of the so-called challengers about the victim survey as a 'true' reflection of victimisation was doubt about findings of such low levels of violence among crime survey respondents. The contrast between what was considered a factor of 'risk' – being socially excluded, targeted for threat and intimidation because of the intersection of various forms of disadvantage for a variety of reasons – was expressed in official victim surveys as fear. What was considered a factor of 'risk' by challengers, such as women's advocates and homophile organisations, was being in a disadvantaged social position; what was considered a factor of risk for the traditional surveys was the lifestyle of the victim. But both challengers and traditional victim survey researchers agreed that it was possible to calculate risk of victimisation through such surveys. While the challengers argued that the 'at-risk' calculation muted many of the experiences of special groups, what was not in dispute was being 'at risk'. The tool for deciding the best estimate of that risk was considered the victim survey. When any of us – as citizens or members of the excluded groups – are potential victims, we fail to see the concentration of serious violence among certain categories of the population. We also fail to analyse the way fear of crime – as a contemporary discourse about inequalities and disadvantage – is the metaphor for contemporary life that has not rid itself of the persistent remnants of hierarchies founded in the historical legacies of colonialism, patriarchy, heterosexism and class.

The use of the genre of the crime survey to capture and to demonstrate fear of crime sacrifices its origins to contemporary political discourse about law and order, and the place of citizen safety and security within it. The use of fear of crime, I suggest, as a concept to make visible inequality will ultimately reverberate back on the shoulders of those structurally and socially disadvantaged. The recipients of violence cannot ask for protection from the state to institutionalised racism, homophobia and misogyny, any more than the residents of the ghettos in the USA could ask for income redistribution to combat poverty. What happened in the USA to resolve the anxiety of many white inner-city residents was the abandonment of the cities for the suburbs. Inner-city poverty, ravaging black-on-black violence and poor housing conditions largely were issues left unaddressed by crime surveys. Law and order took centre stage. Victims and victimisation became disconnected from the wider social context. In using the concept of fear of crime as a strategic platform from which to demonstrate discrimination, campaigners import the paradigm 'crime victim' via its methodological tool, the crime survey. Such a paradigm fails to embrace a remedy for reducing the fear of crime that addresses the underlying collective problem of civil rights.

References

Beck, U. (1992) *The Risk Society*, London: Sage.

Douglas, M. (1992) *Risk and Blame*, London: Routledge.

Elias, R. (1986) *The Politics of Victimization*, Oxford: Oxford University Press.

——(1993) *Victims Still*, London: Sage.

Farrell, G. (1992) 'Multiple victimisation: its extent and significance', *International Review of Victimology*, 2(2): 85–102.

Farrell, G., Phillips, C. and Pease, K. (1995) 'Like taking candy: why does repeat victimisation occur?', *British Journal of Criminology*, 35(3): 384–99.

Feeley, M. and Simon, J. (1994) 'Actuarial justice: the emerging new criminal law', in D. Nelken (ed.) *The Futures of Criminology*, London: Sage.

Fitzgerald, M. and Hale, C. (1996) *Ethnic Minorities: Victimisation and Racial Harassment*, London: Home Office.

Gardner, C. (1995) *Passing-by: Gender and Public Harassment*, Berkeley: University of California Press.

Garland, D. (1996) 'The limits of the sovereign state: strategies of crime control in contemporary society', *British Journal of Criminology*, 36(4): 445–71.

Giddens, A. (1984) *The Consequences of Modernity*, Cambridge: Polity Press.

Gordon, M. and Riger, S. (1988) *The Female Fear*, New York: Free Press.

Gottfredson, M. (1984) *Risk of Victimisation: Findings from the 1982 British Crime Survey*, London: HMSO.

Hale, C. (1996) 'Fear of crime: a review of the literature', *International Review of Victimology*, 3: 195–210.

Hindelang, M., Gottfredson, M. and Garofalo, J. (1978) *Victims of Personal Crime*, Boston: Ballinger.

Hope, T. (1995) 'The flux of victimisation', *British Journal of Criminology*, 35(3): 327–42.

Hough, M. and Mayhew, P. (1983) *The British Crime Survey*, London: HMSO.

——(1988) 'The British Crime Survey: origins and impact' in M. Maguire and J. Pointing (eds) *Victims of Crime: A New Deal?*, Milton Keynes: Open University Press.

Madriz, E. (1997) *Nothing Bad Happens to Good Girls*, Berkeley: University of California Press.

Maguire, M. (1994) 'Crime statistics, patterns, and trends: changing perceptions and their implications', in M. Maguire, R. Morgan and R. Reiner (eds) *The Oxford Handbook of Criminology*, Oxford: Oxford University Press.

——(1999) 'Crime statistics, patterns, and trends: changing perceptions and their implications', in M. Maguire, R. Morgan and R. Reiner (eds) *The Oxford Handbook of Criminology*, second edition, Oxford: Oxford University Press.

Mason, A. and Palmer, A. (1996) *Queer Bashing: A National Survey of Hate Crimes against Lesbians and Gays*, London: Stonewall.

Miers, D. (1978) *Responses to Victimisation: A Comparative Study of Compensation for Criminal Violence in Great Britain and Ontario*, Abingdon: Professional Books.

O'Malley, P. (1992) 'Risk, power and crime prevention', *Economy and Society*, 21: 252–75.

Percy, A. and Mayhew, P. (1998) 'Estimating sexual victimisation in a National Crime Survey: a new approach', *Studies on Crime and Crime Prevention*, 125–50.

President's Commission on Law Enforcement and the Administration of Justice (1967) *Task Force Report: Crime and its Impact*, Washington DC: US Government Printing Office.

Quinney, R. (1974) *A Critique of Legal Order*, Boston: Little, Brown.

Ryan, W. (1976) *Blaming the Victim*, New York: Vintage.

Schafer, S. (1968) *The Criminal and His Victim*, New York: Random House.

Skogan, W. (1995) 'Crime and the racial fears of white Americans', *The Annals*, 539 (May): 59–71.

Sparks, R., Genn, H. and Dodd, D. (1977) *Surveying Victims*, Chichester: Wiley.

Stanko, E. (1985) *Intimate Intrusions*, London: Routledge.

——(1988) 'Hidden violence against women', in M. Maguire and J. Pointing (eds) *Victims: A New Deal?*, Milton Keynes: Open University Press.

——(1990) *Everyday Violence*, London: Pandora.

——(1998) *Taking Stock: What Do We Know about Violence?* Uxbridge, Middlesex: Brunel University.

Stanko, E. and Curry, P. (1997) 'Homophobic violence and the self "at risk": interrogating the boundaries', *Social and Legal Studies*, 6(4): 513–32.

van Dijk, J.J.M., Mayhew, P. and Killias, M. (1990) *Experiences of Crime across the World: Key Findings of the 1989 International Crime Survey*, Boston: Kluwer.

Wolfgang, M. (1958) *Patterns of Criminal Homicide*, Philadelphia: University of Pennsylvania Press.

Young, J. (1988) 'Risk of crime and fear of crime: a realist critique of survey-based assumptions', in M. Maguire and J. Pointing (eds) *Victims: A New Deal?*, Milton Keynes: Open University Press.

2

THE ROLE OF ANXIETY IN FEAR OF CRIME

Wendy Hollway and Tony Jefferson

Introduction

Our topic derives from the 'risk–fear' paradox in the fear of crime literature; that is, those least at risk (old women) are most fearful and vice versa. Our hypothesis in starting our research[1] was that the introduction of anxiety into the debate would assist our understanding of this paradox; we assumed that people's fear of crime would not be a direct response to risk of victimisation but would be mediated by anxiety and defences against it. In the event, our hypothesis proved fruitful.

In the argument that follows, first we shall clarify our usage of the key terms: anxiety, fear of crime and risk. Second, we shall take a comparative look at some of those from our sample whose profile showed a conjunction between risk and fear of crime levels (n=13). The rationalist/realist[2] position assumes such risk–fear conjunctions to be the norm, an assumption contradicted by our findings (two-thirds of the sample of 37 were disjunctive). Moreover, even these 13 conjunctive cases reveal considerable diversity once anxiety is taken into account. We needed a theoretical perspective which explained that variability. Third, we take a selective look at the rest of the sample. Using in particular a highly disjunctive group (in risk–fear of crime terms) of women, we will demonstrate the importance of anxiety in explaining their profiles.

Defining key terms

Anxiety

Psychoanalysis provides the only theoretically developed framework for understanding human subjectivity and action which does not assume a rational, unitary subject. It has therefore been influential in perceiving and understanding the world in ways which pick up on the non-rational, unintentional and emotional aspects of people's actions and experience. Anecdotal evidence about people's responses to criminal victimisation and the threat of it – including our own – were more easily understandable in this psychoanalytic light.

According to psychoanalysis, anxiety is a universal feature of being human. The central principle of the dynamic unconscious depends on the idea that threats to the self, which would otherwise cause primary anxiety, are defended against by preventing such threats from becoming conscious. Thus unconscious defences against anxiety are a commonplace and constructive aspect of human response to threats. Where fear is usually seen as a rational response to threats of an external nature (like, say, the threat of a burglary), we would see anxiety as precipitated by threats to the self in which internal and external threats are inseparable. So, for example, an external threat such as a burglary can become a vehicle for biographically based feelings of threat to the self which precipitate defences against anxiety. At its most simple, these may be signalled by excessive worry in relation to a threat.

Psychoanalysis has identified the workings of many different defences against anxiety, the most obvious being denial ('I recognise no threat'). But, so the psychoanalytic argument goes, anxiety is not dissolved away by defences and thus it will manifest somehow, for example through displacement on to some external threat which, although fearsome, is bearable. There is also a category of defences which are inter-psychic, as opposed to intra-psychic. For example, if unable to face and acknowledge a threat, a person, in order to defend their own vulnerability, may project it on to another or others who are easy to position as more vulnerable.

According to Melanie Klein (1988a, 1988b), the capacity to face reality, even when it is threatening, is a feature of emotional development. On the other hand, in sufficiently threatening circumstances (internal or external), everyone will resort to defences which involve a denial or distortion of reality. While recognising that different modes dominate in different circumstances, we were often struck by what appeared to be the dominant operation of one or other of these responses in our interviewees. These patterns of facing or not facing internal and external threats achieve their significance over time, beginning to characterise a person's typical response mode before they are adult. This means that a focus on anxiety requires that attention be paid to biography. What the fear of crime means to a person, what any actual experience of criminal victimisation means, what the significance is of taking risks: these meanings are influenced by someone's ongoing methods of coping with the anxiety precipitated by threats and their characteristic modes of defending against anxiety. In other words, they are a product of biography. We can expect, therefore, significant differences in the relation between risk and fear between interviewees with identical risk, fear and anxiety ratings.

In this view, rather than assuming that people's relation to real threats of criminal victimisation is a rational one (the realist position), we can examine both cases where people appeared to be realistic about a threat of criminal victimisation and their responses (fearful or otherwise) to it, and others where they appeared unrealistic. In practice, this usually meant fearful about risks which were experienced as more likely and/or more dangerous than either local evidence or personal experience would tend to suggest.

In summary, rationality is understood in terms of the capacity to acknowledge potentially threatening aspects of reality without mobilising distorting unconscious defences against that reality. To posit a psychoanalytic subject of research – basically an anxious, unconsciously defended and therefore to some extent irrational subject – poses new and challenging methodological questions, since generally social research assumes respondents who are knowledgeable about themselves. We adapted techniques from psychoanalysis – eliciting narratives structured by free association, interpreting the significance of avoidance, contradiction, error and changes in emotional tone – to identify the workings of anxiety in interviewees' accounts (Hollway and Jefferson 1997a, 2000a).

Fear of crime

Our understanding of fear of crime was derived both from a reading of the existing literature[3] and from an intensive interrogation of our interview data.[4] This produced a more multi-faceted, less singular notion than the term routinely implies. For a start, fear of crime seems to mean different things to men and to women. Whereas for men it may connote fear of assault, for women it more usually connotes specifically fear of sexual assault (cf. Bannister 1997). It also seems to mean different things dependent on location. Thus, for example, some people may be afraid inside the home, but not outside: either because they never go out or because, being long-term residents and hence known locally, they generally feel safe at any hour walking about in their neighbourhood. Others may feel afraid when outside their home but safe inside, because they have one or more of a number of potentially protective factors, such as a dog or a spouse. (The way that external and internal reality interweave is exemplified here by the fact that these may mean security to one person but not to another.) Third, there is the nature of the emotion involved: the idea that the experience of criminal victimisation produces only fear now seems presumptuous in the light of more recent qualitative work, including our own. Ditton and colleagues go so far as to suggest that their respondents generally seemed 'more angry than fearful' (Ditton *et al.* 1999). Fourth, we found a need to distinguish between what we came to call personal accounts of fear and accounts adopting elements from what we called a fear of crime discourse. We called personal accounts of fear the cases where people's stories of criminal victimisation did not stray beyond the fearful effects produced in them by their particular histories of victimisation. Others' stories, however, moved between their own particular victimisation experiences and a more general, politically inflected discourse. This discourse included elements such as the worsening nature of the crime problem and declining standards of behaviour. The nostalgia-driven, backward-looking nature of this discourse sometimes tempted us to call it a 'Golden Age' discourse (cf. Pearson 1983). Finally, it seemed important to make distinctions between those who used a fear of crime discourse, but in a routine way, and those who used it in an invested way: that is, in a way which suggested that some considerable emotional energy was involved.

Risk

As with fear of crime, our conception of risk developed both from an engagement with the existing literature (Hollway and Jefferson 1997b) and an immersion in our own interview data. Once again such an in-depth empirically grounded approach served only to highlight the range of issues subsumed by the one term. Take risk of criminal victimisation, perhaps the core meaning of risk when used in the fear of crime debate. While we found that the high-crime estate justified its label statistically, especially when it came to crimes of violence (mostly male on male) and burglary, we also found that people's personal experiences of victimisation could diverge from this official picture. They often put this down to protective factors, such as being a known local, or having a big, known, local family. Whether or not such factors were responsible for the low victimisation, they often affected how 'at risk' people felt. In any event, it renders problematic any attempt to read off estate characteristics (high- or low-crime) at the level of individual households.[5] The issue of precautions and resources also affects one's 'at-riskness'. Having a reliable guard-dog or fitting well-functioning security lights and/or a burglar alarm does much to reduce the risks of burglary, just as going everywhere in a car reduces one's chance of being a victim of street robbery or assault by a stranger. The degree of risks taken, of necessity or otherwise, also affects the degree of at-riskness. Though the fear of crime literature assumes the rational norm to be a 'risk-aversive' individual, someone who avoids unnecessary risks and takes sensible precautions like locking doors and windows, risk-taking is also a valued part of our culture, perhaps especially for young men (Walklate 1997).

Accommodating all these different dimensions to fear of crime and risk was not easy but necessary to do justice to the complexity of our data. More difficult still was reducing all this to a three-point scale (high, medium or low) in order to be able to attempt some comparative analysis (Hollway and Jefferson 2000a: chapter 6). First, therefore, we devised an 'at-risk' coding for each interviewee, on a high/medium/low scale, taking into account history of criminal victimisation, lifestyle (precautions taken, risks run, etc.) and resources. The idea of reducing the complexity of individual accounts of risk to a three-point scale (high, medium, low) is a radical step and inevitably oversimplifies. This step is mitigated by the fact that we kept each whole case in view. Our use of a scale represented the translation of our judgements, based on several categories, into a single value on a scale which could then be used for comparison. However, the same value did not necessarily mean the same thing.

For example, we coded two of the young men (Sam and Winston) at medium risk, despite their caution, because they were liable to be picked upon. All the young women on the high-crime estate are medium or high risk, but for different reasons: Cherie because she hangs out with some rough youths on the estate; Rachel because she is the daughter of Dick (the evangelical 'Jovo'); and Jane because she is an 'outsider' and a single mother with two mixed-race children, living on the worst road on the estate, and has to leave the house unoccupied during some evenings. The others at high risk were Dick (the 'Jovo') and Liz, a police informer who spent a lot of time in the rough local pub. The low-risk stories exhibit similarly unique combinations of age, location, lifestyle, resources and precautions, a point we illustrate below through the cases of Phil and Juliet.

The use of a three-point scale is shown up in these examples to be an analytical device, defined both theoretically and in terms of our familiarity with all of our case data, which enabled potentially interesting comparisons about risk.

The route to our fear of crime and anxiety codings was similarly protracted. Again, our interviewing produced a range of narratives, reflections, details of practices and speculations relevant to fear of crime stemming from initial questions about safety and fear, follow-up questions, as well as the specific questions which came at the end. At this stage, then, we had three codings for each interviewee, representing our judgement – based on all the information that we had of their levels of risk, fear of crime and anxiety on a three-point scale, high, medium and low. We called this a profile. Our profiles had the advantage of showing us the relations among the three factors at a glance. We came to realise that these relations were more important conceptually than each coding on its own.

The risk–fear of crime conjunctions

Table 2.1 shows our 37 interviewees from high-crime and low-crime estates with their ratings on risk, fear of crime and anxiety, produced out of a detailed look at our interview transcripts. Column 4 shows those (marked X) with risk–fear conjunctions. Since the majority (24 out of 37) exhibit risk–fear disjunctions, this surely suggests something amiss with the assumption that risk and fear levels should equate. Focusing on the 13 risk–fear conjunctions, the assumption that these are somehow self-explanatory is called into question by the very diverse patterns of anxiety evident. That is, there are risk–fear conjunctions with low anxiety (Sam, Jack, Barbara, Brenda), with medium anxiety (Phil, Graham, Len and Juliet) and with high anxiety (Winston, Tommy, Maureen, Ivy and Dot). Can these three different patterns mean the same thing? This seems unlikely. More importantly, once anxiety is taken into account, each individual's particular risk–fear pattern can be explained. If it seems reasonable to assume that only risk–fear conjunctions associated with low anxiety qualify as rational responses to crime, it seems noteworthy that in a sample of 37 we found only four such cases. But let us start with these.

Table 2.1   Relations among risk, fear and anxiety

		1	2	3	4
		risk	*foc*	*anx*	*r/f con*
Young men	Mark	H	L	L	
HC	Craig	H	L	H	
	Ron	H	L	H	
Young men	Sam	M	M	L	X
LC	Billy	L	M	H	
	Winston	M	M	H	X
Middle-aged men	Harry	M	L	L	
HC	Tom	L	L	H	X
	Dick	H	L	L	
Middle-aged men	Duncan	L	M	H	
LC	Phil	L	L	M	X
Old men	Martin	L	M	M	
HC	Roger	L	M	H	
	Hassan	L	H	M	
	Jack	L	L	L	X
Old men	John	L	M	H	
LC	Arthur	L	M	M	
	Graham	L	L	M	X
	Len	L	L	M	X
Young	Cherie	M	L	H	
women	Jane	H	M	L	
HC	Rachel	M	L	L	
Young	Linda	L	H	H	
women	Juliet	L	L	M	X
LC	Ann	L	H	H	
Middle-aged	June	L	H	H	
women	Kelly	L	H	H	
HC	Liz	H	M	M	
	Joyce	M	L	M	
Middle-aged	Fran	L	H	H	
women	Jackie	L	M	M	
LC	Dawn	L	M	M	
Old women	Maureen	M	M	H	X
HC	Ivy	L	L	H	X
Old women	Dot	L	L	H	X
LC	Barbara	L	L	L	X
	Brenda	L	L	L	X

Notes:
H = high
M = medium
L = low
foc = fear of crime
r/f con = risk/fear conjunction
HC = high crime location
LC = low crime location

Sam, Jack, Barbara and Brenda: cases of rationality

The possibility of a more or less undistorted relation to reality is consistent with our psychoanalytic starting point, and we do not dismiss the idea that some people have a relatively realistic relation to the threat of crime. Given that high anxiety undermines such a relation to reality by precipitating defences which involve its denial or distortion, we can expect to find the most predictable relations between risk and fear to be in those who show a risk–fear conjunction and score low on anxiety. Four people fulfilled these criteria: Sam, Jack, Barbara and Brenda (see Table 2.1).[6]

Brenda and Barbara, aged 65 and 71 respectively, both live on the low-crime estate. The most significant difference between them is that Brenda's husband died several years ago, while Barbara's, now retired, accompanies her in the car to do the shopping, visit the family and go out for pub meals. However, Barbara's husband Len, an energetic ex-policeman, is still frequently out until late in the evenings attending committee meetings and the like, so that Barbara is alone in the house after dark more often than not, where she is content to read, undisturbed by fears of intruders[7] (on a recent occasion, however, when Len was away overnight, she confessed to taking a big stick up to bed with her, finding the idea of herself challenging an intruder unexceptional). In recent severe weather, with public transport ground to a halt, she walked home right across town after dark, having visited her husband in hospital, without considering herself to be at risk (except from slipping).

When Brenda's husband died, her adult son still lived with her and it was when he got married and left home that at first she left lights on, started at noises in the house and arranged extra security. Although she has a fear of the dark dating from her childhood, now she can't even go to the bathroom in the night without switching on the light! From a social life defined as a couple, she had to construct one as a single woman. Now she has a group of (mainly younger) friends whom she meets in the pub, not fearing to arrive there on her own (though her car is a significant resource in this respect). She travels abroad on her own to visit her daughter and with friends on holiday.

Both Brenda and Barbara have adapted without excessive fearfulness to life circumstances which involve being on their own at times (unlike Ann, see below). While they are no different from most of the other women we interviewed when it came to preoccupation with their families, they enjoy pleasurable lives in their own right as well. Their low anxiety is consistent with a well-established sense of self which goes along with a capacity to face reality. They are not free from commonplace fears about being out alone after dark, but (with the help of available resources, which reduce external threats) do not allow it to constrain their lives.

Jack, aged 75, has lived in the same house on the high-crime estate for sixty-three years, where he has never been burgled, nor been the victim of any other crime. He never married and continued living with his parents, and, when they died, with his sister in the family home. His sister died recently and although he

37

misses her his routines remain exactly as they were, with a cosy fire burning in the grate and weekend visits to his caravan. Since nothing untoward seemed to have happened to him in 75 years, it appeared as if his secure and predictable life accounted for his low scores. However, we felt that Jack's account presented a misleadingly unanxious, unfearful picture of his past, in which there was no direct evidence to the contrary, only absences.[8]

Sam (medium risk and fear and low anxiety), aged 18, lives on the low-crime estate with his family of origin and a steady girlfriend. He is not involved in criminal activity and his medium risk score reflects the fact that he goes around in a large group of young men (and a few women) who are picked on by other groups of young men. He 'hates' fighting, acknowledges that he has not got the 'bottle' and would rather talk his way out of trouble. Twice he has been singled out and threatened, once inexplicably and once because he continued to talk to his former girlfriend, whose boyfriend became jealous. On these occasions he takes what precautions he can (in one case, the lad was 'looking for him' for two months), which consist of going by the lighted streets when alone (he lives furthest up the estate of all his group) and getting lifts when his many supporters inform him that the threatener is around. His parents also protect and support him. After the threats and when Sam established that he was no longer being 'looked for', he ceased to worry unduly. However, he and his mates exercise caution; for example, they got into a fight at a local bonfire one year; the next year they still went (the fireworks were the best around), but they arrived and left by a safer route. In summary, there is no evidence, in either his codings or his narrative, that a generalised anxiety amplifies Sam's realistic fear.

In the cases of the three old people, it seemed that their low anxiety functioned as both cause and consequence of their safe, predictable and familiar lifestyles. Barbara had always been a calm, unworried person, with little by way of threats in her life, following from a much-loved and secure childhood. Brenda had coped in difficult times, supported by a good marital relationship. Jack's current lifestyle was notable for its cosy, safe order. In Sam's case, it seemed that he acknowledged the risks, took what precautions he could without compromising his lifestyle, and lived with the resultant fear, rather than it mobilising defences against anxiety. In summary, these four cases demonstrate not so much the possibility of accounting for the relation between risk and fear without anxiety, but the benign, mutually reinforcing effects of low anxiety in coping realistically with external threat (usually not great), the meanings of which derive from experiences whose significance has not been saturated with biographically based anxiety.

By way of comparison, let us take two cases whose risk–fear of crime scores are both low, hence apparently showing a realistic conjunction, but whose anxiety is greater. Here we can see how numerically identical profiles have different meanings: meanings which can be best understood by attending to the way that anxiety threads through their biographies.

Phil and Juliet: same profiles, different meanings

Phil's low-risk, low-fear of crime profile might seem initially to require little explanation. He is a 53-year-old man, too poor to own a car, who has lived, free of criminal victimisation, with his wife, adult stepson and two teenage sons on a low-crime estate for the past six years. His time is mostly spent locally on activities related to his role as neighbourhood watch co-ordinator, in committee work or visiting the elderly. Such a bald picture, however, not only fails to tell the more complex story of the role of fear and risk in Phil's life, but, in ignoring the crucial role of anxiety, it tells a misleading one.

An only child, Phil claims his childhood and schooldays were happy. Thereafter, disappointments dogged him. Forbidden to join the RAF by his father (which left him 'deflated'), for many years he worked twelve-hour shifts in the local bakery. After his mother died, he cared for his ailing father, which prevented him taking up a new career in teaching. His father's death quickly followed, and he was made redundant, a two-year period he described as 'difficult'. Getting married in his mid-thirties no doubt helped at this point, but three years into a new job in a new city, a freak and apparently minor accident to his elbow at home left him 'semi-disabled', permanently retired at 39, and feeling 'shattered'. The accident left him suffering from arthritis, unable to do simple household tasks, and feeling 'a burden'. He is also blind in one eye.

Phil's characteristic way of coping with these 'slings and arrows' has been to throw himself into activities on behalf of others. This community-mindedness stems partly from his early upbringing in a mining village where it had been instilled in him to 'always think of other people's safety as well as your own'. His years as an active trade union representative attest to this legacy. Partly it stems from the need to do something now he can no longer work: to fend off boredom and stop himself 'going daft'. But there is also evidence that his self-imposed round of community activities is part of a defensive structure where 'other people's needs' are constantly seen as 'more greater than mine'. Asked about earlier anxieties in his life, he replied: 'No, only for other people.' Asked about his own safety, he replied: 'Well, I always try to give other people safety.' Such extreme other-centredness in response to questions about himself is highly significant in the light of his own situation as a multiply-disabled, jobless man in poor health.

Support for this reading comes from the moments when such self-denial breaks down, such as in his account of a time when an ordinary illness had made him fear he was dying, though even then he claimed it was his wife, not him, who 'panicked and phoned for the doctor'. From this starting point, he associated, through vulnerability, to the importance of family to him: 'I think the best time is when I sit with family round me, and … 'ave family discussions … and you suddenly think "My God, it's great to have a family round you." '[9] The implied but denied sentiment is how awfully lonely and vulnerable he'd feel without his family, as he was, presumably, after the death of his parents. In this sense, then, Phil's family is undoubtedly a resource which helps contain some of his fears and anxieties.

Phil's messianic concern with community safety provides evidence that displacement is characteristic of his defensive structure. It is true that he picked up a strong sense of the importance of being safety-minded from his father who, having fallen off some scaffolding as a young man and having his abdomen 'ripped out', became very safety conscious as a building contractor employing others in similar situations. His thwarting of Phil's RAF ambitions was to do with the unsafety of flying. Later, Phil's trade union years were dominated by health and safety, being at one time regional Vice-Chair of Health and Safety and later, knowing he was finished with work, going on a union-sponsored health and safety course. So, in many respects, it is unsurprising that when Phil had to give up paid work for voluntary work in the community, issues of community safety should become a core focus. But that fails to explain the somewhat obsessional way in which Phil has approached his community role: for example, his determination to set up a neighbourhood watch scheme on a high-crime estate where he lived previously. He continued to campaign for such a scheme despite apathy ('nobody wanted to know') and outright opposition from those who didn't want a 'police-estate'. This included a vendetta against him and his family by one local teenager which involved five attempted arsons over nine months, and which led to them being rehoused in their present low-crime location. Though he describes this whole time as 'a frightening experience', his first associations, characteristically, were to the welfare of others in the block of maisonettes if the fire had caught. Also characteristically, he transformed a frightening personal experience into something that 'made us more aware on 'ealth and safety grounds of other people as well as meself'.

The threat to his family appeared to affect neither his fear of crime ('I don't worry about crime for myself') nor his keenness to be involved in neighbourhood watch activities. Once settled on his new estate, he continued to campaign for the establishment of a neighbourhood watch, this time successfully. But not content with matters of crime, such as issuing the elderly with personal alarms and talking to the council about improving the area's lighting, he sees danger everywhere: wet fallen leaves in autumn constitute a threat to the elderly, and so he is campaigning to get the council to cut down the old and beautiful broad-leaved trees which line the estate's roads.

Considering Phil's low risk, low fear, moderate anxiety scores in the light of the above, we can see how misleading were first impressions. His disclaimers about not being fearful of crime 'for himself' seem odd in relation to his extreme responses to community dangers and his excessive concern for the safety of others. Given his disabilities and the resulting vulnerability, we can see how the projection of his own feelings of unsafety on to the elderly, along with his investment in family, are the means which help him to cope with his anxieties. His long-standing fears about safety, bequeathed by his father and reactivated throughout the traumas of his own biography, were projected on to the safety of the elderly.

Like Phil, Juliet's low risk and low fear match. According to a realist theory, there is apparently nothing to explain. At 25 years old and having lived for twenty of those years in the same house on the low-crime estate where she still lives, Juliet's present risk and fear are both low largely because she rarely goes anywhere without her boyfriend, with whom she has lived for five years and whom she trusts deeply. The house has never been burgled. This risk–fear of crime conjunction seems to be a product of her current feelings of safety, both external and internal, since before meeting her boyfriend she led a very risky lifestyle but claimed to have been without fear.

Juliet's biography would lead us to expect considerable anxiety, which, however, might not manifest in fear of crime. Her mother resented her from birth, for reasons which Juliet only worked out in her teens when she discovered that her father had disappeared on the day that her mother gave birth to her: a cause, she considered, for the resentment and lack of love that her mother showed her. When her younger sister was born, her jealousy led Juliet to attack the sister constantly, which in turn led to the regular harsh physical punishment that her mother dealt out to Juliet. The risks she was wont to take when in her teens resulted from this experience: 'I used to think I were indestructible when I were younger … I'd 'ad it all – you couldn't 'urt me.' Her claim clearly puts this feeling in the past, and since then her relationship with her mother has improved immeasurably. She also claims that she has 'always' felt an intense fear of rape – according to her, her worst fear – and this remains the case, feeding into, and probably feeding off, her boyfriend's strong feelings of protectiveness towards her. The terror rape holds as a threat to her core self was conveyed by her claim that she would 'flip' if it happened: that is, she would lose her sanity. This is one place where her anxiety feeds into her fear of crime and may account for her rather fearful tendency to avoid pub doorways when walking away from work on winter evenings.

The other suggestion of excessive feelings accompanying her experience of criminal victimisation was over her car, which had been stolen twice, and had also had things stolen from it. When she went with police to reclaim it, she said she felt 'horrible' about the car, so much so that she ceased to enjoy it and sold it soon after. Her strong feelings, which were conveyed in the interview long after the event, implied that her identification with the car was so great that she felt herself violated by its theft and the wanton damage that had been done to it. Her first car had been given to her by the grandparents whose reliability and care had provided the only respite from her own family. Her subsequent relationship to owning a car appeared to contain many of the positive feelings associated with this relationship, so that the external threat of the car being stolen signified an internal threat of considerable proportions. As a result, she would have felt intensely at risk if she had still owned a car, a threat she preferred not to experience.

There was also evidence that Juliet's money worries, which she reported as her main worries, were a site for the safe expression and control of her biographical anxieties. She and her boyfriend were indeed faced by the threat of debt, since both of them were in low-paid jobs. Whereas his response to this reality had been to avoid it by spending what he had, for example on a huge collection of CDs, Juliet's approach was to control their joint income so tightly that, at the cost of rarely going out, every bill was anticipated and they never got into debt. This corresponds to the depressive form of coping with anxiety.

In summary, we believe that Juliet's low risk–low fear conjunction is not adequately explained as a realistic calculation of the risks she faces rationally translated into a low fear of crime. While the main reason for her low risk and low fear is contingent on the internal and external security she has experienced as a result of her relationship, there is some evidence that anxiety feeds into aspects of fear to do with sexual safety, which for her is profoundly connected with the safety of her core sense of self. While her relationship helps to mitigate her anxiety and to contain her fierce anger at her position in life, her rather obsessive approach to money serves to channel anxiety into an area where she exercises some real control.

The similarity between these two profiles does not imply that risk and fear of crime mean the same thing in each case. Once anxiety is factored in, their similar profiles, albeit achieved by unique biographies, become explicable, as we have tried to show here. Finally, let us turn to the more numerous risk–fear disjunctions.

Risk–fear of crime disjunctions

In Table 2.2, we grouped our sample on the basis of their risk, fear of crime and anxiety ratings. When those with identical risk/fear/anxiety profiles were placed together, this produced sixteen clusters. Note that the clusters do not neatly coincide with social demographics, a finding which supports the need to look at the unique biographical factors associated with anxiety. We intend to focus briefly on Cluster 14, which are all low risk but high fear and high anxiety. We want to show how anxiety helps to explain these risk–fear disjunctions (for other examples, see Hollway and Jefferson 1999, 2000b).

Cluster 14 consists of five women (Linda, Ann, June, Kelly and Fran) who are similar with regard to their fear (which we judged to be excessive) of being out on their own after dark. The five women do not all live on the same estate: June and Kelly live on the high-crime, the others on the low-crime estate. All of them have a child or children, except for Linda, aged 17, who lives with her mother and brother. June's husband is unemployed and is usually at home, while Ann's husband has a job which takes him away a lot. Linda depends a great deal on her boyfriend and Fran recently moved on to the council estate (from a private estate) when she separated from her husband after more than fifteen years. Their worries about crime centre on known dangers, notably burglary and physical and sexual assault. Each has relatively low records of victimisation, but Ann's appears to have been more threatening.

Table 2.2   Sixteen clusters based on shared risk, fear of crime and anxiety profiles
(H=high; M=medium; L=low)

1   HLL: Highly at risk, fearless, but not anxious.
Two men, Mark and Dick, both from the high-crime estate, neither of them old.

2   HLH: Highly at risk, fearless and highly anxious.
Two young men, Craig and Ron, both from the high-crime estate.

3   MML: Somewhat at risk and somewhat fearful, but not anxious.
One young man, Sam, from the low-crime estate.

4   LMH: Not at risk, somewhat fearful and highly anxious.
Four men, Billy, Duncan, Roger and John, all except Roger from the low-crime estate.

5   MMH: Somewhat at risk and somewhat fearful, and highly anxious.
Two people, Winston and Maureen, with only the profile in common.

6   MLL: Somewhat at risk, but neither fearful nor anxious.
Two people, Harry and Rachel, neither of them old, both from the high-crime estate.

7   LLH: Not at risk, fearless, but highly anxious.
Three people, Tommy, Ivy and Dot; the former were son and mother. None of them was young.

8   LLM: Not at risk, fearless, and somewhat anxious.
Four people, Phil, Graham, Len and Juliet. All were from the low-crime estate and three were not young.

9   LMM: Not at risk, but somewhat fearful and somewhat anxious.
Four people, Martin, Arthur, Jackie and Dawn. There were no young in this group and three came from the low-crime estate.

10   LHM: Not at risk, but highly fearful and somewhat anxious.
One old man, Hassan, from the high-crime estate.

11   LLL: Not at risk, fearless, and not anxious.
Three people, Jack, Barbara and Brenda, all of them old.

12   MLH: Somewhat at risk, not fearful, but highly anxious.
One young woman, Cherie, from the high-crime estate.

13   HML: Highly at risk, somewhat fearful, but not anxious.
One young woman, Jane, from the high-crime estate.

14   LHH: Not at risk but highly fearful and highly anxious.
Five women, Linda, Ann, June, Kelly and Fran, none of them old.

15   HMM: Highly at risk, somewhat fearful and somewhat anxious.
One middle-aged woman, Liz, from the high-crime estate.

16   MLM: Somewhat at risk, fearless and somewhat anxious.
One middle-aged woman, Joyce, from the high-crime estate.

Characteristic of each woman was a fear of being out by herself after dark (or even in daytime, except locally). Linda has always feared walking alone after dark. In this connection, she remembered hearing, when she was about eight, that a rapist lived round the corner. Now, after college in winter, she arranges for her boyfriend or mother to meet her. She doesn't like being in the house alone and follows her mother's example of asking callers for identification before she lets them in. Recently, Linda's fears seemed justified when a man posing as a gas company employee tried to gain entry to her home. She remains fearful even though she coped with the threat and he did not get in. Ann remembers being warned of the danger of being out after dark by her parents and was afraid by the time she was 11. June says she is very wary around people; even a tap on the shoulder in broad daylight by someone she knew would cause her to jump. Kelly is afraid to get out of her car, even in broad daylight, when visiting her brother on the street next to the one she grew up on (she may have been more afraid for the car than for herself). She expected her husband to garage the car at night, but if he was away she would only do so accompanied by her large dog. Fran's recent fear of crime centres on her fear of male sexual violence, illustrated by her experience, at a bus stop outside the hospital in the middle of the day, of a somewhat shady-looking man who was the only other person there. She waited for the bus imagining how easy it would be for this man to overpower her, pull her behind the wall and rape her. Inside the home the fear is similar: after being out with her mother and step-father, she obliged her step-father to check the house for hidden intruders before he and her mother went home.

This is a common feature of women's lives and arguably reflects a realistic assessment of the risk to women of sexual assault, which may be improbable but would be extremely serious. Nonetheless, as we saw with Barbara and Brenda among others, it did not characterise all the women we interviewed. Rather, it seemed to be a defining feature of a fearful femininity in which anxiety had become attached, often from an early age, to the idea of being the victim of a male stranger when unprotected. Fran's daughter (but not her son) is learning her fear: she is fearful walking the short distance home from her friend's house on winter evenings, even though it is along a busy well-lit road.

The other side of this coin is the experience of security that women habitually feel when they are accompanied by a husband, male partner or male family member. As in the case of Ann, who only sleeps soundly when her husband is back, we heard time and again from women that they felt safe both inside and out as long as their man was with them. The capacity to protect appears to be projected on to known men, despite the practical protection that these women are involved in as mothers, wives and daughters (where it is called care). The ensuing lack of a sense of control is likely to be experienced as vulnerability to criminal victimisation, notably by strange men.

Fran, aged 35, has recently split up with her husband and moved on to the low-crime estate from a private housing estate with her two teenage children. This life change has precipitated fearfulness in instances where risk remains the same. For example, only since then has she been afraid of flying. Fran's anxiety seems to cover for an intense – and maybe temporary – anxiety about being a single woman, lone mother and council tenant: that is, a loss of many aspects of self on which she had depended. Her fears are not simply a response to the new external threats associated with being a single unescorted woman, since she led a very separate social life from her husband while she was married and was not fearful. She closes the front curtains at dusk because, as she explained, she doesn't want people to know her business. This account, which on the surface was about fears of burglary and intrusion, pointed to a deeper fear that she would be seen by others as a lone mother, belonging to a category of women who are doubly stigmatised for supposedly failing as mothers and as women by not having a man. There is a further piece of evidence that her fears of sexual assault are displaced: when her daughter phones up wanting to be escorted back home after dark from a nearby friend's house, Fran's worries are all for her daughter and not for herself, evidenced by the fact that at these times she walks out to meet her daughter without worrying about her own safety.

Both Linda and Fran have memories of violent and alcoholic fathers assaulting their mothers (who both subsequently left their marriages and brought their children up single-handed for many years). It may be that their excessive fears of strange men are a repository for anxieties about men, precipitated early in their lives but kept separated from their feelings about known men; neither have any reason to fear known men now. (Kelly and June, on the other hand, were closer to their fathers than their mothers.)

In short, the higher anxiety and fear of crime, not commensurate with risk, illustrated in this group of women reflects a specifically gendered expression of anxiety. This involves an unrealistic projection of control and the capacity to protect into known men. It manifests in a gendered fear of crime, where threats to the self and the extension of these into their children (especially daughters) are experienced as coming from other men – strangers who are imagined to be threatening.

Let us now look at the way in which we can understand this phenomenon more generally. In the results of survey research, the preponderance of women who may fear sexual assault is camouflaged in the blunt gender difference in fear of crime. When it has been the subject of other research, women have been asked directly about their fears of sexual assault, and this has confirmed its importance in women's lives. It has been seen as a realistic response to a real (and serious) danger. The differences among women are rarely made visible nor, when they are, explained.

In our cases, we see girls' early and formless anxiety being channelled into fear of strange men, specifically through a widespread worry about girls' safety on their own after dark. There are real and serious risks to boys, too, of preda-tory paedophiles, but rarely do boys introject such fear and it normally does not become a receptacle for their anxiety (as in Fran's son's case). For women, fear of strange men continues to be available as a receptacle for anxieties when these are precipitated by events, as in Fran's case in her recent change of circumstances. The biography of such women is in this respect a biography of the recursive channelling of anxiety into a culturally sanctioned, gender-specific fear (of strange men's sexual predations). This explanation does not exclude the effects of real events, such as Linda's narrow escape from what could well have been sexual assault. However, biography is not a direct reflection of real events. Rather, past experiences are continuously reconstructed in the light of later meanings (Scott 1996).

While the above explanation emphasises the role of unique biographies, what we are explaining also has a social dimension, in the sense that these fears are expressed almost exclusively by girls and women. However, because of biographical features, not all women are positioned by this discourse of female sexual vulnerability. We have explained these biographical features in terms of anxiety: it may be that people are subject to very different levels of anxiety as a result, for example, of how secure their early experiences were. It is also the case, so we are arguing, that people cope with and defend against their anxieties through using different channels, of which fear of male sexual assault is just one. In summary, in looking at these women's biographies, even at this superficial level, we can see the way that demographic and biographical features are jointly expressed in their fears of going out on their own.

We can use Hassan's case (on his own in Cluster 10) to show that levels of anxiety and fear, incommensurate with risk, are not confined to women, despite their gendered expressions in the above cases. His profile (low risk, high fear, medium anxiety) is similar to the above group of women, though he is marginally less anxious, but he differs from them on most of the demographic categories that were designed into our research (namely, sex and age) and also 'race'. Hassan, an older man (aged 68) who now lives alone, is highly fearful. An immigrant to England in his late teens, he remained single until his forties. He then had a marriage arranged with a much younger woman who joined him in England and they had five children in quick succession. These were happy years; everything was 'smashing'. He was fulfilled as husband, father and provider – and unafraid. Then his wife began to challenge his authority, eventually leaving, taking the children. Later he was persuaded to sign over his half of the house to them, leaving him nothing. Then his health gave out, he retired early from his job as a nursing assistant and he now spends his days in considerable pain.

Now – which seems to refer generally to his years as a divorced, retired man living on the estate – everything is 'terrible'. He is frightened to go out after dark, rarely doing so except to pray during Ramadan, when he usually gets a lift. At home he is afraid to open the door and jumps when the fridge makes a noise. Watching the TV is scary, with stories of old people getting killed. He talked repetitively of all this 'pinching and killing' frightening him, and all the elderly, 'to death', yet had only ever experienced racially abusive behaviour (on two occasions, both mild) and ill-behaved kids knocking on his door and throwing a stone at the window.

Judged by either his present experience of life in a fairly protected corner of the estate in purpose-built accommodation for the elderly, or his 'smashing' past experience as a happy family man and worker, his present fears are, we suggest, excessive and invested. Clues to the purpose served by Hassan's defensive invest-ment are to be found both in his account of his marriage breaking up and the fact that his vehement tirade against crime is part of a general tirade against the ills of modernity, including sexual permissiveness and drugs. A traditional, conservative, religious man, Hassan's marriage broke down when his wife chal-lenged his patriarchal right to order her life. A younger woman, she chose modern independence over traditional religious and patriarchal authority – as did their children in going with her. The loss of all he ever worked for has left him lonely and disappointed, with a painful old age ahead. His devout and fatal-istic Muslim beliefs serve to contain some of his anxiety. However, the fact that he appeared to channel his feelings of loss into fear of crime suggests the need for a bearable fear to replace his deep loss and how threatening it would be to acknowledge.

Hassan's vulnerability to racist harassment and assault provides an external parallel to women's vulnerability to sexual attack, but there is not the same inser-tion of this vulnerability into biography as with the cluster of women above: Hassan was free of such fears as a young single man and a family man. There is an echo of Fran's recent fear in the way that his fear of crime follows the losses to his self-identity, though his were more severe. This is a reminder that psycho-logical mechanisms to do with coping with loss and trauma and ways of defending against anxiety cross demographic boundaries, as well as often being articulated in gendered – and other social – ways.

Conclusions

We started with the risk–fear conundrum at the heart of the fear of crime debate, and suggested that the inclusion of anxiety would prove useful. We went on, first to use the evidence from case examples where risk and fear of crime levels were the same and then cases where fear of crime was higher. We also examined cases with the same profiles of risk, fear and anxiety scores, as well as those with different levels of anxiety. In all cases, even in those of risk–fear conjunction and low anxiety, we found the application of a psychoanalytic concept of anxiety involving unconscious, often interpsychic defences, to be indispensable in understanding people's fear of crime.

The psychoanalytic concept of anxiety has enabled us to question the usual assumptions of a rational, risk-calculating individual whose fear of crime is a direct reflection of their risk. This position, espoused by the 'realist' theorists in the fear of crime literature, has often been adhered to as part of a critique of a political argument which sees those who fear crime as irrational, thereby locating blame effectively with individuals rather than their situations. In this way the debate reflects the wider problems of dualistic explanations which favour either social or individual accounts of social phenomena. In our interpretations, incorporating psychodynamic insights into the analysis still enables us to take seriously the real risks that people face. However, it recognises that the experience of these risks is never unmediated. The meanings which mediate external risks are a product not only of available circulating discourses, but of individual biography. These biographies are not simply accumulations of past experiences, but the outcome of different ways of dealing with anxiety precipitated by threats to the self. In this sense, biography helps to explain if and how discourses concerning crime and fear of crime are taken up and made meaningful to that individual. In demonstrating the various workings of defences against anxiety in the unique biographical contexts of people's ways of coping with their fears of crime, we hope to have shown the inadequacy of assumptions of rationality underpinning the realist position; in Foucault's telling phrase, how 'fictions function in truth'.

References

Bannister, J. (1997) 'Hidden fears? Perceptually contemporaneous offences and the fear of crime', paper presented to the British Criminology Conference, 15–18 July 1997, Queen's University, Belfast.

Box, S., Hale, C. and Andrews, G. (1988) 'Explaining the fear of crime', *British Journal of Criminology*, 28(3): 340–56.

Ditton, J., Bannister, J., Gilchrist, E. and Farrell, S. (1999) 'Afraid or angry? Recalibrating the "fear" of crime', *International Review of Victimology*, 6: 83–99.

Farrell, G. (1995) 'Preventing repeat victimisation', in M. Tonry and D.P. Farrington (eds) *Building a Safer Society: Strategic Approaches to Crime Prevention*, Chicago: University of Chicago Press, 469–534.

Ferraro, K. (1995) *Fear of Crime: Interpreting Victimization Risk*, New York: SUNY Press.

Hale, C. (1996) 'Fear of crime: a review of the literature', *International Review of Victimology*, 3: 79–150.

Hollway, W. and Jefferson, T. (1997a) 'Eliciting narrative through the in-depth interview', *Qualitative Inquiry*, 3(1): 53–70.

——(1997b) 'The risk society in an age of anxiety: situating fear of crime', *British Journal of Sociology*, 48(2): 255–66.

——(1999) 'Gender, generation, anxiety and the reproduction of culture', in R. Josselson and A. Lieblich (eds) *Narrative Study of Lives, 6*, Thousand Oaks, CA: Sage, 107–40.

——(2000a) *Doing Qualitative Research Differently: Free Association, Narrative and the Interview Method*, London: Sage.

——(2000b) 'Biography, anxiety and the experience of locality', in P. Chamberlayne, J. Bornat and T. Wengraf (eds) *The Turn to Biographical Methods in Social Science*, London: Routledge, 167–80.

Hough, M. and Mayhew, P. (1985) *Taking Account of Crime: Key Findings from the Second British Crime Survey*, Home Office Research Study 85, London: HMSO.

Klein, M. (1988a) *Love, Guilt and Reparation and Other Works 1921–1945*, London: Virago.

——(1988b) *Envy and Gratitude and Other Works 1946–1963*, London: Virago.

Mirrlees-Black, C., Mayhew, P. and Percy, A. (1996) *The British Crime Survey: England and Wales*, Home Office Statistical Bulletin, Issue 19/96, Research and Statistics Directorate, London: Home Office.

Pearson, G. (1983) *Hooligan: A History of Respectable Fears*, London: Macmillan.

Scott, A. (1996) *Real Events Revisited: Fantasy, Memory and Psychoanalysis*, London: Virago.

Sparks, R. (1992) 'Reason and unreason in "left realism": some problems in the constitution of fear of crime', in R. Matthews and J. Young (eds) *Issues in Realist Criminology*, London: Sage, 119–35.

Walklate, S. (1997) 'Risk and criminal victimisation: a modernist dilemma?' *British Journal of Criminology*, 37(1): 35–45.

Young, J. (1988) 'Risk of crime and fear of crime: a realist critique of survey-based assumptions', in M. Maguire and J. Pointing (eds) *Victims of Crime: A New Deal*, Milton Keynes: Open University Press.

3

TRUST AND THE PROBLEM OF COMMUNITY IN THE INNER CITY

Sandra Walklate

Introduction

The notion that the inner city constitutes a problematic area is not a new one. Fraser (1997) has usefully identified a number of different ways in which 'those inner cities' have been discussed in contemporary terms: spatially, culturally, ethnically or (potentially) any combination of these. In some respects, these contemporary discourses about the inner city derive from the legacy of the processes of urbanisation and industrialisation of the early nineteenth century. Images of city life emerged from these processes which, not only identified parts of the city as physically dangerous (for example, from a health point of view), but also characterised the people as dangerous. Here lived the pickpockets, the prostitutes and the 'police property' (Lee 1981) of the nineteenth century: that section of society labelled by Marx as the 'social scum'. Arguably, the Chicago School of sociology, exemplified in the work of Park and Burgess, added further weight to these images by focusing attention on the social disorganisation, and the concomitant social problems (including crime), to be found in the 'zone of transition'. Thus it is possible to discern some of the ways in which presumptions concerning the socially disorganised and disorderly nature of inner-city life have become embedded in more contemporary social and political thought. Such presumptions are not only of historical interest. They have a contemporary relevance in the current concern with social exclusion (Social Exclusion Unit 1998) and community (*Policy Action Team 9 Report*; Active Community Unit 1999). Moreover, these are the presumptions which have been particularly salient in understanding the impact of crime.

It is well recognised in officially recorded crime rates, national victimisation surveys and local victimisation surveys that criminal victimisation is a key problem in inner-city areas. The chance of becoming a victim of crime, and the material impact (at a minimum) that such victimisation is likely to have, is accepted as being far greater in inner-city areas. It has also been demonstrated that the problem of 'repeat victimisation' is largely a phenomenon of these localities (National Board for Crime Prevention 1994). Data such as these add further fuel to the image of such areas exemplified in the following extract taken from *The Independent on Sunday* in April 1994 in an article headed 'Fear Rules in No-Go Britain'.

> How else would you describe an area which taxi drivers refuse to serve, where doctors are advised to seek police protection before making house calls, and which the police themselves will only visit in numbers? What do you call an area where the majority of law-abiding residents lock themselves in their homes in fear of a lawless minority?
>
> (*Independent on Sunday*, 17 April 1994)

The empirical work referred to in this chapter was referenced as one such area in that article by *The Independent on Sunday* in 1994. Such areas, then, are not only portrayed as crime-ridden, but it is also assumed that the people who live there are in a state of fearfulness of what goes on around them. Consequently the question is raised, how do people who go to work in, go to school in, live in high-crime areas construct a sense of 'ontological security' (Giddens 1991)? Or, put slightly differently, what is the 'lived reality' (Genn 1988) of people in high-crime areas; to what extent is that lived reality informed by crime or the threat of criminal victimisation; and what informs the routine management of day-to-day life for individuals who live in these areas?

In order to address these questions reference will be made to some key findings from a two and a half year comparative empirical investigation of two similarly structured high-crime areas. This study was embedded in two assumptions. The first was taken from the work of Giddens (1991). He states that:

> All individuals develop a framework of ontological security of some sort based on routines of various forms. People handle dangers and the fear associated with them in terms of emotional and behavioural formulae which have come to be part of their everyday behaviour and thought.
>
> (*ibid.*: 44)

For Giddens, managing this security is a central problem of late modern society. In part he argues that this is a consequence of the extent to which 'The risk climate of modernity is [thus] unsettling for everyone: no-one escapes' (*ibid.*: 124) so that as individuals we 'colonise the future' (*ibid.*: 125) in order to manage (though not necessarily reduce) our anxieties. The research referred to here was concerned to document some of these management strategies.

The second assumption embedded in this research relates to the way in which the concept of community has been utilised in criminological research. The two communities under investigation (as will be seen below) were part of the inner city and local images of them reflected all the presumptions of disorganisation and dangerousness with which this chapter began. Predominantly North American ethnographic research has illustrated the ways in which people living in high-crime areas, such as the inner city, manage their sense of well-being (see, for example, Merry 1981; Anderson 1990). However, with perhaps the exception of the work of Shapland and Vagg (1988), little work in the UK had focused on how people in predominantly white high-crime areas manage their routine daily lives. Given the disturbances of the early 1990s, and given that each of the areas under investigation here featured differently in those disturbances, it was assumed that if the notion of the fear of crime had any saliency then it would be in areas such as these. As will be seen, this was not necessarily demonstrated. However, before this argument can be furthered it will be useful to engage in a brief description of each of the research areas.

The research areas

The research areas were located in the city of Salford, part of the Greater Manchester conurbation. The city of Salford itself is a multiply deprived, predominantly white area battling with the full effects of the closure of the docks in 1972 and years of de-industrialisation. It is an area in which the City Council has attempted to sow the seeds of economic regeneration, including the creation of one of the first Enterprise Zones in 1981, and latterly with the development of its dockland into an office, leisure and residential development akin to London's Dockland scheme. Arguably the economic and structural changes affecting Salford as a whole have taken their toll on particular parts of the city referred to as 'Old Salford' – its inner-city areas – rather than 'New Salford' – the comparatively wealthy and suburban areas which became part of the city of Salford after 1974. These research areas, called Oldtown and Bankhill respectively here, are in 'Old Salford'.

These areas comprise two predominantly white local authority wards with similar unemployment rates (Oldtown 22.9%; Bankhill, 22.8%) and similar youth unemployment rates (32.4% and 37.8% respectively), but with differing patterns of housing tenure (Oldtown: owner-occupied 23.8%, council 61.2%, housing association 7.1%: Bankhill; 34.6%, 28% and 23% respectively). The two wards are, however, physically quite different and have a very different history.

Oldtown was the residential ward that historically housed a great number of the city's industrial workforce and dock labour. It is predominantly a council-owned estate, part of which, known locally as the Oldtown Triangle, is situated in the heart of the estate and now includes much of the area's lowest standard of housing. The ward has undergone a number of transformations in the last three decades, its back-to-back terraces being largely demolished in the 1960s and 1970s and replaced with system-built high- and low-rise housing stock. From the early 1980s, Salford Council controversially embarked on a policy which sold off many of its worst housing in this area to private developers; the developers transformed these hard-to-let estates on the periphery of the ward into owner-occupied 'yuppie' flats. At the same time, some residents of the Triangle area were improving their own housing through the setting up of Salford's (and indeed Manchester's) first housing co-operative.

The defunct and derelict dock area became, by 1990, the city's prestigious docklands development. Situated on the other side of a busy four-lane highway from the main body of the ward's residential area it is visible from all parts of the estate. It is at once separated from, and yet a part of, the ward. In the 1990s the remaining council stock was being improved by Estates Action monies in five distinct phases, so that, in mid-1995, the further one travelled into the estate the more untouched the area was. Nevertheless, housing for owner-occupation has been built – it is a condition of the Estates Action funding that mixed residential tenure is promoted.

Perhaps as a result of the area's strong working-class make-up, Oldtown was always seen as a 'rough' area. Seafarers from all over the world – with their hard-drinking image – frequented its pubs, and prostitution was common on the main route past the dock area. After the docks closed the area gained a reputation for crime and disorder. Whatever the truth of this reputation, the area became isolated and depressed throughout the 1980s as unemployment worsened and local road-building policies literally cut the area off from its surroundings on all sides, with many of its local amenities being demolished in the process. Those amenities that have remained have served as a public arena in which 'grasses' are named through the use of graffiti (Evans *et al.* 1996). With little reason for most city residents to enter the area, this reputation as a problem area has been easily sustained – a reputation further underscored with the reporting of a 'riot' in 1992 in which a carpet warehouse was razed to the ground and gunshots were fired at a police vehicle.

Bankhill, on the other hand, is a more physically diverse area which, in turn, is more physically connected to surrounding areas, so that there is some local confusion as to where the ward boundaries actually are. It is an area of very large early Victorian and Georgian merchants' houses as well as late Victorian and Edwardian terraces. In Engels' *The Condition of the Working Class in England* it is cited as an area of middle-class flight from the squalor of the city. Its reputa-tion as a more middle-class area, a step up from the inner city on the way to the suburbs, persisted well into the latter half of this century. It is at present, however, very much a part of the 'inner city'. Its larger dwellings are, on the whole, residential homes for the elderly or community care hostels. Many are divided into flats, rented out by private landlords. Small pockets of council housing have been built in the ward from the 1960s, including a small number of tower blocks. Many of the smaller terraced houses have been bought wholesale by housing associations and improved for rent. Owner-occupation is the largest form of housing tenure in the area. Bankhill covers a smaller area than Oldtown but is more densely populated and a higher proportion of its properties are of a poor standard, lacking amenities such as central heating.

Alongside this physical diversity lies a cultural diversity unparalleled in other areas of the city. To the north of the ward is an area of predominantly Jewish settlement, and many of its residents are orthodox Hasidic Jews. To the east of the ward there are streets with a high proportion of Asian families, Muslims from Pakistan as well as Indian Sikhs. There is also an unequal distribution of 'social problems' within the ward. Certain streets have had very high rates of house burglary; others remain relatively untouched by this form of criminal activity. Gangs of young males assert territorial control in some areas, hanging around in large numbers and painting walls, roads and boarded-up houses with graffiti denigrating individual police officers, celebrating local gangs and convicted offenders and generally sending out a very public message of 'control' of the streets, though all of this is a relatively new phenomenon.

There are far fewer references to 'trouble' in this area in the local papers before the mid-1980s. However, young people 'on the rampage' in the area were reported in 1985 and there were some disturbances on the very east of the ward in 1992. Local residents speak of the area as being in a cycle of decline, and, paralleling the blaming in Oldtown, the City Council is often cited as the cause of the decline as they moved 'outsiders' into the area, disrupting a formerly stable community. Talk of this area in these terms provides one of the first clues as to how people living in this community have endeavoured to make sense of what they see, feel and know to be going on around them. So how do people living in these two similarly structured though physically different areas manage their routine daily lives, and to what extent does crime or the fear of crime inform that routine daily management?

Routine management of crime in Oldtown and Bankhill

The fear amongst people in this ward that you're pointing to now is that it could be the next-door neighbour that burgles you, you're not sure who to trust. When there's no trust amongst a neighbourhood it perpetuates. They're looking over their shoulder and they're thinking there's a fear and perhaps it doesn't exist ... these people in this ward have no trust of even their own sons.

(Comment recorded in a police focus group discussion, Bankhill)

It's always been a self-policing community, always has been. But I think that is also a weakness in the community. They still dislike vandalism and they dislike most crime that goes on, but they are unwilling to break from the community chapel. The community is strangling itself, because they have to break free from old traditions and the old 'I can't name any names but what's his face up the road will sort it out'.

(Comment recorded in a police focus group discussion, Oldtown)

These two quotes tap some aspects of the ways in which people living in

Oldtown and Bankhill differently manage their relationship with, and understanding of, the problem of crime in their area. In different ways these quotes articulate, both implicitly and explicitly, the central importance of understanding the questions: whom do you trust? how much can you trust? when can you trust? how do you trust? (Nelken 1994) in contributing to a construction of a sense of well-being for people living in these localities. The mechanisms underpinning this construction for people in these areas have been detailed elsewhere (for example, see Evans *et al.* 1996; Walklate 1998; Walklate and Evans 1999), therefore only a brief overview will be presented here: so what about trust?

The concept of trust has been relatively underexplored in sociology and certainly not fully considered within criminology. It has, however, proved to be an important way of making sense of the empirical findings associated with this study. Its usefulness became apparent when, during the course of the investigation, people in Oldtown were recorded as saying that the questions being asked of them did not really make sense because you were 'all right round here if you were local'. This statement, along with the belief that 'people round here don't rob off their own', was repeated often enough to constitute what Elias and Scotson (1965) have called a 'neighbourhood dogma': that is, a set of beliefs that have a salience above and beyond the interview moment. The recognition of the importance of these beliefs in Oldtown and their absence from Bankhill led to a consideration of what underpinned this presence and absence. The concept of trust facilitated an understanding of these processes.

In discussing the question of ontological security, Giddens (1991) has argued that trust is most clearly evidenced in traditional societies through kinship relations, local communities or religious commitment. Moreover, he goes on to argue that the absence of these mechanisms in late modern societies renders trust no more than a matter for individual contractual negotiation. A similar argument is presented by Luhmann (1989). Gellner (1989), too, suggests that urban life is incompatible with trust and social cohesion, implying that such processes are rooted in rural tribal traditions. Yet, without trust, modern life – especially modern economic life – could not flourish (see Fukuyama 1996). Notably, economic relations are also those which cannot be completely controlled. Trust is therefore essential. Fukuyama (1996) argues that trust is the basis on which 'regular honest behaviour' is created. However, as we shall see, it may just as likely be the basis on which regular dishonest behaviour is created. Arguably it is the regularity or otherwise of the behaviour which sustains or threatens social relationships.

Giddens (1991) and Beck (1992) both argue that an increasing awareness of the value of trust goes along with two other processes: the possible future damage of risk-taking behaviour and the challenge posed by post-modernism to the universalism of modernism. As Misztal states:

> By destroying the grounds for believing in a universal truth, post-modernity does not make our lives more easy but only less constrained

by rules and more contingent. It demands new solutions based on the tolerant co-existence of a diversity of cultures. Yet although post-modernism encourages us to live without an enemy, it stops short of offering constructive bases for mutual understanding and trust.

(1996: 239)

This view certainly endorses the need for understanding the changing nature of trust, especially in the context of social relationships that are being increasingly characterised by diversity and the celebration of difference. (This question of the changing context of trust is re-visited below.) 'To live without an enemy' requires trust. But how does trust manifest itself? In the context of the research referred to in this chapter it has been useful to conceptualise the manifestation of these relationships in terms of a 'square of trust' (cf. Young 1992, who talks of a 'square of crime'). See Figure 3.1.

THE STATE   (DIS)ORGANISATION OF
                                             CRIME

the individual

(DIS)ORGANISATION OF   MECHANISMS FOR

COMMUNITY   SOCIABILITY

Figure 3.1 The square of trust

In this square of trust, whom you can trust, how you trust and how much you can trust all depend upon where individuals find themselves between the different points of the square. In Oldtown, it would appear that people trust as much as the local norms and values permit, whilst simultaneously avoiding being labelled a 'grass' (Evans *et al.* 1996). This takes the form, primarily, of trusting other local people, because they are local (mechanisms for sociability), and certainly does not mean offering generalised trust to official agencies (the state). This does not mean that the criminal gangs present in Oldtown (organised crime) have won the hearts and minds of people living here, but it does mean that it is necessary to re-think how social solidarity is produced and maintained (the organised nature of the community). On the other hand, however, in Bankhill older people were willing to offer a generalised trust to 'official agencies' (the state), and there were some friendship and community groups that strove to offer some kind of militating against a totally atomised existence (mechanisms of sociability). Moreover, the level of social disorganisation in this locality and the expressed fear of, and lack of trust in, young people (the disorganised nature of local crime) undermine any sense of belonging on which calling for help from the official agencies might be developed.

For younger people the picture is somewhat different. They know they cannot be seen talking to 'officials' (the state), which might also include older people. They also know that to stay out of trouble they have to manage 'being known', but not to be a 'grass' or participate in criminal activity (the disorganised nature of local crime). For a fuller discussion of these process see Walklate and Evans (1999: chapters 2 and 3).

The different ways in which these relationships of trust manifest themselves in these two areas may be rooted in the different socio-economic histories of the areas, but the relationships themselves are not historical. They articulate real mechanisms whereby individuals create a way of managing their routine daily lives in a way that meaningfully situates them differently in relation to the state, crime, community and social relationships. If, then, understanding the question of trust constitutes a meaningful way of making sense of the empirical reality of the routine daily lives of people living in high-crime areas, what are the implications of this?

The implications of these findings are (at least) twofold. First, they constitute a challenge to the way in which inner-city areas have been traditionally understood. Second, they constitute a challenge to the policy possibilities and policy implementation process in areas like these. Each of these implications raises questions about the relationship between the citizen and the state, and the role of market forces in impacting upon that relationship, and each will be discussed in turn.

Understanding the inner city

Presumptions concerning the lived reality of the inner city abound in academic, political and policy discourses. As was suggested at the beginning of this chapter, the origins of those presumptions are to be found in the political and policy drive to assert some control over the impact of the industrial revolution and the concomitant growth in urban development. Added to this was the Chicago School's concern with understanding and managing the social disorganisation associated with the zone of transition. The image of the inner city as socially disorganised has remained, and some would say has been perpetuated in more recent years in the United Kingdom, through the importation of the underclass debate and the ideas of communitarianism from North America. Each of these interventions has had a different impact upon images of inner-city communities. On the one hand, the underclass debate presumes that those people living in the inner city (*inter alia*) are cynical towards the official societal values (especially with respect to issues of law and order); have distinctive norms and values; and do not possess the capacity for conventional collective political action (see, for example, Murray 1990). Consequently, inner-city communities and the social problems they represent are seen to constitute a threat to mainstream society. On the other hand, the communitarians, as articulated in the ideas of Etzioni (1996), argue for the need to restore such communities with a new sense of moral, social and public order, reflecting a view that such processes are absent from existing community life. In the light of the empirical evidence discussed above, each of these views is flawed in different ways.

One key message from this empirical investigation is the central difficulty of assuming all inner-city areas are the same. The two areas under investigation were less than two miles apart, yet displayed very different ways of managing their relationship with crime. Oldtown, it is possible to argue, is a well-organised, socially ordered, indeed well-defended community, whose mechanisms of social control co-exist with more conventional processes. In this community people for the most part worked with the local neighbourhood dogma. It equipped them not only with a sense of well-being, but also with a sense of moral, social and public order, and simultaneously did not appear to undermine their capability for both conventional and unconventional collective action. They trusted each other and their own socially constructed mechanisms of informal social control and punishment, rather than any official mechanisms, to maintain local social order. (This is discussed more fully in Walklate, forthcoming.) The other community, Bankhill, it is possible to argue, was a relatively disorganised, disordered, frightened community with a shifting sense of moral, social and public order which did appear to undermine the capacity for any kind of collective action (conventional or otherwise), yet at the same time this did not seem to undermine the acceptance of official norms and values. People here still reached out to, and had trust invested in, the official agencies, for help with the problems in their areas. In other words, inner-city communities can be just that – communities, in the very traditional, almost pre-modern sense of that concept; or they can be 'lonely crowds' (Riesman 1963). Each conjures different policy possibilities.

Whose policy? Whose process?

To reiterate what has been stated above, the two areas under investigation during the course of this research were less than two miles apart, yet it is also evident from the brief summary of the findings which have been presented that the question of what might work in each of these areas looks (potentially) very different. So, what might work?

Partnership has become the new buzzword of the crime prevention industry, a buzzword which has become tied to the notion of community. Indeed, it is now a legal requirement as enshrined in the Crime and Disorder Act 1998. Crawford (1997) has situated the appeals to 'community' and 'partnership' in the wider processes of the governance of crime: that is, as part of the increasingly shifting boundaries between the state and other inter/intra-organisational networks (the public, the private, the voluntary sector, etc.) Analyses of the partnership approach such as these make sense if, and only if, researchers and policy-makers alike insist on looking for solutions to the crime problem from the top down. But what about looking from the bottom up (Lewis and Salem 1986)? Can community safety partnerships prevent, reduce or manage crime in areas like Oldtown and Bankhill? If so, how and under what circumstances?

In Bankhill, for example, there was a willingness and desire to work with the 'authorities', and there was a trust and expectation invested in those 'authorities' to make things happen in return. There, people wanted their concerns, which may appear petty and trivial, to be taken seriously by the 'authorities'. Consequently, in an area like this the local authority and the police may be able to take a lead in local developments and will find support for such in the local community, though that support may lead to a broader interpretation of the notion of partnership above and beyond the usual multi-agency approach. This vision of partnership implies a view of crime as a local problem to be managed locally, not necessarily prevented or reduced.

On the other hand, in Oldtown, the local problems are arguably already being managed, not by a community safety partnership strategy as such but through the (fragile) equilibrium which exists between the police, the local community and the organised nature of crime in that area. A very different conception of what might constitute a partnership! Yet the processes underpinning these relationships, in allowing people to feel all right about living in their locality, seem to work for most of the people living there most of the time. Simultaneously, partnerships may well be formed in areas like Oldtown but such partnerships may not have any of the characteristics of more conventional organisational allegiances. Such partnerships may be, for example, with strategically placed individual residents who may be influential in carrying other local people with them. Here again, the result may not be crime prevention or crime reduction, but crime management with the opportunity of maintaining and/or restoring local equilibrium, or at least offering an opportunity to discover what that might look like. (A fuller discussion of these issues in relation to this research is to be found in Walklate 1999.)

The implications of this discussion suggest that it is necessary to move away from universalistic and/or simplistic solutions to crime in localities like Oldtown and Bankhill. The alternatives may be more complex (though not necessarily more expensive); they may have different outcomes than those valued by the crime prevention industry; and they may challenge conventional views of what is, or is not, acceptable as a crime problem. In addition, they raise the questions not only of whose policy and whose process is crime prevention, but also of what is democratically acceptable at a local as well as a national level.

Conclusion: citizen, state and market

Oldtown and Bankhill are not unusual places. Each urban (and increasingly rural) area has its equivalent Oldtowns and Bankhills. These are predominantly white areas, where the traditional working class historically co-existed with the 'social scum' and those who were endeavouring to better themselves as market forces permitted. Oldtown and Bankhill may be at different points on a socio-economic trajectory (which this research was not designed to accommodate); but this trajectory is suggestive (almost) of an ecological historically driven process which Oldtown has found a way of managing and Bankhill is in the process of so doing. Such a process is characterised by a number of features, one of which is understanding the changing mechanisms of social inclusion and exclusion and the shifting relationships of trust formed to manage those mechanisms.

Evans *et al.* state:

> your *place* in relation to crime *places* you in a community of belonging and exclusion … It is consequently important to recognise who is seen to be protecting you and how: for many people it is not the police or the council but local families and/or the Salford Firm. Moreover, it is the absence of confidence in the formal agencies which creates the space for those other forces to come into play.
>
> (1996: 379)

This quote refers to Oldtown, a locality from which the state had, for the most part, withdrawn. It was apparent that parts of Bankhill were also in the process of suffering a similar fate. There are other such localities throughout the United Kingdom, as Campbell's (1993) analysis suggests, some of them peopled by ethnic minorities, just as many peopled by Caucasians. They are all areas that have been left behind by the market forces of the last two decades. These are the locations which have suffered disproportionately as the gap between rich and poor has grown and as we have become increasingly a 30/30/40 society (Hutton 1995).

A critical reflection on the findings produced by this research reveals much about the ways in which the mechanisms of social inclusion and exclusion have operated and been managed at a local level. The question remains, of course, as to how much responsibility we should assume, collectively, for the most vulnerable in our society, however we might choose to define that vulnerability. It is clear that, while the relationship between the citizen and the state has changed in emphasis since 1945 in the UK, there are also strong historical continuities in that relationship, historical continuities informed by notions of a distinction between the deserving and undeserving, the principle of less eligibility and the notion of the dangerous classes. These dangerous classes, of course, provide the criminal justice system with much of its work, so for that reason alone it is important to grasp a clear understanding of the how and why of those relationships.

In a different context Currie (1997: 147) has discussed the marketisation of violence. By that he is referring to the processes whereby the 'pursuit of private gain' is 'likely to breed high levels of violent crime'. In this context, that same pursuit seems to have produced communities which, when left to their own management strategies, have found ways of making life all right for themselves: the marketisation of trust. The consequences of these processes are there to be seen (*inter alia*) in the report of the Social Exclusion Unit: *Bringing Britain Together: A National Strategy for Neighbourhood Renewal* (September 1998). That report highlights communities, notably including Salford, for whom not only crime but health, education, housing, etc., still constitute issues of serious concern. In the foreword to that document, the Prime Minister states: 'Our goal is simple: to bridge the gap between the poorest neighbourhoods and the rest of Britain. Bridging that gap will not be easy. It will require imagination, persistence, and commitment' (Social Exclusion Unit 1998: 8).

The research discussed here certainly supports the view that bridging this gap will not be easy. Those who are socially excluded and have found ways of managing that exclusion will not be easily persuaded that it is in their interests to manage their lives differently.

For example, since the completion of this research local authorities have been required to engage in Crime Audits with a view to developing local partnerships as a way of tackling local crime problems. The Crime and Disorder Act 1998 put these requirements in place. That legislation was wide in its coverage, demanding not only the legal institution of partnership working but also the use of this as one mechanism for addressing the problem of young people and crime. This latter concern is reflected in the desire to render the criminal justice process swifter in its handling of young offenders and at the same time more meaningful: among other initiatives, for example, through the introduction of the final warning scheme and reparation. Given the problematic status accorded to young people in the findings presented from this research, it is of particular value to consider whether or not the strategy proposed by the Crime and Disorder Act will work in areas like Oldtown and Bankhill.

The partnership approach in tackling all kinds of crime has been well embraced. The Audit Commission (1996), for example, recognised the importance of understanding and working with the interconnections between the family, school, local authorities and the criminal justice system in dealing with the problem of young people (young men) and crime. The potential value, or otherwise, of reparation has also been well established. As this research as demonstrated, however, what can be understood by the term 'partnership' is wide and varied, and the ways such partnerships might work are also wide and varied. For example, it is possible to argue that in Oldtown partnership and reparation already exist. Young people who step over the boundaries of what is considered to be acceptable criminality in this area are quickly made to see the error of their ways through various shaming mechanisms, from being labelled a 'grass' or being 'taxed' to more physical forms of punishment (Walklate, forthcoming). Such mechanisms may not be what the professionals have in mind when they talk of 'reintegrative shaming' (Braithwaite 1989), but they are public and they do seem to work; in other words, they seem to contribute to a local sense of equilibrium. How might the Crime and Disorder Act improve on this for the people of Oldtown? In Bankhill, however, the fluidity of social relationships suggests that there is much more room for manoeuvre and thereby room for meaningful inter-agency work around these issues.

So the question remains as to whether or not the proposed policy strategies designed to tackle these issues are sufficiently imaginative, persistent and committed to face this social reality: 'to think the unthinkable'. If the lived experiences of those people living in high-crime areas are taken into account, there is clearly another layer of questions to be considered concerning what works, for whom, how, why, where and when. However, in order for such an accounting process to occur it is important that academics, politicians, policy-makers and the locally powerful pay constant vigilant attention to the questions of 'whose policy?' and 'whose community?'. As Giddens states:

> In order to work, partnerships between government agencies, the criminal justice system, local associations and community organisations have to be inclusive – all economic and ethnic groups must be involved ... To be successful, such schemes demand a long-term commitment to social objectives.
>
> (1998: 88)

As he goes on to point out, such an approach does not necessarily mean that any link between unemployment, poverty and crime is denied, but does mean that policies need to be co-ordinated with common goals and objectives.

However, to reiterate, a genuine desire for policy to work for change needs above all to be cognisant of the importance of the local context in which that policy is set. This desire needs to work with rather than against the historical and socio-economic circumstances which structure that local context. Such a desire does demand imagination, commitment and persistence. It also requires that desire for policy to work to be both authentic and genuine for the communities themselves and couched in terms which make sense to such communities. The question remains as to whether or not the proposed policy strategies to tackle this issue are sufficiently imaginative, persistent and committed to face this social reality and work with it, since there are opportunities here for this to happen. Unfortunately, I doubt it.

Acknowledgements

The research referred to in this chapter was funded under the ESRC's Crime and Social Order Initiative grant no. L210252036

References

Active Community Unit (1999) *Policy Action Team 9 Report*, London: Home Office.

Anderson, E. (1990) *Streetwise: Race, Class and Change in an Urban Community*, Chicago: Chicago University Press.

Audit Commission (1996) *Misspent Youth: Young People and Crime*, London: Audit Commission.

Beck, U. (1992) *The Risk Society*, London: Sage.

Braithwaite, J. (1989) *Crime, Shame and Reintegration*, Oxford: Oxford University Press.

Campbell, B. (1993) *Goliath: Britain's Dangerous Places*, London: Virago.

Crawford, A. (1997) *The Local Governance of Crime*, Oxford: Clarendon.

Currie, E. (1997) 'Market, crime and community: towards a mid-range theory of post-industrial violence', *Theoretical Criminology*, 1(2): 147–72.

Elias, N. and Scotson, J.L. (1965) *The Established and the Outsiders: A Sociological Enquiry in Community Problems*, London: Frank Cass.

Etzioni, A. (1996) *The New Golden Rule*, London: Profile.

Evans, K., Fraser, P. and Walklate, S. (1996) 'Whom can you trust? The politics of "grassing" on an inner city housing estate', *Sociological Review*, August: 361–80.

Fraser, P. (1997) 'Those inner cities', *Critical Social Policy*, 16: 4.

Fukuyama, F. (1996) *Trust: The Social Virtues and the Creation of Prosperity*, London: Penguin.

Gellner, E. (1989) 'Trust, cohesion and the social order', in D. Gambetta (ed.) *Trust: Making and Breaking Co-operative Relations*, Oxford: Basil Blackwell.

Genn, H. (1988) 'Multiple victimisation', in M. Maguire and J. Pointing (eds) *Victims of Crime: A New Deal?* Milton Keynes: Open University Press.

Giddens, A. (1991) *Modernity and Self Identity*, Oxford: Basil Blackwell.

——(1998) *The Third Way: The Renewal of Social Democracy*, Oxford: Polity.

Hutton, W. (1995) *The State We're In*, London: Random House.

Lee, J.A. (1981) 'Some structural aspects of police deviance in relation with minority groups', in C. Shearing (ed.) *Organisational Police Deviance*, Toronto: Butterworth, 49–72.

Lewis, D.A. and Salem, G. (1986) *Fear of Crime: Incivility and the Production of a Social Problem*, New Brunswick: Transaction.

Luhmann, N. (1989) 'Familiarity, confidence, trust: problems and alternatives', in D. Gambetta (ed.) *Trust: Making and Breaking Co-operative Relations*, Oxford: Basil Blackwell.

Merry, S.E. (1981) *Urban Danger: Life in a Neighbourhood of Strangers*, Philadelphia: Temple University Press.

Misztal, B. (1996) *Trust in Modern Societies*, Oxford: Polity.

Murray, C. (1990) *The Emerging British Underclass*, London: Institute of Economic Affairs.

National Board for Crime Prevention (1994) *Wise after the Event: Tackling Repeat Victimisation*, 2 May.

Nelken, D. (1994) 'Whom can you trust? The future of comparative criminology', in D. Nelken (ed.) *The Futures of Criminology*, London: Sage.

Riesman, D. (1963) *The Lonely Crowd*, London: Collier Macmillan.

Shapland, J. and Vagg, J. (1988) *Policing by the Public*, London: Routledge.

Social Exclusion Unit (1998) *Bringing Britain Together*, London: Stationery Office.

Walklate, S. (1998) 'Crime and community: fear or trust?' *British Journal of Sociology*, 49(4): 550–69.

——(1999) 'Some questions for and about community safety partnerships', *Crime Prevention and Community Safety: An International Journal*, 1(1): 7–16.

——(forthcoming) ' "I can't name any names but what's his face up the road will sort it out". Communities and conflict resolution', in K. McEvoy and T. Newburn (eds) *Criminology and Conflict Resolution*, London: Macmillan.

Walklate, S. and Evans, K. (1999) *Zero Tolerance or Community Tolerance? Managing Crime in High Crime Areas*, Aldershot: Ashgate.

Young, J. (1992) 'Ten points of realism', in R. Matthews and J. Young (eds) *Rethinking Criminology: The Realist Debate*, London: Sage.

4

AFTER SUCCESS?

Anxieties of affluence in an English village

Ian Loader, Evi Girling and Richard Sparks

In his recent book *After Success* (from which we have borrowed part of our title), Ray Pahl postulates that anxiety is part and parcel of the human condition, something that 'in some form or other has plagued people for as long as they have been literate – and probably earlier' (Pahl 1995: 15). He is also quick to point out, however, that thinking about anxiety in this kind of generic way is of little *sociological* interest, it being something – like that old Home Office (1983: 15) finding about the crime risks of the statistically average citizen – that tells us both everything and nothing. According to Pahl: 'The task for the sociologist is not simply to address the general question of what causes people to feel anxious but rather to explore the *specific* contemporary conditions that cause anxieties for *specific* categories of the population' (Pahl 1995: 15; emphasis in original).

It is this latter task that we attempt in this chapter. Our aim is to document and interpret some of the worries about crime and disorder found among residents of one very specific location in which we have recently conducted research: the elite village–suburb of Prestbury, in Cheshire.[1] An affluent enclave situated in the midst of the county's 'swell-belt' (Turner 1967), some three miles north-west of its near neighbour, Macclesfield, and fifteen miles south of Manchester, Prestbury has long provided a home to the rich, famous and infamous – including, over the years, such luminaries as 1970s pop-icon Noddy Holder, the convicted fraudster Peter Clowes, and ex-Manchester United footballer Eric Cantona. More commonly, this is a place for those who are climbing up, or who have prospered in or retired from, the worlds of global finance, enterprise and the professions, one that doesn't so much reproduce itself (the house prices lie far beyond the reach of all but a few first-time buyers), as constantly replenish itself from outside. The 1991 census records that 33.4 per cent of the 5,272 residents hold degrees or professional qualifications and that 65.6 per cent occupy professional or managerial positions. As of 1991, 87.8 per cent of properties were owner-occupied and 63.2 per cent of households owned two or more cars. Unemployment stood at 3.6 per cent. Prestbury, in short, is a place to which people resort while striving for, or having accomplished, success: an exclusive bit of England that represents not merely somewhere to live, nor merely a significant financial investment, but also an act of positional consumption, a mark – in Bourdieu's (1984) terms – of 'distinction'.

In order to understand more fully the crime-related anxieties of this specific fragment of the English middle class and the specific contemporary conditions from which they arise, we want in this chapter to develop two – related – lines of thought. We are concerned first – together with a number of other writers in this field – to transcend the somewhat stale polarisation that has characterised much of the fear of crime debate in Britain since its inception in the early 1980s, one that has sought either to attribute to people's fears a rational kernel (on the grounds that they more or less accurately reflect the material risks of victimisation) or else tried to dismiss them as the irrational products of media-inspired moral panics.[2] Between these two positions – as Karl Kraus nearly said – we refuse to choose. Instead, we take as our theoretical point of departure the conjecture that public discourse on crime (through which people's worries are articulated) will inherently exceed the simple estimation of victimisation risks. It does so, we believe, because crime operates as what Victor Turner (1974) calls a condensation symbol, a means of registering, and making intelligible, what might otherwise remain some unsettling, yet difficult to grasp, mutations in the social and moral order. As such, people's worries and talk about crime are rarely merely a reflection of behavioural change and objective risk (though they represent lay attempts to make sense of such changes and risks), but are also bound up in a context of meaning and significance, involving the use of metaphors and narratives about social change (Sparks 1992: 131).[3] In this respect, we want a further understanding of the fear of crime by starting where many studies of fear among citizens conclude (cf. Hale 1992: 28–34): namely, with the recognition that much crime-talk (Sasson 1995) takes the form of stories, anecdotes and gossip that fold together elements of personal biography, community career and, indeed, perceptions of national change and decline. Moreover, we hope to demonstrate that these issues (which are commonly acknowledged gesturally rather than investigated) are both researchable *and* policy-relevant.

We want to argue, second, that the specific anxieties of Prestbury's prosperous middle-class residents can be rendered more explicable in the light of a thicker contextual understanding of *place*, or, more particularly, *sense of place*. In large measure, we share with a number of other recent commentators on the middle-class condition (both in England (Taylor and Jamieson 1998) and in the USA (Ehrenreich 1990)) the view that fear of crime now works to condense a series of other interconnected anxieties about the current experience of middle-class life (Taylor and Jamieson 1998: 173), and find persuasive the contention that such fears arise from the massive sense of insecurity about the future of their positions in the labour and housing markets that confronts the middle classes at the beginning of the twenty-first century (*ibid.*: 163). Yet we do not think that this analysis holds in any straightforward sense in the present case. For Prestbury's citizens are generally not representative of that strata of middle England for whom – in a post-Fordist downsizing age – such 'fear of falling' (Ehrenreich 1990) appears as either a real prospect or a preoccupying concern (although many of its inhabitants have taken on large financial commitments to live there, commitments whose maintenance depends upon a continued climb up the corporate ladder). As such, their 'fear of falling' adopts a particular form: one, we suggest, that has intimately to do with questions of crime and place. It is a fear that the exclusive pastoral corner of the English social and spatial landscape in which they have invested heavily, both materially and emotionally, can no longer exempt itself (as it properly should) from the malign currents that flow through the wider world, and that its established social and moral order is being threatened, perhaps even eroded, by a combination of outsiders (professional criminals) and strangers (drug-using, disorderly local youths). We hope to make good this interpretation in what follows, when we will have more to say about the nature and meanings of these specific threats. Let us start, though, by taking a closer look at Prestbury itself.

'A special place': the social meanings of Prestbury

In October 1995, a feature in the *Sunday Times Magazine* set out to advise an imaginary 'horde of barbarians' where in Britain to go in search of the best plunder. Having trotted through the usual list of candidates – Bond Street, Hampstead, the 'stockbroker suburbs' of Surrey – the invaders are told to head north:

> The richest village in Britain is not in the spoilt self-satisfied south: it is near Manchester, in Cheshire, and its name is Prestbury. It is, per square mile, the home of more millionaires than any other place in Britain. Prestbury is an old-fashioned English village: after all, it still has a post office and a railway station. But it is not an American Golden Ghetto, such as Tuxedo Park in New York State, where a wall, anti-tank traps and a private armed police force protect the wealthy in their mock-tudor palaces. No. This is a village of 5,000 jolly, welcoming people in the Byzantium of the North.

This article proved to be a major talking point – and irritant – in the village, and was variously described during the course of our focus groups (it had appeared shortly before we began interviewing) as 'scurrilous', 'pretty dreadful', 'in bad taste' and 'totally unacceptable'. This was due in large part to residents having felt misrepresented (the feature went on to make reference to the prevalence of Mercedes Benz, foreign villas and servants, and had described the local 'ladies' as 'blonde, rich, thin as beanpoles'); but it arose also from a sense that the piece had reinforced the already dim view of the village held by outsiders. As one member of the local Women's Institute said of Prestbury: 'It has a reputation for being very snobby, millionaires all over the place, unfriendly, dreadful.'

There are, however, aspects of the *Sunday Times* account with which Prestbury's residents would heartily concur. The first of these concerns the imaginative placing of Prestbury in the 'South of England' (see Figure 4.1).[4] Our respondents

– a number of whom had in fact moved up from the Home Counties – were fond of remarking just how 'out of place' Prestbury seems when set against prevailing cultural images of 'the North' (cf. Shields 1991: ch. 4). As one local parent put it:

> There are many villages that are just the same as Prestbury in the south-east. On the Kent/Essex border where we lived, they're ten a penny. When we came back to Cheshire and we looked around for something like a village with a school, a pub, a hotel, etc., the only one you could find was Prestbury.

Prestbury residents would also take little exception to the *Sunday Times'* depiction of the place as 'an old-fashioned English village'. This particular 'key

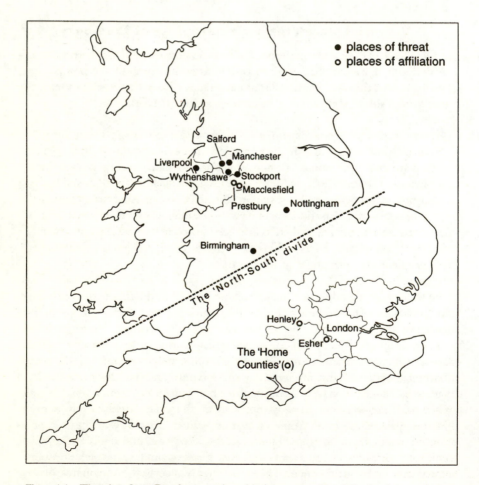

Figure 4.1   The view from Prestbury: an imaginative geography of England

concept in English social life' (Strathern 1982: 249) was deployed time and again by our respondents as a means of communicating what it was they liked about the place. The term is used to convey Prestbury's aesthetic qualities – 'attractive', 'picturesque', 'well-kept', 'pretty' and 'quaint' being among the characteristic phraseology (Prestbury is a frequent winner of Cheshire's Best Kept Village competition). It is also mobilised – as in the above account – in association with Prestbury's 'integrated facilities', the ready availability of post office, pubs, railway station, restaurants and good schools. And it is employed to say something about the character of local social relations, denoting both the rich variety of activities, clubs and organisations, and the 'friendly', 'close-knit' quality of relations between its inhabitants. This – according to one of the retired businessmen we spoke to – is a place where all-comers are able to get along (cf. Strathern 1981; Rapport 1993):

> You've got a very good mix of old Prestbury, people that have been here a lifetime, or a good many years, twenty, thirty-odd years. And you've got, you might describe us as the incomers, people who have worked abroad, internationally, come in with the likes of Zeneca, ICI as it was, CIBA GEIGY, the major companies. We found that the mix works extremely well and it's one of the most pleasant places that we've ever lived, certainly in the United Kingdom.

Such glowing praise was not, however, universally employed to characterise contemporary Prestbury. Some residents evidently found 'the village' rather less hospitable than the terms used above might indicate, contending variously that 'lots of people think they're too good'; or 'there's lots of cliques, you're either in or out'; or, as with this parent who has resided in Prestbury for some eleven years, that 'the neighbours surrounding us are totally appalled that we have children. They go out of their way to be awkward.' Others appear resigned to Prestbury no longer being the distinctive village it once was, or at least no longer corresponding with their received expectations of the 'English village'. One home watch co-ordinator put the matter thus: 'It's a dormitory suburb. It doesn't have, for me, the atmosphere of a village because it's too transitory. Not many people live here very long.'

There is little disputing that Prestbury is a cosmopolitan, evidently urban place of some 5,000 or so generally mobile people, akin in many ways to what urban sociologists call 'exurbia'. But, the foregoing reservations notwithstanding, there is equally little doubt that the *idea* of Prestbury as a village – and an archetypal 'English' one at that – is pivotal to many residents' sense of place; nor that this 'village-in-the-mind' (to use Pahl's (1970: 61) term) is a 'thing real, powerful, political and moral' (Matlass 1994: 8). With its evocative suggestion of scenic and social harmony, its rich and warm associations – long celebrated in literary renditions of the pastoral (Williams 1973) – with order, tranquillity, meaning and security, and its corresponding distancing of the chaos, anonymity and violence of 'the city', 'the village' is a powerful and compelling icon of English culture. It is as such something that many of Prestbury's citizens have actively sought (and taken on large mortgages for), hold dear and are prepared to defend.

Thus it is that many of the anxieties of this prosperous fragment of the English middle-class concern what they perceive as threats to their village and its attendant way of life. Two aspects are of initial interest here. The first centres upon the possibility of Prestbury being subsumed – due to the growth of either – by Macclesfield (or, more remotely, if more troublingly, by Greater Manchester), something evident in the keen desire of many we spoke to to emphasise the 'separate identities' of each and, in particular, 'the distinct, different character' of Prestbury. As one resident put it: 'I think you'll find that most people put their address as Prestbury, Cheshire. They don't mention Macclesfield at all.' A second, more pressing concern surrounds the volume and speed of commuter and freight traffic passing through the village, an issue that was not only a central preoccupation of the Parish Council, but one which also figured highly (and certainly *more often* than crime) when people were asked to name items of troubling change or to select 'the worst thing' about living in Prestbury (the growth of the number of houses and people in the village also featured prominently in this regard). The traffic 'problem' and its attendant dangers are felt to be exacerbated by the lack of pedestrian walkways on some roads, and by the absence in Prestbury of *any* street lights.

People's powerfully felt impression of Prestbury as what one resident called 'a special place' is not then organised solely around its positive qualities, central though these undoubtedly are. The idea that 'this place' (and 'our home') is being assailed by, and needs to be defended against, threats from the outside world is also a constitutive part of what Prestbury means to its citizens. The sense of troubled times, of a place not quite being as it should be, of Prestbury being 'a postcard olde-worlde village full of English charm, until you get to know it more' (primary school parent) pervades not just residents' worries about traffic or the threat of 'Greater Macclesfield' swallowing them up; it similarly permeates their talk about travelling crime, and about the presence in the village high street of what are felt to be disorderly, drug-consuming local teenagers. It is to these issues that we now turn.

Travelling crime: calculated criminals and other intruders

Prominent among the crime-related anxieties of Prestbury residents is the threat of property crime, especially thefts of and from cars, and burglaries. Occupying – as many do – 'relatively secluded' houses which lack immediate neighbours and are left unoccupied for long periods of the day, the threat posed by burglary is of particular concern. Stories detailing the prevalence of housebreaking or the *modus operandi* of burglars arose commonly during our focus group discussions. The following exchange between two retired businessmen is typical:

Harold: I think the amount of burglary, housebreaking is pretty high. Even living in cottages, my neighbour has been burgled, my next-door neighbour but two has been burgled, a neighbour probably about seven or eight cottages away has been burgled within the last two or three weeks. As far as the big houses are concerned, I'm sure Gilbert will be happy to fill you in.

Gilbert: Yes, certainly, we've been broken into three times.[5]

In respect of property crime, Prestbury residents, and for that matter the police, believe the village to be the target of both petty opportunist offending and more organised forms of professional theft: what one retired businessman termed 'calculated criminals' in search of jewellery and antiques. Some of the responsibility for petty offending in the village was laid by adult residents at the door of (local) children and teenagers (and linked in many cases with drugs – see below). But for the most part residents' concerns about property crime did not attach to people from either Prestbury or neighbouring Macclesfield. (None of the town's council-built estates, not even the adjacent Upton Priory, were construed as preying on Prestbury, in the latter case perhaps because many Prestbury teenagers attend the same successful state school as children from the estate.) Rather, the criminal threat to Prestbury is seen as being posed by those travelling from further afield; the following 'crime-exporting' locations appearing most frequently in our respondents crime-talk:

Helen: You mentioning Liverpool does bring one point to mind. I think so far as burglary is concerned, it's the close proximity to Liverpool.

Max: It's very easy to get on the motorway.[...]

Mark: I think the police would say they come from Manchester.

                                                                      (Home watch co-ordinators)

For many, Prestbury's vulnerability to travelling criminals – one church official called it a 'burglar's paradise' – is viewed as the product of both a good system of road communications and the difficulties of conducting informal surveillance in such an unlit place. As one resident put it: 'One of the advantages, in my opinion, of street lights would be that these vehicles could be seen. The chances are that somebody would at least get a description of them, and might even get the number plates.' It is, however, Prestbury's reputation for wealth that residents deem to be the chief attraction for undesirable criminal outsiders (one of the things that bothered people about the *Sunday Times* feature was that it might attract such outsiders to the village; recall the journalist's use of a 'horde of barbarians' as a rhetorical device with which to introduce Prestbury). As one resident said of the frequent reference to Prestbury being 'the richest village in

England': 'That's nice in its way, [but] that could attract the criminal fraternity. There are more millionaires per capita here than anywhere else.' The following extract – taken from our focus group with members of the Women's Institute – encapsulates the foregoing concerns especially well:

Jill: But I think the outsiders, they really do … This wonderful place with motorways, they do use the motorways to get to us. Liverpool, Manchester, Macclesfield to a certain extent, Stockport. We're so handy.

Mary: I think that the reputation that there's a lot of money about, they think that the houses are good pickings. Such a lot of the houses are stood by themselves or up drives that they can get round. Particularly while they're away.

These anxieties of affluence are not, however, confined to burglary alone. Residents also believe they attract more than their fair share of 'pedlars': people either hawking their wares from door to door around the village, or those 'who call on spec, always wanting to do the driveway, or do your guttering'. The presence of such traders is rarely framed in a manner that denotes positive 'initiative' or 'enterprise'. They are for the most part classified as suspicious intruders; at the very least forcing unwanted goods and services on people in invasive and discomforting face-to-face encounters, and at worst potential burglars. As such, pedlars are able to provoke a complex of emotions, including not only suspicion but also fear (especially among those who live alone; the calls, it seems, are often made after dark), engulfment and guilt:

Alice: Look at all the pedlars we have round the door. They come from Nottingham, Birmingham, Liverpool, and they come in by Dormobile, and they saturate the place, don't they?

Max: On wet nights.

Alice: On wet nights when they look pathetic, and you feel really mean saying no.

(Home watch co-ordinators)

In the midst of these various worries, residents remain divided over the extent to which the village has 'a crime problem'.[6] For some the criminal threats posed to their homes and property are clearly of concern and can impact in significant ways upon people's daily life and consciousness. One Prestbury parent spoke of expecting to have been burgled 'virtually every time' he returned home. Another described herself as 'very conscious' about burglary before proceeding to participate in the following discussion:

Laura: We lock our doors when we're gardening. We never used to.

Jill: I don't put the alarm on when I'm gardening, because the doors are locked. I don't leave downstairs windows open at the front when I'm not in the room.

EG: Do you think that Prestbury has a lot of burglar alarms compared to other areas?

Jill: Oh yes.

Kim: Absolutely.

EG: How would you compare then crime in Prestbury to crime in other places?

Kim: Oh, it's not so bad.

Liz: I think it's about the same.

Jill: I would think it's about the same.

(Women's Institute members)

This exchange ends with what is perhaps the prevailing feeling among Prestbury residents about the village's 'crime problem', a feeling that intersects often closely and explicitly with people's sense of 'this' and 'other' places. For some here, it is important to keep the matter of crime in perspective and not let it overshadow the village's abundant positive attributes: 'Although we do have a lot of crime, I think one has to get it in proportion, that it is still a very pleasant part of the world.' Others – such as this home watch co-ordinator – are clearly keen to distance Prestbury from the kinds of places that readily and negatively surface in English popular and political discourse at mention of the word 'crime':

> The other part of the area that I know is Salford and that's a den of thieves if ever there was one. I suspect that we are probably more on a par with somewhere like Henley, or Esher, where they're affluent. It's a different sort of crime.

But these sensibilities towards place can also operate in a reverse direction: to heighten and structure people's feelings about, and responses to, crime. For while many residents felt that crime levels in Prestbury were fairly modest relative to other places, such offending as does occur can nonetheless jar with what they hope and expect to be the case in their village. As one resident put it: 'I think it [the local crime problem] must be on a minor scale compared with other areas. It's just that it's more noticeable in Prestbury because you just don't think that things like that could happen in such a lovely place.'

Youth, drugs and disorder: anarchy in the village

At the time of our research, a group of male and female teenagers (the section of the local population we found least likely to share the prevailing view of Prestbury as 'a lovely place') had taken to congregating in the centre of the

73

village, either in the churchyard or in the village high street by the off-licence and 'traditional' telephone box (dubbed 'the office' by the youths concerned). This had become the preferred site for hanging around since the old meeting place – the sports pavilion on the recreation ground – had been burned down under suspicious circumstances a couple of years previously, and anything from five to twenty or so teenagers were to be found there of an evening. For the young people involved (the majority of whom also attended the local youth club), such hanging around is both a response to having 'nothing else to do' and an assertion of their 'membership' of the village:

Josh: What else are we supposed to do?
Vicky: It's our village as well, not just theirs.
Josh: When we ask them [adults] where they hang about and everything they say where, but when they ask us where we've got to hang about, what have we got?
Vicky: We've got a youth club, yes, fair enough, but there's weekends. In the summer there's nothing to do.

(16/17-year-old teenagers)

Some among the adult residents we spoke to appeared largely untroubled by the presence of these youths, believing them either to occasion few problems, or else evincing some sympathy for the plight of the local young. Some felt these young people were neither 'hard nuts' nor 'violent', and did not find their 'exuberant showing off' especially frightening. Others pointed to the lack of youth facilities in Prestbury – 'it's got something for everybody, apart from maybe the teenagers', as one put it; or believed such young people – often on the basis of parental experience – were at what one resident called 'an awkward age'. Having recounted – during our focus group with home watch co-ordinators – her 'nightmare' trying to keep her daughter in the youth club and away from consuming alcohol with her friends in the village, Alice endeavours to under-stand rather than merely condemn:

> Yes, but they actually go through a period when they want something a little different. My daughter was in the choir for years, was head chorister, and she had swimming, horse riding, she had the vicar's horse for years that she looked after. We filled their lives, then they come to a point when, I suppose it's the old hormone business, and it's far more exciting to be out in the churchyard with a couple of your friends in the dark, when you should be in the youth club. It's far more exciting than anything Mummy has written down as your hobby for tonight. I'm not making excuses, believe me.

The plea that ends this account indicates Alice's awareness that she is speaking, not only against the prevailing weight of 'law and order' discourse, but

74

also counter to the dominant mood among Prestbury residents. This mood is one of anxious concern about the impact on the village and its quality of life of what Arthur Harris (a resident of some twenty-five years' standing with whom we conducted a life-history interview) called 'anarchy in the village among the village youth'. The Parish Council newsletter of Spring 1993 articulated these concerns in the following terms:

CRIME

A pity to open on a sad note, but it has become increasingly evident that a section of our society does not share the values of the majority in relation to respect for the property of others. This has shown itself in two main areas – apparently mindless vandalism and carefully targeted theft. In the former category one thinks of the arson and damage to the football pavilion at the Recreation Ground, the burning of the building at the rear of the Post Office and the general despoliation of the Churchyard and Village with litter and worse.

This 'litter and worse' was reckoned to be the responsibility of that small minority of *local* teenagers who colonised the centre of the village, and was seen as taking two main forms. People's talk centred, first, on what was alleged to be disorderly or criminal behaviour of various kinds. Some preferred to speak here of specific incidents (sometimes observed, more often picked up third-hand) foremost among which were: vandalism to the church, telephone box and local shops; youths swearing at, harassing or obstructing passers-by; petty theft (in one instance, of the church collection); shoplifting; and the making of reverse-charge calls to friends from the phone box. Among others, the presence of young people was characterised as a problem in more diffuse terms; one spoke of them as 'cheeky, but threatening', another of having to 'push your way through them', a third of 'a sense of oppression' and of 'feeling under pressure in certain areas of the village'.[7]

A second – related – worry surrounded the question of drugs, the consumption of which was felt by many to be rife among local teenagers. At the time of our research, this was a major concern and talking-point locally (Arthur Harris reported being told that 'practically every child in the village has experimented at some time with cannabis'; a local shop assistant we spoke to described Prestbury as 'an upper-class Moss Side'), and gossip and rumour abounded about how the gathering of teenagers in and around the churchyard provided both a target for dealers and a breeding ground for consumption. Speaking of the former, one parent described the youths as a soft target for traders to come in from Wythenshawe, while we were frequently told stories about a drugs-car that – it was alleged – descended on Prestbury twice a week from Manchester (the teenagers we spoke to derived much amusement from this tale, which they took as a sign of the ignorance and gullibility of local adults). With respect to the latter, cognate stories circulated about apparently repeated discoveries in the village of the detritus of consumption, common among those narrated to us being that 'When the cricket pavilion was burned down a few years ago ... the firemen discovered it was full of hypodermic syringes underneath', and that 'The church caretaker sweep[s] up syringes on a daily basis, dozens and dozens of injection needles'.

There is little doubt that these worries about youth, drugs and disorder are acutely felt by many of Prestbury's residents, and that their crime-talk represents – in part – an attempt to make some sense of material practices (and social changes) that appear both strange and without immediate precedent, and as a threat to the quality of life (after all, the youths *do* hang around and *can* be cheeky; cannabis *is* available in the village, and it must have come from *somewhere*). This seemed most clearly the case among the parents we spoke to, many of whom expressed great worries about either the prospect of their offspring falling in with what they viewed as 'bad company', or about the possibility of their sons or daughters being 'picked on' by teenagers in the village.[8] Such concerns, it seems, have as much if not more to do with people's role and status as *parents* as they have to do with their place of residence:

Terry: The concern to us as parents is that I don't like my son, who's fourteen years of age, and is responsible, I don't like him walking through Prestbury, and there are occasions when he may have to walk through, because they are accosted by undesirables.
          [*He had earlier recounted how his two sons had experienced 'several youths jump on them and rough them up' at the church gate following choir practice.*]
Geoff: Is this people coming from outside?
Terry: They grab hold of them and say 'Do you take drugs?'
RS: Are you talking about undesirable adults or ...?
Terry: No, undesirable teenagers, who are sitting on the benches outside the church trying to cause trouble. Friday night especially, at quarter to ten, and elderly people are petrified to walk through the village because they're being taunted and being abused.

It is also evident, however, that these worries are shaped in important ways by people's sense of the kind of place Prestbury ought to be, and the kinds of behaviour and social interaction that is expected to flow from this. This generates, first, a set of expectations about the tranquillity, orderliness and polite sociability that is supposed to attend village life and a set of cognate conventions as to the appropriate use of village spaces, conventions that don't extend to its unsupervised, noisy occupancy by groups of young people. But it also gives rise to hopes about the kinds of children and young people who ought properly to inhabit such a place, something that the 'congregation' of teenagers who improperly hang around the churchyard fail to live up to. As Arthur Harris remarks: 'These are kids that are not involved with the church choir, they're not involved in the scouts, they're not involved in the cricket club, which they could be. They're not involved in any of these.' Here, again, as with travelling crime, it is not, in relative terms, that Prestbury is seen as having an especially acute problem of teenage incivility, but rather that it is bedevilled by such difficulties at all. For the existence of drugs and disorder not only runs counter to the residents' sense of what 'an English village' aesthetically and socially should be all about, and undermines the cherished possibility that they have found – in the midst of an England in seeming moral decline – a safe and orderly place in which, as one parent put it, 'you know your children are going to mix with other decent children': it is also powerfully emblematic of the fact that Prestbury is no longer able to insulate itself from the troubles that afflict the wider world:

> I didn't say it [drugs] was any worse than anywhere else. What I'm trying to say is that it's become more and more obvious that this is happening in this little postcard village where everything is in equilibrium, has never been disturbed, and all of a sudden the outside world is creeping in.
>
> (Primary school parent)

Conclusion: crime and the defence of one's place

Towards the end of his recent book on the human consequences of globalisation, Zygmunt Bauman makes the following observation:

> In an ever more insecure and uncertain world the withdrawal into the safe haven of territoriality is an intense temptation; and so the defence of the territory – the safe home – becomes the pass-key to all doors which one feels must be locked to stave off the threat to spiritual and material comfort.
>
> (Bauman 1998: 117)

This seems particularly apposite in the present context. We have seen in this chapter that Prestbury residents view the village's 'crime and disorder' problems as, relatively speaking, 'small scale' (indeed, they remain proud that this is so and would recoil from the suggestion that it is otherwise). Local manifestations of these problems stand out, however, because a place imagined as a protective cocoon from the troubles that afflict English society elsewhere has been violated. Pivotal to the cultural value of this 'English village' is that it is seen to offer a shelter of tranquillity, order and stability which contrasts starkly with the violence, disorder and insecurity of the city (and the wider 'risk profiles' of late modernity). No matter that Prestbury is thoroughly permeated by larger 'social systems and organizations' (Giddens 1991: 184), nor that many of its inhabitants are powerful players in the globalising, risk-generating corporate world of late modernity. To buy into Prestbury is to purchase a pleasurable, exclusive retreat, a place of rest and recreation, a 'safe haven for oneself, one's family and one's children', an environment bracketed-off from the troubles of the outside world. This is something that many of its residents have taken on hefty – often anxiety-inducing, success-dependent – financial commitments in order to enjoy. Hence the intensely felt feelings of disquiet, disappointment and anger that attach to locally occurring instances of crime and disorder; a reaction not only to the objective harm that these problems cause but also to the apparent withering of the order and security in which people have invested so much economic and emotional capital:

> *Terry:* When they [our teenage children] do get free time we try and keep them away from Prestbury, and that shouldn't be, that should not be.
> *Pam:* No, the whole point of being in the village …
> *Terry:* We're paying a healthy premium to live in Prestbury to start with. We're paying £50,000 or £60,000 more to live in a house in this area than we would if we lived in another area, so why should we be penalised?
>
> (Primary school parents)

We have seen that two threats to the safe home loom large in the crime-talk of Prestbury's residents – professional burglary and teenage disorder. It is also evident that these threats remain almost entirely disconnected from one another in people's minds (we found little here to support the view, often propounded in the 'fear of crime' literature (Wilson and Kelling 1982; Skogan 1990), that social incivilities form some kind of 'symbolic cue to the heightened possibility [of] more serious criminal victimization' (Hunter 1978: 9) and that, of the two, it is teenage incivilities in the village high street which prompt the greatest exasperation and anger and which impinge most deeply on people's sense of Prestbury as a liveable place). But why should this be so? Why is it that these troubles have such different levels and kinds of significance attached to them, and vary so markedly in the anxieties and responses they evoke?

There is little doubt that the threat to the sanctity of one's home generated by burglary was a genuine cause of anxiety among many of our respondents, not least because of the possibility of coming face-to-face with a hostile, dangerous other (something that accounts for much of the concern aroused by pedlars). Yet people's relatively modulated response to property crime provides some evidence to support Garland's (1996: 446) contention that such offences have become 'a routine part of modern consciousness, an everyday risk to be assessed and managed in much the same way that we deal with road traffic'. This is due in part to the fact that (prosperous, middle-class) individuals retain a capacity to insure and insulate themselves against criminal threats, that they can protect their properties by taking such defensive precautions as their resources, levels of anxiety and *Weltanschauung* lead them to see fit. By placing themselves in fortified homes behind (often) high walls and imposing iron gates, individuals can to a large extent keep the hostile world at bay, and a good number of Prestbury residents have endeavoured to do precisely that.

But this response also has something to do with what property crime signifies (and, *pace* Garland, such offences continue to galvanise moral discourse in ways that clearly distinguish them from traffic accidents). We have seen that Prestbury's residents interpret burglary and car crime largely in terms of the threats posed by malign outsiders, principally, it was felt, those from the nearby conurbations of Liverpool and Manchester. Far from exacerbating people's concerns, however, this way of couching the issue may in fact contribute to the relatively low levels of anger that attach to property crime. For these outsiders (a category of people towards whom one has little affinity and about whom one possesses at best vague and fragmentary knowledge) represent what might be called a reassuring threat. While coveting and imperilling one's possessions and property, they also stabilise and reinforce social categories and expectations. They remind people that the world beyond Prestbury's borders is a troubled and stressed place from whose dangers our village is not completely immune, while providing a means by which Prestbury's difference from that world (as a pleasant, pastoral English village) is imaginatively sustained. In short, travelling criminals obey the established stereotypes of self and other.

The teenagers who gather in the centre of Prestbury village offer no such solace – for two main reasons. Anxieties arise here, first, from people's uncertainty as to whether and how best to act in response to the 'problem' of youth, and from the fact that this problem has no readily available (or purchasable) solution. For while many Prestbury residents take the boundaries of their home to encompass the village itself (this being one of the constitutive features of the English village as an idea and settlement (Williams 1973: 281)), this more extended home cannot so easily be defended. Despite their worries about teenage disorder and the threat they feel it represents to the quality of local life, Prestbury's residents remain steadfastly reluctant to mobilise their (collective) economic and social capital in pursuit of the kinds of protective measures (CCTV, shop shutters, gating and so forth) that might resolve this problem, or at least displace it elsewhere. The reasons for this are fairly apparent. In part it flows from these being local kids, with all the difficulties this presents for a strategy of exclusion. It also helps that (more serious) undesirables are already kept from Prestbury by the operation of the housing and labour markets. But it has principally to do with the fact that while such measures might make the community more overtly civil and free(r) of disorder, they would do so at the cost of destroying the very thing that Prestbury's citizens are concerned to preserve – the English pastoral appearance of their village.[9]

These anxieties about youth have to do, second, with congregations of *local* teenagers appearing, not as outsiders, but – in sociological terms – as *strangers* (Simmel 1950), something that stands in stark and troubling contrast to the unseen and unknown intruders who might threaten one's individual property:

Strangers are people whom I see and hear. It is precisely because I note their presence, because I cannot disregard this presence and cannot make this presence irrelevant simply by refusing to give it my attention, that I find it difficult to make sense of them. They are, as it were, neither close nor distant. Neither a part of us nor a part of them. Neither friends nor foes. For this reason, they cause confusion and anxiety. I do not know exactly what I should make of them, what to expect, how to behave.

(Bauman 1990: 55)

As an account of the disquiet prompted among adult residents by young people's occupancy of and behaviour in Prestbury's high street, this can hardly be bettered. For it not only pinpoints the disruption congregations of teenagers cause to (many) people's sense of Prestbury as home – 'a space in which one seldom, if at all, finds oneself at a loss, feels lost for words, or uncertain how to act' (Bauman 1998: 13) – but it also captures nicely the anxieties that flow from the realisation that these teenagers (and their neglectful, blameworthy parents) are part of, rather than exogenous to, Prestbury (even if they have also been got at by more global influences, such as drugs, the media or the prevailing cultural and moral climate). In a very direct sense, loitering youths bring the disorder of the outside to the inside. While the burglar and car thief cross the border between us and them (and in so doing sustain it as a border), young people gathering on the street threaten to dissolve both that distinction and 'the clarity of the social world that results from [it]' (Bauman 1990: 54). They are, in Ulrich Beck's (1998: 127) terms, 'a living refutation of the apparently clear borders and natural foundations through which affiliations and identities are expressed', one that threatens to erode *from within* the idea of Prestbury as a safe home, free of the troubles that bedevil so much of contemporary English society elsewhere.

References

Bauman, Z. (1990) *Thinking Sociologically*, Oxford: Basic Blackwell.
——(1998) *Globalization: The Human Consequences*, Cambridge: Polity.
Beck, U. (1998) *Democracy Without Enemies*, Cambridge: Polity.
Bourdieu, P. (1984) *Distinction: A Critique of the Social Judgement of Taste*, London: Routledge.
Cloke, P., Phillips, M. and Thrift, N. (1995) 'The new middle classes and the social constructs of rural living', in T. Butler and M. Savage (eds) *Social Change and the Middle Classes*, London: UCL Press.
Douglas, M. (1992) *Risk and Blame: Essays in Cultural Theory*, London: Routledge.
Ehrenreich, B. (1990) *Fear of Falling: The Inner Life of the Middle Class*, New York: Pantheon.
Garland, D. (1996) 'The limits of the sovereign state: strategies of crime control in contemporary society', *British Journal of Criminology*, 36(4): 445–71.
Giddens, A. (1991) *Modernity and Self Identity: Self and Society in the Late-Modern Age*, Cambridge: Polity.
Girling, E., Loader, I. and Sparks, R. (2000) *Crime and Social Change in Middle England: Questions of Order in an English Town*, London: Routledge.

Hale, C. (1992) *Fear of Crime: A Review of the Literature*, Canterbury: University of Kent.

Hamner, J. and Saunders, S. (1984) *Well-Founded Fear*, London: Hutchinson.

Hollway, W. and Jefferson, T. (1997) 'The risk society in an age of anxiety: situating fear of crime', *British Journal of Sociology*, 48(2): 255–66.

Home Office (1983) *The First British Crime Survey*, London: Home Office.

Hunter, A. (1978) 'Symbols of incivility: social disorder and fear of crime in urban neighbourhoods', paper presented to the Annual Meetings of the American Society of Criminology, Dallas.

Jones, T., MacLean, B. and Young, J. (1986) *The Islington Crime Survey*, Aldershot: Gower.

Matlass, D. (1994) 'Doing the English village 1945–1990: an essay in imaginative geography' in P. Cloke, M. Doel, D. Matlass, M. Phillips and N. Thrift (eds) *Writing the Rural: Five Cultural Geographies*, London: Paul Chapman.

Maxfield, M. (1984) *Fear of Crime in England and Wales*, London: Home Office.

Pahl, R. (1970) *Whose City? and Other Essays on Sociology and Planning*, Penguin: Harmondsworth.

——(1995) *After Success: Fin-de-Siècle Anxiety and Identity*, Cambridge: Polity.

Rapport, N. (1993) *Diverse World-Views in an English Village*, Edinburgh: Edinburgh University Press.

Sasson, T. (1995) *Crime Talk: How Citizens Construct a Social Problem*, New York: Aldine de Gruyter.

Scraton, P. (ed.) (1987) *Law, Order and the Authoritarian State*, Milton Keynes: Open University Press.

Shields, R. (1991) *Places on the Margin: Alternative Geographies of Modernity*, London: Routledge.

Simmel, G. (1950) 'The stranger', in *The Sociology of Georg Simmel*, trans. K.H. Wolff, New York: Free Press.

Skogan, W. (1990) *Disorder and Decline: The Spiral of Decay in American Neighborhoods*, New York: Oxford University Press.

Sparks, R. (1992) 'Reason and unreason in a left realism: some problems in the constitution of the "fear of crime"', in R. Matthews and J. Young (eds) *Issues in Realist Criminology*, London: Sage.

Strathern, M. (1981) *Kinship at the Core: An Anthropology of Elmdon, a Village in North-West Essex in the Nineteen-Sixties*, Cambridge: Cambridge University Press.

——(1982) 'The village as an idea: constructs of village-ness in Elmdon, Essex', in A.P. Cohen (ed.) *Belonging: Identity and Social Organisation in British Rural Cultures*, Manchester: Manchester University Press.

Taylor, I. (1995) 'Private homes and public others: an analysis of talk about crime in suburban South Manchester in the mid-1990s', *British Journal of Criminology*, 35(2): 263–85.

Taylor, I. and Jamieson, R. (1998) 'Fear of crime and fear of falling: English anxieties at the approach of the millennium', *Archive Européenne Sociologique* 39(1): 149–75.

Taylor, I., Evans, K. and Fraser, P. (1996) *A Tale of Two Cities: Global Change, Local Feeling and Everyday Life in the North of England – A Study in Manchester and Sheffield*, London: Routledge.

Turner, G. (1967) *The North Country*, London: Eyre and Spottiswoode.

Turner, V. (1974) *Dramas, Fields and Metaphors: Symbolic Action in Human Society*, Ithaca: Cornell University Press.

Walklate, S. (1998) 'Excavating the fear of crime: fear, anxiety or trust', *Theoretical Criminology* 2(4): 403–18.

Williams, R. (1973) *The Country and the City*, London: Chatto and Windus.

Wilson, J.Q. and Kelling, G. (1982) 'Broken windows: the police and neighbourhood safety', *Atlantic Monthly*, March: 29–38.

Young, J. (1988) 'Risk of crime and fear of crime: the politics of victimization studies', in M. Maguire and J. Pointing (eds) *Victims of Crime: A New Deal*, Milton Keynes: Open University Press.

5

INEQUALITY AND THE CLUBBING OF PRIVATE SECURITY

Tim Hope

We could provide absolute security, eliminate every source of violence except domestic violence, if we put a street light every ten yards and stationed a policeman every thirty yards throughout the city. But that would be very expensive, and so we settle for something less. How much less can only be decided politically.

(Walzer 1983: 67)

the market provision of 'security' generates its own paranoid demand. Security becomes a positional good defined by income access to private 'protective services' and membership in some hardened residential enclave or restricted suburb. As a prestige symbol ... 'security' has less to do with personal safety than with the degree of personal insulation, in residential, work, consumption and travel environments, from 'unsavory' groups and individuals, even crowds in general.

(Davis 1990: 224)

What steps do people take in their everyday lives, or would wish to have taken on their behalf, to protect their property from the threat, as they see it, of appropriation by others? If apparently higher risks of crime victimisation have become a 'normal social fact' (Garland 1996), how have people reacted in their everyday lives; does this differ, in type or scale, from what people have done or thought in the past (Young 1998); and what are the collective consequences of individuals acting to attain security from such risks? This chapter is concerned with *private security* – considered here as the security of private household property (dwellings and contents) from criminal victimisation – and is mainly addressed to the latter question: what do contemporary patterns of property crime risk and private security in everyday life look like and how are they produced? To address this question, however, we need to explore the interplay between private property owners' 'needs' for security, the nature of the risks which are perceived to threaten their security, and the supply of 'goods' which promise either to reduce their risks or to strengthen their security.

Some explanations of the growth of 'private security' have been criticised for their tendency to over-emphasise 'supply' factors – either in terms of the limitations of the 'sovereign state', and its agents such as the police, to supply security to its citizens (see Garland 1996), or as a consequence of a growth in 'mass private property' and competition with the state from corporate actors in the supply of private security goods and services (Shearing and Stenning 1983). In contrast, it is argued, explanation for the growth in private security practices should be looked for in 'the micro-environment of everyday consumption' (Spitzer 1987: 58). The driving forces behind the 'commodification' of security are the 'subjective' anxieties, fears and ontological insecurities (Giddens 1990) which people experience in, and use to make sense of, their everyday lives (see Chapter 4). Thus 'we might learn more about security in contemporary capitalist societies by exploring its relationship to the sphere of consumption than to the sphere of production' (Spitzer 1987: 50). Consequently, the stimuli and dynamics of contemporary 'demands' by private citizens for security can be seen as reflecting needs, crises and anxieties about personal identity and social position (see Taylor 1995; Loader 1997).

Yet while apparently insatiable ontological needs may provide a powerful dynamic for growth in private security, they do not by themselves guarantee particular outcomes, especially collective ones, any more than do 'supply' factors alone. A 'market' in private security, as in other goods, is an *institutional structure* – a collective or systemic entity which brings together its constituent components in a particular way. 'Markets' are not uniquely defined by their components – producers, consumers, traders, products – but also by the mechanisms – rules, values, modes of exchange – which bind the components together as a systemic entity. Analysis of the contemporary 'market' in private security needs to address the latter as well as the former. Crucially, analysis needs to find ways of linking macro and micro levels of explanation, particularly in understanding how emergent macro phenomena, which characterise a market, result from interactions among individuals (see Coleman 1990).

The collective good of private security

In the first place, we need to ask about the nature of the 'good' for which needs are felt. The 'need' to protect one's property from appropriation by others derives both from the intrinsic nature of the need and from the meaning and source of the threat to meeting that need. In the first place, in any society which values the right of its members legitimately to possess and enjoy private property, and for anyone who derives an identity from membership in such a society, then the security of private property may be thought of as a citizenship right reflecting human need (see Doyal and Gough 1991). Similarly, because the threat to this need comes from the actions of others who have membership rights in the same society, the need for security is intrinsically 'social': actions which satisfy individuals' needs for the protection of their right to possess and enjoy private property are those which, in one way or another, prevent or dissuade others from abrogating those rights.

The norm of private security

It can be argued that the social meaning of the 'good' of private security implies that it cannot be allocated by mechanisms resembling those found in markets for commodities without adversely affecting those rights, particularly their just distribution (see Loader 1997). There are, however, two strands in this argument – the first is clearly normative, the second may be so but depends upon the substantive consequences of particular market *outcomes* in practice. The normative argument is that the intrinsic social meaning of the good of the right to possess and enjoy private property means that it would be abrogated were the state (as the legitimate guarantor of the good) to sanction the trade or appropriation of private property without the right-holder's permission. A just society is thus one which prohibits (i.e. 'blocks') these exchanges and the use of power – in the form of money, fraud or force – to accomplish such exchanges (see Walzer 1983). Where they exist, every member of a society, by virtue of membership, has a right to enjoy such property rights, and no other member has a right to remove those rights by the exercise of domination. A purpose of justice is thus to protect citizens' dominion over their persons or property and prevent domination by others (Braithwaite and Pettit 1990). Since the right to the security of legitimate private property protects the individual from others, and since every member possesses that right, the good is a collective one – 'part of the "rights and goods enjoyed in common" that help generate people's sense of a "citizen identity"' (quoted in Loader 1997: 382). In this sense, the good of secure property rights is a collective citizenship good, neither the whole nor the parts of which can be auctioned or otherwise divided without undermining the basis of citizenship (i.e. membership) itself (Walzer 1983).

Intermediate security goods

The second argument, however, is more contingent upon the particular *institutional arrangements* which actually exist to deliver or supply the collective good. While the legitimacy of the state stems from its guarantee that transgression of individual property rights will be sanctioned, it cannot so readily guarantee that it can also deliver this good in practice, nor prevent such transgressions from occurring in the first place. Although, as Walzer (1983) argues, once the meanings of a social good are clarified it becomes possible to work out how and on what criterion the good *ought* to be distributed justly, there is equally nothing intrinsic to the meaning of the good which guarantees how, and by what means, it *can* be distributed feasibly in practice. In the case of private security, as with the delivery of many other social goods, that becomes a political task. Even if the intrinsic meaning of the collective good of private security is unlimited and

85

indivisible, the various educative, preventive, protective, detective and punitive *resources* available to deliver this good – comprising a range of *intermediate security goods* – are, by themselves, evidently scarce and finite, at least relative to the needs expressed for them.

Property owners ideally expect to acquire security for their property from a combination of available intermediate security goods. Typically, they may spend a certain amount of personal resources (including income and time) on home security, mainly technical devices and hardware; and they take a variety of avoidance and risk-protection measures during their everyday lives. Additionally, they pay to defray their losses from property crime victimisation through private insurance which may also provide them with a sense of security. These goods are the kinds which individuals can secure by private actions and contracts: that is, *private goods*, some of which are 'commodities' and some private behaviour. In contrast, residents also benefit from public protection – chiefly from the property guardianship services supplied publicly by police activity (including detection and patrol) and the prospect of punishment which lies behind them. Ideally, this latter takes the form of a *public good*.[1] Last, but certainly not least, individuals also opt into the *collective* protection provided by the 'community' in which their private property is permanently located. Not only do they benefit from the collective good of security generated within their society, but also they move into, stay and invest in particular locales or neighbourhoods, thereby deriving their security from the trust they hold in their neighbours' conventions, norms and routines of behaviour and surveillance (see chapters in this volume by Walklate, Loader *et al.*), as well as from their neighbours' more specific individual and collective security practices. Although such neighbourhood 'bundles' of private security have public goods qualities, since it is difficult for residents to be excluded from their benefits, nevertheless, as non-residents do not benefit, they more resemble a *club good* – one that remains collectively available to members of the 'club' but where non-members' permanent access to the good can be wholly or partially denied, controlled or charged (see Sandler 1992).

The political problem for governments in the face of high crime rates has been seen as that of ensuring, by one means or another, a *level* of provision of such intermediate security goods sufficient to meet at least some minimum level of need (demand) for the collective good. For these reasons, Garland (1996) identifies two strategies which have been pursued by governments: one consists of greater investment in the punitive, deterrent and incarcerative services provided by the state (see chapters in this volume by Sasson and Sparks); the other, the *responsibilisation strategy*, summarises efforts to generate more 'private' (including citizen) investment in the production of collective security. An optimistic prognosis is the hope that by raising the overall (national) aggregate level of provision of intermediate security goods of any kind, the collective need for private security will be met.[2] For example, British governments for the past fifteen years have pursued campaigns and programmes of exhortation, demonstration and (modest) investment in crime prevention with the principal aim of raising security levels for and among private citizens. And governments remain attached to the 'performance indicator' of achieving reductions in national reported crime rates (Barr and Pease 1990). In a potent political sense, the reduction of the crime rate is what governments see as their mandate from the electorate as a whole.[3]

Nevertheless, it appears – on available measures, discussed in the next section – that the threat to the collective good of private security, *when it is disaggregated as individual risk*, is inequitably distributed among members of the population. Not everyone seems actuarially 'at risk' of property crime victimisation to the same degree, notwithstanding their 'subjective' apprehensions. For example, according to estimates derived from the British Crime Survey, members of half the residential communities in England and Wales between them suffer less than a fifth of the total amount of household property crime, while over half of all property crime is shared among the residents of just a fifth of the countries' local communities (Hope 1997; see also Figure 5.1, below).[4] This apparent inequality in need poses problems for the project of maintaining the collective provision of private security, particularly through growth in the total amount of privately provided, intermediate security goods.

It is not that inequality in the distribution of a social harm itself poses a problem for social justice, but that the available goods to remedy the harm are distributed not on the basis of need but on some other criteria (say, income and wealth) which come to dominate their provision, irrespective of the way in which the meaning of the good implies that it ought to be distributed (Walzer 1983). Thus, we may be far more egalitarian about the distribution of the collective good of private safety than we are about the distribution of private wealth. So it becomes unjust if we allow the distribution of wealth to dominate the distribution of safety – the inequality which we tolerate in one sphere becomes intolerable when it comes to determine the distribution of another separate and more equitably regarded sphere. It is not so much that the 'commodification' of intermediate security goods is unjust in an intrinsic sense – that fetishistic, private consumption corrupts the nature of the collective good – but rather that the injustice lies in the *consequences* of commodification: that is, the facility which commodification allows (i.e. money purchase) for those with greater capital to distort the basis on which the good might otherwise be distributed (see also Waldron 1995).

Tackling inequality in the distribution of private safety, then, lies not in the direction of redistributing insecurity (see Barr and Pease 1990) – it is not feasible to assume that members of a society predicated on the pursuit of individual self-interest would accept or let such a redistribution of harm take place – but in safeguarding the autonomy of the just criteria for distributing private security. To paraphrase Walzer (1983: 20): private security should not be denied to people who do not possess some other good – for example, wealth – merely because they do not possess wealth and without regard to the way we think private security ought to be distributed. The problem in implementing this principle, however, as will be illustrated below, is that the distribution of private *insecurity* is intimately connected to the distribution of private *security*. That is, the strategies which are adopted by private actors to provide security for themselves usually, at best, do not benefit others less protected than themselves and, at worst, reinforce the latter's insecurity.

The externalities of private security

In one sense, of course, governments acting in the public interest are right to seek to stimulate private security actions since the collective, public good of security is partly the sum of all the private security goods which are produced. However, actions taken by individuals to protect their own property also have the potential for benefiting others – for example, they might reduce the available pool of accessible opportunities for crime (see below); or the social costs of crime – e.g. of prisons, police and household insurance – to which citizens otherwise have to contribute; or, in a broader sense, reinforce the social norm of the security of private property. In other words, in addition to the benefits which private security actions provide for those taking them, they can also create *externality benefits* of protection for others (Field and Hope 1990). The external benefits generated by private security actions have political significance. If the task of government is to ensure equality of access to the collective good of private security, then it has two basic choices: on the one hand, it might take steps to ensure that everyone has an equal capacity to meet their own needs for private security – if those needs vary according to households' levels of income, or the risks they face, then it becomes the task of government either to *eradicate* the cause of excessive risk or to *compensate* in some way for inequality in access to collective security. Yet the costs of these strategies are substantial. On the other hand, it may be considerably less costly, and socially more efficient, to try to *redistribute* the externality benefits of private security so as to benefit those who do not have the means to produce as much private security for themselves as they need. The alternative to these courses of action is the *laissez-faire* approach of letting private action thrive where it can, though, as illustrated below, this may increase inequality of access to private security.

Yet, while redistributing externality benefits is a more attractive and efficient option, there would seem to be two limiting factors to attaining this goal: first, that private security actions may also generate externality *costs* for others – that is, private-interest security actions may increase the risk of insecurity to others by producing 'malign displacement' of risk in encouraging offenders to seek other, less-protected targets (Barr and Pease 1990); and second, that those with the capacity to generate genuine externality benefits of private security do not see an incentive to produce them, or are able to retain all the benefits exclusively for themselves, with no social benefit from their actions shared among others. The political problem, then, for governments in providing private security for all, when citizens have a differential capacity to produce it for themselves, is compounded by an inability either to distribute externality benefits, to prevent the redistribution of externality costs, or to secure additional resources to compensate for inequality in private security provision.

The distribution of private security

Though not without its real problems, it is arguably easier to estimate the distribution of the risk of private property *insecurity* than it is to estimate the distribution of the outcomes of security activity – i.e. 'non-risk'. Operationally, we may have little choice but to assume that the distribution of private security is the obverse of the distribution of the risk of insecurity. Conventionally, we have tended to assume that such observed distributions merely reflect the distribution of 'offenders' – both their prevalence and their actions (Bottoms and Wiles 1997). However, in as much as aggregate crime rates reflect the distribution of victimisation incidents, they also represent the observed *outcomes* of criminal activity – and there are other elements contributing to this outcome in addition to the motives and activities of offenders. It is necessary to look at the components of these criminal outcomes in order to locate the role, if any, played by (unequal) access to intermediate security goods.

The growth of crime

What has become known as the *routine activities* perspective (Cohen and Felson 1979) is a useful heuristic for conceptualising the array of micro-social interactions which lead to property crime victimisation. Property crimes may be the probable outcome of the interaction of the presence or absence of various conditions, including: the presence of motivated offenders; the absence of those able to exercise moral control over the offender; the presence of suitable or desirable targets and victims; and the absence of agencies capable of exercising protection or guardianship over targets and victims (Felson 1994; Cohen and Felson 1979). While the routine activity framework may not be a *sufficient* explanation of crime,[5] nevertheless its particular usefulness, at least for our purposes, is that it describes 'ecological' regularities in the occurrence of victimisation events across space and time as the outcome of a *convergence of conditions necessary for criminal events to occur*.[6]

Macro-level trends and patterns of crime have been seen as a result of structured variations in some of these micro-level conditions for crime. Thus, Cohen and Felson (1979) explain rising crime rates in America during the post-war period chiefly as a consequence of the diffusion of lightweight, durable consumer goods – such as TVs, hi-fis, VCRs, PCs – and the dispersal of routine activities away from families and households (Felson 1997; Cohen and Felson 1979). The former has increased the supply and attractiveness of suitable targets available for theft; the latter has reduced the degree to which both 'stealable' property and young people – who are the most likely offenders attracted to it – are under routine and capable supervision (Felson 1994).[7]

Yet, despite its intuitive appeal, this explanation does not have general applicability. First, not all societies in which these changes in routine activities may have occurred have seen comparable crime trends: residential property crime victimisation rates in the United States have fallen consistently since their peak in the mid-1970s (the end of the period of growth studied by Cohen and Felson (1979)) while they have increased markedly in England and Wales over the same period, now apparently having surpassed those in the United States (Langan and Farrington 1998) despite broadly similar and continuing trends in consumption and activity between the two societies.[8] Second, trends in property crime rates in England and Wales, particularly in the short run, are *negatively* correlated with consumption growth (Pyle 1998; Hale 1998; Field 1990): property crime seems to rise faster when personal consumption slows down, despite a presumable reduction in the availability of goods to steal and the greater opportunity enjoyed by those who are now unemployed to guard their private property (Land *et al.* 1995)! While the apparent increase in opportunities may account for the 'paradox' of the growth of crime alongside economic growth in the post-war period (see Wilson 1975), it seems less capable of explaining differing social trends in crime – including the stabilisation or decline of crime rates, short-run changes and differing societal crime-trajectories – despite a 'global' convergence of consumption and 'lifestyles' within the post-industrial world.

A resolution of some of these difficulties is provided by van Dijk (1994) who proposes a 'dynamic equilibrium model' of crime rates which derives from the macro-level interactions between 'offenders' and 'victims'. In this model, while social conditions may lead to increased offending – whether through an increase of opportunities, or an increase in offenders, or in offender motivation – the resulting 'crime boom' may nevertheless stimulate a reaction among potential victims, primarily to increase their efforts of self-protection by available means (see also Cook 1986). Consequently, 'the collective implementation of extra security ... in response to a crime boom reduces the net yields of [crime to] offenders and thereby eventually the number of crimes committed' (van Dijk 1994: 108).

Paradoxically, despite efforts to link the 'routine activity' approach to ideas about crime prevention, the everyday reactions of 'potential victims' to crime risks, as they perceive them, are given relatively scant attention (Felson 1994).[9] Yet individuals may seek actively to provide themselves with private security, and to 'react to crime' in their everyday lives, albeit with imperfect knowledge of the risks confronting them or the means which might be available for their protection (Skogan and Maxfield 1981). What are of interest, though, are the *collective consequences* of these individual actions, not only on the level but also on the *distribution* of private security. In the interests of distributive justice, we need to know whether the 'collective' implementation of extra security is likely to benefit everyone equally.

The distribution of private security

Based on data taken from the 1994 British Crime Survey (BCS) covering England and Wales, Figure 5.1 shows that not only the number of different types of 'stealable' property possessed by households but also the number of property security measures adopted by them increases along with household income, with the highest income grouping adopting nearly twice as many different types of security measure as the lowest grouping.

In much research, the most consistent predictors of the adoption of security measures have been higher incomes and home-ownership (Lab 1990; Hope 1995). This tendency is reflected in Table 5.1 where, respectively, higher- versus lower-income households and owner-occupiers versus other (mainly rental) tenures are *consistently* more likely to adopt the various prevention measures surveyed.[10]

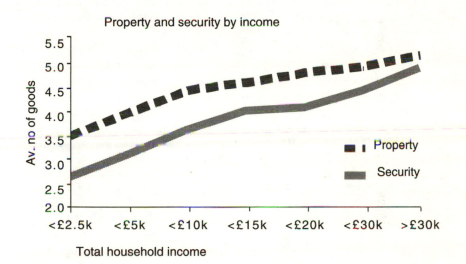

Figure 5.1   Property and security by income

Source   1994 British Crime Survey (weighted data)

Notes:
1   Total household income before tax and deductions in previous twelve months (missing data = 3.8 per cent of sample).
2   Security goods – number of security measures adopted by households (max. = 11) including: household contents insurance; intruder alarm; deadlocks/double locks; window locks; indoor/outdoor timer/sensor lights; window bars or grilles; police security survey; property marking; telling neighbours when home is unoccupied; membership of neighbourhood watch; paying for organised security.
3   Property – number of goods within the household (max.= 6) including: colour TV; video player or recorder; stereo or hi-fi (including CD player); mobile phone; camera; jewellery.

This tendency applies across the range of the intermediate security goods: not only are the better-off and home-owners more likely to purchase 'target-hardening' products but they are also much more likely to benefit from 'collective' services, including being able to arrange private household contents insurance, membership of neighbourhood watch schemes, and free household security surveys provided by the police.

Table 5.1   Household property security measures: differences between high- and low-income households, owners and other (rental) tenures

Security measure	Prevalence (%)[a]	High / low income (relative odds)[b]	Owners / renters (relative odds) [c]
Household contents insurance	83	1.274	1.676
Double locks or deadlocks	70	1.155	1.292
Window locks	62	1.272	1.476
Tell neighbours when home unoccupied	62	1.087	1.345
Lights on timer or sensor switches	32	1.564	1.933
Member of neighbourhood watch scheme	25	1.309	1.979
Security marking of property	19	1.555	1.881
Burglar alarm	18	2.060	3.194
Window bars or grilles	7	0.985[d]	0.792
Security survey by police	6	2.180	2.793
Paid for, organised security	1	0.769[d]	0.474

Source: 1994 British Crime Survey. Weighted data.

Notes:
[a]Prevalence – percentage of sample using the measure.
[b]High/low income (odds) – ratio of the probability of households with above-median income taking the measure to households with below-median income taking the measure.
[c]Owners/renters (odds) – ratio of the probability of owner-occupier households taking the measure to household in other (rental) tenures taking the measure.
[d]Differences not statistically significant (chi-square test). All other differences significant at $p<0.5$.

In terms of distributive justice, however, this inequality in access to private security only 'matters' if

1   the less well-off face an equal or higher risk than the better-off,
2   there are no external benefits generated by the private security actions of individuals, and/or
3   these are not shared by those on lower incomes.

In the first instance, with regard to private self-guardianship, the only study of its kind found negligible crime displacement and benefit-diffusion effects between immediate neighbours (Miethe 1991). If we can extrapolate from these findings, it would seem that there are no immediate externalities generated from private actions – the benefits of private security goods are unlikely to be transferred directly between proximate households, nor can risks be successfully displaced to others.

Yet the macro-level distribution of risk is highly and negatively correlated with the distribution of income and wealth. Figure 5.2, derived from data collected in the British Crime Survey, illustrates the distribution of the incidence rate of household property crime victimisation among residential areas in England and Wales, alongside area-level indices of the distribution of private wealth.[11] There seems little doubt that the more 'affluent' one's community of residence, the less risk to private residential security one faces; conversely, the poorer the conditions in which one's neighbours live, the more at risk is one's own private property – and the disparity of risk is most marked in the most disadvantaged neighbourhoods.[12] Multivariate statistical modelling of household property crime risk shows that these area-level effects remain even after individual household characteristics have been taken into account (Ellingworth et al. 1997).

Property crime rates in high-crime communities in England and Wales are characterised more by an unexpectedly higher *rate of victimisation* (producing, among other things, a greater concentration of repeat victims) than by higher rates of victim prevalence – though these too are, of course, higher than in other areas (Trickett et al. 1992).[13] Since the early 1980s, this inequality has increased:

> the distribution of property crime between areas … experienced a 'double concentration' – a smaller number of areas during the 1980s suffered an increasing proportion of property crime victimisation not only because they contained more victims than other areas but also because victims in those areas were becoming more frequently victimised than were [victims resident in] other areas.
>
> (Trickett et al. 1995: 350)

A substantial part, then, of the increased property crime rate in England and Wales since the early 1980s may be due to the increasing rate of victimisation in high-crime (high-prevalence) communities. In these places, more conjunctions of necessary crime conditions resulted in more crimes (Hope 1996). The structural

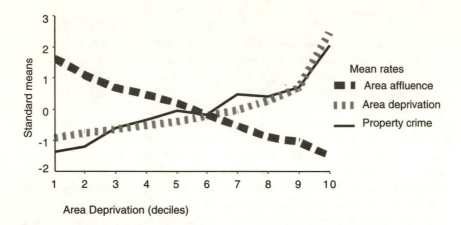

Figure 5.2 Inequality and property crime

Source 1992 British Crime Survey/1991 Census

Notes:
1   Data from the 1991 Census were attached to individual responses in the 1992 BCS (N=10,059) according to the respective postcode 'sector' in which respondents' home addresses were located (n=576). Respondents and sectors were randomly selected in the BCS sample design. Mean rates for each sector were calculated and sectors were further aggregated into deciles according to the measure of area deprivation, where 1 denotes the 10 per cent least deprived and 10 denotes the 10 per cent most deprived. Mean rates for each decile were then calculated and standardised to a normal distribution.
2   Property crime includes burglary, theft from a dwelling, and criminal damage to household property.
3   'Area deprivation' is an additive variable composed of the proportion of households in each area in: overcrowded households; large families; housing association rental tenure; and unemployment.
4   'Area affluence' is an additive variable composed of: the average number of cars per household; and the proportion of detached dwellings.

conditions associated with this redistribution are similar to those giving rise to the phenomena of locally concentrated poverty (Pitts and Hope 1997; Hope 1996; see also Wilson 1996; Sampson and Wilson 1995) which has also increased in Britain (JRF 1995). But, as Figure 5.2 prompts us to ask, why has property crime victimisation imploded in areas of deprivation rather than 'spilling over' into more affluent places where there are likely to be more rewards and opportunities? Or, to put it differently, how have the better-off been able to avoid their 'share' of the increased burden of crime victimisation?

The clubbing of private security

Fight or flight?

From the perspective of the private property owner, there are two broad kinds of intermediate security goods and practices: those which aim to respond to risk *in situ* – that is, measures which might be taken as correctives to existing arrangements, particularly reducing the 'suitability' of targets for crime – and there are those which aim to *anticipate and avoid risks* which are foreseen. The former correspond, though not completely, with physical security or target-hardening measures: the latter, to making changes in routines and lifestyles (see Clarke 1992). Target-hardening measures are relatively widespread, even though the better-off adopt more of them (Table 5.1). Yet in explaining the occurrence of criminal events, the 'routine activity' framework also tends to emphasise the idea of *exposure* to risk. People's 'lifestyles' may increase the risk of crime to their persons or property by bringing them into closer proximity with 'potential offenders'.[14] Therefore, in addition to target-hardening, an alternative strategy for *avoiding risk* would be to ensure that one's person and property are as infrequently exposed to perceived sources of risk as possible. In this way, a convergence of necessary crime conditions does not occur. Thus, not only do we need to know which property-owners have the *capacity* to take what kinds of self-protective action – and it seems that the better-off have a greater capacity for converting their capital into protective measures – but we also need to know the conditions under which they would be prepared either to take *in situ* defence of their property or to remove themselves from such risk altogether. With what considerations, then, do property-owners choose what to do to provide themselves with private security?

'Location, location, location'[15]

A purely 'rational' calculation of the costs and benefits of private security action requires a degree of reliable knowledge about risk which is largely unavailable to private citizens – for the most part, they are unable to attach a separate 'value' of crime risk to their property. They are, however, able to read the 'signals' in the exchange-values emanating from other markets, notably in housing and, to a lesser extent, private insurance, even if such signals about risks, and the value of private security, are bundled together with other values attaching to their property. Nevertheless, it is through the operation of these markets that information, albeit imperfect, is gleaned about private security. Information on crime risk is transmitted to present property owners and prospective 'investors' through commonly shared perceptions and images about residential neighbourhoods. Studies of English high-crime areas – notably in public housing – have pointed consistently to the stigmatising effects of the image of crime and 'disorder' on neighbourhood reputation (Bottoms and Wiles 1997; Foster and Hope 1993). Housing markets, which aggregate and reflexively feed back such information in the valuation of property, thus create an objective pricing yardstick for private security decisions. For example, Taub *et al.* (1984) show how housing property prices in Chicago neighbourhoods served as a general index of perceived neighbourhood change for residents, and how the local housing market mediated their decisions not only about selling or investing in their residential property but also in how they perceived and reacted to local crime.

The consequences of these processes can also be detected in English data. 'Dwelling detachment' is highly valued in English housing markets – the degree of detachment of the dwelling structure reflecting a constellation of both use and exchange values (Hope 1984).[16] The corollary of high property-values is the degree of *affluence* of owner-occupiers and, consequently, the *value* of private property contained within the dwelling (Winchester and Jackson 1982). There is also a fair degree of research evidence that these attributes – especially easy physical access, low surveillance and valuable contents – provide attractive opportunities for burglary (Litton 1997; Hope 1984; Bennett and Wright 1984; Winchester and Jackson 1982; Maguire 1982). Table 5.2 shows the risk for households of becoming a victim of property crime by their type of dwelling. The first column shows risks weighted only to represent the population. In this estimation, both detached and semi-detached dwellings have significantly *lower* risks than other dwelling types, whose risks do not differ much from each other.[17] However, the second column shows the odds re-estimated from a multivariate, logistic regression model (Table 5.2, note c) which takes into account various characteristics both of the households and of the areas in which they are located. In this context, detached houses and, to a lesser extent, semi-detached houses now appear, as in previous research, to have *higher* risks than other dwelling types, particularly flats (apartments).[18] The broad reason for this change in the risk-ranking of dwelling-types is, of course, the effect of other individual and

Table 5.2 Property crime victimisation likelihood by dwelling and area type: univariate and multivariate odds

	Bivariate (sample) odds[a]	*Multivariate odds (p)*[b]
Detached house	1.000	1.000
Semi-detached house	1.254	0.845 (.054)
End-terrace (row) house	1.726	0.986 (.901)
Mid-terrace house	1.505	0.763 (.005)
Flat (apartment)	1.569	0.664 (.000)
Affluence of area[c]	0.803	0.846 (.000)

Source 1992 British Crime Survey/1991 Census

Notes:
[a]Bivariate odds calculated from weighted data.
[b]Multivariate odds estimate from a logit regression model including: characteristics of of the household (age and occupation of 'head', number of children, housing tenure, ethnicity, mobility); perceptions of community (area satisfaction, community reciprocity); and area socio-demographic characteristics (age structure, ethnic composition, rental tenure, inner-city location and household composition). Details in Trickett, appendix to Hope 1999; see also Ellingworth *et al.* 1997.
[c]'Affluence of area' is an additive variable composed of the average number of cars per household, and the proportion of detached dwellings.

area-level variables, either amplifying or suppressing risks which might be associated with the dwelling alone.

The 'affluence' of the area in which the dwelling is located – represented here by the proportion of households living in detached dwellings, combined with the average number of cars per household – represents a powerful suppressant of property crime risk.[19] Risks are reduced the more that higher-value property is surrounded by similar property; when such protection is hypothetically 'removed', the crime-risk of dwelling-detachment is exposed. Thus, as far as avoiding the risk of property crime is concerned, 'affluent' suburbs offer property-owners a *club good* of security – if they wish to dwell in 'desirable' houses (i.e. detached or semi-detached dwellings), then they can provide themselves with private security by selecting a house in a neighbourhood composed of similar dwellings with similarly affluent occupants, thereby partaking in the collective good of security available in the area (Figure 5.2).

Market signals

Market 'signals' from the private housing market may generally attract property-owners towards such desirable – and therefore 'safe' – neighbourhoods. Perhaps not surprisingly, the protective effect of location is mirrored in the actual distribution of dwelling types: 74 per cent of detached dwellings in the sample (which could be at higher risk) are located in the top third of these 'affluent' areas (which are actually at low risk, see Figure 5.2); while 59 per cent of flats and 48 per cent of terraced houses (which could be at lower risk) are located in the third least affluent areas (which are actually at high risk). The housing market, however, is not isolated from the rest of the economy, and the specific security amenities of suburbs form probably only a relatively minor, and unacknowledged, part of the valuation which residents attach to the bundle of use-values they contain.[20] Nevertheless, as better-off residential areas on this score appear to offer a reasonable bet that the security of property is assured (Figure 5.2), it would seem likely that this private security good contributes to the general 'sense of physical and psychic security that comes with a familiar and dependable environment' (Logan and Molotch 1987: 105; see also Walklate and Loader *et al.* in this volume).

Of course, as with the phenomenon of 'gentrification', the better-off could choose to dwell in 'inner-city' neighbourhoods, from which they may indeed derive particular values. Unfortunately, private security, in the sense we are talking about here, is unlikely to be one of them.[21] The outcome, in terms of how they choose to deal with their private insecurity, may depend upon a balancing of risk against use-value, at least as long as the exchange-value of private property remains buoyant and not too many other property-owners decide to depart (see Taub *et al.* 1984). Yet it is also likely that property-ownership (both of dwellings and contents) – whether in the suburbs or elsewhere – induces a high degree of *risk aversion*, otherwise there would be no market for household contents insurance (Field and Hope 1990). On the contrary, household insurance has a high participation rate, particularly among higher income groups and property-owners (see Table 5.1). And, to the extent that 'gentrifiers' take out insurance against risk and collectively make claims, they will in turn receive a signal about their higher risk from the insurance market in the form of higher premiums.[22] Thus, for higher-income groups in lower-income neighbourhoods, the price of private insurance – and its associated costs such as additional security hardware and the excess (deductible) losses which insurers may insist upon (Litton 1997) – is likely to force itself into the calculus of their private security, alongside that of property prices themselves, and the sense of insecurity which 'fortification' itself induces (Taylor 1995).[23]

Security as a positional good

Entry into the private security 'club' of the better-off neighbourhood is, of course, determined by property prices. Yet the collective security goods available to residents may be quite fragile unless their exclusive nature can be maintained. In part, this is because private security resembles what Hirsch (1977) called a *positional good* – something which has value to its possessor only because others cannot possess it to the same degree and whose supply cannot be increased greatly by changes in the basic factors of production. In this sense, the greater demand there is for private security the more *congested* its supply becomes. Thus, for example, the supply of property guardianship services provided by public police is subject to crowding as a result of increased demand (via calls for service), especially if police resources cannot be increased commensurately and yet are still to be offered on a universal basis. Therefore, congestion in supply occurs, reducing the quality of public police for any individual the more that overall demand for public policing goods increases. Consequently, the cost of supplying police guardianship on demand rises at the same time as its effectiveness diminishes, because the public police are having to absorb the costs of congestion (see Bayley 1994).

The bundle of security goods offered by the 'exclusive' suburb itself diminishes through congestion unless external demand for those goods can be resisted (Hirsch 1977). Positional goods, which residents might once have enjoyed exclusively, lose their value if everyone has equal access to them. If the cost of private security can be reduced by avoiding risk in the first place – particularly by avoiding proximity to a 'supply' of offenders – then the private security value of the suburb depends upon the extent to which it can maintain its exclusivity by preventing others, including would-be offenders, from encroaching upon it (Hope, 1999). Yet the spatial and social accessibility of contemporary suburbs (Felson 1994; Logan and Molotch 1987) means that the security of all but the most exclusive suburb becomes devalued (crowded) as more people are able to encroach upon it. Although rising house prices may serve to restrict residential membership of the suburb, they cannot necessarily protect its boundaries.

Thus the defence of the community against 'encroachment' becomes an important weapon in the preservation of neighbourhood values and amenities, including security.[24] Much community action in suburbs is 'preservationist' (Savage *et al.* 1992), not least with regard to anti-crime efforts (Skogan 1988), and better-off communities do have some advantages in generating resources to defend themselves. The 'weak' overlapping ties which characterise social relationships in better-off suburbs (see Baumgartner 1988; Loader *et al.* in this volume) provide linkages between sources of power and influence within a community (Granovetter 1973). These also provide opportunities for network 'closure', creating a collective reciprocity of social obligation from which *social capital* can be generated (Coleman 1990). In turn, social capital can be mobilised to create collective goods like community organisations and residents' associations. These groups can then cash in the (symbolic and cultural) capital which the neighbourhood holds with extra-communal sources of power, such as public police and local government, thus mobilising resources to preserve neighbourhood amenities, including security (Skogan 1988).

Yet the 'associationalism' of suburban interest groups in market society is also fragile:

> liberalism is distinguished less by the freedom to form groups ... than the freedom to leave the groups ... behind. Association is always at risk in a liberal society. The boundaries of the group are not policed ... that is why liberalism is plagued by free-rider problems.
>
> (Walzer 1990: 15)

Predicated upon the values of the market (i.e. individualism and self-interest), suburban interest groups also cannot inhibit 'exit' from community participation in the form of free-riding and outward mobility.[25] Thus, the availability of market-produced incentives to free-ride or exit continually undermines the production of collective goods. Only by creating non-market incentives or penalties can the public goods dilemma of suburban security be resolved in favour of the provision of collective neighbourhood defence.

Mobilising residential defences

Over the past twenty years, governments have encouraged (or at least not prevented) the growth of resident-based community groups – such as 'neighbourhood watch' – as a means of providing security goods through collective self-help. Yet the overwhelming finding from research is that, first, such efforts are most common in the (low-crime) neighbourhoods where they seem least needed and, second, that these groups appear to have a somewhat tenuous and intangible existence (Hope 1995). Analysis of BCS data on English private security practices (described in Table 5.1) offers some clues towards resolving these abiding paradoxes (Lab and Hope 1998). In the first place, membership of neighbourhood watch groups (NW) is highest among households who also security-mark their property, ask neighbours to watch their homes when unoccupied, and have household contents insurance.[26] These are the club goods associated with NW membership – public police encourage residents to form NW groups and intro- duce them to the idea of marking their property to deter theft and/or aid its recovery; the groups introduce neighbours to each other and encourage them to share their routine activities; and British insurance underwriters (accepting their lower risk) have offered discounted premiums to NW members (Laycock and Tilley 1995). While such measures individually may have limited value in reducing risk (Hope 1995; Mayhew 1984), they provide, nevertheless, a collec- tion of non-physical *assurances* about risk, addressing particularly the needs of risk-averse property-owners (Field and Hope 1990).[27]

Second, Table 5.3 lists the most significant variables associated with the household consumption of these security club goods.[28] Not surprisingly, this is highest for older, owner-occupied, higher-income households. Participation is also high not only in areas of predominantly owner-occupied tenure – i.e. communities 'defended' by the property market – but also among owner- occupiers in chiefly public housing areas. As we noted for this latter group, the club goods of NW may offer a 'subsidy' to their otherwise high private security costs. Finally, as we have suggested, those more likely to be involved in local community groups – for example, residents' associations, local youth or sports groups – are also likely to participate in the benefits of NW club goods.

Much of the literature on the emergence and distribution of anti-crime community organisations in the United States since the 1970s shows a strong tendency for such groups to be initiated, and to survive, as an adjunct of existing

Table 5.3 Predictors of participation in the neighbourhood watch security club good: reduced regression model

Variable	Beta weight	Significance (p)
Age of respondent	0.155	0.000
Owner-occupied housing tenure	0.295	0.000
Total household income	0.227	0.000
Proportion of owner-occupier households in area	0.225	0.000
Proportion of households renting from public authorities in area	0.184	0.000
Number of types of local groups respondent belongs to (0–3)	0.129	0.000
R-squared	0.260	

Source 1994 British Crime Survey/1991 UK Census

organised community activity (Skogan 1988). Likewise, specifically anti-crime groups fail to become implanted in communities where general group activities are low (Hope 1995). This reflects not only the availability of social capital in the community but also its capacity to spawn further groups as needed. Their success in sustaining themselves – thus countering free-riding – is that continuing access to the benefits of belonging to the 'security club' depends not simply on residing in a conducive area, but is also reinforced by the benefits accruing from membership or support of other community groups delivering social and cultural benefits. Thus, members who wish to benefit from security club goods may be unable so readily to free-ride without risking sanction or opprobrium within the other groups in which they also have a continuing interest or need to participate. The web of group activity in suburbs may generate not only activists who are able to deal in social capital so as to mobilise community defences in the form of security club goods, but may also provide them with a means of enforcing the participation of others (see Olson 1965). Without such social support it is unlikely that external agents, such as the public police, would be able to sustain these groups over the long term, whatever institutional bias they may have towards them (see McConville and Shepherd 1992). And given that membership of such 'security clubs' overlaps with membership of local groups generally, it is also likely that collective neighbourhood norms of property security may strengthen over time, eventually becoming self-sustaining, both organisationally and normatively.[29]

Exclusive club goods

The principal benefit of a club good to its members is that it is 'an institutional solution to the collective action problem that internalises an externality through tolls' (Sandler 1992: 64). With the kinds of social sanctions available, members can trust that their fellows will continue to contribute to the collective generation of private security goods and that they will not free-ride, thus undermining and diluting the efforts of those who do participate in private security production. Such social sanctions may become less necessary the more 'exclusive' the club, since membership exclusivity ensures that the externalities of individual private security efforts will be retained within the club for the benefit of club-members only, and will likewise not be seen to suffer from the threat of congestion of the club's security from external parties wishing to share in the benefit.

Generally, the price-mechanisms of the housing market tend to ensure that the more affluent suburbs are the most exclusive, usually through increased social and spatial 'distance' placed between itself and the perceived sources of risk (Hope, in press). Membership exclusivity is preserved by insulating the club's boundaries. In open, urban environments, insulation may come from the 'buffering' effect of being surrounded by similar suburbs.[30] Yet in environments where security is more congested, such as with our urban gentrifiers or Davis' frenetic suburbanites (1990), more specific means of policing the boundaries may be needed to retain security for the club, including the use of private police. And the rise of 'common interest developments' (McKenzie 1994) and 'gated communities' represent the ultimate means of preserving the exclusive club benefits of private security for their subscribing members.

Conclusion

The argument advanced in this chapter is that inequality in the distribution of private security is politically important if, first, some groups in society are able to purchase more private security than others whose needs may be greater and yet remain unmet; and second, that the (externality) benefits of the private security goods generated by those who can provide for themselves are not shared by those who cannot. On both counts, the evidence presented here suggests that these should be matters of concern to the public interest in contemporary Britain. The distribution illustrated in Figure 5.2 calls for explanation. Aside from the not inconsiderable issue of why it is that the economically disadvantaged have a disproportionately high risk of property crime (Hope 1996), there is the other issue of how it is that the better-off have apparently been able to avoid and insulate themselves from risk so effectively.

The chief reason for the relative success of the more affluent in attaining a higher level of private security for their residential property than the less affluent is not so much that they have been able to purchase more private security measures (Figure 5.1) – which in themselves may have doubtful efficacy – but that they have been able to use their capital to avoid risk while, at the same time, retaining for themselves the externality security benefits generated by their private actions. The principal mechanism for delivering this good has been the private housing market. Individual households pursuing their private strategies for maximising the use and exchange values of their property have been guided by the markets in housing and household insurance towards more 'exclusive' suburbs. The more 'exclusive' the suburb, the more it can exclude unwarranted risks by maximising avoidance of risk through spatial and cultural distancing from 'criminogenic' places and people (see Hope, 1999). The suburb's capacity to exclude others, primarily via the price mechanism, also guarantees that its positional advantage – that is, its capacity also to retain private security externalities (club goods) – is not diluted by the demands from those excluded from the suburbs' security.

I have followed an argument similar to that developed by Jordan (1996) in respect of the wider task of explaining how the economically marginal have also become excluded from social citizenship.[31] What has been missing from contemporary debate has been a broader view of how:

> groups form, organise and act collectively in pursuit of their interests, and how vulnerable individuals come to be excluded and marginalised in such interactions ... club theory is specially relevant ... because it

explains in detail how groups that form to supply each other with a range of collective goods respond to incentives to include or exclude members.

(Jordan 1996: 4, 62)

The process of club-formation stands in contrast to the collectivisation of social risk – the sense in which inequalities are compensated through sharing the common benefits consequent upon universal, inclusive membership and collective contribution (Jordan 1996). If one of the 'limitations of the sovereign state' (Garland 1996) has been the failure to provide universal (i.e. public goods) private security for citizens, the better-off have responded, consciously or not, by seeking to compensate for their perceived security deficit in their everyday lives. In pursuing their individual strategies, they have become the beneficiaries of a market which, reflexively, has allowed them to transform erstwhile public goods into club goods which they are better able to enjoy for their own exclusive benefit.

Not that the market works perfectly to meet the needs of the better-off, nor are all their security needs met. The downside of neo-liberal associations is the liberty to exit and free-ride, continually undermining the production of club goods. Neither can suburbanites impose tolls on their borders to repel those whom they see as a threat to their positional goods; nor can they insulate their communities entirely from the positional instabilities of global capitalism. Yet if 'crime prevention [is] a new social movement' (Taylor 1997: 63; also Taylor 1996) the crime-talk of the suburbs through which members communicate (Taylor 1995; see also Chapter 4) is not just a middle-class protest movement but may also serve specific positional purposes (Davis 1990). Arguably, not least of these is the generation and maintenance of the social capital which is necessary to establish and preserve the security club goods of the suburbs.

References

Barr, R. and Pease, K. (1990) 'Crime placement, displacement and deflection', in M. Tonry and N. Morris (eds) *Crime and Justice 12*, Chicago: University of Chicago Press.

Barry, B. and Hardin, R. (ed.) (1982) *Rational Man and Irrational Society?* Beverly Hills: Sage.

Baumgartner, M.P. (1988) *The Moral Order of a Suburb*, New York: Oxford University Press.

Bayley, D.H. (1994) *Police for the Future*, New York: Oxford University Press.

Bennett, T. and Wright, R. (1984) *Burglars on Burglary*, Aldershot: Gower.

Bottoms, A.E. and Wiles, P. (1992) 'Explanations of crime and place', in D.J. Evans, N.R. Fyfe and D.T. Herbert (eds) *Crime, Policing and Place*, London: Routledge.

——(1997) 'Environmental criminology', in M. Maguire, R. Morgan and R. Reiner (eds) *The Oxford Handbook of Criminology*, second edition, Oxford: Clarendon Press.

Braithwaite, J. and Pettit, P. (1990) (eds) *Not Just Deserts: A Republican Theory of Justice*, Oxford: Oxford University Press.

Budd, T. (1999) *Burglary of Domestic Dwellings: Findings from the British Crime Survey*, Home Office Statistical Bulletin 4/99, London: Home Office.

Clarke, R.V. (ed.) (1992) *Situational Crime Prevention: Successful Case Studies*, New York: Harrow and Heston.

Cohen, L.E. and Felson, M. (1979) 'Social change and crime rate trends: a routine activities approach', *American Sociological Review*, 44: 588–608.

Cohen, L.E., Kluegel, J.R. and Land, K.C. (1981) 'Social inequality and predatory criminal victimization: an exposition and test of a formal theory', *American Sociological Review*, 46: 505–24.

Coleman, J.S. (1990) *Foundations of Social Theory*, Cambridge, MA.: Belknap Press.

Cook, P.J. (1986) 'The demand and supply of criminal opportunities', in M. Tonry and N. Morris (eds) *Crime and Justice 9*, Chicago: University of Chicago Press, 1–27.

Davis, M. (1990) *City of Quartz*, London: Verso.

Doyal, L. and Gough, I. (1991) *A Theory of Human Need*, Basingstoke: Macmillan.

Ellingworth, D., Hope, T., Osborn, D.R., Trickett, A. and Pease, K. (1997) 'Prior victimisation and crime risk', *Journal of Crime Prevention and Risk Management*, 2: 201–14.

Farrell, G. and Pease, K. (1993) *Once Bitten, Twice Bitten*, Crime Prevention Unit Paper, London: Home Office.

Felson, M. (1987) 'Routine activities and crime prevention in the developing metropolis', *Criminology*, 25: 911–31.

——(1994) *Crime and Everyday Life*, Thousand Oaks, CA: Pine Forge Press.

——(1997) 'Technology, business and crime', in M. Felson and R.V. Clarke (eds) *Business and Crime Prevention*, Monsey, NY: Criminal Justice Press.

Field, S. (1990) *Trends in Crime and their Interpretation: A Study of Recorded Crime in Post-War England and Wales*, Home Office Research Study 119, London: HMSO.

Field, S. and Hope, T. (1990) 'Economics, the consumer and under-provision in crime prevention', in R. Morgan (ed.) *Policing Organised Crime and Crime Prevention*, British Criminology Conference 1989, volume 4, Bristol: Bristol Centre for Criminal Justice.

Foster, J. and Hope, T. (1993) *Housing, Community and Crime: The Impact of the Priority Estates Project*, Home Office Research Study 131, London: HMSO.

Garland, D. (1996) 'The limits of the sovereign state: strategies of crime control in contemporary society', *British Journal of Criminology*, 36: 445–71.

Giddens, A. (1984) *The Constitution of Society*, Cambridge: Polity Press.

——(1990) *The Consequences of Modernity*, Cambridge: Polity Press.

Gottfredson, M.J. and Hirschi, T. (1990) *A General Theory of Crime*, Stanford, CA: Stanford University Press.

Granovetter, M.S. (1973) 'The strength of weak ties', *American Journal of Sociology*, 78: 1360–80.

Hale, C. (1998) 'The labour market and post-war crime trends in England and Wales', in P. Carlen and R. Morgan (eds) *Crime Unlimited? Questions for the 21st Century*, Basingstoke: Macmillan.

Hargreaves Heap, S., Hollis, M., Lyons, B., Sugden, R. and Weale, A. (1992) *The Theory of Choice: A Critical Guide*, Oxford: Blackwell.

Hirsch, F. (1977) *Social Limits to Growth*, London: Routledge.

Hirschfield, A. and Bowers, K.J. (1997) 'The development of a social, demographic and land use profiler for areas of high crime', *British Journal of Criminology*, 37: 103–20.

Home Office (1998) *Annual Report*, Cmnd. 3908, London: HMSO.

——(1999) *The Government's Crime Reduction Strategy*, London: Home Office.

Hope, T. (1984) 'Building design and burglary', in R. Clarke and T. Hope (eds) *Coping with Burglary: Research Perspectives in Policy*, Boston, MA: Kluwer Nijhoff.

——(1987) *Residential Aspects of Autocrime*, Research Bulletin no. 23, London: Home Office Research and Planning Unit.

——(1995) 'Community crime prevention', in M. Tonry and D.P. Farrington (eds) *Building a Safer Society: Strategic Approaches to Crime Prevention. Crime and Justice 19*, Chicago: University of Chicago Press.

——(1996) 'Communities, crime and inequality in England and Wales', in T. Bennett (ed.) *Preventing Crime and Disorder: Targeting Strategies and Responsibilities*, Cambridge: Institute of Criminology.

——(1997) 'Inequality and the future of community crime prevention', in S.P. Lab (ed.) *Crime Prevention at a Crossroads*, American Academy of Criminal Justice Sciences Monograph Series, Cincinnati, OH: Anderson Publishing.

——(1999) 'Privatopia on trial? Property guardianship in the suburbs', in K. Painter and N. Tilley (eds) *Surveillance of Public Space*, Crime Prevention Studies 10, Monsey, NY: Criminal Justice Press.

Hough, M. and Mayhew, P. (1983) *The British Crime Survey: First Report*, Home Office Research Study 76, London: HMSO.

Jordan, B. (1996) *A Theory of Poverty and Social Exclusion*, Cambridge: Polity Press.

JRF (1995) *Joseph Rowntree Foundation Inquiry into Income and Wealth*, volumes 1 and 2, York: Joseph Rowntree Foundation.

Lab, S. (1990) 'Citizen crime prevention: domains and participation', *Justice Quarterly*, 7: 467–92.

Lab, S. and Hope, T. (1998) 'Assessing the impact of area context on crime prevention behavior', paper presented to the 7th International Seminar on Environmental Criminology and Crime Analysis, Barcelona, June.

Land, K.C., Cantor, D. and Russell, S.T. (1995) 'Unemployment and crime rate fluctuations in post-World War II United States: statistical time series properties and alternative models', in J. Hagan and R.D. Peterson (eds) *Crime and Inequality*, Stanford, CA: Stanford University Press.

Langan, P.A. and Farrington, D.P. (1998) *Crime and Justice in the United States and in England and Wales, 1981–96. NCJ 169284*, Washington, DC: US Department of Justice.

Laycock, G. and Tilley, N. (1995) *Policing and Neighbourhood Watch: Strategic Issues*, Crime Detection and Prevention Series Paper 60, London: Home Office.

Litton, R.A. (1997) 'Crime prevention and the insurance industry', in M. Felson and R.V. Clarke (eds) *Business and Crime Prevention*, Monsey, NY: Criminal Justice Press.

Loader, I. (1997) 'Thinking normatively about private security', *Journal of Law and Society*, 24: 377–94.

Logan, J.H. and Molotch, H. (1987) *Urban Fortunes: The Political Economy of Place*, Berkeley: University of California Press.

McConville, M. and Shepherd, D. (1992) *Watching Police, Watching Communities*, London: Routledge.

McKenzie, E. (1994) *Privatopia*, New Haven: Yale University Press.

Maguire, M. (1982) *Burglary in a Dwelling*, London: Heinemann.

Mayhew, P. (1984) 'Target-hardening – how much of an answer?' in T. Hope and R.V. Clarke (eds) *Coping with Burglary: Research Perspectives in Policy*, Boston, MA: Kluwer Nijhoff.

Miethe, T. (1991) 'Citizen-based crime control activity and victimisation risks: an examination of displacement and free-rider effects', *Criminology*, 29: 419–39.

Olsen, M. (1965) *The Logic of Collective Action*, New York: Schocten Books.

Pitts, J. and T. Hope (1997) 'The local politics of inclusion: the state and community safety', *Social Policy and Administration*, 31: 37–58.

Pyle, D. (1998) 'Crime and unemployment: what do empirical studies show?' *International Journal of Risk, Security and Crime Prevention*, 3: 169–80.

Rengert, G.F. and Wasilcek, T. (1985) *Suburban Burglary*, Springfield, IL: Charles C. Thomas.

Sampson, R.J. and Wilson, W.J. (1995) 'Toward a theory of race, crime and urban inequality', in J. Hagan and R.D. Peterson (eds) *Crime and Inequality*, Stanford, CA: Stanford University Press.

Sandler, T. (1992) *Collective Action*, New York: Harvester Wheatsheaf.

Savage, M., Barlow, J., Dickens, P. and Fielding, T. (1992) *Property, Bureaucracy and Culture*, London: Routledge.

Shearing, C. and Stenning, P. (1983) 'Private security: implications for social control', *Social Problems*, 30: 493–506.

Skogan, W.G. (1988) 'Community organisations and crime', in M. Tonry and N. Morris (eds) *Crime and Justice: A Review of Research, 10*, Chicago: University of Chicago Press.

Skogan, W.G. and Maxfield, M.G. (1981) *Coping with Crime*, Beverly Hills: Sage Publications.

Spitzer, S. (1987) 'Security and control in capitalist societies: the fetishism of security and the secret thereof', in J. Lowman, R.J. Menzies and T.S. Palys (eds) *Transcarceration: Essays in the Sociology of Social Control*, Aldershot: Gower.

Taub, R.P., Taylor, D.G. and Dunham, J.D. (1984) *Paths of Neighborhood Change*, Chicago: University of Chicago Press.

Taylor, I. (1995) 'Private homes and public others: an analysis of talk about crime in suburban south Manchester in the mid-1990s', *British Journal of Criminology*, 35: 263–85.

——(1996) 'Fear of crime, urban fortunes and suburban social movements', *Sociology*, 30: 317–38.

——(1997) 'Crime, anxiety and locality: responding to the "condition of England" at the end of the century', *Theoretical Criminology*, 1: 53–75.

Trickett, A., Osborn, D.R., Seymour, J. and Pease, K. (1992) 'What is different about high crime areas?' *British Journal of Criminology*, 32: 81–9.

Trickett, A., Ellingworth, D., Hope, T. and Pease, K. (1995) 'Crime victimisation in the eighties', *British Journal of Criminology*, 35: 343–59.

van Dijk, J.J.M. (1994) 'Understanding crime rates: on the interactions between the rational choices of victims and offenders', *British Journal of Criminology*, 34: 105–21.

Waldron, J. (1995) 'Money and complex equality', in D. Miller and M. Walzer (eds) *Pluralism, Justice and Equality*, New York: Oxford University Press.

Walzer, M. (1983) *Spheres of Justice: A Defence of Pluralism and Equality*, Oxford: Blackwell.

——(1990) 'The communitarian critique of liberalism', *Political Theory*, 18: 6–23.

Wikstrom, P.-O. (1995) 'Self-control, temptations, frictions and punishment: an integrated approach to crime prevention', in P.-O. Wikstrom, J. McCord and R.V. Clarke (eds) *Integrating Crime Prevention Strategies: Propensity and Opportunity. BRA 1995:5*, Stockholm: Fritzes.

Wilson, J.Q. (1975) *Thinking about Crime*, New York: Basic Books.

Wilson, W.J. (1996) *When Work Disappears: The World of the New Urban Poor*, New York: Alfred A. Knopf.

Winchester, S. and Jackson, H. (1982) *Residential Burglary. Home Office Research Study*, London: HMSO.

Young, J. (1986) 'The failure of criminology: the need for radical realism', in R. Matthews and J. Young (eds) *Confronting Crime*, London: Sage.

——(1998) 'From inclusive to exclusive society: nightmares in the European Dream', in V. Ruggiero, N. South and I. Taylor (eds.) *Crime and Social Order in Europe*, London: Routledge.

6

NO MORE HAPPY ENDINGS?

The media and popular concern about crime since the Second World War

Robert Reiner, Sonia Livingstone and Jessica Allen

Introduction: mediaphobia and fear of crime

Anxiety about media representations of crime has flourished for as long as the modern media of communication have existed. Mediaphobia is particularly prominent in various discourses about why crime rates and patterns have changed since the Second World War (although such respectable fears have a much longer ancestry, as shown in Pearson 1983). The most familiar of these discourses is that of moral decline and fall: the media are said to sensationalise deviance more and more, to glamorise offending, and to undermine moral authority and social controls of all kinds.[1]

Anxieties about the media have also figured prominently in liberal and radical discourses about crime and criminal justice changes, although with very different concerns and inflexions. A common theme is that media representations unduly accentuate fears of crime, hence bolstering public support for more authoritarian forms of criminal justice policy and practice.[2]

In the last two decades, fear of crime has increasingly become a prominent concern of policy-makers across the political spectrum. Mirroring the way that left realist criminology recaptured the issue of crime after its 'theft' by the Conservatives (Downes 1983), fear of crime has come to be perceived as an acute problem by the right as much as the left. At times it has been regarded as equally problematic as crime itself. In 1989, for example, a Home Office Working Party declared that fear of crime was an 'issue of social concern' that 'has to be taken as seriously as ... crime prevention and reduction' (Home Office 1989: ii). Although the official policy emphasis has now shifted back to prioritising crime reduction, fear of crime remains a prominent concern. The media have consistently been seen by policy-makers as a major source of the problem, stimulating unrealistic and irrational fears by exaggerating and sensationalising the risks and seriousness of crime (Sparks 1992).

There is a large research literature on media representations of crime and their sources and possible consequences (recent reviews include Reiner 1997;

Surette 1998). However, virtually all studies examine only one relatively brief period in time. Changes in representations may be looked at to some extent by comparing the results of research conducted in different periods. However, this is problematic as the data have been collected using differing definitions of variables and techniques of measurement. A few studies have provided data using consistent methods for different periods, but usually these have looked only at a handful of isolated years (for example, Roshier (1973) analysed newspaper reports in 1938, 1955 and 1967; and Sumser (1996) compared television mystery shows in 1968/9, 1974/5 and 1985/6). The sole exceptions to the dearth of material systematically examining change over time are a pair of recent studies of the changing content of American television and cinema over the last half-century, which include some material on crime and law enforcement images (Lichter *et al.* 1994; Powers *et al.* 1996).

The research reported in this chapter was intended to plug this gap, by providing an account of changing content in the main British media concerning crime over the period since the Second World War, as well as looking at how audiences interpret these changes. The research gathered data from two specific sources:

1   a historical content analysis of how mass media representations of crime and criminal justice have changed since the Second World War, across a range of media in Britain;
2   Focus group discussions with samples of people of different generations, analysing their interpretations of media output and the issue of law and order as these have changed over their lifetimes.

The data collected cannot directly assess the extent to which changing media representations of crime are causally related to changing levels or patterns of crime or fear of crime. Even to the extent that there are parallels between developments in media images and the extent of crime or fear of crime as recorded in various ways, the causal interpretation of such correlations is problematic.

Certainly most content analyses suggest that media representations vastly exaggerate the extent and seriousness of crime and the success of the police and criminal justice system in combating crime. 'If all we knew is what we saw' (Pandiani 1978) it would be plausible to conclude that the media do fan fear of crime and support for tough policing and penality as the answer. Many studies do indeed find associations between media consumption patterns and various measures of fear of crime (Howitt 1998: chapter 4).[3] Heavy viewing of TV crime fiction, for example, is linked with more fearful perceptions of crime and support for authoritarian solutions (Carlson 1985; Signorielli 1990: 96–102). Readers of newspapers which present violent crime stories more frequently and more sensationally express more fearfulness in response to survey questions (although not in behavioural manifestations such as not going out after dark), even controlling for age, gender and socio-economic status (Williams and Dickinson 1993).

The problem lies in deciding what causal relationship can be inferred from these associations. Do media crime stories cause fearfulness, or do more fearful people read or watch more? Given that the majority of stories, especially in the past, feature 'happy' endings with crime and conflict resolved neatly, perhaps they reassure rather than disturb viewers who are already fearful because of personal or vicarious experience of actual victimisation (Wakshlag *et al.* 1983; Zillman and Wakshlag 1987). Or do particular life experiences or social positions, such as living in high-crime areas, generate more risk, heightened anxiety *and* more media consumption? Our reviews of the voluminous existing research literature on these issues led us to the conclusion that the most plausible model is a dialectical process of interaction between changing media representations and patterns of criminality, fear of crime and criminal justice policy and practice (Livingstone 1996: 31–2; Reiner 1997: 216–19, 224–5). There is a complex intertwining of different life positions and experiences with the reception of media texts, which quantitative content analyses can hardly penetrate, requiring interpretive approaches more sensitive to the subtleties of analysing meaning (Sparks 1992; Schlesinger *et al.* 1992).

It was our objective, however, to gather historical and interview data which could test the validity of particular elements of the competing discourses about the part the media have played in the changes in criminality and justice since the Second World War. These discourses all assume particular accounts of how media images have changed. For example, the conservative discourse of moral decline presumes that the media have become increasingly focused on crime, present offenders in more attractive ways and portray the criminal justice system less favourably. The widespread concern about fear of crime similarly assumes that the media are increasingly representing crime in ways that exaggerate its extent and seriousness. Historical content analysis is necessary to assess such claims.

The historical content analyses and the focus group discussions reported in this paper converge in suggesting a particular picture of the changing discourse about crime and criminal justice, both in the public arena constituted by the mass media and in everyday life and experience. In many ways this echoes Durkheim's theorisation of the 'modernisation' of sentiments about punishment (Durkheim 1973), originally published nearly a century ago. Criminality comes to be seen less as an offence against the sacred and absolute norms of a *conscience collective*, and more a matter of one individual harming another.[4] This process is reflected in a transformation of representations of the moral status of offenders, the criminal justice system, victims, punishment and fear of crime. Moral status is no longer automatically conferred by a role in the social order; it is subject to negotiation and constructed by particular narratives.

Research methods

This study examined representations of crime and criminal justice in three mass media from 1945 to 1991, together with audience understandings of and relations to them. Clearly it could not examine all mass media, due to practical constraints of availability and resources. It focused on the two media which have been prominent throughout the twentieth century, cinema and newspapers, and the pre-eminent medium of the post-war period, television.

The historical content analyses

For each medium we examined sizeable random samples of narratives about crime. The *cinema* research combined a generic analysis of all films released in Britain since 1945 (which included an increasing proportion of US films over the period), and detailed quantitative and qualitative content analyses of box-office hits. The latter were chosen as approximating the most influential films of the period – or at any rate, those which were most widely viewed. For *television*, we focused on fictional crime series. The ephemeral character of television news presents insuperable problems of non-availability for the study of long-term changes in content. The *press* study analysed representative samples of stories from *The Times*, the newspaper of record for most of the period, and a paper which contrasts with it in terms of both market (tabloid versus quality) and politics (left of centre versus right), *The Mirror* (previously the *Daily Mirror*). Although inevitably limited, this is a larger sampling across media and time than hitherto found in the criminological research literature.

The category 'crime' is, of course, subject to enormous definitional and conceptual debate and difficulties (Maguire *et al.* 1997: part I). For the purposes of this research a straightforward legal positivist definition was adopted: a crime in a media narrative was any act which appeared to violate English criminal law. Measuring crime is also a notoriously fraught enterprise (Reiner 1996; Maguire 1997). The guidelines for this research were again drawn from officially sanctioned procedures, the Home Office counting rules, to facilitate comparison of the representation of crime in the media and the official statistical picture.

Using these definitions and procedures, the historical content analysis considered:

1 how the quantity of crime stories in the media had changed since the Second World War;
2 how the dimensions and structure of crime stories had changed, through detailed qualitative analysis of samples of narratives.

All quantitative data was analysed using SPSS.

The *film* study was based on two different samples. A random 10 per cent sample of all films released in Britain since 1945 was drawn from a source which also provided synopses of these (F. Maurice Speed's *Film Review*, which has been published annually since 1944). This sample was coded by genre to calculate the proportion of crime films (i.e. which had narratives centred on the commission and/or investigation of a crime). For non-crime films, the same sample was coded to see if they nonetheless had significant representations of crime in their plots (Allen *et al.* 1997). A smaller sample of 84 films was drawn randomly out of the 196 crime movies which had figured since 1945 among the top box-office hits in Britain. These were viewed and analysed in detail to assess qualitative changes. The major coding categories included: types, rates and violence of crimes; characteristics and attitudes of offenders, victims and criminal justice personnel; images of society and social relations; depictions of criminal justice; conceptions of authority and morality.

The *press* study also used two related samples. To assess the proportions of crime and criminal justice stories a random 10 per cent sample of all 'home news' stories since 1945 in *The Times* and *The Mirror* was coded. A more detailed qualitative analysis along the lines of the cinema study was conducted for a smaller random sample of stories. Ten days were selected randomly for both newspapers for every second year since 1945. In those issues all front-page stories, editorial or op-ed items and letters which concerned crime were analysed, as were the most prominent crime news stories on the home news pages.

The *television* study examined all the top twenty television programmes for every year since 1955 (when audience ratings first became available). These were coded according to genre to see the changing proportion which was focused on crime or criminal justice. The crime series were then subject to more detailed study to ascertain the changing representations of crime, criminals and law enforcers.

Audience reception of crime media

Historical study of how audiences interpret mass media representations of crime and criminal justice clearly raises profound methodological difficulties. While past media may have been archived, at least erratically, past audiences do not exist. The project combined methods from oral history with audience reception methods, using homogeneous focus groups to interpret specific media contents.

While most audience research focuses on gender and social class or on self-selected fan groups, the key dimension here was age. Audience age indexes two phenomena: position in the life course (e.g. young person, parent, elderly); and generation (e.g. 'post-war' generation, 'sixties' generation), popularly understood by the particular historical period through which people live.

Selected examples of images and texts were used to stimulate focus group discussion of each media period and to encourage general discussion about crime, social change, notions of authority and responsibility. Four age-groups (approximately 20, 40, 60 and 80 years old) discussed these media which, depending on the group's age, involved discussing media from before they were born, from when they were in their mid-teens, mid-thirties, mid-fifties or mid-seventies.

Following a pilot group, 16 focus groups (4 age $\times$ 2 gender $\times$ 2 social class) were recruited from seven locations in the south-east of England (urban, suburban and rural) by a professional market research agency. Ninety-six people were interviewed in all. The interviews were audio-taped, fully transcribed and analysed using NUDIST. The analysis was based on the major issues identified by the analyses of crime representations.

Changing patterns of media crime since 1945

The pattern and characteristics of media representations of crime have changed in many ways since the Second World War. This section will consider these trends, and their possible significance for popular fears about crime.

The frequency of crime narratives in the media

Crime narratives and representations are, and always have been, a prominent part of the content of all mass media. The proportion of content devoted to crime is highly sensitive to the differing definitions used in particular studies. It also varies between different outlets, according to medium and market (Reiner 1997: 194–9). There may also be change over time, although until now it has only been possible to examine this by comparing separate studies conducted in different periods. This is unsatisfactory because they use varying definitions and methods. The present research attempts to assess the long-term trends in crime content since the Second World War. For the cinema and newspapers it measured the proportion of all narratives which were primarily crime stories,[5] and those which had significant crime content even if not primarily focused on crime. While the absence of change in the quantity of crime represented would not falsify any claims about possible relationships between trends in media content and developments in crime and criminal justice, a significant increase or decrease would be of considerable interest in examining the validity of the different discourses about the media/crime link.

In the random sample of cinema films there did not appear to be any significant pattern of change in the extent of representation of crime. There is no clear trend for the proportion of crime films to either rise or fall, although there are many sharp fluctuations in individual years around this basic steady state (Allen *et al.* 1997, 1998). Crime has been a significant concern of the cinema throughout the post-war period (and probably before that as well). In most years around 20 per cent of all films released are crime films.

The results of the analysis of a random sample of newspaper stories between 1945 and 1991 suggest a more complex picture. By the end of the period the proportion of stories about crime had increased considerably. This was true of both *The Times* and *The Mirror* although the rise was more marked in the former. In the *Daily Mirror* the average proportion of stories which were centrally about crime in the years 1945–51 was 9 per cent, while in *The Times* it was 7 per cent. By 1985–91 this had risen to 21 per cent for both papers (the drawing level of the two papers suggests the general process of tabloidisation of *The Times*). The proportion of stories about the criminal justice system or policy (as distinct from specific crimes) also rose in both papers: from an average of 2 per cent in the *Daily Mirror* between 1945 and 1951 to 6 per cent between 1985 and 1991, and from 3 per cent to 9 per cent in the same periods in *The Times* (this echoes Downes and Morgan's 1997 analysis of the politicisation of law and order policy over the same period). While newspapers' concern with crime and criminal justice appears distinctly higher in the last period of our study than in the first, the years in between show a marked pattern of cyclical fluctuation around this overall rising trend.

Changes in the extent of fear of crime (or indeed in recorded crime rates) cannot be attributed to a sheer quantitative increase in crime content in the cinema – this has not occurred. There has, however, been an increase in crime content in newspaper stories. Although this is nowhere near as marked or as continuous as the rise in recorded crime over the same period, it may be a factor in increasing concern about crime, as well as a reflection of it. Changes in the way that crime narratives are constructed are of more interest than their sheer quantity, and the next sections indicate the key changes in representations of crime, criminal justice, offenders, victims, and authority more generally.

Media crime rates and patterns

The analysis of cinema films distinguished between three categories of crime in terms of their function within the narrative: principal, consequential and contextual crimes. Adapting Hitchcock's terminology for the object which is pursued in a story, we call the crime which provides the principal focus or motive for a story the McGuffin. Consequential crimes are those which are necessary adjuncts of the McGuffin, either before or after (for example, in order to escape capture). Contextual crimes are those which are represented in the narrative but are not related to the McGuffin (for example, the bank robbery Clint Eastwood encounters while munching a hamburger in *Dirty Harry*).

Throughout the period 1945–91, the single most frequent McGuffin crime is homicide, but to a slightly diminishing extent: in 50 per cent of crime films between 1945 and 1964; 35 per cent for 1965–79; 45 per cent 1980–91. There is a marked tendency for McGuffins which are property crimes (e.g. bank robbery) to decline: 32 per cent of films 1945–64; 20 per cent 1965–79; only 5 per cent 1980–91. Sex-related McGuffins such as rape or prostitution have become more frequent: 3 per cent 1945–64; 10 per cent 1965–79; 15 per cent 1980–91. Drugs have shown a curvilinear pattern: 2 per cent 1945–64; 10 per cent 1965–79; 5 per cent 1980–91. There has also been an increase in assault as the McGuffin: none between 1945 and 1964; 5 per cent 1965–79; 10 per cent 1980–91. In short, murder remains the most common crime stimulating a narrative, but to a slightly diminishing extent. Property crimes have plummeted (unlike the picture given by official statistics or crime surveys), while other violent, sexual and drug-related offences have become more common McGuffins.

113

The extent of violence depicted in the presentation of the McGuffin has increased considerably. The proportion of films in which it was associated with significant pain rose from 2 per cent between 1945 and 64, to 20 per cent from 1965 to 1979, and 40 per cent from 1980 to 1991. This has consequences for the typical representation of offenders, victims, police and the criminal justice system.

The representation of consequential crimes has changed even more markedly. Between 1945 and 1964 14 per cent of films depicted no consequential crimes, 43 per cent showed one, and 43 per cent featured multiple consequential crimes. After that there are hardly any films without consequential crimes, and over 80 per cent feature multiple offences of this kind. The extent of violence depicted in these crimes has also multiplied considerably. Whereas between 1945 and 1964 74 per cent of films had consequential crimes involving little or no violence, and only 5 per cent featured significant levels of violence, by 1980–91 these proportions had changed to 16 per cent and 47 per cent respectively.

The representation of contextual crimes is perhaps the most striking change. These crimes are especially significant because a proliferation of contextual crimes connotes a society pervaded by crime, unrelated to the central narrative. Between 1945 and 1964 32 per cent of films had no contextual offending at all, 9 per cent showed just one contextual crime, and 59 per cent had multiple crimes of this type. By 1980–91 only 15 per cent of films showed no contextual crimes, and 80 per cent featured multiple offences unrelated to the central narrative. An increasing proportion of contextual offences are violent and/or sex and drug-related, and a diminishing proportion are property offences (as with the McGuffin crimes). The extent of violence portrayed in these offences has increased. In 1945–64 90 per cent had no or only minor violence; by 1980–91 these proportions had changed to 29 per cent and 65 per cent respectively.

Overall, then, the findings show that although murder has always been the most common McGuffin crime in films, there is over the period since 1945 a diminishing proportion featuring property crime, and an increase in the representation of violent crimes of all kinds. The extent of violence inflicted in these offences has sharply increased. The large rise in the depiction of consequential and especially contextual offences conveys a picture of a society much more threatened by all-pervasive violent crime.

The sample of newspaper stories shows a rather similar pattern of change. Murder (including attempts) is the most common single offence type throughout the period, although to a slightly increasing extent: it accounted for 20 per cent of all newspaper crime stories between 1945 and 1964; and 28 per cent in both the later periods analysed, 1965–79; and 1980–91. In newspaper stories the most rapidly increasing single type of crime reported was terrorist offences: 0.7 per cent of stories in 1945–64; 5.3 per cent in 1965–79; 8.8 per cent in 1980–91. Overall there was a clear shift from stories featuring property crimes (such as burglary and car theft) to offences against the person, including homicide, assault and sexual offences. The proportion of stories reporting property offences went down from 20 per cent in 1945–64 to 12 per cent in 1965–79 and 8 per cent between 1980 and 1991. Offences against the person stories rose from 33 per cent between 1945 and 1964 to 44 per cent in 1965–79 and 46 per cent in 1980–91. This means that a standard finding of research on crime and the media – that the media over-report violent and sexual offences disproportionately – requires some qualification. Although violent offence stories are the most common category throughout the post-war period, the extent of the imbalance has increased markedly. Stories purely about property offences were once fairly common but have virtually disappeared, while almost half of all crime-related stories are now about violence and/or sex.

The changes in media crime patterns are congruent with increasing public anxiety about crime. This is not only because of the even greater emphasis on serious violent crime, but also because of the increasing representation of this as essentially random, implied by the growth of contextual and consequential offences represented in stories. There is clear research evidence suggesting that when risks of victimisation are represented as random and meaningless they are particularly fear-provoking (Box *et al.* 1988: 342).

Criminal justice

The representation of the criminal justice system and its agents has changed substantially. One of the most interesting aspects is the pattern as distinct from the substance of change. As seen above, the pattern of change for most aspects of the representation of crime is unilinear. For example, the proportion of news stories concerning crime increases continuously; there is an increasing emphasis on violent crime against the person rather than property crime; and crime is represented ever more often as a ubiquitous threat, not a one-off event. On other dimensions there is an absence of change: the proportion of cinema films centrally concerned with crime, or the dominance of murder as the most frequently represented crime in either news or fiction. However, on most dimensions the representation of criminal justice alters in a curvilinear pattern. Variables are at their highest or lowest in the middle years (1964–79) of our period. The implications of this will be considered in our final conclusions below.

One central finding of the cinema research is the increasing prevalence of criminal justice agents as heroes, or at any rate the central protagonists, of narratives. This too is subject to something of a U-shaped pattern. The key aspect is the rise (and partial fall) of police heroes. The police are the protagonists of only 9 per cent of films between 1945 and 1964, but 50 per cent of those between 1965 and 1979, and 40 per cent of those between 1980 and 1991. Other criminal justice agents (DAs, customs agents, etc.) were the protagonists of 7 per cent, 5 per cent and 10 per cent of films in these periods, respectively. Lawyers were the protagonists in 9 per cent of films in the first period, none in the second and 5 per cent in the third. Private eye heroes featured in 20 per cent of films from 1964–79, but none in the earlier or later periods. There was a continuous decline in amateur investigator heroes: 36 per cent in 1945–64; 5 per cent in 1965–79; none 1980–91. Victim-related protagonists increased, but in a curvilinear pattern: 13 per cent in 1945–64; none 1965–79; 25 per cent 1980–91. Overall there is a clear decline of amateur sleuths in favour of criminal justice professionals, especially the police, and an increase in victim or victim-related heroes. The police predominance is especially marked in the middle period, although it remains substantial.[6] The prevalence of police protagonists is congruent with the previously noted move to representing crime as an ever-present, ubiquitous threat, not a one-off disturbance in a generally ordered existence. Crime becomes a routine business for bureaucratically organised professionals, not amateurs and first-timers.

Overall, the representation of police protagonists has become less positive over time, although there is a clear curvilinear pattern. Critical and negative images are most common in the period 1964–79, although they are more frequent in 1980–91 than 1945–64. This applies both to the success and the integrity of the police protagonists.

The police and criminal justice system are portrayed as less successful over time. Throughout the period the overwhelming majority of movie crimes are cleared up. However, there is a marked change in how this is achieved. In the period 1945–64 the most common method of clear-up was that the offender was brought to justice (39 per cent), but this has become very infrequent (15 per cent 1965–79, 10 per cent 1980–91). The most frequent method of clear-up becomes the killing of the offender – in 35 per cent of films 1965–91.

The police come to be represented more frequently as vigilantes than as enforcers of the law. In 89 per cent of films 1945–64, the police remain within the parameters of due process of law in their methods, but they break these in 80 per cent of films between 1965 and 1979 and 67 per cent from 1980 to 1991. The police are also shown as more likely to use force (both reasonable and excessive force). Between 1945 and 1964, the police protagonists are not shown using force in 54 per cent of films, and in 40 per cent the force used is reasonable and proportionate (e.g. minimal self-defence). Only in 3 per cent of films were they shown using excessive force. But this is shown in 44 per cent of films from 1965 to 1979 and 25 per cent from 1980 to 1991.

The police protagonists are represented as entirely honest in personal terms in 89 per cent of films 1945–64; but in only 67 per cent between 1965 and 1979, and 77 per cent 1980–91. In no films in the early period are cops shown as seriously corrupt ('meat-eaters', in the parlance of the Knapp Commission Report on police corruption in New York), but they are seriously corrupt in 13 per cent of films 1965–79 and 15 per cent 1980–91. They are shown as engaged in petty corruption ('grass-eaters' in the Knapp Commission's terms) in 11 per cent of 1945–64 films, 20 per cent between 1965 and 1979, and 8 per cent between 1980 and 1991. They are also represented as more personally deviant (in terms of such matters as excessive drinking, swearing and extra-marital sexual activity).

The criminal justice system is also portrayed as increasingly divided internally.

Conflict within police organisations features in only 15 per cent of films 1945–64, but 79 per cent from 1965 to 1979, and 56 per cent 1980–91. Conflict between criminal justice organisations, e.g. the police and prosecutors or the courts, also becomes more frequent. It is represented in only 20 per cent of films 1945–64, but 70 per cent from 1965 to 1991. Police officers themselves become more internally divided: conflict between buddies occurs in only 9 per cent of films 1945–64, but over 50 per cent thereafter. Police protagonists are portrayed as stressed in 23 per cent of films in the earlier period, but well over half after 1965.

Similar trends can be found in newspaper representations of criminal justice. The increasing proportion of stories about criminal justice which has already been referred to is an indication of the increasingly politicised and controversial character of criminal justice issues. News stories in which the police are mentioned critically have increased (6 per cent 1945–64, 10 per cent 1965–79, 17 per cent 1980–91). Stories with approving or even neutral accounts of the police have declined. Approving stories were just over 11 per cent from 1945 to 1979, but only 6 per cent from 1980 to 1991. Neutral mentions declined from 13 per cent to 11 per cent and then 8 per cent through the three periods (the police were not mentioned at all in about 69 per cent of crime news stories in all three periods).

The police and criminal justice system are represented in news stories as less successful in dealing with crime, especially in the middle period. Between 1945 and 1964, 23 per cent of news stories feature crimes which are not cleared up, but this rises to 37 per cent from 1965 to 1979, although there is a slight decline thereafter to 31 per cent. Crime is explicitly represented as out of control in a growing minority of news stories: 3 per cent 1945–64, 6 per cent 1965–79, but 13 per cent 1980–91.

As with the changing representation of crime, the portrayal of the police as less successful, less honest and beset by conflicts and internal problems is congruent with increasing anxiety about crime. Not only is the problem itself represented in more frightening terms, but the safety blanket is seen as becoming threadbare.

Criminals

Unlike the representation of crime, criminal justice and (as we shall see) victims, there are few significant trends in the portrait of the personal characteristics of offenders. Throughout the period they are predominantly middle-aged or older (though there is a slight tendency to portray young offenders more frequently), white (although the proportion of ethnic minority offenders is increasing slightly in both fiction and news stories) and male. This all confirms earlier studies. One way our findings challenge the orthodoxy is that we find that only a minority of stories feature middle- or upper-class offenders, and this does not change significantly over time.

Criminals are overwhelmingly portrayed unsympathetically throughout the period, in both fiction and news. There is little change, and what there is suggests an increasingly unfavourable image of offenders. For example, they are shown using excessive or sadistic force in an increasing proportion of films (80 per cent between 1980 and 1991 as compared to 50 per cent 1945–64). They are portrayed as committing crimes only under pressure in a decreasing minority of films (30 per cent 1945–64; around 15 per cent thereafter). Increasingly they are represented as purely evil and enjoying their offending (from around 60 per cent 1945–64 to 85 per cent 1980–91). Films in which some sympathy is shown for offenders have declined over time: 40 per cent 1945–64; 20 per cent 1965–79; 15 per cent 1980–91).

This predominantly (and slightly increasingly) unfavourable portrayal of offenders goes against the claim that crime has been stimulated by more attractive media representations. However, crime is represented as increasingly rewarding. In 91 per cent of films between 1945 and 1964, 'crime does not pay' for the central offenders, but after 1965 this is true in only 80 per cent of the stories – although this still suggests an overwhelming message about the folly of offending (especially in the light of the low and diminishing clear-up rates found in official statistics).

Victims

Probably the most clear-cut and significant changes we have found are in the representation of victims. In essence, victims have moved from having a shadowy and purely functional role in crime narratives to an increasingly pivotal position, their suffering increasingly constituting the subject position or the *raison d'être* of the story (mirroring the 'discovery' of, and increasing concern about, victims in criminal justice systems around the world; cf. Rock 1990; Zedner 1997). In the film sample, no concern is evinced for the plight of the victim in 45 per cent of cases 1945–64; 35 per cent 1965–79; but only 11 per cent 1980–91. Victimisation is shown as having traumatic consequences in 74 per cent of films between 1980 and 1991, 40 per cent 1965–79, and only 25 per cent 1945–64 (similar trends are evident in the depicted consequences for the victim's family or friends). Victims are increasingly often represented as the protagonists of films, i.e. as the principal subject position. They are protagonists in 56 per cent of the films where they are presented as characters at all (as opposed to corpses or case-files) between 1980–91, but only 26 per cent 1965–79, and 16 per cent 1945–64.[7] News stories also increasingly present the plight of victims in sympathetic or concerned terms, in 11 per cent of stories 1945–64, 18 per cent 1965–79 and 24 per cent 1980–91.

The presentation of victims as the sympathetic yet traumatised centre of gravity of crime narratives is likely to enhance public concerns. Crime ceases to be portrayed primarily as an offence against legal codes and more as a serious risk confronting individuals with whom the narrative invites the audience to identify, and for whom there is no happy ending.

Audience perceptions of media representations of crime

The popularity of crime media

In the interviews, people varied in which type of crime fiction they enjoyed, but most liked fiction involving an intellectual puzzle. Young women are particularly keen on media which are realistic and offer them information (about the nature, consequences and prevention of crime). Men preferred action plots, with fast pace, special effects and humour. Most people were ambivalent about press crime reporting, wanting to know but not to be voyeuristic. Older people recalled past media largely in terms of notorious events, prominent drama series and television and film stars, and little was recalled of specific narratives. Young people showed little interest in past media and much enthusiasm for contemporary media.

Perceptions of past crime media

Despite age and other differences, respondents were remarkably consensual in their characterisation of the post-war period. This consensus tells a story of change in which crime representations (and society generally) shift from the 'pre-sixties' days, of little, mild crime where difficult issues were largely hidden, crime was largely non-violent and the police were your friends, to the 'post-sixties' present where crime is much more prevalent, media images are more explicit and upsetting, violence has increased and police are themselves more distant and more violent.

This shift is interpreted, again consensually, as a transition in morality. An era when good and bad were clearly distinguished and authority structures were respected (a culture of discipline) has been replaced by one in which the boundary between good and bad has blurred, criminals are sympathetic and authorities are corrupt (a culture of disrespect and desubordination).

However, the generations differed markedly in their relation to this perceived overall shift. Older people tell a story of decline – the do-gooders in the 1960s upset the proper social order. Media representations are now too much 'in your face', voyeuristic and disrespectful of authority. Young people, on the other hand, tend to see this as a story of progress. They are optimistic, because they welcome the media championing civil rights in areas like gender, sexuality and ethnicity and the greater legitimation accorded to alternative viewpoints, and are glad that controversial issues are no longer hidden. They approve of the idea that morality should be decided by context, and respect must be earned, not given automatically to those in certain social roles.

Life course also mattered. What is most striking is that people are almost universally positive about the media they encountered during their youth (and into their mid-thirties), irrespective of whether this was, in fact, media from the 1950s, the 1970s or the 1990s. With the exception of the youngest group, people were far more tolerant of the media from before they were born than they were of media from later in their adulthood. The importance of life course suggests that the media of one's youth sets the interpretive framework, the expectations for subsequent experiences of media.

Positioning the audience in relation to crime

Respondents continually 'commute' (Liebes and Katz 1995) between a concrete concern with crime in the media and crime in everyday life. They also commute between a concern with the concrete, such as who commits what kinds of crimes, and the moral (what does this say about the moral and social order?). This suggests that everyday perceptions of crime in society provide a salient context within which media crime is interpreted; conversely, media crime triggers thoughts and feelings which are central to daily life.

Audiences seem more powerfully positioned in relation to crime media according to their perceived positioning in relation to the reality of crime and criminal justice. Particularly in our early period, crime media typically offers audiences the subject position of 'criminal justice protagonist', the criminal becomes 'other' and the victim is virtually invisible. However, real world crime offers three subject positions: police/law enforcer, criminal and victim; and our different groups perceived the media through the lens of these positions.

Those aged 80 perceived media throughout the period not only through the lens of their youth (the culture of respect) but also through the lens of their present-day perceived vulnerability, as potential victims of crime. The loss of a culture of respect weakens their identification with authorities. While both the media and everyday experience tell older people that they are muggable, our youngest groups felt they were continually portrayed as 'dangerous youth', potential perpetrators of crime. Thus they welcome a civil rights focus and the questioning of police authority.

Recalling that each generation is most positive about the media of their youth, we suggest that young people are positive about present-day media because they, like it, are ambivalent about police heroes, seeing themselves as often positioned as suspected criminals in daily life. Their desire is to understand both sides through the media, to question both authority and the 'criminal mind'.

Gender and generation

This picture is cross-cut by gender. Unlike the men, young women are aware of their potential victim status, particularly their vulnerability to male violence, and so welcomed coverage of such crimes. The oldest women shared their generation's pessimism, yet also expressed some approval of the destruction of the 'fairy tales' of their youth – the glamorous images of femininity and masculinity which some perceived to have trapped and distracted them.

The youngest women, on the other hand, shared their male peers' scepticism about the criminal justice system, and so turned not to a reliance on authorities but to themselves. Their orientation to media centred on how media provided information and opportunities to think through situations offering self-protection through realism. It was mainly when police heroes are female or feminised (as in *The Silence of the Lambs* or *Cagney and Lacey*) that younger women showed some approval or identification with the criminal justice system.

Neither younger nor older men in our groups would accept views of themselves as potential victims. Rather, the older men accepted the proffered identification with the protagonist, typically a law enforcement hero. Younger men were particularly interested in forms of crime media in which the criminal was as much a focus as the law enforcers and in which the moral boundaries between the two were ambiguous or unresolved.

Conclusion: insubordination and insecurity, shifting media images of crime

The data presented so far suggests some complex processes of change in media representations of crime since the Second World War, and in audience interpretations of them. Some key variables in our analysis exhibit no pattern of change (for example, the proportion of films which are centrally about crime). Others show a marked degree of change throughout the period: the graphic representation of violence, for instance. Yet others show a curvilinear pattern of development: most aspects of the representation of the legitimacy, integrity, and effectiveness of criminal justice follow this pattern.

These results suggest a rough periodisation in terms of three ideal-type patterns of representation of crime. The first post-war decade is a period of consensus and social harmony in representations of criminal justice (and, more debatably, general social and political debate; cf. Marquand 1996). Crime stories – news as well as fiction – present an image of society as based largely on shared values and a clear yet accepted hierarchy of status and authority. Crime was as defined by Durkheim: it united all healthy consciences to condemn and extirpate it. Criminals were normally brought to justice: crime did not pay. The forces of law always got their man. The criminal justice system was almost invariably represented as righteous, dedicated and efficient.

During the mid-1960s the dominant mode of representation of crime and justice shifts discernibly. The values and integrity of authority increasingly come to be questioned. Doubts about the justice and effectiveness of criminal justice proliferate. Increasing prominence is given to conflict: between ethnic groups, men and women, social classes, even within the criminal justice system itself. While street cops feature increasingly as protagonists, they are more frequently morally tarnished, if not outright corrupt. However, the increasing criticism of the social order and criminal justice is from a standpoint of reform, the advocacy of preferable alternatives.

121

Since the late 1970s another shift is discernible, the advent of what could be called a post-critical era. Stories are increasingly bifurcated between counter-critical ones, which seek to return as far as possible to the values of consensus, and those which represent a hopelessly disordered beyond-good-and-evil world, characterised by a Hobbesian war of all against all. It is this division of narratives which accounts for the curvilinear pattern of many variables: there is some attempt to restore the values of the past, challenged by those which portray the exacerbation of the conflicts of the middle period.

Underneath the shifts in the mode of representation of concrete aspects of crime and justice, however, can be discerned a more fundamental shift in discourse, encompassing both media representations and popular discussion (as captured in our focus groups). This is a demystification of authority and law, a change in the conceptualisation of criminal justice from sacred to secular.

The marked changes in the representation of victims are the clearest emblem of this. Crime moves from being something which must be opposed and controlled *ipso facto* because the law defines it thus, to a contested category. It may be wrong, but this is a pragmatic issue, turning on the harm which may be done to individual victims, not from the authority of the law itself. The moral status of characters in a story (news or fiction) is no longer ascribed by their formal legal role. It has to be established from scratch in each narrative, depending upon the demonstration of serious suffering caused to the victims who are in the subject position of the narrative. Increasingly these may be the legally defined offenders, who may be represented as victimised by a criminal injustice system.

Although the majority of narratives continue to work ultimately to justify the criminal justice viewpoint, this has to be achieved by demonstrating particular harm inflicted by crime on identifiable individual victims. In this sense, the media continue both to reproduce order and to function as sources of social control, while also reflecting the increasing individualism of a less deferential and more desubordinate culture.

This shift in media and popular narratives is isomorphic with changing features of criminal justice policy which have been identified by several influential interpretations. At a concrete level, the increasing attention given to victims by the criminal justice system (and criminologists) has achieved the status of cliché (Rock 1990; Zedner 1997), and is clearly paralleled in media narratives and popular 'crime talk' (Sasson 1995). More fundamentally, the increasing secularisation and individualism of media narratives about crime echoes the increasingly pragmatic and actuarial character of much of contemporary criminal justice policy (Feeley and Simon 1994). This is increasingly directed at finely calculated, highly practical tactics to prevent or reduce individual criminal victimisation by 'criminologies of everyday life' (Garland 1996). Like other dangers, in the 'risk society' crime becomes a matter for systematic 'scientific' assessment and management by experts (who are nonetheless viewed with increasing scepticism and suspicion), not a morality play (Sparks 1997: 424–6).

This is punctuated only by occasional media feeding frenzies, in which moral panics are sparked by spectacular crimes that perform the Durkheimian function of defining what moral boundaries do remain, around which 'healthy consciences' can regroup. However, these are usually prompted by the victimisation of a quintessentially vulnerable and sympathetic individual (like the Liverpool toddler Jamie Bulger), not by the violation of generalised moral codes or values. Both the front-stage spectacles of the exceptionally shocking crime and the back-stage everyday routines of actuarial risk calculation and control testify to an increasingly individualistic and demystified discourse about crime.

References

Allen, Jessica, Livingstone, Sonia, and Reiner, Robert (1997) 'The changing generic location of crime in film: a content analysis of film synopses', *Journal of Communication*, 47: 89–101.

——(1998) 'True lies: changing images of crime in British post-war cinema', *European Journal of Communication*, 13: 53–75.

Box, Steven, Hale, Chris, and Andrews, Glen (1988) 'Explaining fear of crime', *British Journal of Criminology*, 28: 340–56.

Carlson, J.M. (1985) *Prime-Time Law Enforcement: Crime Show Viewing and Attitudes to the Criminal Justice System*, New York: Praeger.

Cohen, Stanley (1972) *Folk Devils and Moral Panics*, London: Paladin.

Cohen, Stanley and Young, Jock (eds) (1973) *The Manufacture of News: Social Problems, Deviance and the Mass Media*, London: Constable.

Dennis, Norman (1997) 'Editor's introduction', pp. 1–28 in *Zero Tolerance Policing*, edited by N. Dennis, London: Institute of Economic Affairs.

Downes, David (1983) *Law and Order: Theft of an Issue*, London: Fabian Society/Labour Campaign for Criminal Justice.

Downes, David and Morgan, Rod (1997) 'Dumping the "hostages to fortune"? The politics of law and order in post-war Britain', pp. 86–134 in *The Oxford Handbook of Criminology*, edited by M. Maguire, R. Morgan and R. Reiner, Oxford: Oxford University Press.

Durkheim, Emile (1973) 'Two laws of penal evolution', *Economy and Society*, 2: 278–308, (first published 1899).

Feeley, Malcolm, and Simon, Jonathan (1994) 'Actuarial justice: the emerging new criminal law', pp. 173–201 in *The Futures of Criminology*, edited by D. Nelken, London: Sage.

Garland, David (1996) 'The limits of the sovereign state: strategies of crime control in contemporary society', *British Journal of Criminology*, 36: 445–71.

Gerbner, George (1970) 'Cultural indicators: the case of violence in television drama', *Annals of the American Academy of Political and Social Science*, 338: 69–81.

——(1995) 'Television violence: the power and the peril', pp. 547–57 in *Gender, Race and Class in the Media*, edited by G. Dines and J. Humez, Thousand Oaks, CA: Sage.

Hale, Chris (1996) 'Fear of crime: a review of the literature', *International Review of Victimology*, 4: 79–150.

Hall, Stuart (1979) *Drifting into a Law and Order Society*, London: Cobden Trust.

Hall, Stuart, Critcher, Chas, Jefferson, Tony, Clarke, John, and Roberts, Brian (1978) *Policing the Crisis*, London: Macmillan.

Harbord, Jane, and Wright, Jeff (1992) *40 Years of British Television*, London: Boxtree.

Hollway, Wendy, and Jefferson, Tony (1997) 'The risk society in an age of anxiety: situating fear of crime', *British Journal of Sociology*, 48: 255–65.

Home Office (1989) *Report of the Working Group on Fear of Crime*, London: HMSO.

Howitt, Dennis (1998) *Crime, Media and the Law*, Chichester: Wiley.

Lichter, S. Robert, Lichter, Linda S., and Rothman, Stanley (1994) *Prime Time: How TV Portrays American Culture*, Washington DC: Regnery Publishing.

Liebes, Tamar, and Katz, Elihu (1995) *The Export of Meaning: Cross-Cultural Readings of Dallas*, Cambridge: Polity.

Livingstone, Sonia (1996) 'On the continuing problem of media effects', pp. 305–24 in *Mass Media and Society*, edited by J. Curran and M. Gurevitch, London: Arnold.

Loader, Ian, Girling, Evi, and Sparks, Richard (1998) 'Narratives of decline: youth, dis/order and community in an English "Middletown" ', *British Journal of Criminology*, 38: 388–403.

Maguire, Mike (1997) 'Crime statistics, patterns and trends: changing perceptions and their implications', pp. 134–88 in *The Oxford Handbook of Criminology*, edited by M. Maguire, R. Morgan and R. Reiner, Oxford: Oxford University Press.

Maguire, Mike, Morgan, Rod, and Reiner, Robert (eds) (1997) *The Oxford Handbook of Criminology*, Oxford: Oxford University Press.

Marquand, David (1996) 'Moralists and hedonists', pp. 5–28 in *The Ideas that Shaped Post-War Britain*, edited by D. Marquand and A. Seldon, London: Fontana.

Medved, Michael (1992) *Hollywood vs America*, London: HarperCollins.

Newburn, Tim (1992) *Permission and Regulation*, London: Routledge.

Pandiani, J. (1978) 'Prime-time crime: if all we knew is what we saw ...', *Contemporary Crises*, 2: 437–58.

Pearson, Geoffrey (1983) *Hooligan*, London: Macmillan.

Powers, Stephen P., Rothman, David J., and Rothman, Stanley (1996) *Hollywood's America: Social and Political Themes in Motion Pictures*, Boulder: Westview.

Reiner, Robert (1996) 'The case of the missing crimes', pp. 185–205 in *Interpreting Official Statistics*, edited by R. Levitas and W. Guy, London: Routledge.

——(1997) 'Media-made criminality', pp. 189–231 in *The Oxford Handbook of Criminology*, edited by M. Maguire, R. Morgan and R. Reiner, Oxford: Oxford University Press.

Rock, Paul (1990) *Helping Victims of Crime*, Oxford: Oxford University Press.

Roshier, Bob (1973) 'The selection of crime news by the press', pp. 40–51 in *The Manufacture of News*, edited by S. Cohen and J. Young, London: Arnold.

Sasson, Ted (1995) *Crime Talk*, New York: Aldine de Gruyter.

Schlesinger, P., Dobash, R., Dobash, R., and Weaver, C. (1992) *Women Viewing Violence*, London: British Film Institute.

Signorielli, N. (1990) 'Television's mean and dangerous world: a continuation of the Cultural Indicators Project', pp. 85–106 in *New Directions in Media Effects Research*, edited by N. Signorielli and M. Morgan, Newbury Park: Sage.

Sparks, Richard (1992) *Television and the Drama of Crime*, Buckingham: Open University Press.

—— (1997) 'Recent social theory and the study of crime and punishment', pp. 409–35 in *The Oxford Handbook of Criminology*, edited by M. Maguire, R. Morgan and R. Reiner, Oxford: Oxford University Press.

Sumser, John (1996) *Morality and Social Order in Television Crime Drama*, Jefferson: McFarland.

Surette, Ray (1998) *Media, Crime and Criminal Justice: Images and Realities*, Belmont: Wadsworth.

Taylor, Ian (1995) 'Private homes and public others: an analysis of talk about crime in suburban south Manchester in the mid-1990s', *British Journal of Criminology*, 35: 263–85.

Wakshlag, J., Vial, V., and Tamborini, R. (1983) 'Selecting crime drama and apprehension about crime', *Human Communications Research*, 10: 227–42.

Williams, Paul, and Dickinson, Julie (1993) 'Fear of crime: read all about it? The relationship between newspaper crime reading and fear of crime', *British Journal of Criminology*, 33: 33–56.

Young, Jock (1971) *The Drug-Takers*, London: Paladin.

Zedner, Lucia (1997) 'Victims', pp. 577–612 in *The Oxford Handbook of Criminology*, edited by M. Maguire, R. Morgan and R. Reiner, Oxford: Oxford University Press.

Zillman, D., and Wakshlag, J. (1987) 'Fear of victimisation and the appeal of crime drama', in *Selective Exposure to Communication*, edited by D. Zillman and J. Bryant, Hillsdale NJ: Erlbaum.

Part II

PUBLIC ISSUES
The new politics of order

7

PERSPECTIVES ON RISK AND PENAL POLITICS

Richard Sparks

Introduction

These days the language of risk appears to be everywhere in social analysis (and perhaps increasingly in everyday social exchange, too). Having broken its original bounds in economic theory and the analysis of techno-environmental hazards, this protean notion shows no sign of being reconfined. Moreover, the tendency in recent social theory to affirm that thinking *in terms of risk* is a pervasive condition in late modernity (Giddens 1990, 1991; Beck 1992) leads us to expect more rather than less of such talk, even if some lament the loss of conceptual specificity or precision thereby implied.[1]

The domains of crime, criminology and penal politics are in no way immune from these developments, even if the grander forms of theory have been late in noticing such movements in the underbrush of social analysis.[2] Lately, by contrast, students of crime, criminal law and the penal realm have responded to the stimulus provided by the language of risk with gusto. They have noted its points of connection with many of their traditional concerns (and by extension its role in shaping the histories of their disciplines and domains). Latterly, and more particularly, they have begun to document the marked reconfiguration of many existing forms of crime control and penal practice by novel and increasingly refined systems and techniques for risk analysis, risk reduction, prediction and control (see *inter alia* Peters 1988; O'Malley 1992; Feeley and Simon 1992; Simon 1993; Bottoms 1995; Ericson and Haggerty 1997; Garland 1997).

This paper takes up the latter theme, albeit in a somewhat quizzical spirit. It attends to the somewhat less theoretically well-developed issue of the infiltration of such risk discourses into the public culture of discussion of crime and punishment, and thereby to their articulation with (or competition with or even perhaps, on occasion, their submergence by) other – and more venerable – features of that landscape. It thus takes as given the *presence* of the vocabularies and outlooks generated by the expert systems of risk regulation but not their *predominance*, at least not so far as the public spheres of media discourse, electoral competition and legislation are concerned. Whatever else we may say about contemporary penality and its associated politics, it seems clear that the discourse and practice of risk management do not have the field all to themselves. But *on what terms* do they co-habit with the existing occupants of that terrain?

Analysts of the 'new penology' of risk regulation are generally correct in arguing that some of the most far-reaching shifts in routine practice (broadly those which partake of a trend from 'discipline' to 'management') have low public visibility. They have an infrastructural, sub-political quality. However, for reasons already well explained by students of crime and mass media (especially Ericson *et al.* 1991) penal questions come to public notice – and enjoin political responses and spark arguments about accountability – when things go wrong (Sparks 2000a), or when the legitimation claims of the responsible authorities are otherwise in jeopardy. For this reason, critical or scandalous moments in criminal justice may have much in common with the sorts of accidents and system-failures that preoccupy students of risk-perception and risk-communication in other fields, both in their capacity to engender dread and in their sometimes profound influence over subsequent political decisions. In other words, some readings of the social theory of risk would draw particular attention to those events and interventions whose dramatic impact or symbolic significance crystallises societal responses and sets in train subsequent chains of action and reaction. This somewhat dramaturgical and dynamic notion of risk, however, is not one that currently receives much attention in social analyses of penality. My point here is just that different *notions of risk* may be activated by many different actors at particular times for diverse purposes. 'Risk' is a more complex word than is sometimes acknowledged, and the effects of its uses in penal politics correspondingly more various (O'Malley 1999).

Attaining a clearer sense of how the dynamics of risk and politics intersect in contemporary criminal justice and penal systems is therefore one of my main aims here (as it is in various ways for several of the contributors to this volume: see in particular Melossi and Selmini, Stenson, Sasson). I therefore begin by briefly reviewing the development of thinking on the 'new penology' of risk management. I then try to locate that work in relation to other social theories of risk, especially to Douglas's views in *Risk and Blame* (1992). Third, I briefly indicate the relevance of these bodies of work to an understanding of the tortuous risk politics of crime and punishment in countries such as Britain and the United States in recent times. In conclusion, I argue that this review sharply qualifies any view of the infiltration of risk-regulation in criminal justice as a seamless, inevitable (and presumably transnational) process. Rather, we must also contend with the continuing relevance of distinct national political cultures and concerns, including their attendant events, accidents and moments of political opportunism. What we seem increasingly to encounter are various local penal hybrids, formed at the meeting points of the ostensibly 'placeless' vocabulary of risk-management and the recent travails of particular states and societies.

A new penology?

In a strikingly provocative and influential statement, Feeley and Simon (1992) have argued that, almost unremarked, a set of transformations have occurred in the routine discourse and practice of criminal justice in the United States. These incremental developments have begun to displace older penological concerns with individuals and their moral or clinical defects, and to deploy instead an actuarial language of risk calculation. Whereas former penologies have variously taken as their focal concern individual culpability, specific deterrence or clinical dangerousness,

> In contrast the new penology is markedly less concerned with responsibility, fault, moral sensibility, diagnosis, or intervention and treatment of the individual offender. Rather it is concerned with techniques to identify, classify and manage groupings sorted by dangerousness. The task is managerial, not transformative.
>
> (Feeley and Simon 1992: 452)

Feeley and Simon do not dispute that shifts in crime control rhetoric and policy also have other and more obviously political sources. But, they argue, the intrusion of risk-management technique has proceeded largely independently of overt swings in political fashion. Indeed

> The new penology is neither about punishing nor about rehabilitating individuals. It is about identifying and managing unruly groups. It is concerned with the rationality not of individual behavior nor even of community organization but of managerial processes. Its goal is not to eliminate crime but to make it tolerable through systemic coordination.
>
> (Feeley and Simon 1992: 455)

Thus the new penology is in part the product of a societal accommodation to routinely high volumes of crime, as well as of the refinement of professional practices for monitoring, surveillance and aggregate management. For Feeley and Simon, this explains how disappointment (especially pessimism about projects of rehabilitation) and reduced expectations about the effectiveness of criminal sanctions can nevertheless coincide with a significant extension of penal supervision and control.[3]

The most *visible* signal of new penological thinking is the trend towards selective (or, more accurately, categorial) incapacitation as a rationale for imprisonment (e.g. Greenwood and Abrahamse 1982; Zedlewski 1987). Here 'incapacitation effects' are sought not on the traditional grounds of confining individuals who present a 'clear and present danger' of committing further grave (usually violent) offences[4] but rather on the rationale that confining a sufficient number of 'high rate' offenders (principally burglars, drug dealers and robbers) for a long enough portion of the active phase of their careers will produce appreciable decreases in the volume of crime. The logic of this position is to sentence on the basis of the offender's risk-profile rather than on the gravity of his current offence. This is self-consciously an expansionist measure, as some of its advocates are unabashed in acknowledging (e.g. Barr 1992).

The further logic of the position is that for less risky cases interventions short of imprisonment may suffice. There thus develops an array of intermediate 'disposals' (sometimes described by their advocates as 'smart' sentences: Byrne *et al.* 1992) which fall short of imprisonment but still involve significant forms of monitoring and/or restrictions of liberty (home confinements, curfews, electronic tagging, intensive probation, drug testing and so on). The key point, so far as the new penology thesis is concerned, is that individuals are allocated to these interventions by *sorting* (for risk) rather than by *tailoring* (for either culpability or need) and that their prime rationales are managerial and preventive rather than transformative or strictly punitive (Feeley and Simon 1992: 459). Feeley and Simon (see also Simon 1993) thus also contend that various existing penal measures, especially parole, have shifted their function. Where the purpose of parole is no longer resettlement, re-employment or rehabilitation but rather supervision, revocation of parole is no longer a 'failure'. Indeed, they propose, parole revocation is an indicator of productivity in risk management. Neither is proven commission of a fresh offence necessary for revocation – other indicators of risky behaviour are enough. Hence, in California, an increasing proportion of prison admissions are now for parole violations arising from failed drug tests. This change in practice provides a significant motor of growth in the Californian prison population (Simon 1993; Zimring and Hawkins 1994).

Although Feeley and Simon term the new penology an 'emergent' strategy, acknowledge the presence of other discourses and priorities and note some continuities between 'new penological' and prior perspectives, they are clearly proposing that a profound reconfiguration of the penal realm is under way. The nature of criminology, the analysis of the criminal career, the purpose and scale of intervention are all in transition. Hand in hand with this development, they suggest, goes the reconstitution of poverty in the language of *underclass* 'understood as a permanently marginal population, without literacy, without skills and without hope' (Feeley and Simon 1992: 467). The context, in their view, is therefore the hardening of poverty in America and the entrenched perception of a detached and disreputable sub-stratum (see further Wacquant 1996, 1999). In this setting, the 'lowered expectations' characteristic of the new penology and its extensive scope conjoin to provide 'the imperative of herding a specific population that cannot be … transformed but only maintained – a kind of waste management function' (Feeley and Simon 1992: 470; see also Simon 1993: 259; see further Bauman 1997, 2000).

In subsequent work these authors (Simon and Feeley 1995, and Simon writing alone 1993, 1995, 1996) have significantly revised their position. The 'new penology' view originally emphasised the discontinuity with prior practices (the

'old penology') and tended to represent its nature as a 'technocratic rationalization' (Feeley and Simon 1992: 456). It was a new 'strategic formation' (*ibid.*: 449)
comprising novel forms of actuarially based expert knowledge, adjusting to
systemic problems and having primarily system-level effects (albeit that these
contributed to something as publicly visible as a steeply rising prison population).
In these respects it was a strongly 'internalist' account.[5] Elsewhere, Simon has
developed a more supple and sociologically imaginative position. This acknowledges, *inter alia*, that:

1   Risk-calculation in the penal realm does not proceed in isolation from other
    areas of social practice. Indeed, Simon's proposition that 'Security is the
    great commodity of our time' (1993: 258) expressly draws attention *both* to
    the proliferation of security industries in private transactions *and* to the obli-
    gations of the state in guaranteeing the protection of its citizens. Moreover,
    Simon recognises that for those largely excluded from the private market in
    security products, 'the hard edge of traditional social control remains the
    predominantly experienced means of security' (*ibid.*).
2   Even those penal innovations that self-consciously claim to fall between the
    'deep end' of the penal system (the prison) and its 'shallows' (probation) –
    and which hence partake of the trend to 'smart' or 'intermediate' sanctions
    – are ambiguously coded and often include powerfully recognisable
    elements of both discipline and retributive severity. Thus, Simon suggests
    that the popular credibility of the 'boot camp' relies upon an iconography of
    wholesome masculine military discipline that provides 'an infusion of mean-
    ingfulness through nostalgia' (1995: 46).
3   Although new forms of penal sanction draw upon current advances in
    knowledge about prediction and control, they are not for this reason entirely
    discontinuous with older ones. In this respect, the stiffening of sentencing
    and parole provisions under so-called 'three strikes' laws clearly recall earlier
    versions of 'habitual offender' legislation (Simon 1996). Although Simon
    rightly continues to insist that the notions of the recidivist individual acti-
    vated in 'old' (Progressive Era) and 'new' penologies are distinctly different,
    they have in common criminology's chronically 'tense proximity to power'
    and its inability to escape 'highly politicized conceptions of crime as a social
    problem' (Simon 1996: 25).[6]

In consequence of these qualifications, Simon and Feeley now note some paradoxical features of the 'new penology'. Its success among agents of the criminal
justice system and their academic associates has not been matched by a
successful capture of public discourse on crime and punishment. Its technicist
emphasis fails to displace other, older and more emotively potent vocabularies.
Although its language and practices have become 'commonplace' they have not
become correspondingly appealing. The 'new penology', Simon and Feeley
conclude, faces a problem of 'cultural sterility' (1995: 169). It does not address

the relationship of crime and punishment to the 'more fundamental tasks of government' (*ibid.*: 171), nor to the passions involved in the public's fears and feelings about crime. It exhibits a 'blindness ... to the cultural effects of penality itself' (*ibid.*: 172).

In the course of this auto-critique, Simon and Feeley move closer to the views set out by Garland on the 'crisis of penal modernism' (Garland 1990: 4). Garland argues that the roles of modern penality as a specialised administrative sub-system and as a theme in culture and high politics are chronically marked by contradiction and ambivalence. For Garland:

> There are two contrasting visions at work in contemporary criminal justice – the passionate, morally toned desire to punish and the administrative, rationalistic, normalizing concern to manage. These visions clash in many important respects, but both are deeply embedded within the [modern] social practice of punishing.
>
> (Garland 1990: 180)

Indeed, the very sequestration of punishment – its enclosure in professional low-visibility institutions such as prisons – may leave the popular imagination to roam free, to fall prey to rhetorical exploitation, and to re-connect with its antique sources of fear and fascination (Garland 1990: 239; see also Ericson and Haggerty 1997: 40–1). In Garland's view, penal cultures inevitably include the accumulated influences of historical traces and comprise elements that are expressive as well as those that are (at least apparently) instrumental in character. This makes them more open to the influences of 'governmental example and political persuasion' (1990: 246) than Feeley and Simon (Mark I) acknowledge, as well as more vulnerable to the effects of specific episodes, events and *causes célèbres* (see also Garland 1995: 200; O'Malley 1992). Perhaps, then, the present configuration of penal politics, although particular, is not so unique or unprecedented as Feeley and Simon originally appeared to want to claim (Garland 1995: 201).

On the other hand, practices redolent of a 'risk society' would now appear to be quite deeply embedded both within the criminal justice apparatus as such and in the private consumption of security products (Ericson and Haggerty 1997). Garland indicates as much in setting out the ways in which the 'new criminologies of everyday life' enjoin us to participate in individual and collective projects of securing persons and property against the opportunist rationally choosing offender ('situational man') (1996: 6–14). What remain distinctive, however, are the politics of punishment as such, especially insofar as these involve the authority and legitimation-claims (what Garland calls the 'sovereignty') of the state. In this respect, Garland argues, one response of contemporary states to the predicaments of crime control (the routine presence of high volumes of crime) is to engage in an implicit denial of those predicaments by resort to punitive 'display'. Here, tough punishment 'magically compensates a failure to deliver security' (1996: 16); it is 'an act of sovereign might, a performative action' (*ibid.*: 17) against feared and reviled alien others. The logic of state punishment remains at bottom 'political ... rather than penological' (*ibid.*: 18).

Garland draws a distinction between the 'relatively fixed infrastructure of [penal] techniques and apparatuses' and those 'mobile strategies that determine aims and priorities' (1995: 204–5). Developing this theme, he argues elsewhere that many varieties of routine crime control and security management are plausibly regarded as an 'adaptation' by the state (and non-state actors) to the chronic and embedded presence of high volumes of routine crimes in most economically advanced countries for the indefinite future (1996: 15). However, Garland also recognises that one of the more marked features of British and US penal politics of the last few years has been their 'punitive counter-tendency' (1996: 13). In Garland's view, there is an increasing ambivalence on the part of contemporary states: the limited capacities that are recognised by the 'adaptation' strategies are implicitly denied by the 'punitive counter-tendency'. Thus:

> A show of punitive force against individuals is used to repress any acknowledgement of the state's inability to control crime to acceptable levels. A willingness to deliver harsh punishments to convicted offenders magically compensates a failure to deliver security to the population at large.
>
> (Garland 1996: 16)

On this view, therefore, the punitive display is a sign of weakness. It arises as an attempt to recover the state's eroded powers of sovereign command. If the nation-state has indeed been 'hollowed-out' (from below by the complexity of contemporary social relations and the failure of top-down planning, from without by the globalising tendencies of late modernity (see Giddens 1990) it may be correspondingly more likely to focus upon those instruments of power and indices of legitimacy over which it retains exclusive control; among these, varying punishment levels traditionally enjoys a privileged eloquence (Garland 1990), perhaps more especially so in an era of mass communication whose principal media are preoccupied with the representation of order (Ericson *et al.* 1991; Sparks 2000b).

This seems convincing, at least in general outline. It is, moreover, quite consistent with a lengthy tradition of experience and reflection which stresses that such populist demonstrations of power, and the cultural politics of national exhortation that generally accompanies them, are associated with a felt or invoked sense of threat from internal and/or external enemies (Hall *et al.* 1978). However, in order to provide an account of the 'punitive counter-tendency' as it occurs *in any particular nation-state*, such a view still requires to be given content and context. The content here would be the particular myths, narratives and structures of feeling within which the cultural politics of punishment in that society are conducted; and the context is given by the particular disposition of conflicts and competitions which then characterise it. In this respect, the question of how what happens in the penal realm intersects with its surrounding political culture remains in need of a good deal of substantive exploration. We know (we can hardly avoid knowing) that political campaigns around sentencing, or latterly about prison regimes, or other 'law and order issues' take place – but we are in general less clear about *how* they work.

How far do these debates illuminate the particular features of the recent penal histories of the societies best known to us? It seems very likely, as Garland and others argue, that the dynamic underlying the transition to a strategy of mass incarceration in the United States (see further Beckett 1997; Tonry 1999), and to a very steeply rising prison population in other countries such as Britain (see Morgan 1999; Benyon and Edwards 1997; Wacquant 1999), is indeed primarily political. However, Garland's distinction between risk management and punitive display (the latter *in denial of* the failure of the former) may be over-drawn (Ericson and Haggerty 1997: 12). Indeed, Garland goes so far as to suggest that the expert and populist registers are 'twinned, antithetical phenomena' (1997: 203). We may equally plausibly suggest that there is neither a harmonious union nor an acrimonious divorce here but a *liaison* of some other sort, often stormy but creating offspring of its own. For example, at the levels of *process* and of *justification*, we perhaps observe (with Simon 1996) not so much an intensification of 'punitiveness' *tout court* as an increasing preoccupation with confinement as such (not just its extent and duration but also, as I have shown elsewhere (Sparks 1996a, 2000a) its conditions and the perfection of its security). The state cannot any longer simply perform punishment as a matter of sovereign right. It must also thereby promise something. And increasingly what it promises is protection. Neither for the most part does the public discourse on crime simply *demand* 'retribution' (as an unmixed idea that is something about which only philosophers speak). Rather, the motifs that dominate public discussion have to do with the brittle patience of hard-pressed citizens, their overburdenedness, their fears, their demands for order and safety. Even if these expressed fears could be shown to be in some sense proxy for other (and less easily voiced) anxieties and passions, they focus on the prison because it is understood to provide what no other penalty provides: namely an impregnable defence against that fraction of one's fellow citizens regarded as irredeemable bearers of intolerable risks.

A number of recent contributions in comparative criminology draw attention to the specificity of local constructions of crime and punishment and their embeddedness in national political settlements (Melossi 1994, and Melossi and Selmini, this volume; Nelken 1994). This seems to suggest that we look for examples not so much of 'punitiveness', however defined, but rather for rhetorics whose peculiar features are marked by their *englobement* (Goldmann 1976) in the culture and ideology of the settings in which they occur. The hope here is that we may achieve some sense of perspective on which features of the current scene are simply the latest iterations of entrenched postures, and which are in any sense novel departures. For example, what was revealed in the intense politicisation of sentencing issues in England and Wales in the early and mid-1990s (see *inter alia* Windlesham 1996) was not just a generic issue of 'sovereignty', but rather a moment in the history of the *British state* (and specifically that moment at which 'Thatcherism' as a *state project* began to unravel; see further Hay 1996).

Risk and blame

The understanding of risk most directly germane to the concerns discussed by Simon and Feeley and by Garland is the one espoused by Mary Douglas in *Risk and Blame* (1992).[7] It is not difficult to grasp why Douglas's work should have particular resonance for analysts of crime and punishment. They share a common interest in understanding how the organisation (or in Douglas's term the 'constitution') of communities relates to their attributions of threat and blame; and Douglas acknowledges that her original arguments about blame were an extension of Durkheim's account of the relations between crime and the *conscience collective* (Douglas 1992: 6–7).[8] Douglas's approach to risk centres on the political implications of judgements (including ostensibly technical and dispassionate ones) (1992: 8), on the relation between notions of risk and the structure of institutional authority (1992: 14) and on risk as the contemporary vestment for societal conversations about morality and identity (1992: 15–16).

Douglas introduces two arguments that are particularly relevant to the present discussion. First, she proposes that in contemporary culture it is the language of risk that provides 'a common forensic vocabulary with which to hold persons accountable' (1992: 22). In this process the notion of risk becomes 'prised away' from its more original and particular application to probability calculations properly so-called, and becomes a cultural key word with much wider reference within 'a debate about accountability':

> This dialogue, the cultural process itself, is a contest to muster support for one kind of action rather than another ... The cultural dialogue is therefore best studied in its forensic moments. The concept of risk emerges as a key resource in modern times because of its uses as a forensic resource.
>
> (Douglas 1992: 24)

In other words, moments of intense controversy or recrimination (such as those engendered in debates about criminal sentencing or prison escapes) crystallise societal anxieties and expose lines of division about the competence, trustworthiness and legitimacy of authorities. But this is also why, in Douglas's view, the vocabulary of risk cannot be confined to the bloodless calculations of new penologists or other technocrats. Instead it has 'fallen into antique mode':

Risk, danger and sin are used around the world to legitimate policy or to discredit it, to protect individuals from predatory institutions or to protect institutions form predatory individuals. Indeed, risk provides secular terms for rewriting scripture: not the sins of the fathers, but the risks unleashed by the fathers are visited on the heads of their children, even to the nth generation.

(Douglas 1992: 26)

Douglas's second proposition is that 'fear of danger tends to strengthen the lines of division in a community'. Fear 'digs more deeply the cleavages that have been there all the time' (1992: 34). The stigmatic effects of such fears attach with particular vehemence to visible feared or despised minorities. Here again, danger is not easily tamed or civilised. It does not 'unload its ancient moral freight' (*ibid.*: 35). This is surely a topic on which criminology can richly inform the cultural theory of risk (e.g. Hall *et al.* 1978; Nelken 1994; Pavarini 1997; and, of course, Cohen 1972, 1985, 1996). In general, the cultural theory of risk clarifies the uneasy suspension of current criminal justice between expertise and populism that occupies its analysts (Bottoms 1995; Simon and Feeley 1995; Garland 1996).[9]

Also, and more specifically, cultural theory draws attention to the mixing of discourses inevitably involved in the punishment of offenders (Garland 1990) and which is not limited to the severity of penalties (their frequency and duration). Rather, public discourse on punishment continues to betray a preoccupation with the morality and propriety of the form and conditions of confinement (Simon 1995; Sparks 1996a; Pratt 1997) and with the absolute perfection of their security. The fact that a given field of activity acquires new technical vocabularies and that these restructure some of its practices in no way lifts it outside politics. For Douglas and others (Rayner 1992; Schwarz and Thompson 1990) the cognitive and affective formations that cultural theory terms 'political cultures' act as filters for risk – they select problems for attention, suggest images of threatening people and situations, propose diagnoses and so on. But this makes risk inherently a plural and conflictual idea. To affirm that contemporary western societies increasingly think their crime and punishment problems *in terms of risk* may in itself be to say rather less than initially appears. It tells us something about the templates for the ensuing debates but not much about their substantive topics, still less about the strength of the emotional charge they carry or the precise positions that actors take up within those debates at any given place and time (cf. O'Malley 1997; 1999).

New penologies and old penal politics

Throughout the 1990s there have been many developments in the penal politics of Britain and other advanced societies that resemble those cited by Feeley and Simon (Mark I) and which impel professional practice in the direction of risk management. In the British case these primarily include pressures on the probation service (and other personal social services) to enhance the supervisory aspects of their work, to make more formal risk assessments for the courts and to work with higher risk clients (Kemshall *et al.* 1997; Kemshall and Pritchard 1997; Parton 1996). That leaves probation officers and social workers not just talking the language of risk more routinely but also, as Kemshall *et al.* (1997) make clear, in some respects working *in a riskier environment,* because of the accountability demands upon them when things go wrong. The infiltration of risk-oriented thinking does not stop there, of course, but also, as I have indicated above, revises parole decisions and, latterly and increasingly, sentencing. Nor does thinking *in terms of risk* only affect the penal system as such but, as is well known, contributes to the refocusing of policing practice and objectives and their intersection with the whole field of 'community safety' in ways that exceed the scope of this paper (Garland 1996; Crawford 1997; Ericson and Haggerty 1997). There is in all these respects ample grist to the mill of readings of British criminal justice discourse and practice as pervaded by the concerns of 'the new penology'.

But these are not the only readings possible, and nor will they suffice taken alone. As Garland has made clear on several occasions (including 1990, 1996, 1997), not only are the 'old' and 'new' penologies *adjacent* rather than antithetical positions in the development of modern penality, but they also both co-exist and sometimes conflict with other motors of penal politics which are less clearly instrumental, more deeply involved with sources of cultural and personal anxiety, rage and resentment, and more clearly prey to overt political manipulation (see especially Garland 1997: 202–3). Moreover, if the *explananda* in the present case include the quite intense politicisation of the penal question in Britain in the 1990s, the reversal of fortunes in sentencing rationales between 1991 and 1996/7 and the rapidity of the increases in the prison population over the period, then the necessary explanatory resources lie mainly in those domains (see, *inter alia,* Windlesham 1996; Benyon and Edwards 1997; Shapland and Sparks 1999; Sparks, in press). In short, signs of 'the new penology Mark I' are present in abundance but they do not provide (in the British case) a complete account of the main lines of force, nor even perhaps the primary 'motor of growth'.[10]

In this respect, the balance of the argument appears to lie with those who suggest that the current penal politics are not ideologically univocal nor even co-eval in their sources (O'Malley 1997; Garland 1996, 1997). Moreover, in certain of its usages the risk-concept easily falls prey to general strictures against evolutionary metaphors in the social sciences (it 'unfolds', as it were, without agency or context) (cf. Giddens 1984: 244–5). This reminds us of the importance of Melossi's (1985) focus upon the differing 'wavelengths' of historical time upon which the formative influences on penal affairs are carried. Even the most significant of long-term 'secular trends' may be countermanded in the short run by priorities that are political and 'local' in their inspiration. The most immediate and urgent pressures upon penal politics are still in this sense *conjunctural,* and it remains to be shown what the most significant elements in the recent conjuncture might be.

To return again to the British example, there is a striking contrast between the tenor of penal politics (as Andrew Rutherford, David Faulkner and others have commented) in the mid to late 1980s when, as it happens, the Thatcher project was most fully in possession of state power, and the tilt back towards alarmism and penal austerity that occurred in the early 1990s. The former was the period in which the Criminal Justice Act 1991 (with its systematising 'just deserts' rationale and its modestly decarcerationist agenda) took shape, when youth imprisonment fell, and when police cautioning became a standard diversionary practice. It was not until 1993 (with economic conditions and political scandals conspiring to produce a terminal decline in the popularity of the then Conservative government; with a newly hard-nosed Labour opposition snapping at its heels and in the immediate aftermath of the Bulger murder) that the climate reverted in earnest to a more visibly 'authoritarian populist' mood. None of this would have surprised Rusche and Kirchheimer (1939) (or their contemporary, Hermann Mannheim). They would have *expected* both a hardening of public rhetoric and imputed sensibility, and a reorganisation of imprisonment around the objectives of deterrence and compliance under such conditions. It was in this moment that an energetic and ambitious Conservative Home Secretary embarked on a campaign to invest the whole arena of criminal justice and penal politics with renewed political force and meaning. 'Prison Works!' was his slogan; and the legislative programme that followed drew together several strands into a powerful rhetoric. It claimed justification both in the instrumental aims of incapacitation and deterrence (it works!) *and* sought to target a fund of public anger and resentment to promote a view of richly merited severity. That's why it went along with an emphasis on 'austerity' in prison regimes – as Mr Howard put it at the time, 'Prisoners enjoy a standard of material comfort which *taxpayers* find hard to understand.' 'Prison Works!' stitched all these disparate elements together in a single potent rhetorical package. Moreover, that stance framed reactions to subsequent events. This in part explains why, for example, the controversies and official responses that followed the prison disturbances and escapes of 1994/5 were so different in nature from the modernising, reflective and justice-oriented focus of Lord Woolf's (1991) response to the 1990 prison disturbances only four years earlier (see further Sparks 2000a). That this move did not succeed in strict electoral terms (but rather preceded the Conservatives' disaster at the polls on 1 May 1997) should come as no surprise. It was precisely a phenomenon of, in John Gray's apt expression, 'the Tory endgame' (1997). It was an attempt to recapture something of the populist magic of early Thatcherism in its glory days, but it came after the point at which Thatcherism as a *state project* had already begun to unravel and to descend into crisis management (Hay 1996).

Conclusions

These English episodes confirm that Garland is correct to re-emphasise the complex interconnection between the penal realm and problems of state sovereignty and legitimation. It is also clear, though, that none of the relevant terms (state/sovereignty/punishment) can be assumed to be already known and transculturally applicable. The tendency to have recourse to punishment as a tactic for relegitimation may be quite culturally specific; and the particular terms on which it is attempted are bound into their particular historical location in rather eloquent and indicative ways (cf. Melossi 1993, 1994). Thus, O'Malley is surely right to propose that we take care before deploying notions of either 'discipline' or 'punishment' as general 'logics' outside an understanding of their position within 'substantive political programs' and their associated 'moral inventions' (O'Malley 1992: 257–9). What is less convincing, however, is the view that there are two 'twinned, antithetical' (Garland 1997: 203) varieties of penal discourse in play, only one of which (the measured, dispassionate, calculative one) is *really* about risk. If instead we follow Douglas's account of the politicisation of risk, we can argue by contrast that contemporary penal populism is *also* in some sense a risk discourse, but in the more highly moralised and controversial form that that notion assumes when it breaks the bounds of professional specialisms and enters the open terrain of political conflict.

More liberal side ignored

What is finally at stake here is an interpretation of the place of the penal realm within contemporary statecraft. Neither those perspectives which stress the *generic* (and hence presumably transnationally applicable) frailty of the sovereign state in the global age (Garland 1996), nor those which emphasise the emergent sub-structure of neo-liberal governmentality (Barry *et al.* 1996) alone convincingly convey the particularities of these encounters and their attendant passions. Colin Hay (1996) is probably very largely correct to portray British politics in the 1990s as characterised by 'neo-liberal crisis management', and both elements in that formulation would seem to be equally important. In this respect it seems plausible to suggest that the crises in British criminal justice of the early 1990s provided an opportunity (albeit that its original proponent was already electorally doomed) to diagnose and redefine the problems of the penal realm in more vivid and urgent terms. Delving deeply into the anxieties of respectable citizens, and accentuating their weary impatience with a sense of distance from deviant and irresponsible others, 'Prison Works!' promised *more*: more protection *and* more retribution in a form more closely attuned to the officially desired version of contemporary common sense. What ensued was a strategy that offered at the same time radical modernisation (spanking new cost-efficient private prisons; an end to the clinical–rehabilitative anachronism of the parole system; revised forms of institutional management whose working assumptions we can more readily comprehend; new and more prudent forms of risk-assessment in making confinement decisions) while in no way attempting to offload the 'ancient moral freight' (Douglas 1992) of blame and censure. One reason, therefore, why the delivery of punishment can increase in ways that have few if any 'natural' limits (Christie 1993; Simon and Feeley 1995) in the absence of countervailing political resources counselling restraint is the liminal nature of the criminal sanction. It can straddle registers of discourse usually otherwise held separate, by promising in the same breath to limit risk (an appeal to an intuitive realism) and to do what is morally fitting (an appeal to intuitions of another sort).

References

Adams, J. (1995) *Risk*, London: UCL Press.

Austin, J. (1996) 'The effects of "Three Strikes and You're Out" on corrections', in D. Shichor and D. Sechrest (eds) (1996) *Three Strikes and You're Out: Vengeance as Public Policy*, London: Sage.

Barr, W. (1992) *The Case for More Incarceration*, Washington: National Institute of Justice.

Barry, A., Osborne, T. and Rose, N. (eds) (1996) *Foucault and Political Reason: Liberalism, Neo-Liberalism and Rationalities of Government*, London: UCL Press.

Bauman, Z. (1997) *Postmodernity and its Discontents*, Cambridge: Polity Press.

——(2000) 'Social issues of law and order', in D. Garland and R. Sparks (eds) *Criminology and Social Theory*, Oxford: Oxford University Press.

Beck, U. (1992) *Risk Society*, London: Sage.

Beckett, K. (1997) *Making Crime Pay: Law and Order in Contemporary American Politics*, Oxford: Oxford University Press.

Benyon, J. and Edwards. A. (1997) 'Crime and public order', in P. Dunleavy, A. Gamble, I. Holliday and G. Peele (eds) *Developments in British Politics 5*, Basingstoke: Macmillan, pp. 326–41.

Bottoms, A. (1995) 'The philosophy and politics of punishment and sentencing', in C. Clarkson and R. Morgan (eds) *The Politics of Sentencing Reform*, Oxford: Oxford University Press.

Byrne, J., Lurigio, A. and Petersilia, J. (1992) *Smart Sentencing*, Newbury Park, California: Sage.

Canovan, M. (1981) *Populism*, London: Junction Books.

Castel, R. (1991) 'From dangerousness to risk', in G. Burchell, C. Gordon and P. Miller (eds) *The Foucault Effect*, London: Harvester Wheatsheaf.

Christie, N. (1993) *Crime Control as Industry*, London: Routledge.

Cohen, S. (1972) *Folk Devils and Moral Panics*, Harmondsworth: Penguin.

——(1985) *Visions of Social Control*, Cambridge: Polity Press.

——(1996) 'Crime and politics: spot the difference', *British Journal of Sociology*, 47(1): 1–21.

Crawford, A. (1997) *The Local Governance of Crime*, Oxford: Oxford University Press.

Douglas, M. (1992) *Risk and Blame: Essays in Cultural Theory*, London: Routledge.

Ericson, R.V. and Haggerty, K. (1997) *Policing the Risk Society*, Toronto: University of Toronto Press.

Ericson, R.V., Baranek, P. and Chan, J. (1991) *Representing Order*, Buckingham: Open University Press.

Feeley, M. and Simon, J. (1992) 'The new penology: notes on the emerging strategy of corrections and its implications', *Criminology*, 30(4): 449–75.

Foucault, M. (1991) 'On governmentality', in G. Burchell, C. Gordon and P. Miller (eds) *The Foucault Effect*, London: Harvester Wheatsheaf.

Funtowicz, S. and Ravetz, J. (1992) 'Three types of risk assessment and the emergence of post-normal science', in S. Krimsky and D. Golding (eds) *Social Theories of Risk*, New York: Praeger.

Garland, D. (1990) *Punishment and Modern Society*, Oxford: Oxford University Press.

——(1995) 'Penal modernism and postmodernism', in S. Cohen and T. Blomberg (eds) *Punishment and Social Control*, New York: Aldine de Gruyter.

——(1996) 'The limits of the sovereign state', *British Journal of Criminology*, 36(4): 445–71.

——(1997) ' "Governmentality" and the problem of crime: Foucault, criminology, sociology', *Theoretical Criminology*, 1(2): 173–214.

Giddens, A. (1984) *The Constitution of Society*, Cambridge: Polity Press.

——(1987) *Social Theory and Modern Sociology*, Cambridge: Polity Press.

——(1990) *The Consequences of Modernity*, Cambridge: Polity Press.

——(1991) *Modernity and Self-Identity*, Cambridge: Polity Press.

Goldmann, L. (1976) *Cultural Creation*, Oxford: Blackwell.

Gray, J. (1997) *Endgames: Questions in Late Modern Political Thought*, Cambridge: Polity Press.

Greenwood, P. and Abrahamse, A. (1982) *Selective Incapacitation*, Santa Monica, California: RAND Corporation.

Greenwood, P., Rydell, C., Abrahamse, A., Caulkins, J., Chiesa, J., Model, K. and Klein, S. (1996) 'Estimated benefits and costs of California's new mandatory-sentencing law', in D. Shichor and D. Sechrest (eds) *Three Strikes and You're Out: Vengeance as Public Policy*, London: Sage.

Hacking, I. (1991) *The Taming of Chance*, Cambridge: Cambridge University Press.

Hall, S., Clarke, J., Critcher, C., Jefferson, T. and Roberts, B. (1978) *Policing the Crisis*, London: Macmillan.

Hay, C. (1995) 'Mobilization through interpellation: James Bulger, juvenile crime and the construction of a moral panic', *Social and Legal Studies*, 4(2): 197–223.

——(1996) *Re-Stating Social and Political Change*, Buckingham: Open University Press.

Hay, W. and Sparks, R. (1992) 'Vulnerable prisoners: risk in long-term prisons', in A. Bottomley, T. Fowles and R. Reiner (eds) *Criminal Justice: Theory and Practice*, London: British Society of Criminology.

Kasperson, R. (1992) 'The social amplification of risk: progress in developing an integrative framework', in S. Krimsky and D. Golding (eds) *Social Theories of Risk*, New York: Praeger.

Kemshall, H. and Pritchard, J. (eds) (1997) *Good Practice in Risk Assessment and Risk Management*, London: Jessica Kingsley.

Kemshall, H., Parton, N., Walsh, M. and Waterson, J. (1997) 'Concepts of risk in relation to organizational structure and functioning within the personal social services and probation', *Social Policy and Administration*, 31(3): 213–31.

Krisberg, B. (1994) 'Distorted by fear: the make-believe war on crime', *Social Justice*, 21(3): 38–49.

Melossi, D. (1985) 'Punishment and social action: changing vocabularies of motive within a political business cycle', *Current Perspectives in Social Theory*, 6: 169–97.

——(1993) 'Gazette of morality and social whip', *Social and Legal Studies*, 2: 259–79.

——(1994) 'The economy of illegalities; normal crimes, elites and social control', in D. Nelken (ed.) *The Futures of Criminology*, London: Sage.

Morgan, R. (1999) 'New Labour "law and order" politics and the House of Commons Home Affairs Committee Report on *Alternatives to Prison Sentences*', *Punishment and Society*, 1(1): 109–14.

Nelken, D. (1994) 'Whom can you trust? The future of comparative criminology', in D. Nelken (ed.) *The Futures of Criminology*, London: Sage.

O'Malley, P. (1992) 'Risk, power and crime prevention', *Economy and Society*, 21(3): 252–75.

——(1997) 'Policing, politics and post-modernity', *Social and Legal Studies*, 6(3): 363–82.

——(1999) 'Volatile and contradictory punishment', *Theoretical Criminology*, 3(2): 175–96.

Parton, N. (1996) 'Social work, risk and the "blaming system"', in N. Parton (ed.) *Social Theory, Social Change and Social Work*, London: Routledge.

Pasquino, P. (1991) 'Criminology: the birth of a special knowledge', in G. Burchell, C. Gordon and P. Miller (eds) *The Foucault Effect*, London: Harvester Wheatsheaf.

Pavarini, M. (1997) 'Controlling social panic: questions and answers about security in Italy at the end of the millennium', in R. Bergalli and C. Sumner (eds) *Social Control and Political Order*, London: Sage.

Peters, A. (1988) 'Main currents in criminal law theory', in J. van Dijk, C. Haffmans, F. Ruter and J. Schutte (eds) *Criminal Law in Action*, Arnhem: Gouda Quint.

Pratt, J. (1997) *Governing the Dangerous*, Sydney: Federation Press.

Rayner, S. (1992) 'Cultural theory and risk analysis', in S. Krimsky and D. Golding (eds) *Social Theories of Risk*, New York: Praeger.

Rusche, G. and Kirchheimer, O. [1939] (1968) *Punishment and Social Structure*, New York: Russell and Russell.

Sasson, T. (1995) *Crime Talk*, New York: Aldine de Gruyter.

Schwarz, M. and Thompson, M. (1990) *Divided We Stand: Redefining Politics, Technology and Social Choice*, Hemel Hempstead: Harvester Wheatsheaf.

Shapland, J. and Sparks, R. (1999) 'Les politiques penales et la politique', in P. Robert and L. van Outrive (eds) *Crime et Justice en Europe depuis 1990*, Paris: L'Harmattan.

Shichor, D. and Sechrest, D. (eds) (1996) *Three Strikes and You're Out: Vengeance as Public Policy*, London: Sage.

Simon, J. (1988) 'The ideological effect of actuarial practices', *Law and Society Review*, 22: 24–50.

——(1993) *Poor Discipline*, Chicago: University of Chicago Press.

——(1995) 'They died with their boots on: the boot camp and the limits of modern penality', *Social Justice*, 22(2): 25–48.

——(1996) 'Criminology and the recidivist', in D. Shichor and D. Sechrest (eds) (1996) *Three Strikes and You're Out: Vengeance as Public Policy*, London: Sage.

Simon, J. and Feeley, M. (1995) 'True crime: the new penology and public discourse on crime', in T. Blomberg and S. Cohen (eds) *Punishment and Social Control*, New York: Aldine de Gruyter.

Sparks, R. (1992) *Television and the Drama of Crime*, Buckingham: Open University Press.

——(1996a) 'Penal austerity: the doctrine of less eligibility reborn?', in P. Francis and R. Matthews (eds) *Prisons 2000*, London: Macmillan.

——(1996b) 'A system in contra-flow', *Criminal Justice*, 14(1): 4–5.

——(2000a) 'Risk and blame in criminal justice controversies: British press coverage and official discourse on prison security (1993–6)' in M. Brown and J. Pratt (eds) *Dangerous Offenders: Punishment and Social Order*, London: Routledge, pp. 127–44.

——(2000b) ' "Bringin' it all back home": populism, media coverage and the dynamics of locality and globality in the politics of crime control', in K. Stenson and R. Sullivan (eds) *Crime and the Risk Society*, Devon: Willan Publishing.

—— (in press) 'Penal austerity and social anxiety at the century's turn: governmental rationalities, legitimation deficits and populism in British penal politics in the 1990s', in Loic Wacquant (ed.) *From Social State to Penal State*, Oxford: Oxford University Press.

Sparks, R.., Bottoms, A. and Hay, W. (1996) *Prisons and the Problem of Order*, Oxford: Oxford University Press.

Tonry, M. (1999) 'Why are US incarceration rates so high?', *Overcrowded Times*, 10(3) (June): 1–16.

Wacquant, L. (1996) 'The rise of advanced marginality: notes on its nature and implications', *Acta Sociologica*, 39: 121–39.

——(1999) *Les Prisons de la Misère*, Paris: Editions Liber/Raisons d'Agir.

Walker, N. (1996) *Dangerous People*, London: Blackstone Press.

Windlesham, Lord (1996) *Responses to Crime, vol. 3: Legislating with the Tide*, Oxford: Oxford University Press.

Wolfgang, M., Figlio, R. and Sellin, T. (1972) *Delinquency in a Birth Cohort*, Chicago: University of Chicago Press.

Woolf, Lord Justice (1991) *Prison Disturbances April 1990*, London: HMSO.

Wynne, B. (1992) 'Risk and social learning: reification to engagement', in S. Krimsky and D. Golding (eds) *Social Theories of Risk*, New York: Praeger.

Zedlewski, E. (1987) 'Making confinement decisions', *Research in Brief*, Washington: National Institute of Justice.

Zimring, F. and Hawkins, G. (1991) *The Scale of Imprisonment*, Chicago: University of Chicago Press.

——(1994) 'The growth of imprisonment in California', *British Journal of Criminology*, 34(1): 83–95.

——(1995) *Incapacitation*, Oxford: Oxford University Press.

8

SOCIAL CONFLICT AND THE MICROPHYSICS OF CRIME

The experience of the Emilia–Romagna *Città sicure* project[1]

Dario Melossi and Rossella Selmini

Città sicure is a project of social intervention on crime and other sources of lack of public safety, created in 1994 by the regional government of Emilia–Romagna, an Italian region that has traditionally been characterised for its progressive political and social orientation (Putnam 1993). In our view, this project – in which the two authors of this chapter have both been in some ways involved – is best characterised as being situated at the intersection of two axes or dimensions. On the one hand, the project developed, and was in part also a response to, the emergence of 'crime' in Italy as a major feature of public discourse. On the other, it unfolded within a deep turmoil in the structure of the Italian political landscape, marked by the demand of local powers (especially regions and cities) to play a much more decisive role *vis-à-vis* the central government.[2] As we will see, we claim that these two aspects are deeply related, because the level at which the issue of crime emerged was the day-to-day level of local life, much better known and manageable by localities than by the central state.

The preliminary question that we would like to address, however, is about the emergence of crime as a mundane feature of public discourse. Given that this is a relatively new discourse in Italy and is, in our opinion, relatively new also in many other developed countries, under what conditions did such discourse emerge, and why? The answer we can give is, of course, only tentative, and is linked with the more general structure of social relationships, and particularly with social conflict.

Elsewhere, Melossi has maintained that, after periods of deep social transformations, characterised by unrest and turmoil, elites usually try to furnish society with a renewed sense of 'unity' (Melossi 2000). A particularly important aspect of this process of social 'unification' is its *moral* aspect, which often unfolds through the singling out of 'internal enemies'. Following classical reconstructions of these nexuses (Durkheim 1895; Erikson 1966), representations of criminality loom large among 'internal enemies'. An aspect, however, which has often been overlooked, even by classical interpreters, is the linkage of these processes with class composition and especially with transformations in the structure and composition of the working class. We argue that, once an 'old' type of working class has become incorporated within the main structure of society, first 'structurally' – by becoming the most representative and significant segment of the working class – then 'politically' – by reaching participation in government – a 'new' type of working class emerges which becomes identified, at first, with 'outsider' or 'deviant' figures.

History offers plenty of examples of such early deviant representations that would later gain respectability. One has only to think of the 'vagrants' that constituted the 'original' proletariat in the process of so-called 'primitive' accumulation (Marx 1867; Melossi and Pavarini 1977); of the 'classes dangereuses' of the nineteenth century (Chevalier 1973); of the 'hoboes' and the 'wobblies' during the great transformation of North American working class in the early decades of this century (Anderson 1923); of the mass migration of former southern and eastern European peasants to the Americas around the turn of the twentieth century, and the panic about their 'criminality' (Teti 1993; Salvatore and Aguirre 1996); of the mass migration of Afro-American rural workers from the south to the north of the United States between the 1920s and the 1960s, a mass migration that eventually went to feed what would come to be called the 'American underclass' in recent years (Wilson 1987); of the mass migration of southern Europeans beween the 1950s and early 1970s, towards central and northern Europe, and there too the ensuing panic about crime (Ferracuti 1968); finally, the most recent example is probably the migration of northern African and eastern European workers towards the countries of the European Union, this time including southern Europe, also marked by an outcry about the 'criminal' invasion (Tonry 1997; Marshall 1997). In all these very different examples, we witness a bifurcation in the 'moral economy' of the working class between a respectable 'old' working class, expressing moral indignation at the mores of the newcomers, and a 'new' working class, subject of extensive processes of criminalisation.

The dialectics of 'the political' and 'the criminal'

Indeed, if 'anomie' is connected to periods of dislocation and transformation, when society becomes unable to 'support', so to speak, individual morality (Durkheim 1893), then periods of rationalisation are prime targets for anomie – and the sectors of the working class hardest hit by these processes are the ones destined to become most anomic. Whereas the 'old' sectors of the working class vent their moral indignation against the immoral habits of the 'new' working class, the latter is certainly more likely to engage in, or anyway be perceived as engaging in, behaviour that is criminalised or defined as characterised by a lack of 'civility'. For the new working class (often the product of processes of social disorganisation of previous social groupings, such as rural workers), the transformation crisis in fact brings about the impossibility of both decent livelihood and the understanding of self as dignified human beings. In other words, the devalorisation of labour goes hand in hand with criminalisation, in the two senses of the term, i.e. an increasing involvement of some sectors of the 'new' working class in criminal behaviour and an increasing visibility of those same sectors by agencies of formal control.

Therefore, the conflicts in which the new emerging working class is involved are at first defined as 'criminal'. It is only when, in turn, this 'new' working class becomes central to production, organised and socially recognised, that the root conflicts within which it dwells can be redefined as 'political' and eventually incorporated within the new structure of power. To a large degree, such process of politicisation is connected to the increasing weight and organisation of the new working class, which, through organising, becomes able to affirm its human and political dignity. On the contrary, the ability of the ruling class to define the main social conflicts as 'criminal' rather than 'political' is a sure sign of its hegemony – a hegemony, however, that is not only constructed ideologically through persuasion but is also deeply rooted in the 'reality' of social relationships.

In our view, David Garland's discussion about the emergence of 'crime' in contemporary societies, as well as the social reaction to such emergence, as facts of major concern in post-industrial societies, should be understood in this light (Garland 1996). In the same way in which a rhetoric of the 'public enemy' emerged in the United States around the time of the New Deal – the period, that is, which marked the first pioneering entry of organised labour into the establishment – so only today, with the coming to maturity of a 'respectable' and non- 'anti-system' Left in Italy and other European and Latin-American countries, the spectre of 'crime' (as opposed to that of 'political violence', whether from governmental or non-governmental agencies) is appearing in these societies for the first time as a matter of public concern.

First in North American societies, and only later in Europe, this process has unfolded together with the maturation of a democratic form of government that has put an end to very deep and divisive lacerations in civil society and has emphasised at the same time the need for social unification. 'Crime' becomes then the rallying cry for the reunification of society, as David Matza indicated in *Becoming Deviant* (1969): the 'outsiders' are not really any longer those 'antagonists' to power but a fragmented reality of marginalised, excluded outcasts: 'deviant', 'predators', 'suitable enemies' (Christie 1986).

In this sense, whether the rhetorical appeal is to punishment or to social prevention, these are simply (not indifferent) variations on the same motif, namely the reconstitution of a symbolic community. This is particularly the case in Europe today, where the root causes of crisis are multifarious: from the deep transformations in state sovereignty (Garland 1996) to the crisis of the welfare state, from the emergence of a *European* society to what Etienne Balibar (1991) has called 'identity panic', and the consequent rise and emergence of 'localities'/'regions'/'stateless nations' (Jauregui 1986; Melossi 1990, 1997). In other words, paradoxically, the very process of democratisation of European societies in conjunction with the end of the Cold War has facilitated the emergence of a common internal enemy, even if, as we will see, the enemy turns out to involve 'immigrants' – i.e. its 'internal' character remains controversial and negotiable. We will see the case of Italy in greater detail below. Similar reconstructions have, however, been presented for developments of the police in France (Monjardet 1999; Laurent 1999), on the transformations following Franco's death in Spain (Cid and Larrauri 1998), or on the current situation in Turkey (Green 2000) and in Northern Ireland (Mulcahy 1999).

The 'turn' of the 1970s: the Italian case

If that is the case we would like to develop, the emergence of 'crime' in recent Italian history as a central question of public debate took place in the midst of a crucial transition of Italian society from being strongly divided along class and political lines (or anyway so perceived and described by its members), to a society where the central sections of the working class became incorporated inside the established system of governance. From this perspective, a crucial protracted transition took place in the late 1960s to 1970s, when a number of social processes began to unfold. First, starting with the centre–Left coalitions in 1962, the role of the police slowly began to change from being a public order force engaged in the control and repression of the Left and the working class to a force that was more and more supposed to deal with 'ordinary' crime (Della Porta and Reiter 1994; Della Porta 1996; Reiter 1996). Between 1946 and 1962, 126 citizens and 12 police officers were killed in street clashes (D'Orsi 1972), without counting the peasants killed by landowners' organised gangs in the south in the period immediately after the end of the war. With the increasing force of the organised working-class and the Left starting to emerge in 1967–8, terrorisms of all colours, directions and sources came to occupy centre-stage and in a sense 'replaced' direct fights with the police as a source of politically motivated violence. The estimated number of victims of political violence between 1969 and 1988 was 428.

Second, crime (as represented in official statistics) increased dramatically, especially the kind that Garland has recently termed a 'criminality of the self', i.e. property crime (Barbagli 1995), as shown in Figure 8.1.

Third, socio-economic change brought 'to power' the organised working class but also at the same time brought its nemesis, 'post-Fordism' (decline of the factory, decline of work ethics, etc.). A general process of class fragmentation ensued that marked both a deep decline in the self-understanding of large sectors of the population as 'working class', and increasing symptoms of social disorganisation, especially among working-class youth (such as the sudden and huge creation of a drug culture and market after the mid-1970s).

Until recently, therefore, phenomena of fear and 'moral panic' have not been very relevant in the public field and the political agenda. In the second half of the 1970s and in the 1980s, elective institutions, public opinion and political parties directed their attention towards the Mafia – and related forms of organised

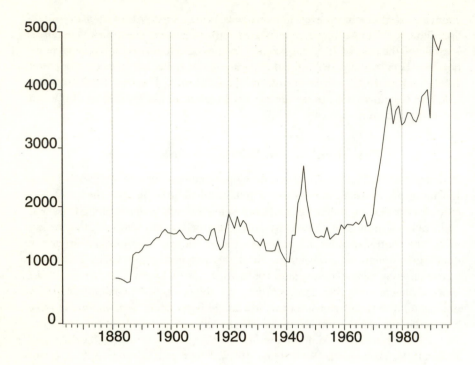

Figure 8.1 Felony rate, Italy 1863–1997 (per 100,000 inhabitants)

crime – and especially towards political terrorism. In both cases, there is no doubt that Italy experienced the outbreak of a widespread moral panic and the emergence of a law and order campaign, accompanied by strong law enforcement tendencies in criminal policy. In only a few cases, however, did Mafia activity and political terrorism give rise to a community-based reaction, except of course for the most politicised sectors of public opinion, especially within the Left. Even then, public opinion did not orient its requests towards more punishment, the death penalty, and so on. The alarm surrounding events of Mafia activity and terrorism did not extend to other less serious forms of crime, nor did it give rise to a widespread feeling of lack of safety, such as we are experiencing today. If one analyses the articles appearing in the journal that marked the appearance of a 'critical criminology' in Italy, *La Questione Criminale* (1975–81), one will find that topics of 'law and order' are very present – they are, however, never coupled with so-called 'common' crime but always with 'political repression'. It is true, on the one hand, that in post-war Italy murder and imprisonment rates are quite correlated (see Figure 8.2) (Melossi 1998), bringing one to hypothesise that the murders linked to organised crime and terrorism may have brought about a substantial social reaction. However, these murders were those of 'excellent cadavers', as Sicilians call them (Stille 1995) and, correspondingly, the following social reaction was much more one from the political and judicial elites than from the general public. In Italy there have been two strong increases in the recorded crime rate, the first in the 1960s and the second in the 1990s (Barbagli 1995; Colombo 1998) (see Figure 8.1). A rise in fear of crime and social alarm developed, however, only around the second of these, coinciding with a decrease in political and social participation (Pavarini 1994).

Research about fear of crime and concern about crime in Italy

In Italy, studies about fear and concern about crime, feelings of lack of safety and also victimisation have been conducted only recently, and in most cases they refer to sections of the country (regions, cities). We have therefore to rely upon a very fragmented type of research, that mainly concerns the last decade. But what seems to be quite incontrovertible, by all accounts, is the fact that, during the 1990s, demands for safety increased dramatically. This is apparent from forms of social reaction to crime and disorder such as, on the one hand, citizens' complaints to the mayors (Barbagli 1999) or to the police (Palidda 1998) and, on the other, the constitution of many community organisations which have become strongly visible, as we will see in a section below.

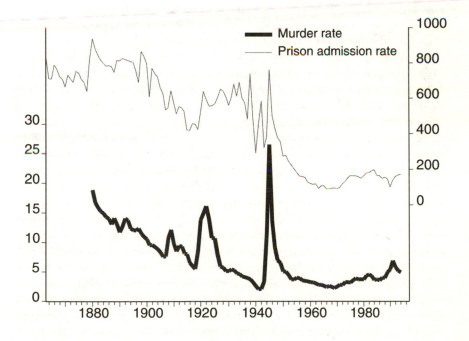

Figure 8.2 Murder rate versus prison admission rate, Italy, 1863–1997 (per 100,000 inhabitants)

As far as fear of crime is concerned, the most interesting results of the few studies conducted are about the kind of crimes which provoke fear and which are supposed to be pervasive in the place where the respondents live: thefts and robberies (52 per cent) followed by 'drugs' (28 per cent), and muggings (*scippi* – 18 per cent) (Doxa 1992). Similar data emerge from studies conducted at a local level. If we consider, in fact, the poll about fear of crime (termed 'Deviance, safety and public opinion') conducted by *Città sicure* each year since 1995 in Emilia–Romagna, we can see that 'ordinary' crime is what alarms the residents of this region the most (Mosconi 1998). In 1998, crime as a reason for personal fear was a matter of concern for 11 per cent of the respondents (6 per cent in 1995), preceded only by fear of illness and fear of losing one's job. If we consider instead what kind of crimes people living in Emilia–Romagna think may happen to them, these are home burglaries, muggings and thefts of vehicles, motorbikes and car radios. Fear of robberies involves about 6 per cent of the respondents, while fear of assaults is negligible.

The most recent – and also the most up-to-date and reliable – source of information about these issues is, however, the first national victimisation survey conducted, at the end of 1997, by the Italian National Institute of Statistics (ISTAT). The sample used in this research is quite substantial (50,000 families) and we can consider the results more reliable than any other information gathered until now. The study's authors come to the conclusion that 'also in our country, the feeling of lack of safety not only exists, but it has become a serious social phenomenon, the importance of which cannot be neglected' (Barbagli 1998: 50). In fact, 29 per cent of Italians say they feel unsafe walking alone at night in the area where they live (ISTAT 1999: 131). Furthermore, the experience of victimisation seriously affects fear of crime at a personal level: those who have been victims of muggings are more afraid of walking alone at night in their neighbourhoods than those who have not been victims of the same crime; the same relation exists for home burglary and fear at home at night.

A further result, which should be taken carefully into consideration, is the difference emerging between the typical victim of crime, and the typical individual who expresses feelings of lack of safety. Risk of victimisation generally, but above all for predatory crimes, is higher in the middle/upper classes, while fear of crime is more widespread among disadvantaged people (workers, unemployed and people with low education) (ISTAT 1999: 131). However, the survey points out also that what mainly affects fear of crime is the perceived presence of disorder in the area in which one lives: social disorder seems to be strictly related to fear of crime, and especially fear of crime outside the home (Barbagli 1998: 67). Related to this last point, a further aspect of safety issues in Italy is the kind of social group considered the main perpetrators of crime and disorder: the immigrants, and especially undocumented immigrants. These groups, sometimes together with urban and marginalised homeless, are frequently associated with forms of 'soft' crimes, such as the 'spectacle' of drugs, prostitution and various 'incivilities'. Their presence, even if in a few cases only, has given rise to strong conflicts and 'riots' with local residents (Petrillo 1995; Belluati 1998; Chiodi 1998). An almost irrelevant role is played instead – contrary to what happens in other contexts, such as France or the United Kingdom – by juvenile delinquency and, specifically, by violent behaviour of young people.

From a journal to a programme: the story of the 'Safe Cities' regional project

How did the political and institutional context react to the reality, and perception, of these phenomena? As we mentioned earlier, for a long time the safety issue did not enter political competition. The right-wing parties certainly included in their agenda concern for public order, but it was a concept unable to embrace the new forms of urban insecurity. In Italy it was the Left that undertook discussion about concern for safety. This was strongly connected to the emergence of the role of localities within a political and legal system ill equipped for federalism.[3]

In 1992, the Democratic Party of the Left (PDS) in Bologna decided to launch a magazine, promoted by researchers, academics, politicians and local administrators, called *Sicurezza e territorio* (*Safety and Territory*). It was through the pages of this journal that the concepts of safety and of a 'new' crime prevention policy developed and spread, at least in Northern Italy, but above all in the Regione Emilia–Romagna. In the first issue of the magazine we can find all the key-words of the new strategies to face crime and lack of safety, in a fashion similar to that spurred by so-called 'left realism' in the United Kingdom:[4] the need, for instance, to take crime and fear seriously; attention to victims; the search for communitarian mobilisation; the importance of the 'local' against the 'central'. From its very beginnings, matters of safety were strictly related to the aim of extending principles of autonomy for regions and cities *vis-à-vis* the central state, and they became part of a more general struggle for federalism. The then president of Regione Emilia–Romagna, interviewed about the role of regions and local authorities in promoting safety, stated:

> [the safety issues] are strictly and increasingly related to the new functions that Regions and Municipalities may assume in many fields, in the general framework of a federalist reform of the State, which gives pre-eminence to the role of the Regions.
>
> (Braccesi 1994: 5, interview with Pier Luigi Bersani)

These considerations, and more generally the development that safety policies have experienced in Italy, lead us to qualify Garland's concept of 'responsibilisation strategies'.[5] What is central in the Italian case is that the redistribution of competencies and responsibilities is strongly demanded by new actors (the local governments) that directly seek to play a role in criminal policies. Institutions which have never been involved in crime control strategy begin to struggle for the recognition of new fields of intervention, and the *central* state opposes and resists this tendency, so that safety issues become central not in the struggle between political parties, but in that between central and local government. This struggle has been facilitated by the fact that traditionally the Italian police forces, for the reasons mentioned above, have not played a very relevant role in ordinary crime prevention, and are not well equipped to face the new feelings of lack of safety in the twenty-first century.

In 1994, *Sicurezza e Territorio* ceased publication: the time was right for the move from a strategy of consciousness-raising of new actors to the implementation of local strategies for safety. In fact, the regional government of Emilia–Romagna, in that same year, started a programme called *Città sicure* ('Safe Cities'), specifically devoted to issues of urban safety.

Città sicure was the first Italian attempt to develop a general programme about urban safety and crime prevention, through research, promotional activities and co-ordination and elaboration of new strategies for reduction of fear and crime prevention. Before this, a few local authorities had developed similar projects, but they were not so ambitious and wide-ranging as *Città sicure* was in its origins.

In the guidelines of *Città sicure* (*Comitato scientifico di Città sicure* 1995), safety is considered one of the most important tasks of local governments, despite the fact that these institutions have no criminal policy jurisdiction whatsoever.[6] Even the local police force, which is a city institution and therefore responsible to the mayor, is allowed to intervene in crime control only when specifically so requested by the prefect (the local representative of central government), and only for the accomplishment of auxiliary tasks.

In relation to social policies, by contrast, local governments cover a large field of intervention, together with socio-sanitary institutions (the *ASL, Aziende sanitarie locali*).[7] Therefore, according to the principles of *Città sicure*, the place for safety policies is to be found partly in an already existing framework of competencies (which we could term *social* prevention) and partly in a new area of intervention for local authorities, in which the right to live safely is considered a public good akin to other citizens' rights, and the responsibility for which belongs with the local government (a better quality of life, a better environment, etc.). However, the conceptualisation of this new field of work remains uncertain, especially with respect to the difficulty of distinguishing between *safety* policies and *crime prevention*, and between *safety* and *public order*. The main actor in safety policies should be, according to *Città sicure*, the mayor, who, after the electoral reform of 1991, is now elected directly by the voters.

Other guidelines elaborated by the Scientific Committee of *Città sicure* recall directly some of the basic principles of 'left realism':[8] the need to take crime and feelings of lack of safety seriously; the importance of giving power and visibility to victims, a category of actors neglected by the legal system and very often constituted of disadvantaged people, the elderly, women; the importance of research, in a mixture of quantitative and qualitative investigations; the attention to differences among the needs and resources of women, men, immigrants, children, adults, etc.; and finally, the need for 'partnerships' among the various levels of government.

During the following years, the programme has been developing along these lines:[9]

- a great deal of research about crime and related social phenomena;
- a strong impulse towards projects managed directly by cities (in the region of Emilia–Romagna, as well as in other parts of the country, *Città sicure* has worked as a sort of consultant, through the scientific committee appointed by the presidency of the region);
- the programme also played a central role in stimulating the national public bodies (police, ministers, prefects) towards introducing the new vocabulary of safety and the new strategies of crime prevention in their everyday work;
- the training of new safety professionals (co-ordinators, mediators, etc.), of local and national police, and of social workers;
- the mobilisation of community participation in safety policies and crime prevention (as we shall see further below).

The Italian way to a 'new' prevention

Since 1994 – the year in which *Città sicure* was established – many Italian cities have been developing programmes to improve safety and to reduce crime and incivilities. Some of these programmes were inspired by the principles of integrating different preventive measures, and especially between social and situational prevention.

Starting from the provisions of the municipalities, social prevention occupies a relevant place in these programmes. It is rather difficult to distinguish between the new and the more traditional welfare measures. Some of the activities of the municipality in the field of social policy are now oriented towards the aim of safety, but the content of the measures does not diverge from rather traditional ones (e.g. professional training for young people 'at risk' and for people released from prison, shelters for battered women and for immigrants, harm-reduction programmes, etc.).

The measures of situational prevention adopted up to now need to be considered in a more detailed way, according to some of the categories developed in the literature (Clarke 1995; Berkmoes and Bourdoux 1986). We find a significant number of measures based on the intensification of formal control, but the agent of such control at the city level is, in Italy, above all the local police, who are becoming an important agent of formal control through various means: a widespread presence in some areas of the town, a stronger professionalisation in prevention tasks, a different organisation of work (for instance, presence at night, new services to victims, etc.). In most cases, as we will see, these activities go far beyond the formal competencies of the local police, thanks to an extension of the boundaries of some administrative tasks. The absence of national police also gives a different feature to the organisation of new forms of informal control. This is managed by local police or by the municipality, and is oriented much more towards a general environmental management than towards control of deviant or criminal behaviours. So, community organisations become engaged – through agreements with the municipalities – in the renewal of parks, revitalisation of public spaces, and a wide variety of other activities. In fact, an orientation which is emerging in Italian prevention programmes is conservative urban renewal, in order to face the decline and disorder of some areas of the cities.[10] It would be difficult, however, to classify these activities as forms of situational prevention, for in most cases they are not directed towards defensive aims, but towards making the neighbourhood a safer place by means of ameliorating the physical environment and the feeling of belonging in the area. These activities are much better seen as forms of community crime prevention.

There is one further dimension of situational prevention in Italy which is worthy of note and which is represented by the approach based on using administrative orders for deterrent purposes. Once again, we are faced with a distortion caused by the lack of partnership with the national agencies strictly responsible for compliance and crime reduction. In the Italian context, the ambiguous overlapping of prevention and dissuasion which often characterises these new strategies of crime control (Hebberecht and Sack 1997: 20; Roché 1999) means that local authorities transfer the dissuasive powers and instruments they have in other fields (for instance, 'public hygiene') into safety policies. Local authorities have the power to control people, to close businesses, to keep some activities under control, but only for reasons unrelated to 'public order' and without the possibility of criminal enforcement. Under the pressure of the public, more and more frequently the mayors of many Italian cities have both asked for more repressive forms of intervention from the state and the police (Pavarini 1998: 25), and tried to apply their own administrative instruments to different ends.

An example of this tendency has been the so-called *ordinanze anti-prostituzione* (anti-prostitution ordinances) adopted in many Italian cities during the summer of 1998. By means of these administrative orders, we have experienced a substantial intervention of local police against street prostitution. These ordinances are grounded not in criminal law powers but in administrative ones. The rules that are applied are those pertaining to traffic, the risk they are ostensibly directed to avert is the risk of traffic accidents. More precisely, these ordinances forbid drivers from stopping their vehicles at specifically designated curbsides, but the obvious purpose is one of removing prostitution from some areas and some streets of the city, to re-establish order, to reassure the citizens.

Prostitution is not the only problem that municipalities try to solve with administrative ordinances: we also find cases in which the intervention of the mayor defines as a problem of 'hygiene' one which is instead perceived by local citizens as an issue of safety or disorder, for instance in the case of empty dwellings occupied by undocumented immigrants.

The tendency towards the use (or misuse) of administrative instruments is not only increasing but also creates a sort of vicious circle, giving the public the impression that the mayor *can* actually do something and so reinforcing the demand for safety and the growing responsibilisation of local authorities for crime problems.

The multi-agency approach: 'partnerships' and 'protocols'

Even if all the projects about safety recall the need of a multi-agency approach, for a long period central governments have disregarded the efforts of local authorities to involve them in safety policies. We find a first acknowledgement of this emerging issue only in 1997, when the prime minister of the period, Romano Prodi, speaking at a conference organised by *Città sicure* in Bologna, admitted that 'the problem of the safety of the country seems to be no longer one of *external* safety, but an *internal* one: the safety of citizens in their everyday life' (Prodi 1997). The issue of safety, in political discourse as well as in the political agenda, came to the forefront for the first time at the beginning of 1999, when a series of homicides and other violent crimes committed in Milan in the space of a few days provoked, for the very first time, the keen interest of the media, the central government and penal agencies. After these events, a group for the study of safety problems – including representatives of central and local authorities – was set up inside the Italian Ministry of the Interior. This was the first example of a partnership between local and central levels.

At a local level, committees were created in which mayors maintain a leading role and in which prefectures, police forces and the judiciary are regularly invited in order to supervise safety projects. The presence of these agencies, however, remained quite formal and rarely acquired the quality of an actual shared responsibility for action. The consequence of such lack of partnership during the past years has been that, on the one hand, the role of co-ordination has been undertaken by a regional government (once again, *Città sicure*) and by an association of cities, the Italian section of the European Forum for Urban Safety; on the other hand, the absence of the police and the judiciary has meant that the safety projects elaborated by many Italian cities have been strictly limited only to the kind of measures local administrations can undertake.

Quite recently, however, things have started to change. The 'protocols'[11] signed by municipalities and prefectures represented, in fact, the first attempt to give rise to and formalise forms of partnership between local and central governments. The first protocol was stipulated in Modena, once again a city from Emilia–Romagna traditionally administered by the Left, in February 1998. At the end of the same year, thirty-eight cities had followed Modena's example. In almost all cases, the municipalities were the ones to initiate the procedure for co-operation, once again confirming their central role in launching the issue of safety policies. What is important to point out is the fact that protocols are used in pursuit of many different goals. First of all, they are adopted with an aim of compelling agencies of the central government to collaborate in local projects managed by municipalities. However, the need for partnership does not respond only to the principle of a multi-agency approach. It depends also on the fact that, in the last few years, mayors have become the most important point of reference for many complaints and demands by citizens in the field of safety, and some of these complaints concern matters in which municipalities have no competencies. The protocols, then, meet both the requirements of collaboration (especially with respect to the exchange of data and information about crime problems at a local level) and the need for a distribution of responsibilities between different agencies. Ironically, however, such protocols often restate the traditional boundaries between prevention and crime control, i.e. between localities and the central government. Given that it was just those boundaries that local institutions were trying to blur in the first period of their activity, protocols therefore represent also a retrenchment in the attempt of local administrations to acquire a larger autonomy in the field of criminal policies. Under the growing pressure of public opinion and the media about 'sky-rocketing crime', many mayors reacted by abandoning the struggle for more incisive powers, and found it politically expedient to go back to a reaffirmation of the traditional framework of competencies and functions.

Until now, there has been no evaluation of the efficacy of these agreements. There is, however, a tendency to make the agreements more binding, on the model of the French 'contracts for safety', a choice strongly supported by the municipalities and by the Italian section of the European Forum (without considering that, in the French case, contractualising the relationships among institutions represented a point of arrival and not of departure, as in the Italian case).

Citizens' committees

So-called *comitati di cittadini* (citizens' committees) have appeared, especially in those areas undergoing deep change in terms of urban renewal and socio-economic development.[12] Inner cities, the old working-class neighbourhoods and the new middle-class suburbs are the areas in which this kind of reaction to crime seems to emerge most frequently. This is especially true for Emilia–Romagna (Selmini 1997), but similar outcomes emerge also from other studies in Milan (A.A.S.TER 1997), Turin (Ires 1995), and Genoa (Petrillo 1995). For inner cities, the major problems are decline, poverty and disorder; for traditional working-class districts, the lack of security perceived with the arrival of immigrants and the consequent difficulty in working towards new common ways of life; for new suburbs, problems usually related to transport and services.

The groups born in working-class neighbourhoods are the most widespread and active. Retired workers, former trade unionists and other persons already familiar with social and political participation often lead them. This feature is more evident in the cities of Emilia–Romagna, but similar elements appear also in Milan (A.A.S.TER 1997) and in Turin (Belluati 1998), while the community organisations studied by Petrillo (1995) in Genoa are mainly characterised by an apolitical orientation. Especially in traditional working-class areas in the north, the community organisations active 'against' crime generally belong to the cultural and political field of the Left[13] and frequently they seem to privilege the discourse of rights and social justice rather than that of defensiveness and victimisation (Della Porta 1996: 334; Selmini 1997).

The attention of these 'communitarian groups' focuses in particular on crime and deviance among recent immigrant groups and their visibility in the everyday life of the neighbourhood. At the core of the problem there no longer seems to be simply a threat to one's property or personal safety, but rather a generalised risk for the whole society, for an idea of order – of *democratic* order, as one of the leaders of a committee in Modena, who had been active in the anti-Fascist Resistance, points out:

> The problem isn't just that they try to push drugs to our boys and girls. It's also the way they behave in public places … The Municipality had to take away the park benches because they used to deface them. They don't use the bins, they just throw everything on the floor, and I think that this shows contempt for everything we've done to make this town nicer to live in.
>
> (Selmini 1997: 82)

These words are no different from those expressed by a component of another group in the same town, less committed to left-leaning positions:

> 'And then there was all the nuisance caused by the pushers; they used to make a real mess in the park; they usually ate here in the park, and they left all the left-overs and rubbish around here'
>
> (Chiodi 1998: 217).

With reference to street prostitutes (usually, in these areas, Nigerian women), one person interviewed (an activist of the 'left wing' of a Catholic party) expressed herself in these words:

> In this part of town we are used to seeing prostitutes. This is a traditional place for prostitution. But once it was different. Now, there are so many girls on the street, and above all, they wash themselves on the road, in the puddles. I ask myself: where is human dignity?
>
> (Selmini 1997: 82)

We can see here how the discourse is not so much about crime but seems to be about disorder, incivilities and, finally, an anxiety about lack of safety related more to a newly perceived distance from local institutions than to the presence of 'crime' as such – almost the feeling of being 'abandoned' by local institutions that have traditionally been 'the people's' institutions, 'our' institutions. The rules of the democratic order are those built during and after the Second World War, starting with the anti-Fascist Resistance:

> We built this town. I remember, we – some friends of mine and I – drained a marsh and made a road, nearby. And we worked for nothing. We wanted to do something for our town, and many of us had this spirit, after the Second World War, when the towns were destroyed ... And now, what we have done is despised.
>
> (Selmini 1997: 83)

> We want the town to come back to the period of the great Mayors after the Resistance period ... We made a lot of sacrifices for the community, to reconstruct the towns ... and now ...
>
> (Selmini 1997: 83)

A great nostalgia pervades the stories told by these leaders: nostalgia for one's town – as it once was – for a sense of community, especially a political community, which seems to have disappeared, for the hegemonic role these citizens once played in the political and social life of their city, and also regret for local institutions, that used to be *their* institutions, but which are now perceived as more and more distant from the citizen.

The fast and deep change in the social and economic structure of some cities and districts, the de-industrialisation of those same areas, the crisis of a 'work ethic' and of work as a means to promote social progress and personal dignity, the disappearance of traditional urban social networks – often related to political participation – and the consequent fragmentation of social identities (Belluati 1998; Martinotti 1993), all of this has created a context in which new images of disorder tend to emerge, often related to the presence of immigrants and, more rarely, of groups of young homeless (who, rather than being regarded as committing crime, are considered responsible for a new 'decay' in the city, and are perceived as opposite to the values and ideals of the former working class).

As Milena Chiodi's research on the specific case of a Modena neighbourhood clearly points out (Chiodi 1998: 241–5) immigrants are *visible*, they are perceived as not used to the rule of democratic participation (nor to the rules of illegal activities, as we have seen); they tend to concentrate in the more vulnerable areas of the city, and where communities are in search of a new identity. Such 'new identities' may be found, however, as in the case studied by Chiodi, in organising the neighbourhood against the immigrants. In the words of the citizens interviewed, they have been able to build a 'renewed unity' in their struggle to 'clean' their neighbourhood of the unwanted guests. Erickson or Matza could not have expressed the matter more clearly: the social cohesion of the Crocetta neighbourhood in Modena was at least temporarily strengthened by the unity of intent and action against North African dealers. This episode is revealing of the contradictions and ambiguities of the processes and feelings involved. A sense of democratic participation mixes with one of parochialism, the old faith in 'the unity of the working class' with outright exclusion and racism. The traditional Left institutions and values seem to be unable to orient and direct the course of events and, in some respects, even the pioneering role of initiatives such as *Città sicure* may appear as having played more the role of 'sorcerer's apprentice' than that of 'Leninist vanguard of the working class'. And in fact, in some cases, when citizen and community organisations' claims have not been catered to, the backlash for this lack of attention has been significant, as in the recent clamorous electoral defeat of the Left in Bologna in 1999, a city that the Left had administrated uninterruptedly since the end of the war (Barbagli 1999).

In concluding this – very sketchy – framework of communitarian reaction to crime and disorder, we have to ask ourselves, therefore, as the literature also reminds us (Nelken 1985; Crawford 1997), is crime or disorder the right means to (re)construct community? Is crime – or disorder – the way to re-establish a link between the Left parties and their grassroots element? These are questions which local institutions and political parties are not able to answer, or worse yet, which, in most cases, they disregard.

In conclusion: microphysics of crime

In former Prime Minister Romano Prodi's words, cited above, 'the problem of the safety of the country seems to be no longer one of *external* safety, but an *internal* one: the safety of citizens in their everyday life' (Prodi 1997). In the still relatively new post-Cold War era, safety is no longer a matter for external security – and, for a concept of internal security as 'public order', an internal reflection of international divisions, as it had been until the 1980s. Crime, and criminals, are 'our' *common* enemy – even better if they can be described as products of a common new 'external' enemy, a 'fifth column' in our midst, the 'undesirable', 'undocumented', 'clandestine' immigrants. 'Coloured' and 'immigrant' sections of the population are already in many countries the core of a new working class. In the most developed cities of Emilia–Romagna, this is already the case in many factories. Thanks to the 'tough' jobs that Italians are unwilling to devote themselves to, in some factories of the town of Reggio Emilia, for instance, nine out of ten workers were not born in Italy. In such cities, the offspring of immigrant and mixed marriages are already one in ten, in a country where only 2 per cent of the population is foreign. It is not difficult to foresee that here, too, very soon the 'foreign' work-force will represent a very substantial section of the 'Italian' working class, in exactly the same way that this happened to Italians in the United States, or Belgium, or Germany. And in the same way in which Italians had to struggle bitterly with prejudice and stereotypes that would link them to images of 'the Mafia' and 'organised crime', so the new immigrants to Italy will have to do the same for the kind of crime and deviance they are associated with. Also in this case, their quantitative and political growth, their capacity to organise and earn human and social dignity in their own eyes and in the eyes of the *other* Italians, will in the end win the day.

At the same time, the lights and shadows of the transposition of the formal social control scenario from that of the centralised state to regions and localities appear now quite clearly. In fact, the old centralised 'state' system was one geared to struggle against forms of *organised* crime, whether criminal or politic, a type of 'crime', or simply of opposition, that as such had to be countered at the national level because it was directed against the very 'core' of the state,[14] within a bitterly divided polity. The current situation is very different. So-called *micro-criminalità*, as Italian media call street crime, maybe unwittingly echoing Michel Foucault's 'microphysics of power',[15] is very remote from the 'grand narrative' of the state: it has to do instead with the very local, mundane, everyday-life, routine series of petty thefts, muggings, burglaries, drug dealing, street-walking, that takes place side by side with the places where 'respectable' citizens live and work. The instruments to counter *microcriminalità* can hardly be, then, the majestic ones of the state – even if governments as well as national police forces have a hard time in coming to deal with such undesired reduction of their 'aura'.

In the Italian context, *Città sicure* pointed the way of these developments. As always with pioneering experiences, the lights and shadows will be clearer to those who are going to write its history than to those who have led the way.

References

A.A.S.TER (1997) 'Dalla comunità rinserrata alla comunità possibile', *Metronomie*, 10: 1–35.

Anderson, Nels (1923) *The Hobo*, Chicago: University of Chicago Press.

Balibar, Etienne (1991) '*Es gibt keinen Staat in Europa*: razzismo e politica nell'Europa d'oggi', pp. 117–37 in E. Balibar, *Le frontiere della democrazia*, Roma: Manifestolibri.

Barbagli, Marzio (1995) *L'occasione e l'uomo ladro. Furti e rapine in Italia*, Bologna: Il Mulino.

——(1998) 'Reati, vittime, insicurezza dei cittadini', paper presented at the seminar 'La sicurezza dei cittadini', ISTAT, Rome, 22 September, unpublished.

——(ed.) (1999) *Egregio signor sindaco. Lettere dei cittadini e risposte delle istituzioni sui problemi della sicurezza*, Bologna: Il Mulino.

Belluati, Marinella (1998) 'Un quartiere in protesta. Il caso San Salvario tra rappresentazioni sociali e immagini mediali', doctoral thesis, University of Milan, unpublished.

Berkmoes, Henri and Bourdoux, G.L. (1986) 'La prevention de la criminalité', *Revue de droit penal et de criminologie*, 8/9/10: 733–82.

Braccesi, Cosimo (1994) 'La politica regionale dell'Emilia–Romagna in tema di sicurezza' (interview with Pier Luigi Bersani), *Sicurezza e Territorio*, 15: 5–10.

——(1997) 'Il progetto, i riferimenti, le attività', *Quaderni di Città sicure*, 10.

Cardia, Clara (1998) *Vitalità e sicurezza in zona 17*, Milano: Comune di Milano.

Chevalier, Louis (1973) *Labouring Classes and Dangerous Classes*, London: Routledge.

Chiodi, Milena (1998) 'Immigrazione, devianza e percezione di insicurezza: analisi del caso modenese (quartiere La Crocetta)', Laurea thesis, Faculty of Law, University of Bologna, unpublished.

Christie, Nils (1986) 'Suitable enemy', in H. Bianchi and R. van Swaaningen (eds) *Abolitionism: Toward a Non-Repressive Approach to Crime*, Amsterdam: Free University Press.

Cid, José and Larrauri, Elena (1998) 'Prisons and alternatives to prison in Spain', pp. 146–55 in V. Ruggiero, N. South and I. Taylor (eds) *The New European Criminology: Crime and Social Order in Europe*, London: Routledge.

Clarke, Ronald V. (1995) 'Situational crime prevention', in M. Tonry and D. Farrington (eds) *Building a Safer Society. Strategic Approaches to Crime Prevention, Crime and Justice 19*: 151–236 Chicago: University of Chicago Press,.

Colombo, Asher (1998) 'Il profilo statistico della criminalità', *La sicurezza in Emilia–Romagna, Quaderni di Città sicure*, 14a: 35–96.

Comitato Scientifico di 'Città sicure' (1995) 'Il Comitato scientifico raccomanda al governo della Regione Emilia–Romagna', *Quaderni di Città sicure*, 2: 175–9.

Crawford, Adam (1997) *The Local Governance of Crime. Appeals to Community and Crime Prevention*, Oxford: Clarendon Press.

Della Porta, Donatella (1996) 'Polizia e ordine pubblico', *Polis*, 10: 333–6.

Della Porta, Donatella and Reiter, Herbert (1994) 'Da "polizia del governo" a "polizia dei cittadini"? Le politiche dell'ordine pubblico in Italia', *Stato e mercato*, 48: 433–65.

D'Orsi, Angelo (1972) *Il potere repressivo: la polizia*, Milano: Feltrinelli.

Doxa (1992) 'La percezione della delinquenza', *Bollettino della Doxa*, 19–20.

Durkheim, Emile (1893) *The Division of Labor in Society*, New York: The Free Press (this edition 1964).

——(1895) *The Rules of Sociological Method*, New York: The Free Press (this edition 1938).

Erikson, Kai (1966) *Wayward Puritans*, New York: John Wiley.

Ferracuti, Franco (1968) 'European migration and crime', pp. 189–219 in M.E. Wolfgang (ed.) *Crime and Culture. Essays in Honour of Thorsten Sellin*, New York: Wiley.

Foucault, Michel (1975) *Discipline and Punish*, New York: Pantheon (this edition 1977).

——(1977) *Microfisica del potere*, Torino: Einaudi.

Garland, David (1996) 'The limits of the sovereign state: strategies of crime control in contemporary society', *British Journal of Criminology*, 36: 445–71.

Green, Penny (2000) 'Crime control without criminal justice: the case of Turkey', in A. Rutherford and P. Green (eds) *Criminal Policy in Transition*, Oxford: Hart.

Hebberecht, Patrick and Sack, Fritz (eds) (1997) *La prévention de la délinquance en Europe. Nouvelles strategies*, Paris: L'Harmattan.

Ires (1995) 'Un caso al microscopio: conflitti e prospettive in un quartiere urbano', pp. 299–316 in M. Maggi (ed.) *Relazione annuale sulla situazione socio-economica del Piemonte*, Torino: Rosenberg and Sellier.

ISTAT (1999) *La sicurezza dei cittadini. Reati, vittime, percezione della sicurezza e sistemi di protezione*, ISTAT: Roma.

Jauregui, Gurutz J. (1986) *Decline of the Nation-State*, Reno: University of Nevada Press (this edition 1994).

Laurent, Vincent (1999) 'Les renseignements généraux à la découverte des quartiers', *Le Monde diplomatique*, 541: 26–7.

Marshall, Ineke H. (ed.) (1997) *Minorities, Migrants, and Crime*, London: Sage.

Martinotti, Guido (1993) *Metropoli. La nuova morfologia sociale della città*, Bologna: Il Mulino.

Marx, Karl (1867) *Capital, vol. 1*, New York: International Publishers (this edition 1970).

Matza, David (1969) *Becoming Deviant*, Englewood Cliffs, NJ: Prentice-Hall.

Melossi, Dario (1990) *The State of Social Control: A Sociological Study of Concepts of State and Social Control in the Making of Democracy*, Cambridge: Polity Press.

——(1997) 'State and social control à la fin du siècle: from the New World to the constitution of the New Europe', pp. 52–74 in R. Bergalli and C. Sumner (eds) *Social Control and Political Order: European Perspectives at the End of the Century*, London: Sage.

——(1998) 'Omicidi, economia e tassi di incarcerazione in Italia dall'Unità ad oggi', *Polis*, 12: 415–35.

——(2000) 'Changing representations of the criminal', *British Journal of Criminology*, 40: 296–320.

Melossi, Dario and Pavarini, Massimo (1977) *The Prison and the Factory: Origins of the Penitentiary System*, London: Macmillan (this edition 1981).

Monjardet, Dominique (1999) 'Réinventer la police urbaine', *Les Annales de la recherche urbaine*, 83/84: 15–22.

Mosconi, Giuseppe (1998) 'Devianza, sicurezza e opinione pubblica', *Quaderni di Città sicure*, 14a: 97–139.

Mulcahy, Aogan (1999) 'Visions of normality: peace and the reconstruction of policing in Northern Ireland', *Social and Legal Studies*, 8: 277–95.

Nelken, David (1985) 'Community involvement in crime control', *Current Legal Problems*, 239–67.

Palidda, Salvatore (1998) 'Domanda di sicurezza e forze di polizia nei capoluoghi emiliano–romagnoli', *La sicurezza nelle città. Quaderni di Città sicure*, 14a: 185–219.

Pavarini, Massimo (1994) 'Bisogni di sicurezza e questione criminale', *Rassegna italiana di criminologia*, 5: 435–62.

——(1998) 'Introduzione', *La sicurezza nelle città. Quaderni di Città sicure*, 14a: 11–31.

Petrillo, Antonello (1995) 'Insicurezza, migrazioni, cittadinanza', doctoral thesis, Faculty of Political Sciences, University of Bologna, unpublished.

Pitch, Tamar (1986) 'Viaggio attorno alla "criminologia": discutendo con i realisti', *Dei delitti e delle pene*, 4: 469–88.

Prodi, Romano (1997) Speech at the seminar 'La sicurezza in Emilia–Romagna', unpublished.

Putnam, Robert D. (1993) *Making Democracy Work: Civic Traditions in Modern Italy*, Princeton: Princeton University Press.

Reiter, Herbert (1996) 'Le forze di polizia e l'ordine pubblico in Italia', *Polis*, 10: 337–60.

Roché, Sebastian (1999) 'Le nuove tematiche della criminalità e della sua prevenzione in Francia', *Polis*, 13: 99–120.

Salvatore, Ricardo D. and Aguirre, Carlos (eds) (1996) *The Birth of the Penitentiary in Latin America: Essays on Criminology, Prison Reform, and Social Control, 1830–1940*, Austin: University of Texas Press.

Selmini, Rossella (1997) 'Il punto di vista dei comitati di cittadini', *Quaderni di Città sicure*, 11a: 77–94.

Skogan, Wesley G. (1988) 'Community organizations and crime', *Crime and Justice*, 10: 39–78.

Stille, Alexander (1995) *Excellent Cadavers*, London: Vintage.

Teti, Vito (1993) *La razza maledetta: origini del pregiudizio antimeridionale*, Roma: Manifestolibri.

Tonry, Michael (ed.) (1997) *Ethnicity, Crime, and Immigration: Comparative and Cross-National Perspectives*, Chicago: University of Chicago Press.

Wilson, William J. (1987) *The Truly Disadvantaged: The Inner City, the Underclass and Public Policy*, Chicago: University of Chicago Press.

Young, Jock (1986) 'Il fallimento della criminologia: per un realismo radicale', *Dei delitti e delle pene*, 4: 387–415.

9

CRIMINAL VICTIMISATION AND SOCIAL ADAPTATION IN MODERNITY

Fear of crime and risk perception in the new Germany

Uwe Ewald

Individual behaviour, social control and fear of crime in late modernity

It is a commonplace that 'the crime problem' and 'fear of crime' have become issues of major concern in almost every sphere and discourse of modern societies: 'Scarcely a day passes that we are not hit anew with penetrating stories of criminal victimisation' (Ferraro 1995: 1). This holds true particularly for Germany after the fall of the Berlin Wall and the collapse of the eastern bloc. For Germany, the transformations of late modernity are characterised by a unique conjunction; namely, an overlapping of the general process of transition in late (western) modernity with the upheaval of state socialism in the former German Democratic Republic (GDR), and its ramifications for a new unified Germany. Naturally, there are different views about the development of crime in Germany but it is only a little simplification to describe the mainstream discourse in criminology and victimology as an echo of the sensationalist public presentation in politics and mass media.

Even those perspectives which do not support the notion of a 'crime explosion' remain uncritical of the traditional conceptualisation of victimisation implicit in the sensationalism apparent during the time of unification. They remain within the limited theoretical framework linking 'fear' and 'crime' as it was developed in conventional 'positivist victimology' during the 1960s and 1970s (see, for critical perspectives, Fattah 1993: 45–63; Mawby and Walklate 1994: 7–9). In contrast, theoretical attempts to conceptualise criminal victimisation in the context of general social development in late modern societies are at an early stage. Nevertheless, they have started to open a new debate about the meaning of victimisation and fear of crime in Germany (Albrecht and Howe 1992; Thome 1992; Heitmeyer 1995; Bilsky 1996a, 1996b, 1997; Boers 1997;

Eisner 1997; Kerner 1997; Sack 1997; Kräupl, 1998; Scherr 1998; Reuband 1993, 1994, 1996, 1999). A particular discourse deals with developments in former eastern bloc countries (see e.g. Ewald 1994, 1997; Sessar and Holler 1997). As part of this debate, this chapter tries to explain criminal victimisation and fear of crime in the course of modernisation and of radically changing social relationships.

The realist perspective on crime – which constructs a *square of crime* consisting of the victim and the offender on the one side, and formal and informal control on the other (Young 1992: 48) – is helpful in understanding ongoing changes in victimisation discourses (see Young and Rush 1994: 156–7). The remainder of this chapter outlines the idea that there has been a shift in the relationship between the four corners of the square of crime. While there was once an emphasis on the relationship between the offender, the state and formal control, there is now an increasing emphasis on the response of state control to victims' requests for safety – which Cohen (1994: 67) calls 'the punitive style'. This shift has been accompanied by a change in the importance of the victim in the discourse about crime: 'We're all victims, OK! ... [Our] belonging comes not from the fact that we are all criminals ... but rather, that we are all victims ... To be a victim is to be a citizen' (Young and Rush 1994: 159). This also means a change in the goal of formal control. The object of social control is now 'the population rather than the individual', a move which is to be explained in the context of the *risk society*: 'Instead of altering individual behaviour, actuarial, surveillance and compliance regimes alter the physical and social structure in which individuals behave' (Cohen 1994: 73). Yet all the changes described in the relationships between victimiser and victim, crime and fear of crime – as well as between social control and the adaptation of behaviour in response to perceived personal risk – cannot be explained ultimately by the 'square of crime'. They must also be contextualised in the wider processes of social change and emerging new forms of risk management.

The basic institutions of modernity, which came into being at the beginning of the twentieth century, are changing rapidly in a way that is similar to the disintegration and dissolution of traditional institutions which occurred at the inception of modern industrialised society. As Burgess and Park stated earlier last century:

> We are living in such a period of individualisation and social disorgani-sation. Everything is in a state of agitation – everything seems to be undergoing change. Society is, apparently, not much more than a congeries and constellation of social atoms.
>
> (Park and Burgess 1967: 107)

This held true also for the system of social control, and of criminalisation by the criminal justice system, which was intended to secure the conformity of mass behaviour in the second half of the twentieth century (Cohen 1994: 67–71; Young and Rush 1994: 154–9; Feeley and Simon 1994: 173–7).

Yet how should we nowadays ensure behavioural conformity in a world of dissolving values and a loss of visions and stable, positive orientations? The immediate and pragmatic answer seems to be 'more of the same' – that is, to extend the use of traditional means of 'law and order' in reaction to social conflicts. Thus, the criminal justice system is promoted as an effective tool for controlling and reducing certain threats and risks in society. Yet, in the process, the 'positive orientations' of modern society – and the values which are attractive to individuals to fulfil their general needs and hopes – fade away, becoming replaced by 'negative orientations' which are represented as threats. For example, Rorty describes a loss of 'metaphysical belief' in something universally valid for human beings (Rorty 1989: 148) and therefore a loss of social hope. Metaphysical values like 'nation', 'God', 'historical mission' are no longer compelling. Instead, the common ground which is shared by all people is a capacity to suffer (Rorty 1989: 286). That is why traditional forms of social control, and in particular the criminal justice system, seem so effective: because they are based on fear and suffering. This manifests itself not only in the ways in which the criminal justice system gains its legitimisation from 'existing' suffering (which it promises to reduce) but also in the way it uses suffering and repression to educate individuals and attain conformity.

Even so, there is a considerable imbalance between those perspectives which see crime as a *threat* – to be addressed by a system of law and criminal justice – and those which see crime as a *challenge* for a new system of risk management. This could be symptomatic of a process of radical social change where uncertainty and insecurity is accompanied by lack of new means (risk management) to control the society and therefore a strong belief in the functioning of traditional but old-fashioned social techniques (punitive system of crime control) still exists. From a perspective which sees modern societies as 'risk societies' (Giddens 1994; Adams 1995; Beck 1986, 1998; Franklin 1998), crime should not be seen only as an 'evil' to be condemned and prosecuted. Such a view obstructs the hidden – and possibly new – meaning of criminal victimisation and fear of crime in late modernity. That is, that criminal victimisation and the related issue of fear of crime can obtain an ambivalent *productive role*: first, in helping individuals to adapt to the continual process of change in a globalising world; and second, in opening a dialogue on changes in social control in general, and crime control in particular, where social discipline and exclusion are losing their central meaning. At any rate, it is argued, discourse about crime and victimisation is part of a process of adaptation to a radically changing world.

While crime – particularly personal crime – is traditionally portrayed as something only 'evil' and dangerous to individuals (in terms of personal disturbance, threat and personal injury), this chapter raises the questions of why and how criminal violence obtains a productive role – mediated by anxiety and fear – in maintaining traditional forms of social control and appropriate adaptations of behaviour. It asks further whether criminal violence could be used as a resource for developing a new understanding of risk management in a changing modern society. To develop this idea I will pursue two major lines of enquiry:

- What do we know about crime, criminal violence and the perception of fear and risk regarding crime in a changing modern society?
- How can we explain the meaning of criminal victimisation in the context of controlling a changing modern society by means of ensuring that individuals' behaviour adapts to conformity?

These questions will be discussed in the context of German unification, and especially pay attention to the specific situation in the five New Federal States (the former state socialist German Democratic Republic). While the theoretical ideas and interpretation refer to 'changing modern societies' in general, the empirical findings are mostly related to the eastern part of Germany.

Fear of crime – questionable concepts?

The discourse on criminal victimisation and related issues like fear and risk of crime is presented in a vast amount of literature (Bilsky *et al.* 1993; Box *et al.* 1988; Hale 1996). This holds true also for Germany since the end of the 1980s, coincidentally also the period following the decay of state socialism in East Germany. A victimological discourse based on many empirical studies developed in Germany after 1989, stimulated by the radical changes in former eastern bloc countries (Kury 1992; Kury *et al.* 1992; Kreuzer *et al.* 1993; Bilsky *et al.* 1993; Boers *et al.* 1994; Neubacher 1994; Mischkowitz 1994; Kaiser and Jehle 1994, 1995; Noll and Schröder, 1995; Shelley and Vigh 1995; Wetzels *et al.* 1995; Pfeiffer and Greve 1996; Trotha 1996; Greve *et al.* 1996; Boers *et al.* 1997; Ewald 1997; Sessar and Holler 1997; Wetzels 1997). Victimological concepts used in the German context were adapted from American victimology (Boers 1991; Kury *et al.* 1992; Bilsky *et al.* 1993) without substantial changes except for some minor modifications with regard to the German situation. Aside from a few methodological modifications – e.g. using facet theory (Bilsky 1997) – the basic aim of this research was to find the *level* of the *fear of crime*, how it was distributed among the national domestic population, and to explain the relationship between the threat from crime and its associated fear.

Nevertheless, in the absence of any noticeable critical distance from the American model, Fattah's general assessment holds true for Germany as well: 'Most of the studies treat "fear of crime" as if it were self-explanatory' (Fattah 1993: 45). For example, Boers assumes (Boers 1997: 299) that the reasons for the increase of fear of crime in transitional former eastern bloc societies are much the same as those which were discussed in the 1960s and 1970s with regard to the USA, Western Europe and West Germany. According to Boers there are three levels of explanation:

- at the *micro level*, there is the *victim perspective*, which explains fear of crime as the result of personal criminal victimisation;
- at the *meso level*, there is the *social control perspective*, which interprets fear of crime as the consequence of a loss of informal social control;
- at the *macro level*, there is the *social problem perspective*, where fear of crime appears as a result of a dramatisation of disorder and insecurity, using crime as metaphor for social threats in general (Boers 1997: 299–301).

Surprisingly, even though Boers attempts a post-modern interpretation, there seems little difference from earlier ones. Also, it is clear that stable empirical evidence cannot be found in transitional Germany for any of these 'perspectives' (Boers 1991; Kury 1992). Yet there is a paradox here: on the one hand, these perspectives are considered to be 'serious' and 'important' since, as Boers assumes, they present 'orientations of criminal politics' (Boers 1997: 300–1); yet, on the other hand, the three perspectives obviously lack theoretical substance (Fattah 1993: 46) and empirical support. Without going back to their point of departure and questioning their traditional victimological conceptualisation, these perspectives merely echo the conventional political discourse on fear of crime, despite their so-called 'critical' posture and their protagonists' warnings not to dramatise the crime problem (Noll and Schröder 1995; Habich *et al.* 1999; Reuband 1999). So far, then, it is simply part of the same political rhetoric used to explain and justify the given mode of governing as the response to the 'insecurity' caused by crime.

At the core of this rhetoric is the construct of 'evil' in the shape of criminality. This is used to gain political consent (see below). As Robins and Post in their book *Political Paranoia: The Psychopolitics of Hatred* put it, 'the paranoid dynamic is always present, even in stable, democratic, and humane societies; it is part of the human condition' (Robins and Post 1997: 3) – a condition which Safranski describes (on the basis of an historical analysis of philosophy) also as a possibility of human freedom (Safranski 1997). Yet, once again, there is no reliable evidence that personal experience of criminal victimisation in general causes fear of crime, represents a lack of informal control (beside some hints) or is a result of media sensationalism.

But are the findings of conventional victimological studies useful at all for interpreting the wider framework? The second part of this chapter presents some empirical findings about criminal victimisation taken from victimological studies carried out in Germany after 1989. Despite being based on conventional victimological concepts, these findings are used to interpret victimisation, fear and risk of crime in the context of a broadened theoretical framework, deriving from a perspective of late modernity (see 'Understanding the transition to late modernity', below). Nevertheless, before presenting the findings it should be mentioned that there is only a narrow range in which they can be interpreted. That is why the vagueness of research on fear of crime has to be emphasised:

Research on fear of crime conducted to date suffers from serious conceptual and measurement problems and the findings, therefore, have to be
treated with extreme caution. One of the major problems has to do with
the concept of fear itself. Fear is an emotion. Like other emotions (love,
hate, etc.) it is difficult to define and hard to measure. Attitudes (such as
concern about crime) or perceptions (such as estimates of the chances of
being victimised) are, on the other hand, easier to deal with on both
counts. … By recognising and treating fear as an emotion we can avoid …
attempts to determine whether the level of fear is, or is not, commensurate
with the real risks to which the group in question is exposed. Emotions,
such as fear, are not based on rational objective assessments of chances of
becoming victim. There is no sense, therefore, in trying to determine
whether they are proportionate or disproportionate to the real dangers
and the objective risks of victimisation.

(Fattah 1993: 45)

Therefore the following presentation of empirical findings should be interpreted chiefly in the context of attitudes towards and perception of safety and
risk.

Empirical findings from (Eastern) Germany

The following findings refer mainly to the situation in Eastern Germany after the
upheaval in 1989. The social changes after the breakdown of state socialism
created a huge social experiment, characterised by radical dissolution in every
sphere of society, leading to an increase in risks for everybody in the former East
Germany. Therefore, the data can be used to analyse how individuals perceive
crimes as threats, evaluate and communicate risks, and how they react if they
have to cope with social problems in the organisation of their everyday lives.

Data presented in this section come from five different victimological studies
carried out in Germany from 1990 to 1995. Through all of these studies, representative samples of the German population (SUK'91 only East Germans) were asked
about their personal and vicarious victimisation and also regarding their fear of
crime. The use of standardised questions in the field of victimisation makes it
possible to compare the findings. The first study (MPI'90) was conducted by
the Max Planck Institute for Foreign and International Penal Law (MPI) in co-
operation with the Bundeskriminalamt, September 1990 (Kury et al. 1992).
Findings for 1991 (SUK '91) and 1993 (SUK'93) have been collected in a representative victim survey (Sozialer Umbruch und Kriminalität – SUK) carried out by
criminologists at universities in Berlin, Hamburg and Tübingen (Boers et al. 1994;
Boers et al. 1997). The Criminological Institute of Lower Saxonia (KFN) carried out
a victimological study (KFN'92) in 1992/1993 (Wetzels et al. 1995). And data for
1995 come from a victim study conducted by the Institute for Criminology,
University of Tübingen (TÜB'95; Boers et al. 1995).

Personal and vicarious victimisation

The comparison of reported victimisation in five representative German victim surveys

Table 9.1 shows an increase in reported victimisation – especially of property and violent crime – in Eastern Germany right after the destruction of the Wall. In Spring 1991, the East German level of victimisation, as reported in the interviews, had reached the level of the former Federal States (Kury *et al.* 1992). Reported victimisation remained relatively stable between 1991 and 1993, with again a slight increase for some property offences and threat in 1995. Victimisation from serious crimes (e.g. assault with weapon, burglary, sexual violence, in particular rape) remained very low and altogether stable.

Table 9.1 Prevalence rates after the upheaval[a]

Offence	MPI'90[b]	SUK'91[c]	KFN'92[d]	SUK'93[e]	TÜB'95[f]
	(n=4.999)	(n=2.011)	(n=2.150)	(n=2.212)	(n=1.095)
Car theft	0.3	0.7	1.5	1.5	0
Theft of parts from cars	5.1	6.4	6.1	4.9	0
Damaging of cars	6.4	11.4	13.6	8.6	0
Theft of bicycles	1.9	2.0	2.7	1.6	0
Theft of a bicycle	11.0	13.1	10.0	7.7	9.0
Burglary	2.1	3.5	1.5	3.5	4.0
Robbery	2.0	2.0	1.3	3.0	5.0
Theft of handbag	0	2.1	1.5	3.6	3.0
Larceny	5.1	8.8	6.0	5.2	7.0
Fraud	0	13.0	7.7	7.4	7.0
Assault	0	3.9	4.5	2.6	3.0
Assault with a weapon	0	0.9	1.2	0.9	1.0
Threat	3.2	7.5	1.5	6.6	9.0
Sexual harassment[g]	1.2	7.4	3.5	6.7	6.0
Sexual violence[g]	0	1.0	0.5	1.8	1.0

Source: Ewald and Langer 1997: 143; for Tübingen 1995 see also Boers *et al.* 1995: 9.

Notes:
[a]Question: 'Has it happened to you [for household offences, additionally: "or to a member of your household"] that ...' (within a five-year period).
[b]Study conducted by Max Planck Institute for foreign and international Penal Law and Bundeskriminalamt, September 1990 (Kury *et al.* 1992).
[c]Findings for 1991 and 1993 have been collected in a representative victim survey (SUK: Sozialer Umbruch und Kriminalität) carried out by criminologists at universities in Berlin, Hamburg and Tübingen (see Boers *et al.* 1997).
[d]The Criminological Institute of Lower Saxony (KFN) carried out a victimological study in 1992/1993 (Wetzels *et al.* 1995).
[e]See note c.
[f]Data for 1995 come from a victim study conducted by the Institute for Criminology, University of Tübingen.
[g]Only women.

Overall, these findings can hardly be interpreted as proof of a dramatic increase in crime, either on a general level or in the case of serious (i.e. violent) crimes. Taking into account also that the official crime statistics do not 'speak' another language – not even for child abuse which is dramatised in the media (Wetzels 1997) – we come to the conclusion that crime as a social problem and an objective threat, although increased through the course of transition after unification, did not increase dramatically in the New Federal States (the former GDR). Of course, there remain certain serious youth crime problems, particularly right-wing violence. But these crimes happen very rarely, despite the public and political attention which is paid to them, and are almost no real threat to the average German population (Merten and Otto 1993).

Table 9.2 shows that, in comparison with perceived personal victimisation, perceptions of vicarious victimisation in the New Federal States (NFS) between 1991 and 1993 increased rather dramatically. Answering the question 'Do you know people from your family, your acquaintances, or friends who became victims of the following ...?' the proportion of respondents answering in 1993 that they knew such persons was significantly higher than in 1991 for burglary, pickpocketing, theft, assault with and without weapons, and (for women only) sexual harassment and violence. Only for robbery did vicarious victimisation remain stable. This contradicts the survey respondents' perceptions of their risk

Table 9.2 Tendencies of perceived personal and vicarious victimisation in the New Federal States

Offences	Personal victimisation (development 1991–3)	Vicarious victimisation (development 1991–3)
Burglary	→	↗
Pickpocketing	↗	↗
Robbery	↗	→
Theft	→	↗
Assault without weapon	→	↗
Assault with weapon	→	↗
Sexual harassment	↘	↗
Sexual violence	→	↗

Source Ewald and Langer 1997: 107

Notes:
→ statistically insignificant differences, relatively stable level
↘ statistically significant decrease
↗ statistically significant increase

of personal victimisation. Only in the case of pickpocketing were perceptions of personal and vicarious victimisation between 1991 and 1993 similar (i.e. increasing). For the other offences there were significant differences. Indeed, with the exception of robbery, trends in perceived personal versus vicarious victimisation were in completely opposite directions: perceived personal victimisation appears to be stable or even decreasing, while vicarious victimisation shows a significant increase. In other words: while dismay at the prospect of being victimised personally remained at a relatively constant level between 1991 and 1995, the 'real' victimisation of 'others' from criminal violence appears as a whole to have increased tremendously.

Such a difference between the perception of victimisation as a real personal threat and crime as known to happen to 'others' or from 'hearsay' raises issues about the communication and construction of crime in society. The belief that 'others' are much more victimised than oneself can be interpreted not only as a probable personal threat but also as a probability of being affected by those threats. As Ferraro (1995: 121) argues, although one might assume that personal victimisation has a stronger influence on risk interpretation and behaviour adaptation, '[that] is not the case, however, for we find that indirect victimization has a stronger effect on constrained behaviour than does direct victimisation' (see also Mawby and Walklate 1994: 33).

Fear of crime and risk perception

As shown in Table 9.3, there is a remarkable gap in the feelings of safety between the New and Old Federal States. In 1993, 16 per cent more East Germans felt unsafe compared to West Germans. Feelings of insecurity in the New Federal States increased from 51 per cent in 1991 to 58.4 per cent in 1993, while feelings of insecurity in the Older Federal States were relatively stable between 1991 and 1993. Although the reporting behaviour to the general question about fear after nightfall in the neighbourhood has to be interpreted with caution – since it is well known that lots of vague insecurities can stimulate the answers to this question – the findings indicate a high level of personal insecurity, more in the East than in the West, which is not directly related to the experience of personal victimisation (see Table 9.1).

Table 9.4 shows that differences between reported feelings of fear on the one hand and estimated personal risks on the other hand (with the exception of getting mobbed by young people in the two parts of Germany and break-in or robbery only in the New Federal States), respondents' estimation of the risk of being victimised was significantly lower than their reported fear regarding the particular crime. This difference appears to be a paradox: although people judge their likely risk of becoming a victim in most of the asked offences as rather low, they express much higher levels of fear. Thus, the perception of victimisation as a personal threat is different on a cognitive from on an emotional level.

Table 9.3 Feeling of personal safety at night

	NFS		OFS
	1991 n = 2005	1993 n = 2,208	1993 n = 2,032
Very safe	9.6	10.8	16.8
Somewhat safe	39.4	30.8	41.2
A bit unsafe	29.4	34.8	31.7
Very unsafe	21.6	23.6	10.3

Note:

Question: 'How safe do you feel today when you walk alone on the streets of your neighbourhood/community at night? Do you feel very safe, somewhat safe, a bit unsafe, very unsafe?'

Table 9.4 Fear and estimated personal risks

Offence	NFS 1993			AFS 1993		
	Fear	Risk	Diff. (risk–fear)	Fear	Risk	Diff. (risk–fear)
Getting mobbed by young people	34.3	35.2	+0.9	25.7	23.8	-1.9
Getting beaten up and injured	36.8	23.5	-13.3	25.7	13.7	-12.0
Getting affected by a break-in to my flat/house	50.9	40.2	-10.7	33.9	23.4	-10.5
Getting attacked and robbed	48.3	33.3	-15.0	31.7	18.8	-12.9
Having something stolen from me, besides a break-in or robbery	39.2	40.3	+1.1	32.9	21.9	-11.0
Getting killed	22.6	11.0	-11.6	13.3	5.2	-8.1
Getting sexually harassed	45.1	31.2	-13.9	34.3	22.8	-11.5
Getting sexually attacked and injured	41.6	24.6	-17.0	30.7	17.9	-12.8
Getting raped	39.1	22.5	-16.6	29.4	15.4	-14.0

Notes:

Question being disturbed/concerned: 'Some people see many reasons to feel unsafe, for others this only applies in certain situations, while others scarcely feel affected by such things. Please tell me in each given situation the degree you are disturbed by these conditions in your neighbourhood in the evening when you are alone and it is dark. Please tell me for every given situation how disturbed you are by them today.' (column 'Fear' contains 'somewhat disturbed' and 'very disturbed')

Question risk/probability estimation: 'Independent from whether you are disturbed by something like this or not, how probable do you think it is that such things could happen to you at night in the dark in your neighbourhood?' (column 'Risk' contains 'somewhat probable' and 'very probable')

An assessment

Hypothetically, these findings about personal and vicarious victimisation, on the one hand, and fear of crime and risk estimation, on the other, can be interpreted as follows: the higher levels of perceived victimisation of 'others' are being experienced by the people of the New Federal States as a direct personal threat, reflected in their higher levels of 'fear of crime', despite lower levels of personal experience with crime. This would suggest that the idea of crime as a metaphor created in societal discourse can become a direct threat in people's lives without any personal experience of being threatened by crime. Thus, *voilà*, the social construction works: *feeling* at risk and threatened by crime without *being* at risk and threatened by crime. The three 'perspectives' on victimisation, discussed in the first part of this chapter, are rather unhelpful for interpreting the empirical findings shown above. They seem to have more to do with criminal politics than everyday experience. And it seems that there are also other reasons accounting for the paradox of a high fear of crime and relatively low risk of being victimised. While there was a dramatic increase in the feelings of insecurity in Germany, especially in the New Federal States, people were much more realistic in estimating their personal risk of becoming a crime victim. Nevertheless, on a societal level, crime is a major topic, expressing feelings of general insecurity and dominating the public discourse. As we have seen, this discourse is inappropriate in view of the real chance of becoming a crime victim, particularly a victim of criminal violence. This gap between 'real' insecurity and 'discursive' insecurity raises the question of crime as a metaphor in political communication, in social control, and as a catalyst for individual behavioural adaptation.

The political and societal reaction to crime obviously creates a symbolic 'evil' which is interpreted as real threat for everybody. For instance, both the issues of drug crime and organised crime are presented by the mass media and politicians as major risks to society which 'challenge' state, society and every (responsible) individual. This is what Nils Christie called a 'useful enemy' (Christie 1991). In June 1998, it became a matter for the United Nations during a three-day special plenary assembly, where all UN members agreed to co-operate in fighting drugs. Yet do we really have to fear drug crime so much as a basic threat in our lives that states of the world unite to fight it? Are there not other issues to be solved more urgently? At any rate, the strengthening of the criminal justice system seems obligatory – and therefore necessary – for a responsible state policy to reduce the threat of drug crime. Similarly, the argument is that crime is also a real threat and, consequently, causes fear. Thus crime control has to manage and reduce the threat which will, ultimately, lead to a reduction of fear in order to achieve a safer society. How this 'logic' can be understood in the perspective of reflexive modernisation will be shown in the third part of this chapter.

Sessar (1997: 118) explains the social meaning of fear of crime in the transitional period in Germany after unification in relation to the development of crime policy. For Germany he sees a repetition of developments in the USA, where the futile 'war on crime' was replaced by the equally vain 'war on fear of crime'. Yet what he does not ask directly is: why are those 'futile wars' being fought? His suspicion is that the shift from a 'war on crime' to a 'war on fear of crime' motivates and legitimates concepts of crime control and prevention which are no longer just concentrated on putative perpetrators but also act upon the complex world of everyday life, which has to be controlled in order to increase feelings of safety and protection and to minimise 'fear of crime'. But is this war really futile? Clearly, the net-widening of crime control is futile, at first glance, with respect to a supposed reduction of crime. Yet, in a wider framework of a complex attempt to maintain social control – where the status quo itself is just a 'torrential river of a modernisation' which has its own momentum and direction – such a 'war' appears not quite so futile (see following section).

Nevertheless, Sessar's remark does allude to a significant development: a visibly *new* effort to strengthen the *traditional* system of crime control. Yet this is being carried out in a widely uncontrolled world by maintaining the traditional foundations of political and social control developed at the beginning of the twentieth century. Ultimately, therefore, fear of crime legitimates a more-of-the-same policy regarding 'law and order'. It is, therefore, a 'century mistake' (Beck 1988: 9) because of the use of concepts of social control which are inappropriate in a globalising world. In the next part of this chapter we will try to make 'sense' of this, in the framework of post-modernism.

Understanding the transition to late modernity – a victimological perspective

From the empirical findings discussed above, one conclusion seems obvious: crime is *not* the most threatening problem in the everyday lives and perceptions of the German population, but the *discourse* on crime and fear of crime *is*. To understand the meaning of fear of crime (particularly violence) and risk perception in the unified Germany – as a transitional modern society in a globalising world – we must explain why the fear of crime has become a general preoccupation of citizens in the changing modern world. The dominant perspective in this discourse is a general *threat-and-fear* scenario: 'We're all victims. OK!' – and fearful! Bruckner calls this the disease of modernity: 'I am suffering, that is why I am' (Bruckner 1997). Suffering is a dominant issue in the risk society not just for citizens of the advanced economies but all around the world (Kleinman *et al.* 1997). Yet specific attempts in German criminology to conceptualise the concept of post-modernism in order to interpret the 'victimisation and fear of crime problem' in the broader framework of late modernity and social transition (Blinkert 1988; Boers 1997; Sack 1997) have not yet developed a new methodological approach.

To understand the nature of the transitional process to late modernity it is necessary to look at the sociological literature on social transition, particularly in Germany. Yet this also shows a confusing picture. While there have been attempts to systematise thinking about social change and transition (Reissig 1994; Hradil 1995; Müller and Schmid 1995), no paradigm of social change has emerged since Wolfgang Zapf's 'Theory of Social Change' (Zapf 1991) faded away as the 'orthodox paradigm' (see Müller and Schmid 1995: 7). Today there are only 'methodological minimal standards'. Hradil mentions two assumptions which all modernisation theories have in common:

- modernisation means rationalisation and differentiation;
- modernisation means an increase of individual autonomy.

(Hradil 1995: 6)

While rationalisation and differentiation refer to the macrostructure of modern society, which is characterised by an increasing complexity and interdependence as well as diversity, these processes are at the same time – more or less – directly linked to the capacity of individuals to act on the basis of personal competence as self-responsible and autonomous individuals. From this starting point two perspectives can be derived about the discourse on late modernity which lead to very different conclusions for a criminological understanding of the function of (in particular, violent) crime and criminal victimisation in modern transitional societies.

Perspective of 'ongoing modernisation' (e.g. Zapf 1991)

Current modern western society is a highly complex and differentiated system comprising competent and autonomous individuals. Risks, disturbances and crime are indicators of malfunction which ought to be avoided, or at least controlled, for the sake of the survival of the whole system. Individuals are subject to these processes of social change but often they are not able to meet the requirements of modernity and are unable to behave like autonomous individuals (Heitmeyer 1995). The implication for criminological/victimological research seems to be obvious – there is a need to measure the social disturbance caused by crime, reflected in the attitudes towards crime, in particular fear of crime.

In much recent German criminology, crime appears as a *risk* of modernisation (Blinkert 1988; Boers 1997). And an effective criminal policy has to organise the protection of the society. In this approach, modernisation is seen as an evolutionary and basically *productive* process. Seemingly destructive phenomena – such as crime – indicate malfunctions and call for limited (but necessary) capabilities to manage the complex process of social change. This concept of 'ongoing modernisation' (Hradil 1995: 6) – where the direction of evolution remains relatively stable and the social structure (market economy, democracy, consumption, welfare state) requires modification to avoid, or at least mitigate, its negative side-effects – considers crime as something deviant but which necessarily exists (according to Durkheim) and thus needs to be kept within certain limits. The important methodological consequence is that crime – and related phenomena like fear of crime – are seen as *pathological phenomena* to be split from the 'healthy

178

body' of society. Thus – with only little simplification – fear of crime need be explained only with respect to the pathology of crime and not with regard to society as a whole.

Of course, this is the way that conventional concepts of fear of crime function. Yet it is like putting old wine in new bottles to leave the concept of fear of crime unchanged while society itself undergoes a radical transition. All this approach actually says is that crime – like poverty, mass unemployment or ecocide – is a modernisation risk, to be explained as a negative and disturbing side-effect which has to be kept under control, while the main processes of modernisation continue to be seen positively. From a methodological perspective, the crucial point is that crime need be thought of only as a separate social phenomenon, complex yet nevertheless distinct from other social systems, actors or agencies (Boers 1997: 305). Thus, crime becomes a *marginal* phenomenon which, although connected to the main processes of modernity (and what criminologist would deny this?), nevertheless remains defined purely as a social malfunction.

Yet the inevitable consequence of this approach is the disconnection of crime from the basic processes of society. Consequently, the current explanations of fear of crime and risk perception in transitional Germany confirm (instead of questioning) the conventional and limited concepts of victimology, and miss a conceptual link which is basic to an understanding of late modernity. Neither the theoretical nor the empirical weaknesses of the conventional concepts of victimology (as noted above) are taken seriously; and this perspective has no ready explanation for the paradox, noted above, of a high level of perceived discursive fear and vicarious victimisation in contrast to relatively low levels of perceived risk. As Sack notes, this explanation – to portray crime only as a 'side-effect' of the modernisation process – appears to be merely a new version of the discredited notion of Marxist–Leninist criminology (Sack 1997: 120) which described crime as a relic of former bourgeois society, meaning that there were actually no 'causes of crime' in the essence of socialist society. This is similar to the perspective which describes crime as just a 'side-effect' of modern society while denying the basic relationship between major societal processes and crime in a society. Thus it is still true – as Kräupl and Ludwig stated with respect to Germany after 1989 – that there is no social theory of recent social changes which is useful for a criminological explanation (Kräupl and Ludwig 1993: 1), a view shared by Sack (Sack 1994). Yet it seems obvious, in the light of the available evidence, that we need to seek a new interpretation of the perception of victimisation as a risk in everyday life.

Perspective of 'reflexive modernisation' (e.g. Lutz 1994; Beck 1986)

In this view, the basic institutions of modernity (state, family, industrial work) are dissolving and the diversity of life is accompanied by a lack of cohesion, attachment, bonds, and a crisis of personal identity of the post-industrial or post-modern society. Everything is at risk – a *risk society*. Loss of values and orientation lead to insecurity, anxiety and suffering as a general phenomenon. And there is no common concept like nation, god or historical mission as a basic belief or vision, particularly among youth. It is a loss of social hope (Rorty 1989: 149).

This second perspective on late modernity characterises crime and victimisation very differently from the first. While the former considers crime as inevitable but mainly accompanying external risk and with negative side-effects, the latter approach sees crime as a *necessary* feature of modernity, to be understood in the context of global insecurity. Thus criminal victimisation as individual risk can be seen as part of people's survival mechanism, indicating a new quality of modern society. Developing the notion of *reflexive modernisation* would seem to be productive for developing an understanding of victimisation and fear of crime in transitional societies and may help to explain both individuals' adaptation processes and changes in crime control. It takes the ongoing transition not as something gradual, but as a consequence of change to an entirely new type of society, where the old mechanism of social functioning becomes replaced by a completely new pattern of social behaviour and social control as a consequence of rationalisation and differentiation as well as of increased individual autonomy.

Reflexive modernisation and risk

From the perspective of reflexive modernisation, the appropriate explanation of modern society is the concept of *risk society*. According to Beck (1986, 1998) and Giddens (1997, 1998), industrialisation, as the rationale of modernity, produces side-effects like poverty, air pollution, unemployment and crime which are no longer on the periphery of mainstream commodity production but rather themselves determine the nature of modern society at the beginning of a new period of modernity. That is why they cannot be administered as external risks to limit their negative impact, as in the nineteenth and early twentieth centuries. It is no longer possible to control negative social side-effects without touching the main processes which produce the side-effects.

The point of departure in a new understanding of criminal victimisation and fear of crime in (post-)modern societies is the new relationship of risks with respect both to the main social processes and to their side-effects. In the perspective of Giddens and Beck we are living in a general situation of *manufactured insecurity* (Giddens 1997: 141–8) which characterises the second period of modernity. This shift from the first to the second phase of modernity – and the changes in the nature of risk and insecurity along with methods to deal with them – is significant for an understanding of the 'fear-of-crime scenario' and traditional 'law and order mentality'. During the first period ('first modernity'), risks appeared as 'external risks' which were distributed in society in a relatively stable way (Giddens 1997: 207). While the main social processes – like the market economy, industrialisation, technical progress – appeared to be predictable, controllable and scientifically understandable, some side-effects like poverty, unemployment, air pollution and crime could not be abolished completely and thus needed to be taken under control as 'external' risks of modernisation. Science could make it possible to predict these risks and their causation as well as help to develop the appropriate (political) means to keep them under control. Thus the continued functioning of the main social processes could be guaranteed. And welfare state security arrangements and insurance systems appeared to be the best way to prevent or cope with those risks without losing control in general.

This understanding of risks in modern society changes rapidly at the beginning of a second period of modernity, also called 'reflexive modernisation'. It becomes clear that it is an illusion to be able to control the risks produced by modernisation through a system of social control, based on scientific methods of prediction, in a more complex and differentiated world. Risks can no longer be understood as external and treated as the side-effects of modernisation. Instead, they should be seen as integral to the main processes of modernisation, leading to a completely new understanding of risks. While in the 'first modernity' risks could be controlled, though the means of risk control were distributed in society unequally (in favour of political and economic elites), under the conditions of reflexive modernity risks appear to be (ultimately) uncontrollable and are not experienced by individuals differentially according to their social position. Instead, manufactured insecurity affects everybody without exception.

Giddens describes the broader context of insecurity and threat in terms of four global risk areas:

- ecology (global warming, etc.);
- the expansion of relative and absolute poverty;
- uncontrolled distribution of mass destructive weapons;
- wide-scale suppression of democratic rights.

(Giddens 1997: 141–8)

Ultimately, these risks do not differentiate between rich and poor. They are characteristics of the main societal processes and can lead to the self-destruction of mankind which no security and insurance system can prevent. Major risks become unpredictable and uncontrollable. Manufactured insecurity unifies all individuals: everything and everybody is interdependent. The general feeling of insecurity is not related to some external risk (represented by side-effects) but created by modernisation and globalisation itself. Consequently the system of social control developed at the beginning of modernity, based on the idea of predictability and ability to control 'external risks', is not appropriate to the new insecurity. The old system of social control – and consequently the criminal justice system – becomes an outdated 'century mistake' (Beck 1988: 9–11). And, in the face of a weakening of the conventional control system, it appears that life is running 'out of control' (Kelly 1997).

The Myth of Modernity

The four global risk areas described by Giddens on a macro level need to be 'translated' into individual threat-perception, fear and feelings of suffering. Using a concept of Klaus Wahl, the personal perception of modernity can be explained as the 'Myth of Modernity' (Wahl 1989: 93). In his book *The Trap of Modernisation* Wahl (1989) says that modernity, beginning during the Enlightenment, held out three promises:

• the development of the autonomous individual;
• partnership and marriage based on inner bonds of love;
• a belief in unlimited (industrial and technical) progress.

But there is one problem in the further development of modernity – there are insufficient resources of society to keep these promises for all people. There is no equal distribution of chances for individual development, partnerships are often fragile, marriages which last a lifetime seem to be the exception. Also, unlimited technical and scientific progress is no longer viable. In the course of their lives, people discover the promises of modernity to be a myth. Instead, they face risks and try to cope with them, but *disappointment* is often what follows. And the loss of hope and trust in the future become general features of mass psychology. According to Wahl, there is a contradiction between individuals' expectations for their personal life, which are created by the 'Myth of Modernity', and their disappointment in everyday life. The capacity to handle the contradiction between expectations and performance ultimately shapes their feelings of self-esteem or inferiority. Thus, the 'trap' of modernisation lies in the contradiction between such myths and the disappointments of everyday experience.

The Myth of Modernity corresponds to the three promises of the Enlightenment (Wahl 1989: 93, 164). For Wahl, the dialectical contradiction between these promises and their fulfilment is experienced as personal disappointment, suffering and bad luck. People internalise the legend of modernity, in particular the promise of free and autonomous personality, but this is denied by their expe-rience of discrimination, and their limited and constrained possibilities of development. 'So the myth of the modern self-confident subject is experienced first of all through its negation, in suffering or by violence against others which is born in suffering or in suffering through this violence' (Wahl, 1989: 101, author's translation).

Yet for people in state socialist societies there was also a fourth promise of modernisation: the *expectation of social security*. While the 'myths' of the Enlightenment refer very much to the free development of autonomous individ-uals in an individualistic way, the 'vision of socialism' – which degenerated to a 'myth' during state socialism too – was derived from the assumption formulated in the Communist Manifesto that the free development of the individual is linked to the free existence of the whole society. The guarantee and protection of the existence of the whole society appeared to be a major proof for the superiority of socialism over capitalism. This principle was not only an ideology during the Cold War, it was also a guiding line for practical politics in state socialism. As a consequence, social security – in terms of employment for everybody, medical care as a state matter, childcare, education and social welfare – was guaranteed by the state, although partly at a low level. Individuals socialised under those circumstances internalised personal demands in this respect as their right from society, which they did not simply give up after the breakdown of the state socialist system. The former promise of state socialism not to be threatened by, for example, unemployment and individual decay through the loss of one's own material basis, became a strong attitude and expectation among East Germans. The end of the state socialist system of social security and the difficulties of the welfare system in the unified Germany thus appeared as a major threat for East Germans.

The particularity of the former state socialist countries

During the transition of the former state socialist societies, patterns of existential threat changed rapidly. Accordingly, this change required a corresponding reaction on the part of the individuals in managing their everyday lives. This change can be characterised as a shift from 'victimization by the state' to 'victimization by crime' (Fattah 1994). Although, under state socialism, the authoritarian state tried to control almost all external risks which were perceived as sources of individual insecurity (poverty, unemployment, crime) – seeking to fulfil the 'historical laws' of Marxism–Leninism – the state also became a major threat to people who rejected the political system or were declared as political enemies. Accordingly, the might of the state found its expression in suppression, authoritarian control, subjugation and obedience.

Yet, although often repudiated, there was also a dowry in the heritage of GDR state socialism. There was another side, too, which can be called the *social dimension* (Ewald 1990). This refers to the capacity within the criminal law for dealing with everyday conflicts by mobilising collective initiatives for integrating the individual into society. Of course, this dimension was shaped and ultimately dominated by the authoritarian and paternalistic nature of state socialist society. Nevertheless, as an unintended consequence, there was the development of particular individual capabilities as a catalyst of modernisation processes. Hradil defines six such properties as 'modern structures' (Hradil 1995: 12–15; see also Lemke 1991; Reissig and Glaessner 1991; Haeder 1991; Wolle 1998; Engler 1999):

- *Collective-oriented attitudes (gemeinschaftsbezogene Einstellungen)* East Germans are more collectively orientated, which holds true in particular for managers who were functionaries in the state socialist economy. Therefore they are committed to teamwork and to associate with others in order to prevent dysfunctional decay caused by egoistic actors.

- *Chaos qualification and persistence (Chaosqualifikation)* Under circumstances of shortage and unreliability in everyday life, as well as in the economy, East Germans had to develop the capability to deal with 'chaos'. This required a strong attitude of persistence to achieve goals, and flexibility of organisation.

- *Economic relation network (ökonomische Beziehungsnetze)* In a situation of economic deficiency, the creation of personal relationships ('social capital') was required to be able to organise personal and societal life. As a result, economic networks emerged in factories as well as neighbourhoods. Such networks were persistent and functional even when normal structures did not work properly.

- *Private networks* Private networks in East Germany are traditionally based more on mutual assistance than on communication and recreation. In situations of economic difficulties they can be used to solve problems.

- *Social–political networks* East German private networks and neighbourhoods are useful in a post-industrial society too. Such networks are reliable and functional in dealing with social problems like the care of the elderly, dealing with drug problems, integration of foreigners, family problems, etc.

- *Local belonging (regionales Wir-Gefühl)* The feeling of belonging to a certain region is part of an identity necessary in a post-modern world where traditional orientations are dissolving and values are ambivalent. The consciousness of a common history and the common experience of breakdown and transition developed a regional 'we-feeling' in the East.

As will be suggested below, following Hradil, these East German capabilities might be considered useful in post-socialist times, too.

While West Germans have to face a transition from the first to the second period of modernisation, for East Germans this social change is combined with the particularity described above. After the decay of state socialism, an entirely new risk pattern emerged in individuals' everyday lives, including crime, which developed rapidly and forced people to adapt to the new system very fast. It is too early to judge whether this legacy of special East German qualities in dealing with conflicts and risks is beneficial in helping people to adapt to change, but we should be open to the possibilities of these apparently unacknowledged capabilities. Thus, both parts of the heritage of state socialism are worth discussing in the context of late modernity, particularly in the search for resources to manage the risks of societal transition and, hence, for dealing with victimisation and crime control.

The complexity of processes of social transition from state socialism on the one hand and ongoing social changes in modern societies on the other hand should urge criminological and victimological research to overcome the conventional concentration and limitation on figures about levels of victimisation and fear of crime. Rather, they call for a search for what could be called the *meaning* of crime and victimisation in the adaptation to transitional late modern society.

We should address the question of whether and why crime is given the role of catalyst and metaphor for the communication of basic social problems. This holds true in particular for criminal interpersonal violence which is communicated as a public, political and informal issue far beyond the real and practical influence of criminal violence on everyday life (Albrecht 1994: 3). On a societal level, this means finding out how crime control is maintained; on an individual level, the question is how crime as risk and threat influences the process of learning about the new society, and the role played by crime and victimisation in helping people to adapt to completely new patterns of behaviour and systems of values.

Although not entirely reliable, changes in responses to standard survey questions on the fear of crime can be interpreted in the light of the above-mentioned perspectives. After 1989, there were changes regarding reported levels of fear of crime and feelings of insecurity in both parts of Germany (Boers *et al.* 1995; Noll and Schröder 1995: 316; Bilsky 1996a; Reuband 1999), yet in 1990 there was a significant increase of fear of crime in the East of Germany with a relatively low level in the Western part. For East Germans, this could represent their insecurity regarding the new social relationships based on individualism and competition, while West Germans experienced the unification as a corroboration of their way of life. Later, between 1992 and 1993/1994, when actual risks of crime increased, the level of fear in the East went down. In his article 'From crime hysteria to normality?' Reuband (1999) recently gave an complex overview on the development of fear of crime and reported crime in Germany.

As Reuband interprets the figures presented in Table 9.5 – in the context of perceived social threats (e.g. unemployment) and reported crime – there is a disjunction in the East between what he calls 'objective' threat and subjective feelings of being threatened. From 1995 to the end of the 1990s, the numbers of reported burglaries and muggings decreased in East Germany. During this time, the level of fear of crime in the New Federal States also went down and developed very close to West German levels. The decrease of perceived fear was stronger than the decrease of reported crime. Explaining these developments, Reuband stresses the point of East Germans getting used to this new pattern of threats which lead to a more realistic view on threats and crime (Reuband 1999: 18).

Another explanation of this apparent paradox could be that East Germans have learned to deal with the meaning of new social risks by remembering and re-activating their particular skills – learned during the days of the GDR – in handling confused and chaotic situations. In their initial reactions to the upheaval, East Germans were often blamed – particularly from a West German perspective – for their seeming 'learned helplessness' (Hradil 1995: 4, 10). Yet, on closer inspection, it could be that the skills of East Germans in dealing with risky situations were, in fact, much more developed but were not deployed initially. After they had become used to the functioning of the new society they regained their confidence and, consequently, lost their fear.

Nevertheless, despite these differences, there is generally a new perception of

Table 9.5 Fear of crime in Germany (in percentages)

Years	Old Federal States									New Federal States			
	75	79	80	82	91	92	93	94	99	92	93	94	99
Getting burgled at home	21	20	21	21	57	43	41	40	32	68	59	59	31
Getting attacked and robbed	20	17	18	23	–	38	35	27	30	60	55	52	31
Theft on the street	12	9	14	15	–	29	30	24	22	51	45	42	25
Loss of savings by fraud	7	9	8	–	–	13	6	10	8	28	17	20	11
Being attacked by aggressive juveniles (skinheads, punks) on the street	–	–	–	–	44	–	37	36	30	–	44	46	40
Some relative or good friends victimised by crime	–	–	–	–	–	–	33	34	34	–	45	51	37

Source: Reuband 1999: 17 (Reuband used published and unpublished polls conducted by the Institut für Demoskopie)

Notes:
– denotes not reported
Respondents were asked: 'Are you more often afraid of something on this list than last time?'

risk and even suffering now common among people in *both* East and West Germany which signals rapid change in individual behaviour and systems of social control (Babl 1993; Gensicke 1995). Starting from the notion – as outlined above – that modernity is characterised by a growth in autonomy for individuals (micro level) and a rationalisation and differentiation on a societal level (macro level), I will now try to show that criminal victimisation and fear of crime can be interpreted as a means for individuals to gauge their position in a changing society, particularly whether they see themselves as 'losers' or 'winners'. Subsequently (in the final section), I go on to discuss the question of whether suffering and fear of crime is a supplement to a new mode of social control, and a 'new penology', in a transitional period.

The winner–loser culture and victimisation

A general feature of victimisation (not only criminal) is the infliction of suffering from external forces. Those external forces could be nature, individuals, groups of people or institutions (Fattah 1991: 5). Victimisation is felt by the victim as the experience of losing control over one's life: 'Victimization implies an imbalance of strength and a disequilibrium in the positions of power: the strong, powerful victimizer and the weak, helpless victim' (Fattah 1991: 4). Thus, threat of crime is translated into anticipated or experienced suffering. This allows us to link the concept of modernisation as a risk society with the experience of criminal victimisation. The main psychological effect of criminal victimisation is to experience (usually as a sudden unforeseen event) personal disequilibrium and helplessness, and a loss of existential properties of personality. This experience is even more hurtful if personal resources to cope with the experience are too weak to compensate for the harm experienced.

This leads to the *central hypothesis* of this paper regarding the understanding of criminal victimisation in modernity, since the experience of criminal victimisation can be explained only in the context of psychological strain in the modernisation process. This is because the impossibility of realising the Myth of Modernity affects the self-perception of individuals and their feelings of personal efficacy. Disappointment in everyday life is felt as personal weakness, with the individual ending up feeling like a 'loser'. Similarly, crime – as a personally experienced phenomena touching the individual physically and psychologically as a concrete and inescapable threat – directly affects individuals' perceptions of their ability to control risks in their everyday life. There is thus an affinity between reactions to victimisation and disappointment in the myth of modernisation – both are experienced as loss of control and both induce a self-perception as a 'loser' rather than a 'winner'. Consequently, the interpretation of a criminal victimisation depends not on the victimising act itself (except for very serious offences of bodily injury and rape) but on those basic and general features of individuals whereby they come to see themselves as 'winners' or 'losers'.

Risk perception and social position

Findings of a multivariate analysis confirm this assumption developed above. Table 9.6 compares people's perceptions of their personal victimisation according to their social position in three of the samples – New Federal States (NFS) 1991; New Federal States 1993; and Old Federal States (OFS) 1993.

Multivariate analysis (via a multinomial logit model) sought to identify the independent correlates of risk perception (personal victimisation, vicarious victimisation) in each of the samples. While the independent variables 'size of location', 'gender', 'age', 'partnership' and 'employment' are self-explanatory, the variable 'socio-economic status' (SES) needs some explanation. The concept of SES is based on a proposal of Hoffmeyer-Zlotnik (1993) to differentiate professional position according to the degree of 'professional autonomy'. Thus Level 1 (the lowest level) is characterised by unskilled or semiskilled workers while Level 5 (the highest level) is characterised by self-employed/freelance professions with more than ten employees, or government officials. SES depicts levels of individual fulfilment of the promises of modernisation, as outlined above. In order to predict personal victimisation perception for assault, robbery and sexual harassment (women only), the multinominal logit model defined correlates between independent variables and selected types of victimisation as reported in the analysis. The analysis allows us to identify which correlates are

Table 9.6 Social position and personal victimisation (multivariate analysis)

	NFS sample 1991 (N=2,011)			NFS sample 1993 (N=2,212)			OFS sample 1993 (N=2,034)		
	Assault	*Robbery*	*Sexual. harrassment*	*Assault*	*Robbery*	*Sexual. harrassment*	*Assault*	*Robbery*	*Sexual harrassment*
Size of location	100–500T >500T	-	>100T	-	-	>100T	>100T	-	>100T
Gender	male	-	only female	male	-	only female	male	-	only female
Age	younger	-	younger	younger (influence of age becomes stronger than 1991)	-	younger	younger	-	younger
Socio-economic status (SES)	unskilled	-	housewife	unskilled*	-	skilled and higher	-	-	skilled and higher
Partnership/ family	divorced, living alone	-	-	divorced, living alone	-	-	divorced, living alone	-	-
Employment	unemployed	unemployed	-	unemployed	unemployed	-	unemployed	-	-

Note:
* Influence of social factors becomes much stronger in 1993 compared to 1991.

common and which unique to each sample, and therefore will allow us to see, for instance, whether Eastern respondents differ from Western respondents in their risk perception, and whether there were any changes in risk perception among Eastern respondents in the period following unification.

There were differences between East and West Germans, post-unification, with regard to perceptions of the risk of assault (including aggravated assault) and (partly) robbery: in the East, unskilled workers and the unemployed were more likely to see themselves at risk than they were in Western Germany; additionally, this perception intensified among unskilled East German workers following unification. Thus, the perception of risk in the East was much stronger among the more economically marginal labour force than in the West, which confirms the assumption that the self-perception of being victimised correlates with weaker economic status in terms of professional autonomy. The breakdown of the whole economic system in Eastern Germany (without the complex functioning of the new economic mechanisms) led to a widespread devaluation of professional skills and education in the East of Germany, which can explain the higher level of general insecurity as well as the higher level of perceived victimisation compared to the West German population. Yet while this model worked in the case of assault, it did not explain perceived victimisation of women (in the case of sexual harassment) and showed that unemployment only correlated with victimisation perception of robbery for East Germans, and not for West Germans. Nevertheless, in the comparison of the two NFS samples for 1991 and 1993 a change becomes visible. The influence of SES in predicting self-perception as victim of an assault in the New Federal States as found for 1991 becomes even stronger for 1993. This goes along with the economic changes in the East at that time, which caused even more structural instability, and therefore individual insecurity as well as feelings of 'losing'. Thus, although these first empirical findings are rather provisional they provide some good arguments that the model of 'winning' and 'losing' is still functioning.

Yet, although there are no 'winners' or 'losers' in the second modernity with respect to major risks since 'we are all victims', we are still trying to regain control of our lives by continuing to believe that we can make ourselves 'winners'. This kind of self-betrayal can happen, since personal victimisation has a very irrational side. It is an attempt to deal with manufactured insecurity *as if it were an external risk*. The modernity trap is, therefore, accompanied by a victimisation trap. The general perception of being a victim co-exists with the desire to succeed personally. Thus, most people still want to see crime as an external and avoidable danger, lending support for policies which extend control against crime while maintaining the basic processes of modern societies. Nevertheless, if the assumption is right that the side-effects of modernisation increase and get more and more out of control, then this outdated method – which only seeks to control the side-effects – will lead to an uncontrollable situation where it is not just the side-effects any more which prevent access to social resources, but the loss of resources itself. It becomes clear that the personal feeling of fear corroborates a process of social exclusion or participation ('loser', 'winner') in modern societies and accompanies the process whereby individuals come to recognise their social position in society and also their acceptance of basic social rules (like individualism, competition, self-reliance, etc.). Not being successful is felt as individual failure. Thus, at the individual level, fear of crime can be interpreted as part of the social process of learning one's basic social position, mainly through becoming aware of the Myth of Modernity as fearful threat or challenging risk.

Fearless 'winners' and fearful 'losers' in transitional Germany

Consequently, the trap-mechanism of modernisation affects people from the former GDR in a very special way. On the one hand, the Myth of Modernity was the moral and political programme invoked to persuade people to break with the old authoritarian state. An analysis of the political speeches at the time of breakdown and shortly before unification shows this well – including Chancellor Kohl's promise of 'blooming landscapes' in the East (Späth 1997). Yet, on the other hand, the reality today is that there are rates of unemployment of up to 30 per cent in the former East German states, on average much higher than in the old Federal states. So, in addition to the common disappointments of modernity, the transformation of the GDR has brought a further disappointment to its former citizens – the end of the promise of social security. Thus, the experience of disappointment – expressing itself in a heightened fear of crime despite no great increase in crime risk – is more marked among the population of Eastern Germany, especially (as Table 9.6 shows) among low-skilled, marginal and economically more vulnerable workers. Those who fear they are losing out in the new Germany are also those who fear crime the most.

Conclusion: fear and social control

The societal side of this process is the system of social control which frames individual and collective behaviour. The way social control – including the criminal justice system – functions is also directly linked to the role of fear and its dominance in public discourses. In a Foucauldian perspective, the *fear state* becomes the other side of the *constitutional state*. Deviance and crime become a basis for the durable existence of constitutional states and due process. They guarantee insecurity and threat and therefore an average level of fear in everyday life (see Lemke 1997: 192). The key issue, then, is how the risk society in general and crime in particular is controlled and why it seems that the discourse of the fear of crime is inevitable to keep this system running.

As noted above, during the first period of modernity risks were perceived and treated as external threats (Giddens 1997: 207, 258). Risks were considered as accidents and exceptions, distributed in a relatively stable way and seemingly predictable. Problems such as crime and poverty were considered as external, predictable threats administrated by specialist agencies (the criminal justice system, insurance companies, the welfare system). A criminal justice system focused on 'law and order' as well as the welfare state was organised in order to maintain a social equilibrium. The disciplining of individuals was necessary for the functioning of the system, which was visibly separated from the disturbing 'evil', which was to be identified and excluded. This definition and separation was made by experts in the control of external risks, mainly using exclusion and suppression. The capacity to ensure social discipline depended on those experts who were trained to use means to exclude and suppress the 'deviant' and keep them away from ordinary society (see Lemke 1997: 134). In addition, insurance systems would guarantee to satisfy victims' needs for reparation and restitution.

Following Durkheim, a healthy society required a certain amount of crime. This notion about a healthy portion of crime serving as an indicator of a functioning modern society goes along with the concept of the controllability of the external risk of crime and a disciplinary vision of control. The only question was 'How much crime was healthy?' The challenge for the system of crime control was to define and control this 'healthy portion' and, in doing so, draw the line between conformity and deviance. Consequently, criminological research should concentrate on the perpetrator as the source and cause of the crime, who should, within certain limits, be kept under control.

This scenario has changed with the emergence of the risk society. The maintenance of the first model of social control in modernity can now be seen as a 'century mistake' (Beck 1988: 9). Risks are no longer external side-effects but a manufactured property of society. Moreover, they are no longer predictable in a reliable way. And insurance is now necessary yet inefficient. Given the extent of loss and suffering caused by major global risks, compensation makes no real sense any more, since the damages are irreversible. To deal with those risks in order to save existential prerequisites would need prevention rather than after-care. That is why the old way of social control can be seen as outdated and a mistake. Beck's main argument is that the dangers we are facing today, and the guarantee of security, belong to different historical time periods (Beck 1988: 9). Although Beck refers to the major threats of industrial society, in a similar way, principles of criminal justice like individual guilt (*Einzeltatschuld*) also ultimately lead to what he calls 'organised irresponsibility'. That is, such principles function as a rationalisation, allowing us to hunt for the guilty single perpetrator, while acquitting the rest of society (Beck 1988: 10).

From this perspective, it makes sense to develop a *new understanding* of victimisation as risk. Like other risks, crimes as social phenomena are by nature no longer side-effects, to be controlled by specialised institutions run by experts. They belong to the class of manufactured risks and cause manufactured insecurity. Crime and its control has to become a general matter for the entire society. Ultimately, though, sensationalism and fear are dysfunctional since they are still part of the business which creates the 'evil' which has to be controlled and excluded. Thus, they have to be replaced by understanding and concern, developed in a broad dialogue. And yet, the question remains whether it is just an admission of failure to seek to maintain the old model of social control. Addressing this issue leads us again to the issue of the relationship between crime control and fear of crime, which will now be discussed further in the context of Foucauldian ideas of governmentality.

A central term in Foucault's historical analysis of the prison system is 'discipline' (see Foucault 1979: 135; Lemke 1997: 68, 134, 188). Discipline becomes a major feature of modern society. Modernity appears as a societal system dependent upon force, pressure and compulsion. Moreover, social identity is being produced by processes of force and procedures of exclusion. Thus, discipline is directed towards producing useful, obedient individuals. The emerging disciplinary system of modern society until the twentieth century ultimately relied on the Benthamite prison system. The basic notion of this system is that external control, symbolised and exemplified by the means of power (prisons, guns), turns into internal control even without the direct intervention of the functionaries of power. In other words, the prison system operates as part of a complex disciplinary system in which all the useful and obedient individuals act according to the demands of a developing industrial society. The disciplinary system limits self-determination and creates a class of experts who 'know' how to control the risks.

Nevertheless, the demands of external control for discipline need to be internalised into psychological principles for steering behaviour; and people need to have personal 'reasons' – internal and/or external – for accepting and following the basic norms of society. Beside prisons, modern discipline requires fear as well. Fear is both the irrational legitimisation of discipline (and prisons) and an expression of being threatened by risks, including criminal victimisation. Fear justifies discipline not only because undisciplined people (deviants) end up in prison but also that prison is understood as a protection against threats from crime. In other words, being subjected to discipline enables participation in society, and being undisciplined is to be excluded and made an object (and example) for the enforcement system of discipline. That is why the 'fear-state' is the other side of the constitutional state.

The maintenance of the disciplinary system by both prisons and the fear of crime expresses the two sides of the modern disciplinary system. There is both a *repressive* and an *ideological* technology of might (Lemke 1997: 71). Crime control by repressive and ideological technologies of might seemed to work up to the arrival of the risk society. Up until then, the ideological side (i.e. the production of 'evil') had grown, finally ending up as paranoia (Robins and Post 1997).

'Victimology', the victim movement and the sensationalised 'fear-of-crime problem' were part of this 'paranoia'. So that the disciplinary model of social control could maintain the functions of industrial society while the power of repressive discipline faded away, it was prudent to concentrate on ideological mechanisms to attain conformity. Thus, conventional victimology manufactured knowledge about crime from the victim's perspective. Regardless of whether it is 'paranoia', a 'century mistake' or a social 'failure', fear of crime remains a feature of the everyday behaviour of masses of individuals, and continues to keep them in conformity to the basic values and norms of the modern society. Thus, the ideological system of crime control defines and mediates both a threat scenario and a 'promising' model of social control, which works nevertheless as a diversion from real threats (Lemke 1997: 87).

The interpretation of the fear of crime as part of the ideological technology to control modern society in a disciplinary mode – alongside the 'demand' during the transition to late modernity to develop particularly the ideological function in order to strengthen conformity through the maintenance of discipline – sheds a new light on the empirical findings presented in the second part of this chapter. These findings also illuminate the question of why it is that the fear of crime seems so useful for attaining conformity. On the one hand, conventional victim surveys deal with the distinction between personal and social level of fear of crime in a very pragmatic way (Boers 1997: 299). At first glance, it seems very plausible to differentiate between those two forms of fear of crime since there is 'seemingly' an individual and a societal level. The higher levels of perceptions of fear of crime on a social level compared to those on an individual level (see Boers 1997: 197, 217) are regularly interpreted as the ultimately realistic judgement of crime as a personal risk in society (see also Table 9.4 in this chapter). Yet, on the other hand, there is no theoretical concept which requires this distinction. Rather, it may be that the fear of crime has a *hinge function*, since it belongs both to the micro level of the body (the individual level) and to the macro level of the population (the societal level) – in terms of the system of values and orientations which should direct mass behaviour.

In this latter perspective, the notion that fear of crime has a hinge function could provide a new interpretation of the distinction between personal and social levels of fear of crime as part of the (ideological) technology of power. On the one hand, the *personal level of fear of crime* could be (hypothetically) interpreted as an individual demand for discipline and the personal capability to fulfil the needs of disciplined functioning in a modern industrial society, ultimately in being a 'winner' or a 'loser'. Thus fear of crime (on a personal level) becomes an expression of self-definition as 'winner' or 'loser' and the capability to deal and cope personally with crime as a risk. So fear is indeed a realistic risk perception – though not so much related to the Yes or No of direct victimisation, but rather expressing whether or not victimisation is a threat. Similarly, fear also expresses whether an individual can regain or lose a sense of control over their lives; and it is a challenge to activate and use appropriate means to deal with their victimisation. That is why victim and fear stories are 'loser stories'. The hypothesis with regard to the relationship between personal levels of fear of crime and punitiveness would be that high levels of personal fear would support stronger disciplinary reactions of power ('law and order') to 'protect' the individual. Ultimately, it should express higher levels of punitiveness as a direct call to suppress and discipline the deviant.

On the other hand, the *social level of fear of crime* can be (again hypothetically) interpreted as a need for a security state which is capable of governing and balancing the risk society through appropriate risk management. So, the observed higher levels of social fear of crime, along with significantly higher levels of vicarious victimisation compared to personal victimisation (see Table 9.2), could represent a demand of social control which can *balance* the risk society as a whole. Thus, the empirical findings of personal and social levels of fear of crime address two *different* discourses: while personal fear of crime refers to the discourse *individual–power–discipline*, the social level of crime refers to the discourse of *population–power–governmentality*.

The rationality of governing, as well as being governed, on a societal level is to limit risks as threats, and to minimise sufferings through discipline and regulation. Thus the politics of fear of crime is part of this rationality and a justification of a style of governing in the transition to late modernity which combines two technologies of power: first, *discipline* – which is the conventional, current technologies (i.e. repression and exclusion) for the production of (economically) functioning individuals; and second, *regulation* which is the administration of social and individual forms of risk management. In the transition to late modernity, the disciplinary system is losing power. However, instead of developing a new system of social control – which might function on the basis of integration, substantial participation and dialogue–democracy by self-directed people (Giddens 1997: 133–7) and which could appear, in the terms of the 'new penology', as a shift from discipline to management (Albrecht 1994; Simon and Feeley 1995) – it still seems natural for policy-makers and parts of the population to re-activate the old strategies of 'law and order' and 'fear of crime' in order to increase the level of social control. Yet the crucial point is that an artificial level of fear actually blocks the possibilities of complex risk management, since management requires the conscious development of an appropriate realistic strategy for dealing with risks. For the sake of a better risk management, the perspective of 'governmentality' promises better results (Lemke 1997: 126) – it should be the function of government to frame social spaces for regulation in addition to the deployment of disciplinary technologies.

As the experience of the former East Germans suggests, fear of crime appears to be part of the rationalisation of governing technologies of new liberalism, where discipline becomes combined with self-responsibility. Governing, in the sense of 'leading human beings', can be considered as a discursive field where the execution of power becomes rationalised. Thus, the fear-of-crime issue is part of the wider political dialogue on security and, particularly, concerns how to place and use the different means of social control: discipline and regulation. As we have seen in the Eastern German situation, these means gain a particular meaning in transitional societies, where old orientations fade away and new normative systems are not fully developed.

References

Adams, J. (1995) *Risk*, London, UCL Press.

Albrecht, G. and Howe, C.-W. (1992) 'Soziale Schicht und Delinquenz. Verwischte Spuren oder falsche Fährte?' *Kölner Zeitschrift für Soziologie und Sozialpsychologie*, 44: 697–730.

Albrecht, P.-A. (1994) 'Das Strafrecht im Zugriff populistischer Politik', *Neue Justiz*, 5: 1–7.

Babl, S. (1993) 'Mehr Unzufriedenheit mit der Öffentlichen Sicherheit im vereinten Deutschland. Eine Zusammenstellung objektiver und subjektiver Indikatoren zur Kriminalität', *Literatur- und Forschungsdokumentation 1985–1992*: 61–73.

Beck, U. (1986) *Risikogesellschaft. Auf dem Weg in eine andere Moderne*, Frankfurt am Main: Suhrkamp.

——(1988) *Gegengifte. Die organisierte Unverantwortlichkeit*, Frankfurt am Main: Suhrkamp.

——(1998) 'Politics of risk society', pp. 9–22 in J. Franklin (ed.) *The Politics of Risk Society*, Cambridge: Polity Press.

Bernal, J.D. (1961) *Die Wissenschaft in der Geschichte*, Berlin: VEB Deutscher Verlag der Wissenschaften.

Bilsky, W. (1996a) 'Die Bedeutung von Furcht vor Kriminalität in Ost und West', *Monatsschrift für Kriminologie und Strafrechtsreform*, 79(5): 357–72.

——(1996b) 'Steigende Kriminalitätsfurcht – Gesichertes Wissen oder Trugschluss?' *Kriminologisches Journal*, 28(4): 284–6.

——(1997) 'Die Bedeutung der Kriminalitätsfurcht in Ost und West', pp. 157–69 in K. Sessar and M. Holler (eds) *Sozialer Umbruch und Kriminalität*, Pfaffenweiler: Centaurus-Verlagsgesellschaft.

Bilsky, W., Pfeiffer, C. and Wetzels, P. (eds) (1993) *Fear of Crime and Criminal Victimization*, Stuttgart: Ferdinand Enke Verlag.

Blinkert, B. (1988) 'Kriminalität als Modernisierungsrisiko? Das "Hermes Syndrom" der entwickelten Industriegesellschaften', *Soziale Welt*, 39: 397–412.

Boers, K. (1991) *Kriminalitätsfurcht. Über den Entstehungszusammenhang und die Folgen eines sozialen Problems*, Pfaffenweiler: Centaurus-Verlagsgesellschaft.

——(1997) 'Sozialer Umbruch und Kriminalität in Mittel- und Osteuropa. Gedanken zu einer Tagung', pp. 277–309 in K. Sessar and M. Holler (eds) *Sozialer Umbruch und Kriminalität*, Pfaffenweiler: Centaurus-Verlagsgesellschaft.

Boers, K., Ewald, U., Kerner, H.-J., Lautsch, E. and Sessar, K. (eds) (1994) *Sozialer Umbruch und Kriminalität*, vols I and II, Bonn: Forum Verlag Godesberg.

Boers, K., Kerner, H.-J. and Kurz, P. (1995) 'Rückgang der Kriminalitätsfurcht', *Neue Kriminalpolitik, Forum für Praxis, Politik und Wissenschaft* 4: 9–10.

Boers, K., Gutsche, G. and Sessar, K. (eds) (1997) *Sozialer Umbruch und Kriminalität in Deutschland*, Opladen: Westdeutscher Verlag.

Box, S., Hale, C. and Andrews, G. (1988) 'Explaining the fear of crime', *British Journal of Criminology* 28(3): 340–56.

Bruckner, P. (1997) *Ich leide, also bin Ich. Die Krankheit der Moderne. Eine Streitschrift*, Berlin: Aufbau Taschenbuch Verlag.

Christie, N. (1991) *Der nützliche Feind*, Bielefeld: AJZ Druck und Verlag GmbH.

Cohen, S. (1994) 'Social control and the politics of reconstruction', pp. 63–88 in D. Nelken (ed.) *The Futures of Criminology*, London, Thousand Oaks, New Delhi: Sage.

Eisner, M. (1997) *Das Ende der zivilisierten Stadt? Die Auswirkungen von Modernisierung und urbaner Krise auf Gewaltdelinquenz*, Frankfurt, New York: Campus.

Engler, W. (1999) *Die Ostdeutschen*, Berlin: Aufbau-Verlag.

Ewald, U. (1990) 'DDR-Strafrecht – quo vadis?' *Neue Justiz*, 4: 134–7.

——(ed.) (1994) *New Definitions of Crime in Societies in Transition to Democracy*, Bonn: Forum Verlag Godesberg.

——(ed.) (1997) *Social Transformation and Crime in Metropolises of Former Eastern Bloc Countries. Findings of a Multi-City Pilot Study 1993*, Bonn: Forum Verlag Godesberg.

Ewald, U. and Langer, W. (1997) 'Opfererleben in Deutschland nach der Wende. Entwicklungen in Ostdeutschland mit vergleichendem Bezug zu Westdeutschland', pp. 89–156 in K. Boers, G. Gutsche and K. Sessar (eds) *Sozialer Umbruch und Kriminalität in Deutschland*, Opladen: Westdeutscher Verlag.

Fattah, E. (1991) *Understanding Criminal Victimization. An Introduction into Theoretical Victimology*, Scarborough, Ontario: Prentice-Hall.

——(1993) 'Research on fear of crime: some common conceptual and measurement problems', pp. 45–70 in W. Bilsky, C. Pfeiffer and P. Wetzels (eds) *Fear of Crime and Criminal Victimisation*, Stuttgart: Ferdinand Enke Verlag,.

Feeley, M. and Simon, J. (1994) 'Actuarial justice: the emerging new criminal law', pp. 173–201 in D. Nelken (ed.) *The Futures of Criminology*, London, Thousand Oaks, New Delhi: Sage.

Ferraro, K.F. (1995) *Fear of Crime. Interpreting Victimisation Risk*, Albany: State University of New York Press.

Foucault, M. (1979) *Discipline and Punish. The Birth of the Prison*, New York: Vintage.

Franklin, J. (ed.) (1998) *The Politics of Risk Society*, Cambridge: Polity Press.

Gensicke, T. (1995) 'Die Stimmung ist besser als die Lage – Stimmungs- und Wertewandel in den neuen Bundesländern', pp. 285–303 in W. Glatzer and H.-H. Noll (eds) *Getrennt vereint. Lebensverhältnisse in Deutschland seit der Wiedervereinigung*, Frankfurt am Mein, New York: Campus-Verlag.

Giddens, A. (1994) *Beyond Left and Right. The Future of Radical Politics (Jenseits von Links und Rechts. Die Zukunft Radikaler Demokratie)*, Frankfurt am Main: Suhrkamp (German edition, 1997).

——(1997) *Jenseits von Links und Rechts. Die Zukunft radikaler Demokratie*, Edition Zweite Moderne, Frankfurt/Main: Suhrkamp.

——(1998) 'Risk society: the context of British politics', pp. 23–34 in J. Franklin (ed.) *The Politics of Risk Society*, Cambridge: Polity Press.

Greene, W.H. (1995) *LIMDEP (LIMited DEPendent variable models). Version 7. User's Manual*, Bellport, New York: Econometric Software.

Greve, W., Hosser, D. and Wetzels, P. (eds) (1996) *Bedrohung durch Kriminalität im Alter. Kriminalitätsfurcht älterer Menschen als Brennpunkt einer Gerontoviktimologie*, Interdisziplinäre Beiträge zur kriminologischen Forschung, Baden-Baden: Nomos Verlagsgesellschaft.

Habich, R., Noll, H.-H. and Zapf, W. (1999) 'Subjektives Wohlbefinden in Ostdeutschland nähert sich westdeutschem Niveau. Ergebnisse des Wohlfahrtssurvey 1998', *ISI 22, Informationsdienst soziale Indikatoren*, Juli: 1–7.

Haeder, M. (ed.) (1991) *Denken und Handeln in der Krise. Die DDR nach der 'Wende': Ergebnisse einer empirisch-soziologischen Studie*, Berlin: Akademie-Verlag.

Hale, C. (1996) 'Fear of crime: a review of the literature', *International Review of Victimology* 4: 79–150.

Heitmeyer, W. (1995) *Gewalt. Schattenseiten der Individualisierung bei Jugendlichen aus unterschiedlichen Milieus*, Weinheim, München: Juventa.

Hoffmeyer-Zlotnik, J.H.P. (1993) 'Operationalisierung von "Beruf" als zentrale Variable zur Messung von sozio-ökonomischen Status', *ZUMA-Nachrichten*, 32: 135–41.

Hollway, W. and Jefferson, T. (1997) 'The risk society in an age of anxiety: situating fear of crime', *British Journal of Sociology* 48(2): 255–66.

Hradil, S. (1995) 'Die Modernisierung des Denkens. Zukunftspotentiale und "Altlasten" in Ostdeutschland', *Aus Politik und Zeitgeschichte*, B 20/95: 3–15.

James, O. (1995) *Juvenile Violence in a Winner–Loser Culture : Socio-Economic and Familial Origins of the Rise in Violence Against the Person*, London, New York: Free Association Books.

Kaiser, G. and Jehle, J.-M. (eds) (1994) *Kriminologische Opferforschung. Neue Perspektiven und Erkenntnisse. Teilband II. Verbrechensfurcht und Opferwerdung. Individualopfer und Verarbeitung von Opfererfahrungen*, Heidelberg: Kriminalistikverlag.

——(eds) (1995) *Kriminologische Opferforschung. Neue Perspektiven und Erkenntnisse. Teilband I. Grundlagen – Opfer und Strafrechtspflege. Kriminalität der Mächtigen und ihre Opfer*, Heidelberg: Kriminalistikverlag.

Kelly, K. (1997) *Das Ende der Kontrolle. Die biologische Wende in Wirtschaft, Technik und Gesellschaft*, Mannheim: Bollmann.

Kerner, H.-J. (1997) 'Kriminologische Forschung im sozialen Umbruch', pp. 331–72 in K. Boers, G. Gutsche and K. Sessar (eds) *Sozialer Umbruch und Kriminalität in Deutschland*, Opladen: Westdeutscher Verlag.

Kleinman, A., Das, V. and Lock, M. (eds) (1997) *Social Suffering*, Berkeley, Los Angeles, London: University of California Press.

Kräupl, G. (1998) 'Angst vor Ungewissheit', *Evangelische Kommentare*, 29(2): 147–57.

Kräupl, G. and Ludwig, H. (1993) *Wandel kommunaler Lebenslagen, Kriminalität und Sanktionserwartungen. Bevölkerungsbefragung in einer städtischen Region Thüringens 1991/92 (Jenaer Kriminalitätsbefragung)*, Freiburg: Max-Planck-Institut für ausländisches und internationales Strafrecht.

Kreuzer, A., Gorgen, T., Kruger, R., Münch, V. and Schneider, H. (eds) (1993) *Jugenddelinquenz in Ost und West. Vergleichende Untersuchungen bei ost- und westdeutschen Studienanfängern in der Tradition Giessener Delinquenzbefragungen*, Bonn: Forum Verlag Godesberg.

Kury, H. (ed.) (1992) *Gesellschaftliche Umwälzung. Kriminalitätserfahrungen, Straffälligkeit und soziale Kontrolle*, Freiburg: Max-Planck-Institut für ausländisches und internationales Strafrecht.

Kury, H., Dörmann, U., Richter, H. and Würger, H. (eds) (1992) *Opfererfahrungen und Meinungen zur inneren Sicherheit in Deutschland*, Wiesbaden: Bundeskriminalamt.

Lemke, T. (1991) *Die Ursachen des Umbruchs 1989. Politische Sozialisation in der DDR*, Opladen: Westdeutscher Verlag.

——(1997) *Eine Kritik der politischen Vernunft*, Berlin: Argument Verlag.

Lutz, B. (1994) 'Das "Projekt Moderne" liegt noch vor uns. Zur Notwendigkeit einer neuen Makrotheorie moderner Gesellschaften', pp. 513–26 in H.-U. Derlien (ed.) *Systemrationalität und Partialinteresse, Festschrift für Renate Mayntz*, Baden-Baden: Nomos Verlagsgesellschaft.

Mawby, R. I. and Walklate, S. (1994) *Critical Victimology*, London, Thousand Oaks, New Delhi: Sage.

Merten, R. and Otto, H.-U. (eds) (1993) *Rechtsradikale Gewalt im vereinigten Deutschland. Jugend im gesellschaftlichen Umbruch*, Opladen: Leske Verlag and Budrich GmbH.

Miers, D. (1990) 'Positivist victimology: a critique. Part 2: critical victimology', *International Review of Victimology*, 1 (3): 219–30.

Mischkowitz, R. (1994) *Fremdenfeindliche Gewalt und Skinheads. Eine Literaturanalyse und Bestandsaufnahme polizeilicher Massnahmen*, Wiesbaden: Bundeskriminalamt.

Müller, H.-P. and Schmid, M. (eds) (1995) *Sozialer Wandel. Modellbildung und theoretische Ansätze*, Frankfurt am Main: Suhrkamp.

Neubacher, F. (1994) *Jugend und Rechtsextremismus in Deutschland vor und nach der Wende*, Bonn: Forum Verlag Godesberg.

Noll, H.-H. and Schröder, H. (1995) 'Öffentliche Sicherheit und subjektives Wohlbefinden in Ost- und Westdeutschland', pp. 305–28 in W. Glatzer and H.-H. Noll (eds) *Getrennt vereint. Lebensverhältnisse in Deutschland seit der Wiedervereinigung*, Frankfurt am Main, New York: Campus-Verlag.

Park, R.E. and Burgess, E.W. (1967) *The City*, Chicago: University of Chicago Press.

Pfeiffer, C. (1997) *Jugendkriminalität und Jugendgewalt in europäischen Ländern*, Hannover: Forschungsberichte des Kriminologischen Forschungsinstituts Niedersachsen e.V. Hannover.

Pfeiffer, C. and Greve, W. (eds) (1996) *Forschungsthema 'Kriminalität'*, Interdisziplinäre Beiträge zur kriminologischen Forschung, Festschrift für Heinz Barth, Baden-Baden: Nomos Verlagsgesellschaft.

Reissig, R. (1994) 'Transformation – theoretisch-konzeptionelle Ansätze und Eklärungsversuche', *Berliner Journal für Soziologie*, 4: 323–43.

Reissig, R. and Glaessner, G.-J. (eds) (1991) *Das Ende eines Experiments. Umbruch in der DDR und Deutsche Einheit*, Berlin: Dietz.

Reuband, K.-H. (1993) 'Kriminalitätsfurcht in Ost- und Westdeutschland. Zur Bedeutung psychosozialer Einflussfaktoren', *Soziale Probleme*, 3(2): 211–19.

——(1994) 'Steigende Kriminalitätsfrucht – Mythos oder Wirklichkeit? Objektive und subjektive Bedrohung durch Kriminalitä', *Gewerkschaftliche Monatshefte*, 45(4): 214–20.

——(1996) 'Gesellschaftlicher Wandel, Kriminalität und Kriminalitätsfurcht', *Neue Praxis*, 26(6): 494–504.

——(1999) 'Von der Kriminalitätshysterie zur Normalität?' *Neue Kriminalpolitik*, 4: 16–19.

Robins, R.S. and Post, J.M. (1997) *Political Paranoia. The Psychopolitics of Hatred*, New Haven, London: Yale University Press.

Rorty, R. (1989) *Kontingenz, Ironie und Solidarität*, Frankfurt am Main: Suhrkamp.

Sack, F. (1994) 'Conflicts and convergences of theoretical and methodological perspectives in criminology', pp. 7–34 in U. Ewald (ed.) *New Definitions of Crime in Societies in Transition to Democracy*, Bonn: Forum Verlag Godesberg.

——(1997) 'Umbruch und Kriminalität – Umbruch als Kriminalität', pp. 91–154 in K. Sessar and M. Holler (eds) *Sozialer Umbruch und Kriminalität*, Pfaffenweiler: Centaurus-Verlagsgesellschaft.

Safranski, R. (1997) *Das Böse oder Das Drama der Freiheit*, München, Wien: Carl Hanser Verlag.

Scherr, A. (1998) 'Alles Gute kommt von oben …', *Vorgaenge* 43(3): 81–92.

Sessar, K. (1997) 'Die Angst des Bürgers vor Verbrechen – was steckt eigentlich dahinter?' pp. 118–38 in H. Janssen and F. Peters (ed.) *Kriminologie für Soziale Arbeit*, Münster: Votum.

Sessar, K. and Holler, M. (eds) (1997) *Sozialer Umbruch und Kriminalität*, Pfaffenweiler: Centaurus-Verlagsgesellschaft.

——(1998) 'Kriminalitätseinstellungen: Von der Furcht zur Angst?' pp. 399–414 in H.-D. Schwind, B. Holyst and H.J. Schneider (eds) *Festschrift für Hans Joachim Schneider zum 70. Geburtstag am 14. November 1998, Kriminologie an der Schwelle zum 21. Jahrhundert*, Berlin, New York: de Guyter.

Shelley, L. and Vigh, J. (eds) (1995) *Social Changes, Crime and Police*, international conference, 1–4 June 1992, Chur, Switzerland, United States: Harwood Academic.

Simon, J. and Feeley, M.M. (1995) 'The new penology and public discourse on crime', pp. 147–80 in T.G. Blomberg and S. Cohen (eds) *Punishment and Social Control. Essays in Honor of Sheldon L. Messinger*, New York: de Gruyter.

Sparks, R. (1992) 'Reason and unreason in "left realism": some problems in the constitution of fear of crime', pp. 119–35 in R. Matthews and J. Young (eds) *Issues in Realist Criminology*, London: Sage.

Späth, L. (1997) *Blühende Phantasien und harte Realitäten. Wie der Umschwung Ost die ganze Republik verändert*, Düsseldorf, München: ECON.

Thome, H. (1992) 'Gesellschaftliche Modernisierung und Kriminalität. Zum Stand der sozialhistorischen Kriminalitätsforschung', *Zeitschrift für Soziologie*, 21: 212–28.

Trotha, T. von (ed.) (1996) *Politischer Wandel, Gesellschaft und Kriminalitätsdiskurse, Beiträge zur interdisziplinären wissenschaftlichen Kriminologie, Festschrift für Fritz Sack zum 65. Geburtstag*, Baden-Baden: Nomos-Verlagsgesellschaft.

Wahl, K. (1989) *Die Modernisierungsfalle. Gesellschaft, Selbstbewusstsein und Gewalt*, Frankfurt am Main: Suhrkamp.

Walklate, S. (1997) 'Risk and criminal victimisation: a modernist dilemma?' *British Journal of Criminology*, 37(1): 35–45.

Weiss, R. (1997) 'Bestandsaufnahme und Sekundäranalyse der Dunkelfeldforschung', in *Informationen aus der kriminalistisch-kriminologischen Forschung*, Wiesbaden: Bundeskriminalamt.

Wetzels, P. (1997) *Gewalterfahrungen in der Kindheit. Sexueller Missbrauch, körperliche Misshandlung und deren langfristige Konsequenzen*, Baden-Baden: Nomos.

Wetzels, P., Greve, W., Mecklenburg, E., Bilsky, W. and Pfeiffer, C. (eds) (1995) *Kriminalität im Leben alter Menschen. Eine altersvergleichende Untersuchung von Opfererfahrungen, persönnlichem Sicherheitsgefühl und Kriminalitätsfurcht. Ergebnisse der KFN-Opferbefragung 1992*, Stuttgart, Berlin: Schriftenreihe des Bundesministeriums fuer Familie, Senioren, Frauen und Jugend.

Wolle, S. (1998) *Die heile Welt der Diktatur. Alltag und Herrschaft in der DDR 1971–1989*, Bonn: Bundeszentrale fuer Politische Bildung.

Young, A. and Rush, P. (1994) 'The law of victimage in urbane realism: thinking through inscriptions of violence,' pp. 154–72 in D. Nelken (ed.) *The Futures of Criminology*, London, Thousand Oaks, New Delhi: State University of New York Press.

Young, J. (1992) 'Realist research as a basis for local criminal justice policy', pp. 33–72 in J. Lohman and B.D. MacLean (eds) *Realist Criminology. Crime Control and Policing in the 1990s*, Toronto, Buffalo, London: University of Toronto Press.

Zapf, W. (1991) 'Modernisierung und Modernisierungstheorien', pp. 23–39 in W. Zapf (ed.) *Die Modernisierung moderner Gesellschaften*, Frankfurt am Main: Campus Verlag.

10

THE PURSUIT OF SECURITY[1]

Lucia Zedner

Introduction

Our historic preoccupation with crime has been overlaid in recent years by growing concern about personal security, community safety and the maintenance of social order. Notwithstanding the inflated currency of political rhetoric which promises to be 'tough on crime', techniques of crime control have become curiously disassociated from crime itself. Rather, they promise some measure of protection, some freedom from anxiety about crime and the insecurities which appear to be the inevitable accompaniment of modern life.[2] The ever burgeoning and aptly named 'security industry' extends well beyond the traditional sphere of crime control to embrace an array of private provisions. In Britain, security arrangements which were once thought necessary only at points of high risk such as airports or national borders have become routine on transport, at theatres, cinemas and shopping malls.[3] General acceptance of searches of person and property, of identification checks and uniformed security guards, were won with remarkably little public debate about the curtailment of personal freedoms that these entail.[4] Policing, public and private, is bolstered by an ever growing arsenal of 'high-tech' surveillance equipment, from CCTV to bugging devices, together with the legal sphere powers to use them ever more widely.[5] The breaking down of constitutional barriers between police and intelligence agencies such as MI5, the expansion of police powers to engage in bugging operations and to employ computer database searches for suspects, are all justified as necessary to the pursuit of security. Yet exactly what security is, who should provide it, for whom and to what ends, remains remarkably unclear.

David Garland has observed that the strength of government and the emphasis it places on security are inversely related. That is, the stronger the political regime, the less likely it is to need to rely upon a tough stance towards crime control and punitive sanctions.[6] Accordingly, he argues, weak political regimes are much concerned about fear of crime, threats to personal security and social order, and the consequent need to bolster sources of security. But it is questionable whether this phenomenon is limited to regimes whose political position or legitimacy is precarious. Rather, it could be argued that the increasing internationalisation of both economic and political life is gradually undermining the power of contemporary national governments with the result that they are casting about for spheres of activity in which they can assert their sovereignty. At the same time, private corporate interests have become major players in meeting and promoting the demand for security.[7] These developments have led to the rise of a 'security society' in which a significant political and financial investment is made in security in and of itself. Security (together with its fashionable analogue 'community safety')[8] attracts increasing attention from national governments as an area in which they can offer citizens evidence of their continuing power and effectiveness. It furnishes the conceptual framework within which contemporary governments promise to deliver social order. Crime and disorder are no longer paramount social or political concerns, but merely specific issues within this more general framework.

In this chapter we examine the meanings of security and ask whose responsibility it is and how this has changed over time. We go on to analyse shifts in power entailed by the redistribution and commodification of security. We explore the ramifications of the privileging of security as a social and political goal for the pursuit of justice. And we conclude with some sobering observations on the limits and costs of security which point towards the paradox that the very pursuit of security contains and propagates the seeds of its own failure. Drawing on comparative research between Britain and Germany, we will suggest that the pursuit of security is at the same time both an international phenomenon and one which is highly differentiated according to local culture.

The meanings of security

One of the more striking features of the security debate is the lack of clarity about its meaning. This arises in part as a result of the very different threats to social order posed in different jurisdictions. The security problems faced by countries like Israel or Northern Ireland[9] are clearly very different from those of less troubled nations. Even within single jurisdictions, the word 'security' embraces several quite distinct ideas simultaneously and its attainment cannot easily be measured. As Freedman has observed, security is best described as an absence: it is achieved precisely 'when bad things do not happen rather than when good things do'.[10] But increasingly, the pursuit of security appears to require not merely an absence of threats but the positive reinforcement of public perceptions of their safety. Threats to security range from large-scale organised violence such as warfare, through economic recession and unemployment, to the starkest, most direct threats posed by individuals or groups against each other.[11] It is with this last form that this chapter will occupy itself. International security has largely taken a back seat to domestic concerns with personal and community safety and social order as the primary preoccupation of political life.[12] The pursuit of security in this sense attracts substantial funds, both public and private, and serves to justify draconian intrusions on personal freedom. Given the ramifications of the pursuit of security for public expenditure and civil liberties, we need a more developed understanding of what is at stake when security is invoked as a justification for public policy and private action.[13]

It is illuminating to differentiate between subjective and objective conceptions of security. While security may be said to have been achieved in the subjective sense that an individual, group or nation enjoys a sense of protection from harm and an absence of fear (irrespective of actual risk), objective security on the other hand requires an absence of actual threats.[14] 'Personal security' connotes that subjective sense of safety enjoyed by the individual and typically tested by the survey question 'how safe do you feel walking in your neighbourhood after dark?'[15] As the question itself reveals, what is at issue here is not an objective calculation of risks actually faced, but rather a highly personal assessment of risk which may owe more to individual temperament, prejudice, or physical strength than any external factor.[16] National crime surveys such as the British Crime Survey have revealed that there is often a significant disjuncture between so-called objective security in the sense of risks faced and subjective levels of insecurity suffered by different groups within the population. Typically, for example, elderly women living alone suffer feelings of insecurity disproportionate to the risks they actually face, while young men who habituate pubs enjoy a confidence not borne out by their high exposure to risk.[17] Rather than dismiss these discrepancies as mere irrationality, we would do better to acknowledge that personal security is a social good whose pursuit extends beyond the minimisation of objective risk and whose subjective appreciation may not be directly correlated with risk at all.[18] Personal feelings of insecurity derive from a multiplicity of secondary indicia of risk: subjective perception, political climate, media-inspired moral panics, or the construction of threats to social order in the wider public sphere at national and even international levels.[19] It follows that the contours and dynamics of both objective and subjective personal security will be likely to vary considerably in different social orders, and that issues of security in contemporary social theory may be illuminated by comparative investigation.[20]

Although the promise of personal security 'has come to be perceived as a condition of life in civilized society'[21], it is questionable whether its pursuit is either realistic or desirable. If high levels of objective personal security are obtainable only at the cost of living in a 'fortress-society' with significant limitations on freedom of movement and civil liberties, then that cost may be too high. Davis describes how on a Los Angeles housing project 'visitors are stopped and frisked, while the police routinely order residents back into their apartments at night. Such is the loss of freedom that public housing tenants must now endure as the price of "security" '.[22] To establish, as a common expectation, a standard of safety which cannot reasonably be met is only to promote dissatisfaction and inevitable disappointment. The complex and often conflictual relation between objective and subjective senses of security is nicely represented in the paradoxical nature of the attempt to promote security by scattering our social world with visible reminders of the threat of crime. To promise personal security is no more rational than to promise universal wealth, freedom from unhappiness or ill health. As such it is a puzzle why the myth of personal security is so powerful and enduring, and why it is that politicians across the political spectrum maintain that this is something which they can plausibly provide. In this context, the extent to which different societies regard the provision of a base level of security as the unambiguous responsibility of public institutions such as government and national police becomes a highly significant variable. Our research shows very clearly that, notwithstanding the growth of private security and local crime prevention initiatives in Western Germany, there is a far stronger consensus that security is a matter for the state there than in Britain.[23] Whether this signifies greater confidence in the state in Germany or an unrealistic faith in the continuing capacity of Federal and Land institutions to deliver social order is open to question. Is Germany a nation relatively untouched by the anxieties of postmodernity and hence with the political salience of demands for mythical security which government has to promise but can never deliver? Or is it rather a nation whose political attitudes suggest an out-dated faith in the state? [24]

Beyond the level of the personal, another important usage of security connotes attempts by the state to act against threats to common values or the social order. Even within this second category we can distinguish between internal threats to social order which are largely the province of the police and external threats responded to variously by border controls, customs, and the armed forces. Our research suggests that the force of this internal/external distinction varies significantly from country to country: whereas in Britain internal and external threats tend to be clearly distinguished, in Germany, the nearest equivalent to the English term 'law and order' is *Innere Sicherheit* – a markedly spatialised conception which marries ideas of internal disorder with fears of external threat.[25] The historic German reluctance to accord full citizenship rights or 'internal' membership even to second-generation guest workers implies a very particular conception of the conditions underpinning social order where security is predicated upon social homogeneity. In the German case, apparently solidarity-based security strategies are in fact premised on a social order which is exclusionary in its very conception.[26]

Security in the sense of national and social order is both a goal – that is, an absence of such threats – and also an activity, pursued by the 'security forces' both civilian and military. This second usage of security as an activity rather than a goal does not necessarily promise immunity from threat, still less an absence of threats. Rather, it describes the pursuit of strategies which purport to avert, minimise or respond to threats which are perceived as an inevitable facet of modern social life even by those whose very task it is to combat them.

The diversification of security

Just as comparative research challenges assumptions derived from over-familiarity with the domestic scene, so historical perspective throws present configurations of security into relief. The current devolution of state provision for security to private bodies is in some senses the reversal of a historical process whereby state responsibility for internal security itself grew out of private practices.[27] In Britain the historic movement from communal self-help through to the development of justices of the peace as purveyors of local justice led only relatively recently to the establishment of a formal state criminal justice system. Until the eighteenth century 'the only police were parish householders who took turns as constables'.[28] Social order was produced less by statute law or the actions of formal agencies than by conformity to local custom secured by fellow inhabitants of the village or town.[29] Only with the development of formal police forces in the nineteenth century was the state confirmed as bearing primary responsibility for security. Today, this trajectory has been stalled by a partial move back to communal self-help. Does this signify a return to a more modest conception of state power, or does it rather signify a diffusion of state power into a diversity of formally non-state bodies?

From the mid-nineteenth century through to the 1960s, Western governments confidently asserted their ability to tackle crime and its causes. State agencies of crime control and the criminal justice professions enjoyed clearly defined roles in combating crime, reforming offenders and seeking their reintegration into civil society. The gradual loss of faith in the rehabilitative ideal which followed the 1960s prompted growing questions over the ability of the state to control crime. As Downes and Morgan have observed, 'it was at this time that many an editorial was written on the "ungovernability" of Britain'.[30] Garland describes this shift as the abandonment of 'the myth of sovereign power', the myth that the state has a monopoly of organised violence and sole right to govern all social life.[31] Yet this is a myth which the state itself is unwilling to relinquish. In consequence, growing recognition of the limits of the state's power is met by a parallel 'recurring tendency towards a kind of hysterical denial, and the emphatic reassertion of the old myth of the sovereign state'.[32] The result is a serious tension between the state, in its attempts to reassert its former hegemony, and newly emergent providers of security. How far this is also true of Germany is open to question. It would seem that, historically at least, faith in the power of the state to solve social problems has been much stronger there than in Britain.[33]

The erosion of the historic state monopoly on security can be imputed to three salient trends: privatisation (and the explosion of the commercial security industry); communitarianism; and the re-emergence of vigilantism. We will examine each in turn before going on to assess the redistribution in political power entailed by these developments.

Privatisation of security has become a billion-pound business with private outstripping public provision in many countries in West Europe and North America.[34] Although the privatisation of security is a worldwide phenomenon, its development is by no means evenly distributed. Van Dijk has suggested that private security is much more prominent in Sweden, Germany and England and Wales than in France or the Netherlands.[35] This raises fascinating questions for close comparative investigation. Certainly, in France cultural attitudes to the power of the central state are still more robust than in Britain or, arguably, Germany.[36] Yet even between Britain and Germany, our research is suggestive of significant differences: as we have already observed, German insistence on state responsibility for crime control is markedly stronger than in Britain while, until recently, concern about crime there has registered far lower on social attitude surveys.[37] In order to draw any firm conclusions, therefore, one would need to know how private security is distributed and in what forms. Merely quantitative comparisons, though an interesting starting point, cannot be more than that.

The rise of private security has been accompanied by the parallel development of voluntaristic ventures which operate on the margins of the state. They vary from grass-roots community activities through charitable initiatives to those operating in close association with state agencies. Rarely are they wholly autonomous either in origin or operation: instead, the language of 'partnership', 'inter-agency co-operation', and 'multi-agency approach' captures the array of interactions between state, charitable and private bodies which characterise these developments.[38] For the past decade, citizens have been encouraged to participate in community crime prevention schemes and to take greater responsibility for securing their homes, property and persons.[39] Successive governments have sought to promote active co-operation with the formal agencies of law and order, with slogans like 'Together we can crack it', inviting public participation in activities once reserved to the police. And yet most of these largely ad hoc initiatives impose few controls or constraints on their membership, lack guidelines on how to respond to sensitive issues such as racial attacks or domestic violence, and are democratically accountable to no one.

Whether these initiatives stem from a loss of faith in state provision, a rejection of welfare state dependency and a determination by citizens to take control, or whether they result rather from attempts by government to instil social responsibility and a commitment to self-protection where none previously resided, is a matter of continuing debate.[40] Tactics described inelegantly but aptly by Garland as 'responsibilisation' strategies promote the duties that non-state bodies and even private individuals must accept in securing social order and their own protection.[41] Even where these initiatives are state-led, they can be seen as reflecting tensions within the state. On the one hand it appears unwilling to relinquish its monopoly of power, on the other it is obliged to acknowledge that it alone can no longer bear responsibility for security. By diffusing responsibility, the state can therefore hope to square the circle by taking credit for both the generation of new 'partnerships' and any positive outcomes of increased (subjective or objective) security.[42] As one might expect given the wider public consensus on state responsibility for security in Germany, community-based and partnership initiatives have been a good deal slower to develop there.[43]

Where the state, the private market and community are all seen to fail to provide sufficient guarantees of security, resort to individual action is an increasingly common consequence. Self-help or vigilantism[44] entails a conscious rejection of the authority or competence of traditional providers of security and a premeditated, and often co-ordinated, attempt to provide protection to the participants and others. The flourishing of vigilantism in recent years has been the subject of considerable political attention and concern. Its existence is troubling at several levels. At very least, it reflects a loss of faith in the guarantees offered by the formal system of state security and a determination to supplement these with self-help measures and local patrols. In its more extreme forms, vigilantism may threaten or even use force, engage in extra-legal activities, and target 'suspect' populations irrespective of the threat they actually pose. What distinguishes the most extreme forms of vigilantism from other forms of security is that they go beyond the pursuit of protection to mete out impromptu 'popular' or 'informal' justice (neither of which is justice at all). Although the delivery of informal justice is not a necessary facet of vigilantism, the temptation to mete out retribution against suspected offenders is high where the pursuit of security is privileged over the values of formal justice (see below). It is a moot point what goal is being pursued when retribution is meted out. As Johnston speculates, is it intended as 'mere revenge or the insertion of a deterrent element into the proceedings which, by discouraging others, will somehow enhance security?'[45] Once again, significant differences in the occurrence and dynamics of vigilantism (or anything resembling it) can be observed in the two countries. In Britain, when 'Guardian Angels' began patrolling the London Underground in the 1980s they received a cautious welcome. Similarly, property owners who engage in pre-emptive attack or victims who resort to post hoc retaliation are often met with a relatively sympathetic response in the courts. In Germany, by contrast, memories of the Nazi Blockwart in the West and the use of informers by the Stasi in the East have bred deep resistance to anything even faintly redolent of vigilantism even – or perhaps especially – when it appears to have state sanction.[46] This resistance is further entrenched by the fact that the most visible manifestations of vigilantism in Germany are the activities of neo-Nazi groups. Groups of skinhead or neo-Nazi youths clearly regarded themselves as defending a certain conception of German social order when they attacked refugee hostels in the months and years following unification and the dismantling of the Iron Curtain. Debate raged in Germany as to whether the official response was sufficiently vigorous to distance the state completely from the implication that those attacked were deemed to be outwith public guarantees of security.[47]

Shifts in security and the relocation of power

The parallel developments of privatisation, what might be called communitarianism, and vigilantism raise intriguing questions about the location, or relocation, of power they entail. At first sight it might appear that all these developments connote a straightforward transfer of power from state to non-state authorities. A more nuanced appreciation of these shifts suggests a rather more complex picture. Opponents of privatisation have argued that transferring security provision from public to private hands necessarily entails a concomitant transfer of power and loss of control by the state.[48] The activities of private security firms have the effect of limiting access to what was once public space and in its place creating privatised streets, housing estates and shopping malls open only to those who are able to buy their right to be there.[49] Yet to the extent that privatisation is subject to state sanction and regulation, it is questionable whether its growth represents a significant attenuation of state power. Fears about the loss of accountability threatened by privatisation have been partially met by the creation of regulatory legislation, provisions for inspection, and auditing.[50] These new regulatory modes, far from diminishing the power of the state, generate new tiers of governmental activity which effectively extend its ambit.[51] Private security firms operating in commercial and shopping centres, for example, are often overseen by local police, and security guards are themselves the subject of police video surveillance.[52] In the Netherlands, for example, every town is now patrolled by uniformed city guards managed by the police. While there is certainly evidence of increasing private provision of security in Germany, auditing is far less pervasive and the linkage of private to governmental provision is markedly weaker, particularly in 'mainstream' areas such as policing or crime prevention.[53] It is dangerous to generalise, therefore, about the movements in power effected by privatisation. Privatisation takes many forms even within one jurisdiction and its significance depends fundamentally on its interaction with prevailing institutional structures and cultures in particular societies.

The development of community-based initiatives would also seem to suggest a transfer of power away from the state. Community organisations, charities and other non-governmental organisations increasingly take responsibility for activities like crime prevention, victim-offender mediation and even community penalties. In describing these, it is common to talk of a diminution of state power. And yet, these developments are arguably better understood as a new mode of exercising state power. Corporatism describes this trend as incorporation of non-state bodies within the realm of the state rather than the dissemination of power outward.[54] The particular forms which corporatism may take are well illustrated through comparative research: we found striking differences between Britain and Germany. In Germany, the development of local initiatives, for example, in crime prevention must be interpreted in the light of a long history of corporatism which has seen governments negotiating with 'private' actors such as local businessmen. Apparently similar developments involving local businesses and other associations have a very different genesis, and one which can draw on longer-term relationships of relatively high trust (hence, arguably, the absence of auditing). There is little to compare with the centrally propelled development of the new 'partnership' approaches in Britain, which have transformed pre-existing community groups by forcing them into the institutional mould of the new agencies, and the accountability procedures and funding imperatives which this entails.[55] In these developments the state extends its control over what were once essentially private and voluntaristic endeavours.

Genuine vigilantism is arguably the one exception to the trend towards expansion of state power described above. Where privatisation and the development of community-based initiatives are state-sanctioned and may even be state-promoted, vigilantism apparently poses a direct challenge to state authority. Where privatisation and 'responsibilisation' strategies may be seen as an extension of state control, vigilantism signifies a rejection and an undermining of state power. Yet even here we may observe attempts by government to 'tame' or 'incorporate' vigilantism by sanctioning quasi-vigilantist activities – for example the Conservative government's promotion of 'walking with a purpose'.[56] It is debatable whether parallel developments in Germany also represent an attempt to incorporate would-be vigilantes. The Bavarian analogue of 'walking with a purpose', the *Sicherheitswacht*, met initially with a mixture of outrage and satire in the national press.[57] More worryingly still, the inadequate police response to xenophobic gang violence against foreign workers in German towns appears to signify a tacit sanctioning of these actions. This inaction reveals the limits of security: where foreigners are deemed outside full citizenship, they are rendered ineligible for the protections offered to those within.[58]

Perhaps one of the most successful bids to co-opt vigilante energies occurred in Israel when the community-initiated 'Civil Guard' swept the country in the 1970s in response to growing fears of terrorism. The government first tamed this grass-roots movement by subjecting it to legal regulation, then co-opted it as auxiliary units to the national police force.[59] What had begun as a clear challenge to state authority was effectively incorporated into state security provision and resulted in a significant expansion of the state.

What becomes clear from these comparative observations is that it is hazardous to generalise about the shifts in power entailed by new developments in security provision. While some undoubtedly represent an erosion of state power, others are better seen as a reconfiguration of the state, and others still signify its overall expansion, albeit in disguised forms.

The commodification of security

A more complex issue still is how the phenomenon of security is itself reconfigured by changes in its provision and distribution. The growth of the commercial security industry together with the burgeoning of voluntary, communal, and individualistic efforts has had the effect of transforming security into a commodity to be bought and sold in the marketplace.[60] Proponents of privatisation argue that state provision of security is overly bureaucratic, unresponsive and expensive. By contrast, the market is lauded as an economic and flexible means of providing consumers with the choice to buy such protection as they need.[61] The danger, however, is that privatisation is liable to create major disparities in the provision and distribution of security. Where security is no longer deemed to be the primary responsibility of the state but rather a commodity to be purchased by those with the wherewithal to do so, it is inevitably distributed according to market forces rather than need.[62] As with so many important social goods, those with greatest need of state protection tend to be those with least purchasing power. The rich and powerful can readily afford personal and property insurance premiums, burglar and car alarms, homes in gated residential areas and even security guards, leaving the poor and unprotected ever more vulnerable to those who are thus driven to prey on their more meagre resources. Commodification of basic social goods like security thus has the effect of reducing citizenship to a brand of consumerism. Those without the financial and other resources essential to exercising the muscle of consumerism are effectively excluded from citizenship and its protections. The danger is that this trend will lead to an increasingly segregated society where basic values of political and social justice are undermined by the differential capacity to buy security.[63]

The creeping replacement of the language of citizenship by that of consumerism is by no means confined to the issue of security.[64] But it is in relation to basic social goods such as security that its implications for social justice are rendered most transparent. The commodification of security and the concomitant loss of public provision erode an integral element of the rights and goods enjoyed in common which are essential to maintaining any sense of 'citizen identity'.[65] The ramifications of privatising security are much larger, therefore, than at first appear: in the name of providing choice, the commodification of security inflicts irreparable damage on the basic goods of equal citizenship and social cohesion. It is for this reason that academics like Loader insist that 'security ought not to be thought of and acted upon as a tradable commodity'.[66]

The social costs of pursuing security

The pursuit of security is clearly not without social costs. Promoted as pursuing the elimination of risk, the security industry in fact presumes the persistence of crime. Arguably it is not even in the interests of those whose professional careers, business interests, or political programmes rely upon the continued threat of crime to seek its eradication. As Feeley and Simon have observed in respect of the 'new penology', the focus has switched from punishing individual wrongdoers to calculating risk and managing suspect or dangerous populations with the purpose 'not to eliminate crime but to make it tolerable through systemic coordination'.[67]

Allied to this shift is the growth of managerialism. Debates about the values and principles necessary to the pursuit of due process and procedural fairness are increasingly superseded by a new emphasis on auditing and 'key performance indicators'.[68] The provision and measurement of the criminal process becomes an end in itself to be evaluated and applauded irrespective of the success of its outcomes. Managerialism permits the reformulation of goals away from the task of controlling or reducing crime and towards more modest system-based criteria of throughput, economy and efficiency.[69] We would argue that the pursuit of security has been central to the success of managerialism, for it allows criminal justice professionals to be judged less by results than by the pursuit itself. For example, in England community safety has been pursued primarily by the readily auditable practices of distributing window stickers, encouraging property marking and advising on home security. Whether or not these activities actually reduce crime is apparently less important than the fact that they are visible and readily counted. Social crime prevention has, by contrast, been marginalised into the spaces left by the imperatives of the audit and objective performance indicia.[70] Managerialism is no less central to the logic of private security systems, in respect of which Robert argues 'repression is far from being a priority: it is counterproductive to the firm's aims'.[71]

The pursuit of security also has important, and arguably adverse, ramifications for the populations targeted by the formal agencies of social control. Whereas traditional modes of punishment focused attention on the individual wrongdoer, on the determination of their guilt and on punishment, attention is now increasingly turned to a target population of potential wrongdoers. The means by which this population is identified is wholly unscientific, relying on race and class prejudice and drawing on questionable presumptions about people's appearance, lifestyles and habits. This suspect population is seen, according to Feeley and Simon, as 'a permanently marginal population ... a self-perpetuating and pathological segment of society that is not integratable into the larger whole'.[72] Permanently excluded from the social body, it is condemned to the status of external threat. Little hope is extended for the transformation, still less reintegration, of this segment of society whose lack of educational qualifications or marketable skills exclude them from social and economic mobility.[73] Security becomes a perpetually elusive goal whose attainment is barred by the continuing and irredeemable presence of this dangerous population. Paradoxically, just as the British government declares itself committed to tackling social exclusion, so the criminal justice system resigns itself to the semi-permanent exclusion of those who form the burgeoning population of our prisons.

Security is thus promoted as a goal only for that part of the population deemed part of the body politic: for a significant minority security is not even sought. This is particularly striking in Germany, where policies towards Ausländer[74] may still be described in terms of a politics of exclusion. Again, this suggests that solidaristic security strategies may themselves be exclusionary. They are predicated upon the existence of a dangerous population without which it would not even be necessary to speak of security as an important social good.[75] Inevitably, the shape and location of this suspect population varies in different cultures: whereas in Germany it is principally Ausländer, in Britain it is that body of economically marginal, often long-term unemployed labelled by social scientists and politicians 'the Underclass'. Although the group designated as outsider varies, it is the consistency with which the pursuit of security appears to require that there be such a group which must cause concern.

These social divisions are exacerbated further still by the rush by those who can afford to do so to insulate themselves from perceived risks. They live in gated communities, avoid travel on public transport and isolate themselves further through their choice of leisure activities. For the residents of Los Angeles, Davis has observed, ' "security" has less to do with personal safety than with the degree of personal insulation, in residential, work, consumption and travel environments, from "unsavoury" groups and individuals, even crowds in general'.[76] His scarifying picture of life in LA neatly exposes the ultimate logic of the security society: the demand for 'walled residential communities' has 'assumed the frenzied dimensions of a residential arms race as ordinary suburbanites demand the kind of social insulation once enjoyed only by the rich ... hence the thousand lawns displaying the little "armed response" warnings'.[77] Living under self-inflicted siege, it is all too easy for middle-class imaginations to demonise the perceived threat posed by the underclass 'Other' and buy with ever greater urgency the products which the security industry is all too happy to sell them.

Conclusion

The pursuit of security presupposes threats against which the individual, group or community must be secured. And just as it presupposes those who must be protected against threat, so it presupposes those who threaten. The pursuit, to say nothing of the attainment, of security necessarily implies the identification and exclusion of this latter group.[78] Similarly, maintaining security relies upon continued communal vigilance against a common 'enemy'. Exclusion, be it of particular economic, social, racial or political groups, is an inevitable concomitant of the security society.[79] Is it that we have some collective psychic need for an external enemy in order to promote collective solidarity[80] or is the construction of an external threat simply a means of justifying the continued existence of our defence and intelligence services? A clue here may be found in the recurrent resort to a vocabulary of 'war' against crime. The language of warfare not only justifies the involvement of agencies whose remit might normally be seen as outside the sphere of criminal justice: it is reflective also of the idea that it is an entire 'enemy' population, rather than individual offenders, against whom security initiatives are targeted. The irony is that the promise of community safety and social solidarity is bought only at the cost of social exclusion.

References

Albrecht, P.-A. (1988) 'Das Strafrecht auf dem Weg vom liberalen Rechtsstaat zum sozialen Interventionsstaat', *KritV*: 182–209.

Barron, A. and Scott, C. (1992) 'The Citizen's Charter programme', *Modern Law Review*, 55/4: 526–46.

Bennett. T. (1990) *Evaluating Neighbourhood Watch*, Aldershot: Gower.

Berki, R.N. (1986) *Security and Society*, London: Dent.

Bilsky, W. (1996) 'Diskussion – Die Bedeutung von Furcht vor Kriminalität in Ost und West', *Monatsschrift für Kriminologie und Strafrechtsreform*, 79: 357–72.

Brake, M. and Hale, C. (1992) *Public Order and Private Lives: The Politics of Law and Order*, London: Routledge.

Christie, N. (1994) *Crime Control as Industry*, London: Routledge.

Crawford, A. (1997) *The Local Governance of Crime: Appeals to Community and Partnerships*, Oxford: Oxford University Press.

Dake, K. (1992) 'Myths of nature: culture and the social construction of risk', *Journal of Social Issues*, 48(4).

Davis, M. (1998) *City of Quartz: Excavating the Future in Los Angeles*, London: Pimlico.

Downes, D. and Morgan, R. (1997) 'Dumping the "hostages to fortune"? The politics of law and order in post-war Britain', in M. Maguire, R. Morgan and R. Reiner (eds) *The Oxford Handbook of Criminology*, Oxford: Oxford University Press, second edition, 87–134.

Ericson, R. and Haggerty, K.D. (1997) *Policing the Risk Society*, Oxford: Oxford University Press.

Feeley, M. and Simon, J. (1992) 'The new penology: notes on the emerging strategy of corrections and its implications', *Criminology* 30: 449–74.

——(1994) 'Actuarial justice: the emerging new criminal law', in D. Nelken (ed.) *The Futures of Criminology*, London: Sage, 173–201.

Fischer, R.J. and Green, G. (1992) *Introduction to Security*, London: Butterworth-Heinemann.

Freedman, L. (1992) 'The concept of security', in M. Hawkesworth and M. Kogan (eds) *Encyclopedia of Government and Politics*, vol. 2, London: Routledge, 730–41.

Frehsee, D. (1981) 'Zu den theoretischen Grundlage "Kommunaler Delinquenzprophylaxe"', *Kriminologische Journal* 13: 64–7.

——(1998) 'Politische Funktionen Kommunaler Kriminalprävention' in H.-J. Albrecht *et al.* (eds) *Internationale Perspektiven in Kriminologie und Strafrecht*, vol. 1, Berlin: Duncker and Humblot, 739–63.

Frehsee, D., Löschper, G. and Schumann, K.F. (eds) (1994) *Strafrecht, soziale Kontrolle, soziale Disziplinierung*, Opladen: Westdeutscher Verlag, especially articles by S. Cohen and D. Nogalia and F. Sack.

Funk, A. (1995) 'Ausgeschlossene und Bürger: Das ambivalente Verhältnis von Rechtsgleichheit und sozialen Ausschlus', *Kriminologisches Journal*, 4: 243–56;

Garland, D. (1996) 'The limits of the sovereign state: strategies of crime control in contemporary society', *British Journal of Criminology*, 36(4): 445–71.

Glatzer, W. *et al.* (1992) *Recent Social Trends in West Germany 1960–1990*, Frankfurt: Campus Verlag.

Graham, J. (1990) *Crime Prevention Strategies in Europe and North America*, Helsinki: Helsinki Institute for Crime Prevention and Control.

Hale, C. (1996) 'Fear of crime; a review of the literature', *International Review of Victimology*, 4: 79–150.

Hay, D. (1980) 'Crime in eighteenth- and nineteenth-century England', in N. Morris and M. Tonry (eds) *Crime and Justice*, vol. 2, Chicago: University of Chicago Press 45–84.

Hollway, W. and Jefferson, T. (1998) 'The risk society in an age of anxiety: situating fear of crime', *British Journal of Sociology*, 48(2): 255–66.

Ireland, P. (1995) 'Reflections on a rampage through the barriers of shame: law, community, and the new conservatism', *Journal of Law and Society*, 22(2): 189–211.

Johnston, L. (1992) *The Rebirth of Private Policing*, London: Routledge.

——(1996) 'What is vigilantism?', *British Journal of Criminology*, 36(2): 220–36.

Jones, C. (1993) 'Auditing criminal justice', *British Journal of Criminology*, 33: 187–202.

Jones, T. and Newburn, T. (1998) *Private Security and Public Policing*, Oxford: Oxford University Press.

Kury, H. (1992) *Opferfahrungen und Meinungen zur Inneren Sicherheit in Deutschland*, Wiebaden: Bundeskriminalamt.

——(ed.) (1997) *Konzepte Kommunaler Kriminalprävention*, Freiburg: Max Planck Institute.

Lacey, N. (1994) 'Government as manager, citizen as consumer', *Modern Law Review*, 75: 534–54.

Lacey, N. and Zedner, L. (1995) 'Discourses of community in criminal justice', *Journal of Law and Society*, 22: 316–18.

——(1998) 'Community in German criminal justice', *Social and Legal Studies*, 7(1): 7–25.

Leadbetter, C. (1996) *The Self-Policing Society*, London: Demos.

Leigh, I. and Lustgarten, L. (1994) *In from the Cold: National Security and Parliamentary Democracy*, Oxford: Oxford University Press.

Lisken, H. (1994) ' "Sicherheit" durch "Kriminalitätsbekämpfung" ', *Zeitschrift für Rechtspolitik*, 2: 49–52.

Loader, I. (1997) 'Private security and the demand for protection in contemporary Britain', *Policing and Society*, 7(3): 377–94.

——(1997) 'Thinking normatively about private security', *Journal of Law and Society*, 3(24): 377–94.

McCorry, J. and Morrisey, M. (1989) 'Community, Crime and Punishment in West Belfast', *Howard Journal of Criminal Justice*, 28 April: 282–90.

Messner, C. and Ruggiero, V. (1995) 'Germany: the penal system between past and future', in V. Ruggiero, M. Ryan and J. Sim (eds) *Western European Penal Systems: A Critical Anatomy*, London: Sage, 128–48.

Miller, D. (1995) 'Citizenship and pluralism', *Political Studies*, 43: 432–50.

Mirrlees-Black, C. Mayhew, P. and Percy, A. (1996) *The 1996 British Crime Survey*, London: HMSO.

Narr, W.-D. (1994) 'Das "System Innere Sicherheit" ', *Bürgerrechte und Polizei*, 48: 6–12.

Obergfell-Fuchs, J. and Kury, H. (1996) 'Sicherheitsgefühl und Persönlichkeit', *Monatsschrift für Kriminologie und Strafrechtsreform*, 79: 97–113.

Osborn, S. and Bright, J. (1989) *Crime Prevention and Community Safety: A Practical Guide for Local Authorities*, London: Safe Neighbourhoods Unit.

Raine, J.W. and Wilson, M.J. (1993) *Managing Criminal Justice*, Hemel Hempstead: Harvester Wheatsheaf.

——(1997) 'Beyond managerialism in criminal justice', *Howard Journal of Criminal Justice*, 36(1): 80–95.

Robert, P. (1989) 'The privatization of social control', in R. Hood (ed.) *Crime and Criminal Policy in Europe*, Oxford: Centre for Criminological Research, 104–20.

Rock, P. (1985) 'Law, order and power in late seventeenth- and early eighteenth-century England', in S. Cohen and A. Scull (eds) *Social Control and the State*, Oxford: Blackwell.

Rose, N. and Miller, P. (1992) 'Political power beyond the state: problematics of government', *British Journal of Sociology* 43: 173–205.

Scherr, A. (1997) 'Sicherheitsbedürfnis, soziale Ausschliessung und Kriminalisierung', *Kriminologisches Journal*, 4: 256–66.

Sharpe, J.A. (1990) *Judicial Punishment in England*, London: Faber & Faber.

Shearing, C. (1992) 'The relationship between public and private policing', in M. Tonry and N. Morris (eds) *Crime and Justice 15*, Chicago: Chicago University Press, 399–434.

Shearing, C. and Stenning, P. (1981) 'Modern private security: its growth and implications', *Crime and Justice: An Annual Review of Research*, 3: 193–245, Chicago: University of Chicago Press.

——(1983) 'Private security: implications for social control', *Social Problems*, 30: 493–506.

Shepticki, J. (1998) 'Policing, postmodernism and transnationalization', *British Journal of Criminology*, 38(3): 485–503.

Short, J. (1984) 'The social fabric of risk: toward the social transformation of risk analysis', *American Sociological Review*, 49: 711–25.

South, S. (1988) *Policing for Profit: The Private Security Sector*, London: Sage.

Sparks, R. (1992) *Television and the Drama of Crime*, Milton Keynes: Open University Press.

Spitzer, S. (1987) 'Security and control in capitalist societies: the fetishism of security and the secret thereof', in J. Lowman, R.J. Menzies and T.S. Palys (eds) *Trancarceration: Essays in the Sociology of Social Control*, Aldershot: Gower, 43–58.

Streng, F. (1998) 'Wie weit trägt das broken windows-Paradigma?' in H.-J. Albrecht *et al.* (eds) *Internationale Perspektiven in Kriminologie und Strafrecht*, vol. 2, Berlin: Duncker and Humblot, 921–41.

van Dijk, J. (1991) 'More than a matter of security: trends in crime prevention in Europe', in F. Heidensohn and M. Farrell (eds) *Crime in Europe*, London: Routledge, 27–42.

Walter, M. and Kubink, M. (1993) 'Ausländerkriminalität – Phänomen oder Phantom der (Kriminal-) Politik?', *Monatsschrift für Kriminologie*, 5: 306–19.

Wildavsky, A. (1988) *Searching for Safety*, Oxford: Transition.

Wolfers, A. (1962) *Discord and Collaboration*, Baltimore: Johns Hopkins University Press.

Wrightson, K. (1980) 'Two concepts of order: justices, constables and jurymen in seventeenth-century England', in J. Brewer and J. Styles (eds) *An Ungovernable People: The English and their Law in the Seventeenth and Eighteenth Centuries*, London: Hutchison, 21–46.

Yanay, U. (1994) 'Co-opting vigilantism: government response to community action for personal safety', *Journal of Public Policy*, 14(3): 383–96.

Young, J. (1988) 'Risk of crime and fear of crime: a realist critique of survey-based assumptions', in M. Maguire and J. Pointing (eds) *Victims of Crime: A New Deal*, Milton Keynes: Open University Press.

——(1999) *The Exclusive Society*, London: Sage.

Zedner, L. (1995) 'In pursuit of the vernacular: comparing law and order discourse in Britain and Germany', *Social and Legal Studies*, 4: 520–1.

11

SOME DAY OUR PRINCE WILL COME

Zero-tolerance policing and liberal government

Kevin Stenson

A Prince ought to have no other aim or thought, nor select anything else for his study, than war and its rules and discipline; for this is the sole art that belongs to him who rules, and it is of such force that it not only upholds those who are born princes, but it often enables men to rise from a private station to that rank.

(*The Prince*, Niccolo Machiavelli)

Introduction

In the beleaguered, media-dominated liberal democracies of the 1990s, one of the most potent sound-bites recurring in the debates about policing and the crises of urban governance is the notion of zero-tolerance policing (ZTP). This is associated internationally with New York's Mayor Giuliani and Police Commissioner Bill Bratton. The knowledge base of this strategy is rooted in James Q. Wilson and George Kelling's famous 'broken windows' thesis (1982). This posits that in neighbourhoods on the cusp of decline, if broken windows and other indicators of community disintegration are not promptly dealt with and informal community controls restored, a spiral of deterioration and criminality will quickly ensue. Among academic commentators and police managers (including some of the key players), a frequent refrain is that the term is resistant to definition, its referents are fluid, slippery, ambiguous and can mean different things in different locations (Johnston 1997). This is seen as particularly so as one moves further from New York City. Nevertheless, in the world of political communication, which involves pressing the appropriate emotional buttons with the bulk of the electorate – the readership of tabloid and middlebrow newspapers – the aggressive and forceful *emotive* message projected through the media is clear enough, even if it selectively focuses only on a fraction of the complex policing structures and practices involved in ZTP (Pollard 1997).

This approach highlights 'quality of life' issues. These include petty disorders and incivilities on the streets associated *inter alia* with: beggars, the homeless, 'squeegee merchants', vandals, street robbers, graffiti artists, street drug dealers (often armed with guns and knives), those who urinate in public and rowdy, drunken young men and women. All of these groups are perceived to degrade the urban aesthetic and make life difficult and intimidating in public urban spaces for the 'law-abiding'. They are also seen as hastening the flight of the middling classes to the suburbs, thus diminishing urban tax revenues, and also scaring away tourists, commuters seeking entertainment and other, hopefully high spending, visitors to the city. Dealing with the supposedly trivial, petty problems is held to be the key to containing the more serious crimes against the person and property, on the premise that minor miscreants often turn into – or are simultaneously – serious career criminals. This is also seen as the key to replacing vicious circles of urban decline and pessimism with virtuous, optimistic spirals of economic and social growth, often led by small businesses once more prepared to make a go of it in the city. More deeply, tough action against crime chimes with a nostalgic wish, fostered particularly by politicians of the right like President Reagan and Mrs Thatcher, to reinstate, in part through tough penal and welfare policies, more civilized, neighbourly ways of living. These allegedly preceded the age of welfare dependency, with citizens taking greater responsibility for their own lives and the discipline of their children.

In June 1997, soon after the election of the new Labour Government, the British Home Secretary Jack Straw, who was raised by a single mother in an area of social housing, affirmed his unwavering and apparently sincere commitment to a zero-tolerance approach. Impressed by seeing ZTP in action during a visit to New York, Straw regarded the programme as applicable not only for the big city but also for the run-down and increasingly disorderly peripheral areas of social housing that, in Britain and France particularly, are increasingly located far from town and city centres (Power and Tunstall 1997; Bailleau 1998).

> The risks of being a victim of violent crime are four times greater in a disorderly neighbourhood than an orderly one. It is now clear from the British Crime survey that whether a neighbourhood is felt to be disorderly – full of graffiti and so on – is a more important predictor of the level of property crime than whether that neighbourhood is a city area or not. This evidence powerfully reinforces the case for a zero tolerance approach to disorder
>
> (Home Office news release 25 June 1997).

Although radical critics see the knowledge base for this perspective as rooted in conservative American criminology, it is arguable that in the UK setting it also harmonises with some of the early arguments of the Left Realist school of criminology (Lea and Young 1982). They helped to make Labour Party policies more responsive to the neglected crime anxieties of working class constituencies in the 1980s (Hopkins Burke 1998). The Left Realists emphasised the need for Keynesian policies of economic redistribution and were careful to criticise a reliance on harsh, overly pro-active policing styles that would further alienate poor populations from the police. Nevertheless, it was stressed that benign or lazy neglect and the failure to deal with crime are held to symbolise a failure not just of policing, but of the very core of public government and the contract in liberal polities between citizens and the state. The apologists of ZTP also stress that this governmental failure is a betrayal of the interests and needs of the old, women, the disabled and all those who lack the capacities and skills to survive in a predatory environment and lack the money to avoid the use of public space.

But, it is important to note the shift in the forms of language with which this message is communicated when it is translated from intellectual to political discourse. Away from the world of the academy and the policy advisers who usually favour conceptually precise, emotionally low key, rationalist discourse, the discourse of law and order employed by politicians and the mainstream media is more likely to be driven by emotionally charged metaphorical discourse. Metaphors do not just embroider language or rational conceptual arguments, they have powerful emotional force as calls to action and operate in clusters to structure our thought and understanding of social relationships (Lakoff and Johnson 1980: 5). For example, a senior London Metropolitan police officer, visiting the New York Police Department perceptively noted how, in regular management meetings with precinct commanders, Commissioner Bratton and his team routinely used metaphors drawn from Winston Churchill's Second World War rhetoric.

> I found that much of the language in a successful NYPD is taken from that great conflict – 'we have taken the beaches' (Manhattan), we now intend to take the fields and hedgerows (Brooklyn). Such references may account for the relaxed attitude that is evident in the NYPD command team to increased complaints about hard policing. To conclude the war analogy, I was struck by the focus on intelligence, the quality of which is likely to contribute significantly to victory to victory in any *battle*... [there are] Four steps to crime control:
>
> * Timely and accurate information
> * Effective *tactics*
> * Rapid *deployment*
> * Relentless follow-up and assessment.
>
> (Griffiths 1998: 128, emphasis added)

Hence, the emotive and popular message is that a failure to confront these issues allows a return to a rival, alternative politics of survival where the strong devour the weak: a primeval hegemony of muscle, youth and those willing and able to use violence to protect and defend illegal economies and practices. This is the riposte to leftist critics who argue that ZTP simply defends the interests of wealthy city residents and powerful businesses like the Disney Corporation which has, since the mid-1990s, invested heavily in the environmental upgrading of mid-town Manhattan (Kelling and Coles 1996).

This argument echoes the seventeenth-century English philosopher Thomas Hobbes' nightmare of the war of all against all, which he saw as characterising the pre-social state of nature, a dark cloud hovering eternally at the edge of civilisation. Hobbes' strongly masculine war metaphors for the human condition emphasise 'security; distrust of enemies; the possibility of invasion; the importance of self-defence, and the atmosphere of mutual fear' (Brace 1997: 142). Following a Hobbesian logic, the modern proponents of ZTP argue that the solutions must include a more hands-on confrontation by police officers, galvanised by strong and decisive leadership, with those who are deemed to be a nuisance or threat to citizens who have a perceivably more secure linkage to the mainstream social bond, through regular work, family responsibilities and respect for the law. It also implies that shrinking from this task amounts to cowardice on the part of those who are paid not simply as security guards to protect against commercial loss, but, more nobly, to act as valiant protectors and defenders of the public order, the core mandate of state policing.

Populist, ambitious politicians tend to be less squeamish than liberals about the phrase zero tolerance, are happy to exploit the huge vote-winning potential of ZTP and leave moral agonising and fine-grained conceptual debate to progressive academics, journalists, lawyers and liberal police managers. The proponents of ZTP, implicitly or explicitly, follow an updated version of the martial logic advocated by Machiavelli to the Medici Princes in sixteenth-century Florence, which has well served subsequent power seekers (Clegg 1989). Those trained in classical sociology will also note affinities here with Max Weber's argument that the valorisation of strong charismatic leadership is heightened in organisations and whole societies that are undergoing the challenges of social change, during which traditional and dry bureaucratic modes of authority lose their appeal and legitimacy.

For those with the courage and savoir-faire, ZTP offers the chance to create a potent political alliance in the war against crime for the politician-prince as helmsman of the ship of state. In this case the alliance would link the prince as 'saviour' of the poor, the decent and the law abiding with *heroic* police officers willing to reinvent and repair the tattered warrior virtues of a devalued masculinity. The presumption seems to be that female officers, insofar as they have a role to play in this male war, must do so as proxy male heroes. This would rescue police officers from being seen as impotent, marginalised bystanders of disorder, failing to measure up to glamorised TV images, or being recast as feminised community/social worker-cops. From this perspective a refurbished patriarchy may provide the underpinnings for the reclamation of the streets and the reinstatement of a civilized social and economic order.

In this chapter, I will, firstly, examine the New York model of ZTP, then explore its international appeal, especially in the European societies facing crises of anxiety and fear. I then explore the links between ZTP and liberalism, understood not simply as an ideology but as a historically emergent, institutional reality, the ground of liberal democratic societies. I then focus more specifically on ZTP in Britain as an instance of an attempt to create hybrid technologies of liberal government. In these conditions war-like metaphors underpin the language of government and help shape the circumstances which foster demands for charismatic, firm leadership, both within police agencies and in the wider society. Yet, though the governmental metaphors and discourses may be war-like, the goal is to recreate nostalgic images of consensual community life, in which informal controls contain the bulk of incivilities, disorder and crime.

The New York model

It is no accident that New York City provided the birthplace of ZTP. For genera-tions the city's Statue of Liberty provided a great immigrant magnet and global beacon of optimism, ambition, energy and prosperity. However, at least in the western world, by the end of the 1980s the city rivalled Los Angeles as the most frightening global icon of the modern urban nightmare. The burgeoning epidemic of crack cocaine use and trading and associated gang wars were accompanied by escalating homicide rates and sensational court cases like the 'jogging trial' in 1990, which attracted global media attention. In this, a group of African-American youths were accused of the violent multiple rape of a wealthy white woman jogging in Central Park. Other cases became staging grounds for politicised inter-ethnic conflict, particularly between African-, Jewish- and Italian-American lobbies and provided an international media platform for Harlem's ubiquitous Rev. Al Sharpton, a perennial critic of the police and crim-inal justice system. In addition, reports of growing fiscal crises, homelessness and other major social problems helped to create the impression that American cities were out of control and a frightening portent of where cities like London, Amsterdam, Paris, Hamburg, Berlin, Rome and Sydney may be heading (*New Statesman and Society*, 25 January 1991, 1 February 1991; Stenson 1991). The unremitting wars between police and criminals, and between criminal groups showing scant regard for the law or state power, were conveyed to a global audi-ence in heightened dramatic form by Tom Wolfe's epic Balzacian New York novel, *Bonfire of the Vanities*, countless movies and TV shows set in the city and, especially, by the gritty glamour of the hit 1990s TV series *NYPD Blue*, which dramatised the work of the New York Police Department. The images of urban nightmare were also transmitted through the hip-hop graffiti movements, associ-ated dress codes and the globally disseminated soundtrack of rap/hip-hop records, many recorded in Brooklyn. Hostile critics of this genre accused artists of celebrating violent lifestyles, showing 'diss'-dain for the police and putting the lives of officers at risk. This fuelled concern among police officers wherever this music became popular, and coalitions were formed across the USA and beyond to fight against the perceived aesthetic and political threat posed by this musical/youth cultural movement (Ferrell 1996). Crime fears were additionally disseminated by morally framed 'crime talk' (cf. Sasson 1995), orally conveyed stories (often exaggerated) of the urban jungle brought back, for example, to Europe, by tourists as intrepid explorers.

These dramatic frames for perception and interpretation provided the cultural back-cloth for the entry of a Machiavellian prince in the persona of New York's new mayor, Rudy Giuliani, who had already brought to the office a formidable reputation as a public prosecutor and scourge of organised crime. Using the law and order issue to displace the long-term hegemony of the Democrats and create a new political base for the Republicans beyond the high-income neighbourhoods, Giuliani secured an additional establishment of 7,000 officers for the NYPD and appointed the (arguably) equally charismatic William Bratton as police commissioner. Between 1994 and 1996, Bratton formulated and implemented the strategy that has popularly become known under the label of 'zero-tolerance policing', even if its architects are reluctant to embrace this term. The complex details of and commentary about this story have been relayed elsewhere (see Bowling 1999). I would simply add that the tough policing of 'quality of life' offenders was supplemented by a range of other innovations, among which the following will be highlighted:

- Greater powers of arrest were restored to patrol officers in relation to drug-related crime and prostitution.
- The arrest of 'petty' offenders provided occasion for interview by detectives about other crime – hence aligning ZTP with the new emphasis on more strategic, less reactive 'intelligence-based' and 'problem-oriented' (POP) community policing practices.
- ZTP does not simply involve blanket law enforcement, but a series of shifting targeted crime control strategies to keep offenders guessing: for example, gun possession, car theft, youth crime, domestic violence and drug trading.
- Managerial innovations were introduced, based on commercial models, which included decentralised responsibility and accountability to precinct commanders and the introduction of Comprehensive Computer Statistics (COMPSTAT). This involved a computerised system for collating and measuring policing and crime reduction targets for precincts agreed with senior managers and discussed at bi-weekly meetings.

(Bratton 1998; Silverman 1998)

Bratton and Giuliani claim, for example, that the ZTP strategy is responsible between 1994 and 1996 for an overall reduction of serious crime by a third, a 24 per cent reduction in burglaries, a halving of the murder rate and a reduction in robberies by 32 per cent (Bratton 1998). The critiques by progressive critics of these claims are by now familiar, but the following points are emphasised. It is argued that:

- Crime rates fell in a wide range of US cities with a range of policing styles, including, for example, in San Diego, which adopted a gentler community policing approach.
- Crime reductions are more plausibly explicable in terms of demographic downturns in the populations at risk and the waning of the crack epidemic and associated gang wars.
- ZTP is best seen as an element in a sharp turn towards exclusionary, oppressive, punitive policies towards the poor and the criminal. These include dramatic increases in the prison population, boot camps, the growth of privatised prisons, the return of the chain gang, and 'three strike' laws in many states that lead to automatic prison sentences for petty crimes (Simon 1996).
- These policies have proved to be hugely expensive, draining tax funding away from education, housing and other areas of welfare, with, ironically, criminogenic effects. Liberal criminologists claim that recycling the homeless in and out of the justice system will not stop violent crime. (Bowling 1996 and 1999; Currie 1997)

International appeal

Despite these criticisms, the successful media presentations of the case for ZTP have proved seductive to politicians from many countries and indicate the ease with which emotive political metaphors, political rationalities and ways of conceptualising both social problems and fashionable solutions to them, can be traded between countries (Stenson 2000). There are familiar narratives that try to explain the search for new governmental solutions to the problems of conceptualising and managing insecurity in European welfare states. The governmental strategies and technologies of the post-war welfare states had given a privileged role to central and local state agencies in attempting to promote an inclusive solidarity. But it is argued that a series of inter-related changes have undermined post-war optimism and faith in 'social' modes of government. These have been associated with a pessimism about capacities of the state to govern and the rapid growth of crime and fear of crime in both the domestic and public spheres. These changes include *inter alia*: the impact of an increasingly globalised economy (including technological change rendering many traditional male jobs obsolete); growing fiscal crises; environmental degradation; demographic movements; the introduction of neo-liberal social and economic policies; and the fracturing of traditional gender roles, family and community structures, informal controls and sources of identity (Castells 1995; Offe 1996; Rose 1996a; Stenson 1996; Ericson and Haggerty 1997; Bailleau 1998).

Decline of the 'social'

The actuarial risk-sharing technologies of the 'social' operated in accordance with Keynesian principles. State co-ordinated protection against sickness, old age, unemployment, crime and the other major risks of life were shared very broadly among citizens, even where costs were not wholly borne by the tax-payer. By contrast, under the impact of neo-liberal innovations, support for Keynesian tax-and-spend policies which underpinned the 'social' has waned. Hence, risk-sharing communities have become prudential: that is smaller, exclusive, less dependent on the state and crystallised in the image of the gated community with 24-hour commercial security (O'Malley 1992). This has created a search for new governmental strategies that blur the boundaries between state, voluntary/not-for-profit and commercial initiatives. These target particular 'communities' of risk sharers, or social categories who pose risks to others. In the sphere of crime prevention, as in health and other areas of policy, state propaganda increasingly encourages individual citizens, families and other corporate bodies beyond the state to be responsible for their own welfare as far as possible, in order to relieve the burdens of over-stretched public agencies (Stenson 1996; Garland 1996).

Increasingly, it is argued, the new social order is creating a residualised 'excluded' population of the poor, often differentiated by ethnicity and increasingly at risk of victimisation and involvement in criminality (European Commission 1996). These people are seen as increasingly ghettoised in areas of poor social housing, and experience multiple compounding social problems (Power and Tunstall 1995). It is feared that some in their midst, through their colonisation of public spaces, especially as beggars, muggers, drug dealers, pimps and prostitutes, are contributing to pervasive moods of pessimism and fear among the wider population. This is seen as exacerbating the retreat from public spaces and perhaps the public sphere of life itself (Taylor 1998). Clearly, these changes have not had uniform effects in Europe; for example, the UK has experienced the impact of neo-liberal policies in more concentrated form than elsewhere (Hutton 1995). More research is required to chart the variations in conditions, especially with respect to the impact on public spaces, but also on the more subtle, psychological and cultural impact on how people feel about fear, insecurity and the emotional climate of the places in which they live and work (Taylor et al. 1996; Loader et al. 1998).

It is no surprise, therefore, that, notwithstanding different social structures and policing institutions and traditions, interest in ZTP has stimulated many fact-finding tours to New York by European members of parliament, civil servants, police chiefs and academics (van Swaaningen 1998). So far, political opinion in Germany has remained more sceptical than in Britain about the relevance of ZTP for its country (Ortner et al. 1998). Yet this may change. With an eye to the British election in 1997, law and order became a key issue in the 1998 German elections, with Gerhard Schröder's new-look Social Democratic Party (SPD) keen to respond to growing anxiety about crime and security. These anxieties were linked, especially, to the perceived threats posed by burgeoning East European organised crime moving their operations into Western Europe and the 1.6 million asylum-seekers who had entered Germany between 1987 and 1994 (Rinaldi 1998). These issues have been associated with the use of extreme violence by skinheads and other disaffected groups against gypsies and other minorities. This has been concentrated especially in the eastern regions, still blighted by high unemployment and the effects of economic transition, and has been readily exploited by parties of the far Right. Writing in the German tabloid *Bild* during his bid for the chancellorship, Gerhard Schröder employed language indistinguishable from that used by Jorg Haider, Austria's charismatic foreigner-baiting right-wing politician,

> You've got to point out, even if some people don't like to hear it: Poles just happen to be conspicuously active in organised car theft, the Russian Mafia dominates prostitution, drugs-related criminals are often from south-eastern Europe or black Africans. For those who abuse their status as guests, there can only be one answer: get out and quick!
>
> (quoted in Rinaldi 1998: 7)

The anti asylum-seeker/foreigner theme has also been exploited in calls for ZTP by Belgium's far-right Vlaams Blok party. So far, in the Netherlands, much of orthodox opinion remains sceptical about ZTP's compatibility with Dutch traditions of tolerance of diversity and the artful negotiated settlement of conflict, yet growing public concerns about crime, urban decline and the perceived problems of absorbing 'foreigners' may be undermining those traditions. In 1998, Amsterdam's police commissioner incorporated zero-tolerance principles into police practice guidelines. In April of that year, serious conflict between police and Moroccan youth, often held responsible for much of the street crime in Amsterdam, was blamed by young demonstrators on aggressive policing styles, using the slogan, 'Zero tolerance, maximum arrogance' (van Swaaningen 1998).

Liberalism and zero tolerance in tension?

The Netherlands has provided a global yardstick for the values and practices of tolerant liberal governance and policing, manifested especially by its coffee houses for cannabis smokers and its harm-reduction drugs policies (Downes 1988; de Haan 1991). The currency, though as yet limited, given to ZTP in that country therefore raises worrying questions about the relationship of ZTP with the tolerance towards deviance and diversity which many would argue lies at the heart of liberal democracy. To what extent does it signify a growing reliance internationally on violence as a routine method of control or conflict resolution? During the crumbling and after the collapse of communism, there has been a growth in the number of zones in which central state power is fragile or non-existent. This was the case, for example, in the Lebanon during the long years of war and inter-communal strife, in large areas of the ex-Yugoslavia, and in Chechnya. With no effective state apparatus to impose order and security, power returns to the most primitive versions of patriarchy. It takes the form of brutal armed warlords prepared to use kidnapping, torture, murder, rape and ethnic cleansing in the struggle to monopolise control over geographical territory and to defend illegal economies (Voronin 1996).

In addition, the existence of a recognisable central state, in Hobbes' terms, can often at best guarantee security only for the wealthy. Amnesty International and other liberal human rights organisations remind us that a large proportion of the world's population suffer under the yoke of modes of policing which are, so to speak, truly zero tolerant (Cohen 1993). Whether in Sudan, Algeria, Iraq or China, policing involves a kind of warfare against much of the domestic population construed as enemies within. These regimes are underpinned by the routine use of harassment, arbitrary arrest, imprisonment, exile, spatial segregation, torture and murder. They rarely lack moral rationales for these practices, since, frequently, such regimes came to power with backing from western liberal democratic governments. It would, arguably, jeopardise the very basis of a liberal order to allow a slide towards this style of policing, targeted at growing proportions of the population seen as in some way ineligible for the rights of citizenship, or even basic human rights. But what underpins a liberal order?

One way to criticise and evaluate ZTP would be to judge it against the benchmark of liberalism, considered as a coherent intellectual construction: a political rationality or set of values of universal, timeless relevance, crystallised in philosophical texts and seminar discussions. For example, in the Anglo-Saxon intellectual tradition from John Locke to J.S. Mill to John Rawls and Isaiah Berlin, it is possible to argue that running through its complex variations and internal disputes is a thread depicting a creed which recognises the universal nature, worth and freedoms of the individual and the need to provide checks and balances on the use of central state power and the administration of justice (Mouffe 1993). On this basis it may be possible to argue that the practices of ZTP involve the abuse of human rights in a way which parallels that of authoritarian regimes. However, this harsh moral beam would obscure much that can only be illuminated by a more subtle light. My conception of liberalism is more concrete and complex, emphasising the linkages it sets up between grounded critical intellectual/political practice and the practices of rule. Liberalism is best viewed, not as a point on the ideological spectrum of liberal democratic societies, but rather as the field within which political contest operates (Gordon 1991; Stenson 1998, 1999). This permits a more sensitive understanding of the relationship between ZTP and liberalism.

Hence, the meaning of liberalism employed here is historical and institutional. The key concerns are, first, with how abstract notions have been operationalised to engage in practical critiques of and resistance to power. During the seventeenth and eighteenth centuries, authoritarian fantasies were produced by apologists of absolutist monarchical regimes in Europe. These included the France of Louis XIV, Prussia and the regimes of the Hapsburgs and the Russian Tsars. They involved the first attempts in the modern era to create 'police states', underpinned by *polizeiwissenschaft* (police science) in which the power of the ruler was represented as the interest of all, that recognised no

224

rights to privacy or legitimate opposition and that attempted to bear over every facet of life (Stenson 1993b). Liberal ideas and practices were forged in opposition to, or in spite of, these absolutist forms. The origins of English, Scottish and Dutch forms of liberalism in the same historical period included the development of abstract theories of social contract, the rights and dignity of the individual, of liberty and the new political economy of the market produced, for example, by Locke, Ferguson and Smith. However, these intellectual creations were significant insofar as they were, in part, operationalised in practical ways by radical reformers, men of commerce and politicians. They became embedded in or provided rationalisations for *inter alia*: the practices of (relatively) free trade and manufacturing; struggles for the right of religious dissent and suffrage; critiques and subversions of absolutist fantasies of unchecked state power; and the forging of a host of ways of muddling through and containing – if not always resolving – conflicts. In this way, practical forms of nascent liberalism included survival skills and modes of social conduct which resisted utopian formulation and were congenial for trading urban peoples (Gordon 1991; van Swaaningen 1998).

Hence, second, the historical conception of liberalism employed here highlights concerns about the ways in which the arts and practices of liberal government developed as self-scrutinising and limiting forms of rule, and how they have made possible the formation and operation of markets, commercial firms, trade unions, political parties, religious and ethnic minority orbits of governance, self-governing professions, the 'private' sphere of family life and other relatively autonomous domains (Barry *et al.* 1993). I have argued that liberalism, as historical reality, in practice has rarely operated in pure universalistic and individualistic forms, but usually in hybrid interaction with other modes of rule and political rationality, particularly strategies of nation building (Stenson 1998, 1999, 2000). Although individual freedoms may have been a convenient banner, in practice they have often denoted, especially in the British context, the rights to (somewhat) separate spheres of governance for a multitude of particularistically defined organisations and religious and ethnic collectivities. Many of these collectivities may provide only equivocal recognition of the rights of individuals in their own spheres of governance. Collective rights can, in this sense, be as central to liberal social orders as individual rights, and liberalism has usually operated in complex relations with (particularistic) competitive nationalisms and the institutions of nation building and citizenship (Dench 1986).

Police and hybrid technologies

Police agencies have played a key role in this process of nation building in liberal orders. Like other liberal modes of government, they tend to operate through interdependent, hybrid technologies. These include, first, sovereign technologies, which aim to monopolise the use of legitimate violence in maintaining control over geographical space. This can involve a range of practices from military-style initiatives to destroy the hegemony of drug dealers in housing estates or of paramilitary groups in cities like Belfast, to more routine practices of order maintenance (Waddington 1998). Second, they include disciplinary technologies, based on systematic surveillance, which aim to transform the behaviour and subjectivity of individuals (for example, through linkages with probation work initiatives) in line with general governmental rationalities and programmes. Third, they involve a range of technologies loosely grouped under the heading of 'governmentality'. These involve the range of ways in which populations, at the collective and individual levels, are made thinkable and measurable for the purposes of government (Foucault 1991). One of the key issues in recent debates about the nature of crime control is the role of actuarial technologies whereby populations are governed in terms of calculations made about the risks they pose to social well-being, or to the bureaucracies charged with managing them. It is argued that older rival technologies that aimed for a (disciplinary) rehabilitation of the offender, or the allocation of punitive 'just deserts' have been largely displaced by a new concern with 'containment policies' involving risk assessment and risk management approaches. These technologies include, for example, drug courier and other offender profiling methods to assess the dangers posed by sex and other types of offender. In essence, the newer actuarial approach to policing and criminal justice is less concerned with curing or punishing the offender than with containing problem individuals, social groups and neighbourhoods at minimal public cost (Feeley and Simon 1994). This is an instance of a post-Keynesian approach to government (O'Malley and Palmer 1996).

The conception of the liberal polity operating through these governmental technologies presents it as complex, unfolding, messy, divided by multiple inequalities and eternally in creative tension. First, there is an ongoing tension between critique and rule, which usually drifts towards authoritarianism and creates the possibility and indeed likelihood, from liberal premises, of immanent critique. Second, the tendency of liberal orders to generate a plethora of self-governing groupings can create the capacity for centrifugal unravelling and even chaos. The struggle for sovereignty is in part the struggle to maintain a centripetal coherence in the relation between centre and periphery, albeit often in ways which reproduce inequalities (Stenson 1998).

I would also point to a third tension, between liberal values, seen as the repository of professional, governmental elites, often represented as the Platonic guardians of the public interest and, on the other hand, representative and participatory modes of democracy (Stenson 1999). This is particularly pertinent to debates about policing and justice, since from the perspective of the liberal elites, in delicate areas like the policing of paedophiles or street robbers, liberal values may be better served by the rule of law and/or bolstering the authority of the tutelary professions over 'deviants'. By contrast, a 'democratic' stance, in making too many concessions to perceivably reactionary strains of public and media opinion and perhaps mob or vigilante justice, could be viewed as under-mining the primary function of law: preventing blood feuds and the unconstrained thirst for revenge.

The implications for liberal policing have, over the generations, been profound. Sir Robert Peel's Metropolitan Police Force was instituted in London in 1829 as a vehicle of policing by consent. In this Peelite model, which became an international reference point for liberal democratic policing, social control became woven into the fabric of civil society, rather than remaining a harsh instrument of central state power, which was to characterise so many other European policing systems (Mawby 1990; Stenson 1993b). Yet Peelite police agencies have, at every stage, played a central role in helping both to construct and to defend national sovereignty at every level from the local upwards and also in helping to regulate the relations between self-governing collectivities. This has inbuilt tensions between, on the one hand, the requirement to use authoritative action to maintain sovereign order, disproportionately advantaging privileged groups even as it provides a measure of security to the poor and middling classes and, on the other hand, the requirement to win consent from the common people (Reiner 1985; Stenson 1993a and b). Let us turn now to explore how these tensions have unfolded recently, with the rise of New Labour in Britain.

Zero tolerance in the UK

It may seem ironic that the rhetoric of zero tolerance, associated with right-wing American criminology and a Republican US mayor, should prove so attractive to British Labour politicians of the centre Left, who modelled their restructuring of 'New Labour' so closely on Bill Clinton and Al Gore's refashioning of the Democratic Party in the 1980s. However, this becomes more intelligible in considering the broader formation of policy. The Democrats' suburban-friendly 'Tough Love' approach to crime control and welfare reform (including welfare to work programmes) conceded much to the Reagan/Bush policy agenda and could be seen as close to Giuliani's ideology. Clinton's administration has coincided with a massive expansion in the prison population and spending on criminal justice, unwarrantable in relation to variations in the recorded crime rate (Zimring and Hawkins 1997). New Labour's promise of reform to reduce dependency through welfare, promote welfare to work initiatives, and Blair's slogan as shadow Home Secretary, 'Tough on crime and tough on the causes of crime', closely mirrored the Clinton strategy and chimed with key neo-liberal themes of the Conservative government. Labour crime policies also provided a sharp challenge to Conservative policies, which, despite tough law and order rhetoric, had failed to prevent a doubling of recorded crime in the Tory years between 1979 and 1992 (Blair 1998: 12). It is argued that the watershed came in 1993. In response to moral panics about youth crime, New Labour exposed the vulnerability of the Conservative government. In an interview on BBC Radio 4 on 10 January 1993, distancing himself from deterministic explanations of crime, Blair emphasised the theme of personal responsibility and duty, key communitarian features of New Labour policy (Hughes 1998),

Anti-social behaviour should 'be punished, if necessary, severely ... Society ... has not merely a duty, it is in its interest, to try to create the conditions in which people get a chance in life. But the other side of that ... is: where people are given chances, they're expected to take them, and they're expected to take responsibility for their own individual actions.'

(quoted in Dunbar and Langdon 1998: 101)

Selective crackdowns and punitive rhetoric stressing that 'prison works' by Conservative politicians and the tabloid papers pressured judges into lengthening custodial sentences. Attacks by Blair and then later by Jack Straw as shadow Home Secretary on Conservative law and order policy led to a 'bidding war', fanned by the tabloids, with the reactionary Home Secretary Michael Howard over who could appear toughest (Dunbar and Langdon 1998). This continued until the election in 1997 and sharpened conflicts between New Labour and progressive opinion in the academy and the criminal justice professions. Yet a powerful case was assembled, arguing that the punitive thrust of neo-conservative rhetoric under the Conservative regime was undermined by the neo-liberal budgetary and managerial disciplines that still drove government policy. These conditions starved the Crown Prosecution Service, the police and other authorities of the necessary resources to develop consistent and coherent prosecution and crime prevention and reduction strategies in deprived areas. Existing research, particularly from the British Crime Surveys, indicated the high concentration of criminal victimisation in these neighbourhoods, yet the control agencies seemed to be failing citizens there. This undermined the morale of control agencies and of the populations most vulnerable to victimisation. It was claimed that despite burgeoning prison populations, the police and criminal justice agencies had effectively abandoned large chunks of British territory to the hegemony of criminal gangs, the drugs economy and ill-disciplined children and young men (Rose 1996b; Davies 1997).

The third way

Law and order policies have from the start been presented as central to the project of New Labour. This political philosophy and policy framework was later described as 'the Third Way' by Blair and other senior ministers and also by sociologist Tony Giddens, director of the London School of Economics and a close political ally. It also represents their struggle to find solutions to the crisis of liberal government and new holistic or 'joined up' strategies, built on pluralistic partnerships between statutory, commercial and not-for-profit agencies and initiatives (Blair 1998: 12–14; Giddens 1998: 86–9). Despite the notorious slipperiness of the concept, in every area of policy there is an attempt to find a position beyond, rather than between, old tax-and-spend social democratic policies and what is deemed to be a naive neo-liberal conservative reliance on market forces. Third Way policies in this field needed to provide the Treasury with a convincing rationale for significant increases in spending on both policing and criminal justice, on the one hand, and, on the other hand, on crime prevention and reduction strategies. A number of initiatives have already emerged, not least being the setting up of the Social Exclusion Unit at 10 Downing Street to co-ordinate targeted policies to regenerate the perceivably most problematic areas. A running thread of these initiatives is to enable the police and other governmental agencies to regain control over the neighbourhoods of the so-called 'socially excluded', the 'problem' housing estates and poor inner-city areas. In this way the aim is to provide congenial conditions for social and economic regeneration. It would be beyond the scope of this chapter to detail the full range of policy initiatives, but the following will be mentioned:

- under the omnibus Crime and Disorder Act (CDA) 1998, partnerships of police and local government agencies are required to prepare audits of local crime problems and formulate holistic community safety strategies, which deal with both crime reduction and preventive strategies, from 'early interventions' to support high-risk families and neighbourhoods through to situational preventive initiatives to protect the victims of multiple burglaries, to CCTV and other initiatives to monitor and protect public spaces from those engaged in incivilities;
- under the CDA a fundamental recasting and speeding up of the billion-pound per annum juvenile justice system, around the partnership principle of Youth Offending Teams;
- new measures to deal with anti-social 'neighbours from hell';
- a £250 million, three-year crime reduction programme, targeted to key 'hotspots' of crime and critically evaluated as a pilot for further policy development;
- a welfare to work programme to reduce unemployment in the at-risk 18–25 age group;
- the appointment of a US-style 'Drugs Czar', to co-ordinate policies to prevent and reduce drug-related offending.

(Bright 1998)

It is against the back-cloth of these policy developments that we should recognise the significance of the powerful attachment of New Labour to the rhetoric of zero tolerance, which has become a mobile trope, applied to a range of policy areas. It is significant that the thrust of zero-tolerance rhetoric is intolerant not just of crime and criminals but, in continuity with Margaret Thatcher's assault on the professions, it is also intolerant of the police, education, local government and other agencies that fail to achieve their agency goals and the neo-liberal market-defined criteria of *economy, efficiency and effectiveness*. This image was featured in Blair's speech to the annual Labour Party Conference in September 1998, in which he said, 'Don't show zero imagination, help us to have zero tolerance of crime ... There are too few good state schools, too much *tolerance* of mediocrity, too little pursuit of excellence' (*Guardian*, 30 September 1998, emphasis added).

Schools and teachers' unions are repeatedly warned by ministers and the school inspection agency, OFSTED, that family poverty is no excuse for low attainment, and that 'failing' schools and local government education authorities will be ruthlessly punished, if necessary, by drafting in new managers and introducing private sector management. The link between educational failure and crime control is particularly apposite, since much stress is placed by New Labour ideology and Home Office research on the impact of poor attainment on truancy, school exclusion and the development of criminal careers by young people (Graham and Bowling 1995).

Zero tolerance as policing technology

Zero tolerance, in this wider policy sense, is primarily a rhetorical device to challenge complacency in the public services and to promote a culture and mindset conducive to continuous change, entrepreneurship, active leadership and the requirement, as in competitive commercial markets, to meet externally set targets (Stenson and Watt 1999). This explains the affinity of New Labour politicians with the proponents of zero-tolerance policing in the UK.[1] One of the striking features of rationales for ZTP in Britain is their stress on its role as a component within a more complex set of strategies. These involve community policing strategies that include intelligence-led measures and problem-oriented policing (POP), which attempt to identify and deal with the underlying problems giving rise to surface incidents (Leigh *et al.* 1998).

For example, in 1996 the Metropolitan Police in London conducted a ZTP initiative in conjunction with the Transport Police, and the City of London Police and local borough authorities. This involved active confrontational measures to deal with homeless beggars, drug dealers, pimps and prostitutes, who were congregating around the Kings Cross railway station. This built upon an earlier initiative, responding to political pressures, which in 1992 had linked the police with two boroughs and commercial and voluntary agencies to reduce criminality and regenerate what had become seen as a run-down intimidating area (Crowther 1998: 73). However, the ZTP label was a new term to describe the latest phase of initiatives to contain crime and incivilities around a transport terminus that, like the Gare du Nord in Paris, had experienced similar problems for generations. While improvements tend to be temporary, with problems displacing to adjoining neighbourhoods until control pressures relax, it is claimed that these measures have resulted in over 400 arrests of drug dealers and a higher levels of public satisfaction with the quality of life in the area (*ibid.*: 73).

In Strathclyde Police Authority, including the city of Glasgow, a new Police Commissioner, John Orr, in 1996 introduced a ZTP initiative in partnership with Customs and Excise and local authorities, in response to evidence of high levels of public fear about crime in a city and region with a grim, if not entirely deserved, reputation for violent crime (Orr 1997). This strategy involved managerial innovations similar to the Bratton model. In addition, force resources were focused on a series of shifting 'spotlight' issues, as defined by public surveys. These included, for example, street robberies, drinking in public and carrying weapons. The first month of operation produced 20,000 stops of citizens. It was claimed, for example, that there was a drop of 9 per cent in recorded offences in this period. This included a drop of 5 per cent in robberies, and serious assaults fell by 12 per cent (Crowther 1998: 74).

Mallon as Machiavellian prince

However, probably the best-known exponent of ZTP in Britain was Superintendent Ray Mallon, who spearheaded ZTP strategies in Hartlepool and Middlesbrough in the rust-belt zone of north-east England, a predominantly white area which had experienced long-term industrial decline and increasing unemployment. By contrast with the other initiators, he did so from a relatively junior managerial position (initially as a Detective Chief Inspector) and with enormous energy and enthusiasm. He rapidly became a media darling, wrote a weekly column in a local newspaper and enjoyed great local popularity (not necessarily endorsed by his senior officers). Mallon's variant of the war metaphors favoured by exponents of ZTP mixed the language of the management guru, exhorting the sales force to fight for market share and win hearts and minds, with a footballing metaphor, with particular resonance in a working-class population which reveres the game. As Mallon put it, 'I was thoroughly sick of police officers who said, "We can't do it." It is like a footballer who says, "We can't score any goals." Of course he won't score any, and he won't help the team' (Dennis and Mallon 1997a: 72).

As with the link between Giuliani and Bratton, until his mysterious suspension Mallon could be viewed as a Machiavellian prince ascending to celebrity status from a humble station and forming alliances with other 'saviour-princes'. In this case, they came in the guise of New Labour politicians for whom crime control was genuinely a key manifesto issue. He was courted by Tony Blair, Jack Straw and also by the Conservative Home Secretary Michael Howard during the election campaign in the spring of 1997 (*Observer*, 7 December 1997; *Guardian*, 2 December 1997; *World in Action*, 17 August 1998). He initiated his own version of ZTP during the same period as Bratton's incumbency in New York. Mallon's strategy was to rouse and inspire rank-and-file officers to believe that they could truly make a difference and win the respect and appreciation of a grateful public. Hence the strategy (the 'what') involved:

- crime reduction by positive, confident policing, denting offenders' sense of confident invulnerability;
- boosting the confidence of police officers and 'decent' citizens;

- replacing vicious circles of decline with virtuous spirals of optimism and community regeneration.

The tactics (the 'how') included:

- allocation of teams of officers to problem estates and other problem locations;
- prioritising crime reduction and co-ordinating detective and uniformed branch work;
- use of charismatic management style, including a preparedness to engage in hands-on work with constables, and moral exhortation to galvanise officers' enthusiasm;
- active law enforcement through targeting quality-of-life offences and burglary to forestall the development of criminal careers in the young;
- involvement of the public through intensive media campaigns and public meetings, locally and nationally.

(Dennis and Mallon 1997a)

With the co-operation of sociologist Norman Dennis, Mallon explained the growth of crime and incivilities in the north-east, which had lost much of its traditional male-employing industrial jobs, in moral terms rather than in those of material deprivation (Dennis and Mallon 1997b). Rooted in a nostalgic longing for a pre-feminist vision of a more orderly and happy working-class way of life in the 1930s, from their perspective, the 1960s had marked a watershed which ushered in a breakdown of gender roles and (particularly male) authority structures in the home and community, leading to faulty socialisation of boys. This was compounded by failed soft policing philosophies and management styles. As a result of ZTP, it was claimed that Hartlepool's recorded crime figures fell by a startling 27 per cent between 1994 and 1996. Domestic burglaries were down by 31 per cent and thefts of motor vehicles down by 15 per cent (Dennis and Mallon 1997a: 63). Mallon joined Middlesbrough in 1996, lasting a year before being suspended from duty. In the first nine months, to September 1997, recorded crime fell by a quarter (*Observer*, 7 December 1997). At the time of writing, Mallon's national presence has all but disappeared, starved of the oxygen of publicity. This curtailed the unprecedented courting of a police officer of modest rank by the political elites, hence casting him out from the cult of celebrity, within which he had been such a celebrated icon.

Radical critics in Britain of the Mallon model echoed their US counterparts. For example, 'Zero tolerance … involves highly discriminatory enforcement against specific groups of people in certain symbolic locations, Where is the "zero tolerance" of white collar crimes, business fraud, unlawful pollution and breaches of health and safety?' (Crawford 1998: 155). This harmonises with the criticisms of the leading police critic of the harsh rhetoric of ZTP, Charles Pollard, Chief Constable of Thames Valley Police (Pollard 1997). He warns that, especially in Britain, with its Peelite policing traditions and slender

232

police/population ratios, ZTP can be a dangerous short-term fix that could damage police–community relations. This is especially so with minorities and could lead to a repetition of the riots associated with similar police initiatives in Brixton in 1981. In addition, feminists have objected that the Mallon model does not take domestic violence seriously, ironically since Edinburgh Council's women's unit launched a successful 'zero tolerance' campaign to reduce domestic violence in 1992 (Campbell 1997).

Conclusion

A recent Home Office study of policing styles noted that Cleveland Police, responsible for Middlesbrough, remained convinced that ZTP is compatible with community policing in a Problem-Oriented Policing form. This is viewed as 'a short-term prelude to the implementation of longer-term measures in high-crime areas where fear of, and intimidation by, a minority of residents is having a detrimental effect' (Leigh *et al.* 1998: 26; Romeanes 1998). Given that this principle is endorsed by the Crime and Disorder Act's emphasis on regaining control over disorderly areas, it is not surprising that a recent major Home Office review of what works in crime control policy gives a qualified endorsement of ZTP, but under the sanitised label of 'order maintenance' (Jordan 1998: 72).

However, ZTP could be seen as an essential component in the hybrid technologies that make up liberal government. It has recently been argued that ZTP can be viewed as an element in the mix of disciplinary and actuarial technologies in the attempt to police communities defined in terms of categories of risk (Johnston 1997). I would agree, but go beyond this argument by stressing that it is also, centrally, a *sovereign* technology of government. As I have argued elsewhere, this remains not only a central feature of New Labour's strategy of crime control, but is also, in sophisticated updated form, an irreducible feature of liberalism and emanates from popular demands for safety as well as those from more privileged social positions. It is not simply a removable atavistic survival from our monarchical past (Stenson 1998, 1999). ZTP may be regarded as incompatible with liberalism, considered as an abstract individualistic philosophy, yet in the way in which I have used the term it may not be so incompatible. We should be wary, therefore, as liberal intellectuals, of being too ready to label this style of policing and the warlike metaphors employed by Mallon and Bratton, as 'authoritarian or punitive populism' (Garland 1996).

This label is perhaps best understood as a construction of liberal professionals, who see themselves as the custodians of liberal values, but who may be out of touch, both with the less palatable aspects of democratically responsive liberal government and with the everyday conditions of life in the more deprived neighbourhoods. This ignorance is compounded by the curious paucity of solid ethnographic research in such areas, leading to an over-reliance on journalistic accounts focusing on a few locations. To some degree, the liberal critique of tough policing may exist in tension with democratic demands. ZTP and the

233

charismatic authority that may be necessary to make it work could be essential elements in the reconstruction of trust between government and a fearful citizenry. Central to this reconstruction is additional pressure from government above and from people below to galvanise police officers into action, when many would, for a quiet less risky life, prefer to allow illegal economies and bullies to operate with unhindered dominion in poor neighbourhoods. However, the first real test is, as Max Weber pointed out, how charismatic authority can be sustained beyond the flush of enthusiasm accompanying organisational change. The second test is whether new economic and social policies have the potential and adequate funding to tackle unemployment, family and community breakdown and the other complex dimensions of inequality, which contribute to the 'causes' of crime (Downes 1998). The third test is to gauge how far the exercise of sovereign government can avoid re-creating, on an ever increasing scale, outcast 'underclass' populations of the Other (Crowther 1999). In addition, in these uncertain times, when older lines of political authority both within the state and in its relations with 'external' agencies are blurred by the declining legitimacy of representative democracy, the increasing politicisation of policing and by formations of power beyond the state (Reiner 1985), older role divisions are also blurred. In these circumstances, it is not so clear who is the discreet Machiavellian counsellor to the powerful prince and who is the prince.

References

Bailleau, F. (1998) 'A crisis of youth or of juridical response?' in V. Ruggiero, N. South and I. Taylor (eds) *The New European Criminology Crime and Social Order in Europe*, London: Routledge.

Barry, A., Osborne, T. and Rose, N. (eds) (1996) *Foucault and Political Reason. Liberation, Neo-Liberation and Rationalities of Government*, London: UCL Press.

Blair, Tony (1998) *The Third Way, New Politics for the New Century*, London: Fabian Society.

Bowling, B. (1996) 'Cracking down on crime in New York City', *Criminal Justice Matters*, 25 (Autumn): 11–12.

—— (1998) 'The Rise and Fall of New York Murder: Zero Tolerance or Crack's Decline?', *British Journal of Criminology*, 39(4): 531–54.

Brace, L. (1997) 'Imaging the boundaries of a sovereign self', in L. Brace and J. Hoffman (eds) *Reclaiming Sovereignty*, London: Pinter.

Bratton, W. (1998) 'Crime is down in New York City: blame the police', in N. Dennis (ed.) *Zero Tolerance, Policing a Free Society*, London: Institute of Economic Affairs.

Bright, John (1998) 'Preventing youth crime', *Criminal Justice Matters*, 33: 15–17.

Campbell, B. (1997) 'A CID is out of control', *Guardian*, 15 December.

Castells, M. (1995) *The Rise of Network Society*, Oxford: Blackwell.

Clegg, S.R. (1989) *Frameworks of Power*, London: Sage.

Cohen, S. (1993) 'Human rights and crimes of the state: the culture of denial', *Australian and New Zealand Journal of Criminology*, 26: 97–115.

Crawford, A. (1998) *Crime Prevention and Community Safety, Politics, Policies and Practices*, London: Longmans.

Crowther, C. (1998) 'Policing the Excluded Society' in R. Hopkins Burke (ed.) *Zero Tolerance Policing*, Leicester: Perpetuity Press.

—— (1999) *Policing the Underclass*, London: Macmillan.

Currie, E. (1997) 'The scalpel, not the chainsaw, the US experience with public order', *City*, 8: 132–8.

Davies, N. (1997) *Dark Heart*, London: Vintage.

de Haan, W. (1991) 'Abolitionism and crime control: a contradiction in terms', in K. Stenson and D. Cowell (eds) *The Politics of Crime Control*, London: Sage.

Dench, G. (1986) *Minorities in the Open Society. Prisoners of Ambivalence*, London: Routledge and Kegan Paul.

Dennis, N. and Mallon, R. (1997a) 'Confident policing in Hartlepool', in N. Dennis (ed.) *Zero Tolerance, Policing a Free Society*, London: Institute of Economic Affairs.

——(1997b) 'Crime and culture in Hartlepool', in N. Dennis (ed.) *Zero Tolerance, Policing a Free Society*, London: Institute of Economic Affairs.

Downes, David (1998a) 'From Labour opposition to Labour government', paper delivered to the Renewal of Criminal Justice Conference, University of Hull, 22 September.

——(1998b) *Contrasts in Tolerance: Post-War Penal Policy in the Netherlands and England and Wales*, Oxford: Clarendon Press.

Dunbar, Ian and Langdon, Anthony (1998) *Tough Justice*, London: Blackstone Press.

Ericson, R. and Haggerty, K.D. (1997) *Policing the Risk Society*, Oxford: Clarendon Press.

European Commission (1996) *Immigrant Delinquency, Social Construction of Deviant Behaviour and Criminality of Immigrants in Europe*, Brussels: European Community.

Feely, M. and Simon, J. (1994) 'Actuarial justice: the emerging new criminal law', in D. Nelken (ed.) *The Futures of Criminology*, London: Sage.

Ferrell, J. (1996) *Crimes of Style: Urban Graffiti and the Politics of Criminality*, Boston: North-East University Press.

Foucault, Michel (1991) 'On governmentality', in G. Burchell, C. Gordon and P. Miller (eds) *The Foucault Effect – Studies in Governmentality*, Hemel Hempstead: Harvester Wheatsheaf.

Garland, D. (1996) 'The limits of the sovereign state: strategies of crime control in contemporary society', *British Journal of Criminology*, 36(4): 445–71.

Giddens, A. (1998) *The Third Way: The Renewal of Social Democracy*, Cambridge: Polity.

Goldblatt, P. and Lewis, C. (1998) *Reducing Offending: An Assessment of Research Evidence on the Ways of Dealing with Offending Behaviour. Research Study 187*, London: Home Office.

Gordon, C. (1991) 'Governmental rationality: an introduction', in G. Burchell, C. Gordon and P. Miller (eds) *The Foucault Effect, Studies in Governmentality*, London: Harvester Wheatsheaf.

Graham, J. and Bowling, B. (1995) *Young People and Crime, Research Study 145*, London: Home Office.

Griffiths, W. (1998) 'Zero tolerance, a view from London', in N. Dennis (ed.) *Zero Tolerance, Policing a Free Society*, London: Institute of Economic Affairs.

Hopkins Burke, R. (1998) 'A contextualisation of zero tolerance policing strategies', in R. Hopkins Burke (ed.) *Zero Tolerance Policing*, Leicester: Perpetuity Press.

Hughes, Gordon (1998) *Understanding Crime Prevention, Social Control, Risk and Late Modernity*, Buckingham: Open University Press.

Hutton, W. (1995) *The State We're In*, London: Cape.

Johnston, L. (1997) 'The politics of zero-tolerance policing in Britain: discipline, civility and risk', paper presented to the Annual Conference of the American Society of Criminology, November, San Diego.

Jordan, P. (1998) 'Effective policing strategies for reducing crime', in P. Goldblatt, and C. Lewis, *Reducing Offending: An Assessment of Research Evidence on the Ways of Dealing with Offending Behaviour. Research Study 187*, London: Home Office.

Kelling, G. and Coles, C. (1996) *Fixing Broken Windows – Restoring Order and Reducing Order and Reducing Crime in Our Communities*, New York: The Free Press.

Lakoff, G. and Johnson, M. (1980) *Metaphors We Live By*, Chicago: University of Chicago Press.

Lea, J. and Young, J. (1982) *What Is to be Done about Law and Order?*, London: Penguin.

Leigh, A. Read, T. and Tilley, N. (1998) *Brit Pop 11: Problem-Oriented Policing in Practice – Police Research Series Paper 93*, London: Home Office.

Loader, I., Girling, E. and Sparks, R. (1998) 'Narratives of decline: youth, dis/order and community in an English "Middletown"', *British Journal of Criminology*, 38: 388–403.

Mawby, Rob (1990) *Comparative Policing Issues: The British and American Experience in International Perspective*, London: Unwin Hyman.

Mouffe, C. (1993) *Return of the Political*, London: Verso.

Offe, Claus (1996) *Modernity and the State: East, West*, Cambridge: Polity.

O'Malley, Pat (1992) 'Risk, power and crime prevention', *Economy and Society*, 21: 252–75.

O'Malley, Pat and Palmer, D. (1996) 'Post-Keynesian policing', *Economy and Society*, 25: 137–55.

Orr, J. (1997) 'Strathclyde's spotlight initiative', in N. Dennis (ed.) *Zero Tolerance, Policing a Free Society*, London: Institute of Economic Affairs.

Ortner, H. Pilgrim, A. and Steinert, H. (1998) *Die Null-Lösung: New Yorker 'Zero-Tolerance' Politi – das Ende der urban Toleranz?*, Baden-Baden: Nomos.

Pollard, C. (1997) 'Zero tolerance: short-term fix, long-term liability?' in N. Dennis (ed.) *Zero Tolerance, Policing a Free Society*, London: Institute of Economic Affairs.

Power, A. and Tunstall, R. (1995) *Estates on the Edge: The Social Consequences of Mass Housing in Northern Europe*, York: Joseph Rowntree Trust, and London: Macmillan.

Reiner, R. (1985) *The Politics of the Police*, Brighton: Wheatsheaf Books.

Rinaldi, A. (1998) 'No Turks, please, we're German', *New Statesman*, 1 January: 23–4.

Romeanes, T. (1998) 'A question of confidence: zero tolerance and problem-oriented policing', in R. Hopkins Burke (ed.) *Zero Tolerance Policing*, Leicester: Perpetuity Press.

Rose, N. (1996a) 'The death of the social? Refiguring the territory of government', *Economy and Society*, 22: 283–99.

——(1996b) *In the Name of the Law, the Collapse of Criminal Justice*, London: Jonathan Cape.

Sasson, T. (1995) *Crime Talk, How Citizens Construct a Social Problem*, New York: Aldine de Gruyter.

Silverman, E. (1998) 'Below zero tolerance and problem oriented policing', in R. Hopkins Burke (ed.) *Zero Tolerance Policing*, Leicester: Perpetuity Press.

Simon, J. (1996) 'Criminology and the recidivist', in D. Shichor and D.K. Sechrest (eds) *Three Strikes and You're Out, Vengeance and Public Policy*, Thousand Oaks: Sage.

Stenson, Kevin (1991) 'Making sense of crime control', in K. Stenson and D. Cowell (eds) *The Politics of Crime Control*, London: Sage.

——(1993a) 'Social work discourse and the social work interview', *Economy and Society*, 22: 42–76.

——(1993b) 'Community policing as a governmental technology', *Economy and Society*, 22: 373–89.

——(1996) 'Communal security as government – the British experience', in W. Hammer-schick, I. Karazman-Morawetz and W. Stangl (eds) *Jahrbuch für Rechts und Kriminalsoziologie*, Baden-Baden: Nomos.

——(1998) 'Beyond histories of the present', *Economy and Society*, 29: 333–52.

——(1999) 'Crime control, governmentality and sovereignty', in R. Smandych (ed.) *Governable Places: Readings in Governmentality and Crime Control*, Aldershot: Dartmouth.

——(2000) 'Reconstructing the government of crime', in G. Wickham (ed.) *Socio-Legal Politics: Post-Foucaultian Possibilities*, Aldershot: Dartmouth.

Stenson, Kevin and Factor, Fiona (1994) 'Youth work, risk and crime prevention', *Youth and Policy*, 45: 1–15.

——(1995) 'Governing youth – new directions for the youth service', in M. May and J. Baldock (eds) *Social Policy Review no. 7*, Canterbury: The Social Policy Association.

Stenson, Kevin and Watt, Paul (1999) 'Governmentality and the "death of the social"?: a discourse analysis of local government texts in South-East England', *Urban Studies*, 36: 189–201.

Taylor, Ian (1998) 'Crime, market liberalism and the European idea', in V. Ruggiero, N. South and I. Taylor (eds) *The New European Criminology, Crime and Social Order in Europe*, London: Routledge.

Taylor, I., Evans, K. and Frazer, P. (1996) *A Tale of Two Cities: Global Change, Local Feeling and Everyday Life in the North of England. A Study in Manchester and Sheffield*, London: Routledge.

van Swaaningen, R. (1998) 'Tolerance or zero-tolerance: is that the question?' paper presented to the Conference of the American Society of Criminology, Washington, November.

Voronin, Y.A. (1996) 'The emerging criminal state: economic and political aspects of organised crime in Russia', *Transnational Organised Crime*, 2(2/3): 53–62.

Waddington, P.A.J. (1998) *Policing Citizens*, London: UCL Press.

Wilson, J.Q. and Kelling, G.L. (1982) 'Broken windows', *Atlantic Monthly*, March: 29–38.

Zimring, F.E. and Hawkins, G. (1997) *Crime is not the Problem: Lethal Violence in America*, New York: Oxford University Press.

12

WILLIAM HORTON'S LONG SHADOW

'Punitiveness' and 'managerialism' in the penal politics of Massachusetts, 1988–99[1]

Theodore Sasson

In early October 1997, spurred on by a string of grisly murders, including the rape and murder of a 10-year-old boy, the Massachusetts Senate voted in favour of a death penalty bill for the third time in a decade. Attention immediately shifted to the House of Representatives, which in each of the past three go-rounds had resisted voting for a death penalty law. In a dramatic gesture, Representative Donna Cuomo, sister of the original murder victim of William Horton – about whom more later – announced that she had abandoned her opposition to the death penalty and would vote in favour of the bill. 'It was really obvious that the people really want the death penalty … I didn't want to deny the people their voice.' The death penalty bill passed in the House by one vote. Local journalists called the moment a 'watershed' event in Massachusetts political history and declared that 'the liberal retreat is a rout'.[2]

Indeed, this seemed to be the case. The death penalty votes came on the heels of a string of law and order initiatives that passed one after another throughout the past decade. The state legislature dramatically expanded the range of offences for which juveniles could be tried and sentenced as adults and made such practices mandatory in cases of murder. It allocated nearly half a billion dollars to add 3,000 cells to a prison system whose population had already increased more than 300 per cent since 1980. It passed a 'truth-in-sentencing' law eliminating 'good time' credits and other mechanisms by which court-mandated sentences have historically been shortened. It established lifetime parole for sex offenders as well as an elaborate system of registration and neigh-bourhood notification to keep tabs on these offenders after they have served their court-mandated sentences. And it adopted harsh new mandatory sentences for drug, firearm and drunk-driving offences.

In the midst of this wave of highly emotional law and order activity, however, a cool-headed *zweckrational* initiative to establish comprehensive sentencing guidelines is under way. Created by vote of the Legislature, a sentencing commission worked for two years drawing up sentencing guidelines, effectively rewriting much of the State's statutory criminal law. Like those being advanced in many US states, the proposed guidelines aim to reduce sentencing disparities by establishing presumptive minimum terms of incarceration based on the current offence and the offender's criminal history. They also aim to increase penalties for violent offenders, expand the use of intermediate sanctions for non-violent offenders, restore limited judicial discretion with respect to drug-offence sentencing, and match penalties to available criminal justice resources. The Commission's proposed sentencing guidelines have been written into a bill that is now awaiting action by the state legislature.

How do we make sense of these twin and apparently contradictory developments? What do they tell us about the impulses and considerations animating legislative decision-making on crime in Massachusetts? What does their commingling portend? Garland (1990: 180) argues that to grasp contemporary struggles over crime penalties we must examine the interaction between the 'administrative, rationalistic, normalising concern to manage' and the 'morally toned desire to punish'. Observing developments in Great Britain in the 1990s, Garland (1996) argues that the routinisation of high rates of crime has generated a range of 'adaptations' by the state including, *inter alia*, new managerial techniques for enhancing system efficiency and new strategies for 'responsibilising' private parties for crime control.[3]

> Modest improvements at the margin, better management of risks and resources, reduction of the fear of crime, reduction of criminal justice expenditure and greater support for crime's victims, have become the less than heroic policy objectives which increasingly replace the idea of winning a 'war against crime'.
>
> (Garland 1996: 448)

In the USA, Feeley and Simon (1992, 1994, 1995) similarly claim that a 'new penology' is gaining ground among criminal justice practitioners and academics. In contrast to old penology's emphasis on punishing or rehabilitating individual offenders, the new penology is 'concerned with techniques for identifying, classifying and managing groups assorted by levels of dangerousness' (1994: 173).

> [The new penology] does not speak of impaired individuals in need of treatment or of morally irresponsible persons who need to be held accountable for their actions. Rather, it considers the criminal justice *system*, and it pursues systemic rationality and efficiency. It seeks to sort and classify, to separate the less from the more dangerous, and to deploy control strategies rationally.
>
> (1992: 452)

New penology represents the application of 'systems analysis' and actuarially based 'social utility analysis' – forms of policy analysis increasingly prevalent in many institutional domains – to the institutions of criminal justice. It is bound to neither liberal 'due-process' nor conservative 'lock 'em up' political postures and thus has steadily gained popularity notwithstanding the 'pendulum-like shifts' of penal politics (1994: 186–90).

The 'punitive counter-tendency', however, has by no means been dispersed by either generic *managerialism* or the more particular formations of *new penology*. For Garland, it returns in the form of neurotic denial by politicians of the profound weakness of the modern state.

> A show of punitive force against individuals is used to repress any acknowledgement of the state's inability to control crime to acceptable levels. A willingness to deliver harsh punishments to convicted offenders magically compensates a failure to deliver security to the population at large.
>
> (1996: 460; see also Platt 1994)

For Feeley and Simon (1995), the drive to 'get tough' with criminals is fuelled by fear of crime in combination with a traditional, moralistic public discourse that has proven impervious to the abstract, disembodied representations of the new penology. In short, according to these writers, contemporary penal policy-making is schizophrenic, animated by discourses and programmes that are 'twinned, antithetical' (Garland 1997: 203).

These analyses have obvious relevance to developments in Massachusetts and most other US states as well. As much as they illuminate, however, they are also confounded by a variety of factors. In this chapter, I discuss the limits of these analyses and seek to reconfigure them in ways that make sense in light of the case of Massachusetts. In the next section, I argue that punitiveness must be viewed not as an irrational response to either the 'limits of the sovereign state' or popular fear of crime, but as a key element in the political strategy of the Right. In the section that follows, I argue that managerialism, in the form of sentencing guidelines, should be viewed less as a response by practitioners and policy-makers to chronically high rates of crime than to the punitive turn in criminal justice practice and the hegemonic discourse that sustains it. In the final part, I argue that the commingling of punitiveness and managerialism in contemporary penal politics portends ongoing expansion of the criminal justice apparatus in the foreseeable future.[4]

Popular punitiveness

The Massachusetts Legislature's votes on the death penalty and juvenile justice bear many of the trappings of what Garland (1996) describes as a hysterical denial of the limits of the sovereign state. In both of these cases, law-makers responded to torrents of news coverage of a sensational crime with bills aimed at 'sending a message' to the public.[5] The juvenile justice bill, for example, was introduced in the context of massive media coverage of the refusal of a judge to 'waive' into adult court a juvenile (Eddie O'Brien) charged with the murder of his next-door neighbour. No hearings were held on the bill in spite of the fact that it proposed significant changes to the rules for dealing with a wide range of youthful offenders. The leadership of the Legislature, moreover, was forthright about the need for a unanimous vote in order to let the public know that state government was capable of responding vigorously to the perceived crisis.[6]

The overheated rhetoric of law-makers during floor debates on each of these issues also suggests their preoccupation with the issue of legitimacy. Many law-makers sought, in effect, to single-handedly embody the outrage of the *conscience collective* against heinous criminals. For example, consider the following excerpts from the 1997 death penalty debate. The speaker is a death penalty opponent:

> It's awful, these last few months. We talk about the killing of police offi-cers on duty. We talk about the crimes of domestic violence. And we talk about the murder of the 10-year-old Jeffrey Curley. And people ask me, 'You oppose the death penalty, would you really object to seeing these two people executed for what they've done?' Absolutely not. I cannot imagine such a horrific crime. It's almost beyond belief that people would do something like that. You almost cannot say that they're human beings. They're some type of degenerates put on this earth just to bother us. They are NOT human beings. But when the death penalty is enacted, it doesn't affect just these horrific, heinous, disgusting cases.[7]

Finally, also pointing to the significance of symbolic politics in these votes is the fact that they were taken during a period of sharp decline in violent crime, especially homicide.[8]

This analysis of the impulse to punitiveness, however, ignores two important issues. First, although the punitive tendency may be a permanent feature of the political landscape of modern society, it varies in terms of prevalence, intensity and relationship to concrete policy-making. It is therefore necessary to ask why it has become such a central aspect of Massachusetts politics and public policy in the past decade. Second, although the need to respond to perceived crises of authority explains several of the law and order initiatives of the 1990s, it does less to explain the Legislature's decisions to build (at considerable cost) new prisons, create a sex offender registry and implement 'truth-in-sentencing'. These latter initiatives were pursued under only a modest media spotlight and absent any sense of legitimacy crisis, and therefore require more ample explanation.

To address these issues, we must expand our inquiry in terms of time and place. Taken as a whole, the punitive turn in Massachusetts penal policy makes sense only as the sedimentation of a set of ideas about crime and welfare policy associated with New Right ideology and political strategy. This story may be quite familiar, but its central importance to the questions at hand justifies a quick rehearsal of its salient elements. In the USA, modern law and order rhetoric originated in the 1960s as a means of expressing conservative opposition to civil rights and Great Society social welfare programmes.[9] It was simultaneously mobilised by conservative politicians such as Richard Nixon as part of political strategy aimed at forging a new conservative majority. The 'southern strategy', as it came to be known, encouraged, by means of coded appeals to white racial fears and resentments, electoral realignment along racial instead of class lines (Edsall and Edsall 1992; Carter 1996). Modern law and order rhetoric had a definite ideological component as well; for New Right intellectuals, the legitimate purpose of the state is social control rather than social welfare (Beckett 1997). Tough-on-crime rhetoric, crack-downs on drugs and initiatives to expand the federal government's role in crime fighting while curtailing its role in the provision of social welfare were centrepieces of the Reagan and Bush administrations. In the mid-1990s, cracking down on crime and welfare, as both political strategy and practical domestic policy, achieved apotheosis in landslide Republican Congressional victories and President Clinton's embrace of the 1994 crime bill and subsequently of 'welfare reform'.[10]

Absent the support of the mass media and segments of the general public, conservative politicians and intellectuals could not possibly have succeeded in keeping crime and drugs at the top of the national agenda almost continuously for three decades. These issues make for dramatic news, however, and journalists have proved more than willing to accept the definitions of reality emanating from Washington, DC (see Beckett 1997; Reeves and Campbell 1994; Beckett and Sasson 1997). Much of the American public, moreover, has resonated quite sincerely to the New Right's moralistic political rhetoric decrying social breakdown and criminal justice leniency (Sasson 1995; Beckett and Sasson 2000). Law and order thinking thus swept the country and the need to appear tough on crime deeply penetrated the political common sense. There were, however, two more direct connections between the New Right project and policy-making in the state of Massachusetts and it is upon these that I would like to briefly dwell. The first concerns the 1988 presidential campaign of then Massachusetts governor and liberal flag-bearer Michael Dukakis.

The Bush campaign assailed the Democratic challenger as an old-style tax-and-spend soft-on-crime liberal. In a gesture construed by some commentators as 'McCarthyist', the Vice-President charged the Massachusetts governor with being a 'card-carrying member' of the American Civil Liberties Union.[11] More notoriously, Bush-for-President supporters aired television ads in selected markets in the southern United States charging Dukakis with complicity in the brutal rape of a white Maryland woman by a black Massachusetts convict named William Horton. In the final stages of his lengthy prison term for a 1974 murder,[12] Horton had absconded to Maryland from a weekend furlough to commit the infamous crime. It mattered little to the Bush campaign publicists that the furlough programme was established by Dukakis's Republican predecessor, or that at the time a similar programme was in place in the federal prison system. The tale of 'Willie' Horton, 'a wonderful mix of liberalism and a big black rapist', in the words of the advertisement's creator, was simply too good to forgo.[13] Journalists soon joined in the fray. In one of a small number of nationally televised debates, CNN anchor Bernard Shaw asked the Massachusetts governor if he would change his view on the death penalty if someone raped and killed his wife Kitty. The Democratic presidential candidate's cool, didactic response – he discussed the failure of the death penalty to deter crime – did nothing to change his image as a 'technocrat' who was 'out of touch' with the people.

The governor returned home after his embarrassing defeat to find Massachusetts in the midst of a fiscal crisis widely attributed to mismanagement of the state budget. In the ensuing two years, the once-popular governor was widely vilified.[14] The Legislature quickly repealed the prison furlough programme and Dukakis became a cautionary tale of what happens to politi-cians who are 'soft on crime'. More than ten years later, death penalty supporters could still gain political mileage by accusing their opponents of 'lining up with Mike Dukakis and the soft-on-crime crowd' (*Boston Herald*, 27 October 1997).

The 1990 gubernatorial election of William Weld further catalysed the New Right project in Massachusetts. Liberal on culture-war issues such as abortion and gay rights, Weld is otherwise a died-in-the-wool Reaganite. In fact, he came to the governorship by way of a position in Reagan's Justice Department. As a candidate twice for governor and once for the US Senate, Weld made 'crime, welfare and taxes' the centrepieces of his campaigns. He frequently claimed that under his leadership criminals would become acquainted with 'the joy of busting rocks'. In terms of policy, he either initiated or actively supported each of the punitive criminal justice initiatives discussed above. Lobbying for a bond bill to build new prisons, for example, he argued that 'Revolving door justice is anathema to victims and all law-abiding citizens. New cells are the wedge that will stop the door from swinging.' During Weld's tenure, the state not only 'got tough' on crime but also implemented one of the harshest 'welfare reforms' in the country, imposing mandatory cut-offs and extensive 'workfare' requirements.

In sum, the string of punitive criminal justice initiatives supported by the Massachusetts Legislature in the 1990s must be understood in a broader political context. These decisions reflect not only the law-makers' preoccupation with the issue of legitimacy but also their acceptance of the basic terms of New Right ideology. Both the timing and harsh tenor of the punitive turn are comprehen-sible in light of this project, as is the determination of law-makers to match rhetoric with instrumental action on issues such as 'truth in sentencing'.

Managerialism

Writers such as Garland (1990), Feeley and Simon (1992) and Bottoms (1995) treat the sentencing guidelines initiatives sweeping the USA as, in part, manage-rial efforts to cope with the routinisation of high rates of crime. Feeley and Simon (1992), moreover, argue that the guidelines movement bears the imprint of the 'new penology'. This is a bit paradoxical. In the official discourse, sentencing guidelines are treated as an effort to implement a scheme of 'just deserts' punishments in which the traditional criminal justice goals of rehabilitation, deterrence and incapacitation are de-emphasised. This was certainly the position of the Massachusetts Sentencing Commission:

> Consistent with the truth in sentencing statute, which directs the commission to recommend sentencing policies and practices which 'punish the offender justly', the commission has established *just punishment* as the central purpose of sentencing. Just punishment should be proportional to the gravity of the offence, taking into account the harm done to the victim or to society and the criminal intent of the offender, along with the seriousness of the offender's criminal history.
> (Massachusetts Sentencing Commission 1996, emphasis in original)

The proposed sentencing guidelines are thus construed, in statute and the official discourse, as the fruit of the movement for determinate sentencing that swept much of the industrialised West in the 1980s (for overviews, see Tonry 1996; Tonry and Hatlestad 1997).

But there are apparently several good reasons to view the Massachusetts sentencing guidelines initiative as in part managerial in nature,[15] first, the drive to establish guidelines originated with the efforts of an ad hoc task force of criminal justice practitioners and policy experts. One of the principal actors pressing for the creation of a sentencing commission, for example, was an agency that has historically been involved in rehabilitation programmes and now sponsors intermediate sanctions programmes. Second, the originators were clearly concerned not only with sentencing disparities but also with resources and expertise. Sentencing guidelines were promoted as a way of more effectively planning for the rationing of scarce prison beds. In fact, the proposal to establish a sentencing commission was situated among a series of other proposals that were purely managerial in nature:

> The Task Force found a justice system overwhelmed, with each element having reached a crisis point. The Commonwealth's courts are so grossly clogged that they are unable to impose timely criminal sanctions. Its probation system is so understaffed that it is unable to provide adequate supervision or monitoring of those on probation. Its prisons and jails are so dangerously overcrowded that they must release through the back door persons who may be more threatening to the community than those they must accept through the front door.
> The Task Force found a criminal justice system that is not a 'system' at all, but rather a myriad of unconnected bureaucracies lacking shared goals, adequate resources or clear policy direction. For example, some sentencing decisions are at the complete discretion of an individual

judge, while others are automatic and mandatory sentences, imposed irrespective of the seriousness of the offence or the dangerousness of the offender. As a result, it is a system that is both too lenient and too harsh.

(Boston Bar Association/Crime and Justice Foundation 1991: 1–2)

Sentencing guidelines were thus promoted, in part, as a practitioner's solution to the resource crisis occasioned by the burgeoning correctional population.

Finally, the language of the task force report that first proposed sentencing guidelines includes 'new penology' rhetoric on sorting offenders on the basis of dangerousness. The task force, for example, urged the repeal of mandatory minimum sentences for 'low risk' drug offenders in order to preserve prison space for more dangerous offenders. More fundamentally, the categorical distinction between 'violent' and 'non-violent' offenders that is at the heart of the sentencing guidelines initiative[16] is ambivalent with respect to time horizon; in the official discourse of the Sentencing Commission, it refers to past offences; in the everyday rhetoric of politicians, it is as likely to refer to future dangerousness.[17] In short, although sentencing guidelines may in fact be the intellectual fruits of the movement for determinate sentencing, their supporters in Massachusetts have included criminal justice practitioners who regard sentencing guidelines as a potential solution to specifically managerial problems.

Does it make sense, however, to think of the sentencing guidelines initiative as a response to chronically high rates of crime (cf. Garland 1996)? In my view, taken as a whole, sentencing guidelines are better viewed as an initiative of progressive reformers, including practitioners, policy advocates and politicians, seeking to reverse the punitive drift in criminal justice policy-making and restore elements of penal welfarism.[18] This is evident in the nature of the political sponsorship of sentencing guidelines, as well as in what the sponsors say about their motives.[19]

In Massachusetts, the political actors promoting guidelines, both from within and outside of the Legislature, have primarily been Left–liberal (i.e. 'progressive'). In advocating on behalf of the guidelines initiative, they have struck the now familiar managerial themes: by restoring a modicum of judicial discretion in drug cases, and increasing the overall range of offenders that can be punished in the community (with 'intermediate sanctions'), the guidelines promise to cut correctional costs and ensure that cells continue to be available to house dangerous and violent offenders. These claims were each expressed in an agenda-setting speech for the 1998 legislative session by the Speaker of the House of Representatives:

> The rationale behind such a proposal is simple and straightforward. Our jail and prison space is very expensive. It should be reserved for violent felony offenders and we should not expose our citizens to the risk of a judicial release of such prisoners because of overcrowding caused in part by inappropriate mandatory sentences … [It is wise to]

calculate the savings and benefits available to all of us if we were to require productive community use [via intermediate sanctions] of a convict's time. To have a non-violent offender occupy expensive prison [sic] seems misguided ... With more than 90 percent of our inmates scheduled to return to their homes and communities, is it not wiser to hold prison over the heads of such non-violent offenders, to require their continued work and support of their dependants, and to impose our society's legitimate demand for punishment in other ways?

(Speaker's Address to the Citizens of the Commonwealth, 12 January 1998)

In private conversations, however, the political actors most responsible for shepherding the guidelines initiative through the Legislature provided more ample and, in my view, persuasive accounts of their motivations. For these politicians and policy advocates, comprehensive sentencing guidelines can achieve a variety of goals beyond those discussed above – including goals that otherwise escape penal progressives:

- Because the guidelines restore judicial discretion over penalties for drug offences, they are a backdoor strategy for eliminating the cruelty and injustice associated with the new mandatory minimum drug sentences. [20]
- Because the guidelines divert a wide range of offenders from prison into community programmes that include significant therapeutic dimensions ('intermediate sanctions' in the jargon of the guidelines), they are a backdoor strategy for expanding opportunities for rehabilitation.
- Because the guidelines vest significant decision-making authority in a Sentencing Commission that meets behind closed doors – out of the media spotlight – they are a vehicle for de-politicising decision-making about criminal punishment.[21]

One policy advocate who played a leading role early in the guidelines initiative explained his motivations in this way:

[It is because] we saw the 'get tough on crime' forces winning hands down that we felt that if we could develop something that would focus attention on resources and how we manage the system we pull the discussion about how we penalise different crimes, pull that out of the Legislature, and into what I always describe as the 'nameless, faceless, body of the sentencing commission' who can, behind closed doors, thrash out what it should be and give to the Legislature ... a package that hopefully they don't get into picking apart ... And give the Legislature ... an opportunity to take a notorious crime and the cry to do something really awful to whoever commits that crime, pull it out of the public policy debate, throw it to the Sentencing Commission and say 'you guys come back with something'. Allow it to be done in a quieter, more thoughtful venue. And, we didn't start out to do sentencing guidelines. We were looking at corrections and in particular were concerned about prison crowding and the major influx of people going to prison, mandatory sentencing.

How do we make sense of the disparity between the public political rhetoric of the guidelines sponsors and their private accounts of their motivations? Why do political actors who are committed to reviving the justice system's emphasis on rehabilitation, de-politicising decision-making about criminal punishment, and moderating some of the harsh new drug penalties translate these ambitions into managerial rhetoric that emphasises cost considerations above all else? Not surprisingly, it is because they believe that the rhetoric of penal welfarism is (pick your metaphor) non-viable, dead-in-the-water, bankrupt. The conventional wisdom among all law-makers, regardless of political stripe, is that any talk that smacks of leniency towards criminals will be used by a future political rival to make the point that the incumbent is soft on crime. In this context, the 'just deserts' and managerial overtones of sentencing guidelines allow progressives to pursue some of their traditional goals while providing them with political 'cover'. As one prominent member of the House of Representatives put it:

> [T]he reason for support of it politically in this state, the reason is because it gives a package with sufficient cover for those who would politically be inclined to embrace that, that would in fact mediate to some degree some of the outrageously harmful and hurtful things that the Legislature has done in the past five or six years in knee-jerk reaction to what they perceived as a politically expedient cause. And things that they have now looked back on with great regret politically, the Eddie O'Brien – the juvenile murder statute that we now have – I think that you would find across the board that most people feel that that's [gone too far] … Sex offender bill … another reaction where we have gone too far.

Managerial rhetoric is simply the only rhetoric available to those who regard discourse on either rehabilitation or proportionality in punishment as either ineffective or downright self-destructive.

There is, of course, a great deal of irony in the resulting state of affairs: in order to move penal practice from the medieval 'sovereign spectacle' of death and branding (death penalty, sex offender registry) into the era of twentieth-century penal welfarism, progressive reformers have embraced sentencing guidelines – a programme with nineteenth-century neo-classical symbolic overtones.[22]

There is nothing ironic or paradoxical, however, about the spectacle of progressive reformers forging an alliance with administrators and bureaucrats.

THEODORE SASSON

Throughout this century, progressives have sought to mitigate social harms through rational planning. Brandishing 'expertise' as a warrant for authority, they have also sought to rationalise the administration of both government and corporation (see Derber *et al.* 1990, especially chapter 15; Hofstadter 1955). In the penal realm, an exemplary case is the 1967 Presidential Commission report, *The Challenge of Crime in a Free Society*. A 'classic statement of 1960s liberalism',

> [t]he report embraced the dominant view among criminologists that crime was the product of social influences, particularly the lack of social and economic opportunities for the poor and for racial minorities. It endorsed the concept of rehabilitation and called for 'more extensive community programs providing special, intensive treatment as an alternative to institutionalisation'.
>
> (Walker 1998: 202–3)

In the view of criminologist Samuel Walker, however, the report's most lasting contribution was its conceptualisation of the various agencies responsible for identifying, processing and punishing crime as a single, potentially integrated *criminal justice system*. 'The systems model emphasised the dynamic relationship among police, courts, and correctional agencies and the critical role of discretionary decision-making in determining whether cases were sent forward or removed from the system' (Walker 1998: 203). Feeley and Simon (1994) regard this coincidence of penal progressivism and managerialism as indicative of a moment of transition between old and new penologies. Be this as it may, it also illustrates the easy compatibility of these two discursive formations.

A look ahead

In the near term, there seems to be little support in the Legislature to pass the sentencing guidelines as they were written by the Sentencing Commission. Although there were prosecutors represented on the Commission, the District Attorneys' association has recommended significant revisions to the proposed guidelines. The DAs and the governor wish to preserve mandatory minimum sentencing for drug offences, establish a more comprehensive and unforgiving approach to 'criminal histories' and ratchet-up penalties for a host of specific offences.[23] Disagreements over these matters have created an apparent stalemate, and already several years have elapsed since the guidelines were first introduced as a bill. If the guidelines pass through the Legislature at all, it will likely be with most of the changes demanded by the DAs. As one law-maker explained, most state politicians are simply reluctant to publicly support any criminal justice scheme that does not enjoy 'more than a majority' of support among law enforcement officials.

Taking a longer view, the managerial perspective may be gaining the upper hand in Massachusetts as costs mount and crime rates remain relatively low.

Absent a critique of the social costs of a system as expansive as the one that now exists in the USA, however, the future is not terribly bright. Innovations may, in this context, correct some of the worst cruelties of the present regime (e.g. by repealing mandatory drug sentences), but at the price of further expansion and intensification of probationary supervision (in the form of 'intermediate sanctions'). Indeed, 'punitiveness' and 'managerialism' increasingly appear to operate as an uneasily integrated hegemonic discourse, the invariable fruit of which is further expansion of the criminal justice system.[24] Progressives grope for alternatives, embracing sentencing guidelines, intermediate sanctions and, more recently, 'restorative justice,'[25] but they are apparently incapable of articulating a programme that might plausibly arrest (and reverse) the growth in the penal system.

Conclusion

In the Commonwealth of Massachusetts, the cool-headed instrumentally rational sentencing guidelines initiative developed in the context of a string of new 'get tough' laws and a rapidly expanding criminal justice apparatus. In this paper, I've argued that these contradictory developments are best understood as the accomplishments of rival political projects. To be sure, growing punitiveness has been catalysed by intermittent crises of legitimacy over particularly horrendous crimes. More fundamentally, however, it reflects the ideological sedimentation of the New Right's struggle to realign the electorate and reconstruct the state. The fact that similar law and order discourse has played well in British politics (Downes and Morgan 1996) is an important indicator of the extent to which penal discourses are becoming global in nature (and consequently ever less sensitive to national conditions). But penal policies are still rooted in particular political projects and therefore must be understood in terms of their local conditions of production. The theory that treats punitiveness as a neurotic denial of the limits of the sovereign state (Garland 1996) might well explain the case of England and Wales, especially the reversal of the 1991 Criminal Justice Act (Downes and Morgan 1996). But it is less helpful in the United States, where criminal justice punitiveness is a key aspect of a coherent, ideologically driven and highly instrumental political programme aimed at electoral success and reconstruction of the state.[26]

Similarly, in the US context, it makes more sense to view managerialism as a response to prison overcrowding occasioned by recent 'wars' on crime and drugs than it does to treat it as a response to chronically high rates of crime. This is especially true in light of the relatively stable rate of serious crime in the USA over the past twenty-five years – a period during which the rate of incarceration more than tripled (Beckett and Sasson 2000). In Massachusetts, moreover, managerialism (in the form of sentencing guidelines) is also a political project of penal progressives. Having abandoned the discourse of rehabilitation, progressive policy-makers and advocates have seized upon managerialism as a way to express their opposition to overheated law and order rhetoric and the punitive policies to which it gives rise. In this sense, the new managerial penology is rapidly becoming the new liberal discourse on crime.

References

Beckett, Katherine (1997) *Making Crime Pay*, Oxford: Oxford University Press.

Beckett, Katherine and Sasson, Theodore (1997) 'The media and the construction of the drug crisis in America,' in Eric Jensen and Jurg Gerber (eds) *The New War on Drugs* (an ACJS Annual), Cincinnati, OH: Anderson Publishing Company.

——(2000) *Crime, Politics and Society*, Thousand Oaks, CA: Pine Forge Press.

Boston Bar Association/Crime and Justice Foundation (February 1991) 'The Crisis in Corrections and Sentencing in Massachusetts'.

Bottoms, Anthony (1995) 'The philosophy and politics of punishment and sentencing', in Chris Clarkson and Rod Morgan (eds) *The Politics of Sentencing Reform*, Oxford: Clarendon Press.

Braithwaite, John and Pettit, Philip (1990) *Not Just Deserts*, Oxford: Clarendon Press.

Carter, Dan (1996) *The Politics of Rage: George Wallace, the Origins of the New Conservatism and the Transformation of American Politics*, New York: Simon and Schuster.

Cohen, Stanley (1985) *Visions of Social Control*, Cambridge: Polity Press.

Derber, Charles, Schwartz, William and Magrass, Yale (1990) *Power in the Highest Degree: Professionals and the Rise of a New Mandarin Order*, New York: Oxford University Press.

Doob, Anthony (1995) 'The United States Sentencing Commission Guidelines: if you don't know where you are going, you might not get there,' in Chris Clarkson and Rod Morgan (eds) *The Politics of Sentencing Reform*, Oxford: Clarendon Press.

Downes, David and Morgan, Rod (1996) 'Dumping the "hostages to fortune"? The politics of law and order in post-war Britain,' in Mike Maguire, Rod Morgan and Robert Reiner (eds) *The Oxford Handbook of Criminology*, Oxford: Oxford University Press.

Edsall, Thomas and Edsall, Mary (1991) *Chain Reaction*, New York: Norton.

Feeley, Malcolm and Simon, Jonathan (1992) 'The new penology: notes on the emerging strategy of corrections and its implications,' *Criminology*, 30: 449–74.

——(1994) 'Actuarial justice: the emerging new criminal law', in David Nelkin (ed.) *Futures of Criminology*, London: Sage.

——(1995) 'True crime: the new penology and public discourse on crime', in Thomas Blomberg and Stanley Cohen (eds) *Punishment and Social Control*, Hawthorne: Aldine de Gruyter.

Garland, David (1990) *Punishment and Modern Society*, Chicago: University of Chicago Press.

——(1996) 'The limits of the sovereign state: strategies of crime control in contemporary society', *British Journal of Criminology*, 36: 445–71.

——(1997) ' "Governmentality" and the problem of crime: Foucault, criminology, sociology', *Theoretical Sociology*, 1: 171–214.

Hofstadter, Richard (1955) *The Age of Reform*, New York: Random House.

Karst, K. (1993) *Law's Promise, Law's Expression*, New Haven: Yale University Press.

Massachusetts Sentencing Commission (April, 1996) 'Report to the General Court'.

Melossi, Dario (1993) 'Gazette of morality and social whip', *Social and Legal Studies*, 2: 259–79.

O'Malley, Pat (1992) 'Risk, power and crime prevention', *Economy and Society*, 21: 253–75.

Platt, Anthony (1994) 'The politics of law and order', *Social Justice*, 21: 3–13.

Reeves, Jimmie and Campbell, Richard (1994) *Cracked Coverage: Television News, the Anti-Cocaine Crusade and the Reagan Legacy*, Durham, NC: Duke University Press.

Rock, Paul (1995) 'The opening stages of criminal justice policy making', *British Journal of Criminology*, 35: 1–16.

Sasson, Theodore (1995) *Crime Talk: How Citizens Construct a Social Problem*, Hawthorne, NY: Aldine de Gruyter.

——(1998) 'Beyond agenda setting: the framing effects of "Nannygate" on a death penalty debate', annual meeting of the American Society of Criminology, November, Washington, DC.

Savelsberg, Joachim (1992) 'Law that does not fit society: sentencing guidelines as a neoclassical reaction to the dilemmas of substantivized law', *American Journal of Sociology*, 97: 1346–81.

Tonry, Michael (1996) *Sentencing Matters*, Oxford: Oxford University Press.

Tonry, Michael and Hatlestad, Kathleen (1997) *Sentencing Reform in Overcrowded Times*, Oxford: Oxford University Press.

von Hirsch, Andrew and Ashworth, Andrew (eds) (1996) *Principled Sentencing*, Boston: Northeastern University Press.

Walker, Samuel (1998) *Popular Justice*, Oxford: Oxford University Press.

NOTES

2   THE ROLE OF ANXIETY IN FEAR OF CRIME

1   An ESRC funded project, Gender Difference, Anxiety and the Fear of Crime, Award Number L21020252018, under the Crime and Social Order Programme.

2   For example, see Young (1988), Hough and Mayhew (1985), and Mirrlees-Black *et al.* (1996).

3   Which is now voluminous. For useful overviews, see Box *et al.* (1988), Sparks (1992), Ferraro (1995) and Hale (1996).

4   Thirty-seven in-depth double interviews, focused on respondents' experiences of criminal victimisation, their risk, their fear of crime and anxiety, with young, middle-aged and old men and women residing on two different estates, one high-crime and one low-crime, in a city in northern England.

5   This point is endorsed by the work being done on repeat victimisation. See Farrell (1995).

6   Barbara and Brenda are also interesting because they contradict the widespread stereotype of fearful old women whose risks are minimal: a stereotype which survey findings have helped to produce through their techniques of averaging and generalising.

7   This was amusingly illustrated when Brenda was telling the interviewer how the Tenants' and Residents' Association (in which her husband is very active) was providing alarms for old people on the estate. She was asked whether she had received one, and after a brief look of surprise she laughed and confessed that it had never occurred to her.

8   His case suggests the methodological paradox that those who predominantly deny or distort reality – unconsciously experiencing it as too extreme in its threats to self to face realistically – can appear to be (and report being) low in fear of crime.

9   The shift from 'I' to 'you' in this manner suggests a distancing from strong emotions conjured by the account.

4   AFTER SUCCESS? ANXIETIES OF AFFLUENCE IN AN ENGLISH VILLAGE

1   Between 1994 and 1996, in Prestbury and the neighbouring town of Macclesfield, we conducted an intensive inquiry into the place and significance of crime in local social relations (a fuller account of the study's theoretical orientations, methods and conclusions can be found in Girling *et al.* 2000). The work in Prestbury, upon which we report here, encompassed: (1) focus group discussions with retired businessmen, members of the Women's Institute, home watch co-ordinators, managers working at the Macclesfield-based pharmaceutical giant Zeneca, and parents with children at the

local primary school; (2) in-depth biographical interviews with three long-standing residents; (3) observation of Parish Council meetings, documentary analysis of Council minutes and Parish newsletters, and an interview with councillors; (4) a period of voluntary work/observation at Prestbury youth club, coupled with two focus groups with local teenagers and an interview with the youth worker; and (5) numerous hours spent in informal conversations with local residents, 'worthies' and professionals, and attendance/observation at various meetings. We gratefully acknowledge the support of the Economic and Social Research Council, who funded the study under its Crime and Social Order research programme (award no. L210252032).

2   Illustrations of the former position – which was associated with 'left realism' and some variants of feminist criminology – can be found in Hamner and Saunders (1984), Jones *et al.* (1986) and Young (1988); for accounts of the latter view, which came in both Home Office and radical guises, see Maxfield (1984) and the essays collected in Scraton (1987). The critiques and revisions include Sparks (1992); Taylor (1995); Taylor *et al.* (1996); Hollway and Jefferson (1997); and Walklate (1998).

3   To adopt this perspective is not to deny that people worry about crime and disorder, nor is it to eschew entirely the connections that exist between levels of anxiety and those of measurable risk. It is to recognise, however, that when people speak about crime they do so in ways that register its entanglement with other aspects of economic, social and moral life; attribute responsibility and blame; demand account-ability and justice; and draw lines of affiliation and distance between 'us' and various categories of 'them' (cf. Douglas 1992). This mode of enquiry is, we believe, best advanced by a hermeneutically sensitive analysis (of the kind attempted here) which aims to disclose the *particular* kinds of entanglement that are acknowledged, and the *specific* sorts of blaming/boundary-drawing practices that are engaged in by *differently situated* citizens (see further, Girling *et al.* 2000: chs 3–4).

4   Figure 4.1 represents all the places mentioned by our respondents during the course of our interviews and focus groups, and distinguishes them according to whether they were cited as locations of affiliation or threat.

5   The names of all those quoted in the chapter have been changed.

6   In 1995, Cheshire Constabulary recorded 228 property offences for the beat covering Prestbury, including 68 domestic burglaries, 31 non-domestic burglaries, 52 thefts from vehicles and 13 stolen vehicles.

7   These worries, however, generate relatively few calls for police assistance. Of the 280 calls made to Macclesfield police station from the Prestbury beat during April and May 1995, only six (some 2 per cent) concerned youths behaving suspiciously or causing annoyance. In 1995, Cheshire Constabulary recorded twelve incidents of criminal damage for the beat covering Prestbury. No incidents of shoplifting and no public order offences were recorded by the police in that year.

8   Though this is not, it would seem, the case among all parents. In what might be inter-preted as a conflict between the (seemingly threatened) cultural norms of those established residents who invest time and effort in 'the village' and its 'character', and the values of those for whom Prestbury offers merely a (temporary) backdrop to their private lives (cf. Cloke *et al.* 1995; Taylor and Jamieson 1998: 166), it was often alleged during our discussions that some among Prestbury's residents permit and even actively encourage their teenage children to 'roam the village till all hours', so that they can pursue unhindered their busy professional and social lives. The following account – provided by a participant in our parents' focus group, but a version of a tale we came across frequently – encapsulates this complaint nicely:

A nice brand new Mercedes will drive through Prestbury at eight o'clock on a Saturday evening, or thereabouts, and drop a child, or two children off, and the parent leans out of the door and is actually seen passing a wad of notes – not a ten pound note, but a wad of notes – across to them [this echoes another common refrain in our discussions: that Prestbury's young have too much money]. This goes on on a regular basis. It's not an isolated incident, there may be several sightings every Saturday night of this happening. Then they are seen to pick them up at half past twelve or one o'clock in the morning, whilst the parents go off doing whatever they are doing.

Needless to say, we never came across one of these parents.

9 Thus it is that residents' demands for order are directed principally at those who are felt able to restore a lost civility and discipline to 'village life' *without* undermining Prestbury as 'a village': namely, the youth club and the – recently 'withdrawn' – 'village bobby' (see further, Girling *et al*. 2000: ch. 5).

5 INEQUALITY AND THE CLUBBING OF PRIVATE SECURITY

1 A public good is usually defined as having two characteristics: non-rivalry and non-excludability (Barry and Hardin 1982). A good can be thought of as *non-rival* if 'one person's enjoying more of the good does not reduce the ability of others to enjoy it' (Hargreaves Heap *et al*. 1992: 345). A good is *non-excludable* in its provision if access to the good cannot be denied to individuals even if they have not contributed in some way to its provision. Rarely are goods purely public but, as will be described below, these characteristics nevertheless comprise useful criteria for analysing the nature of particular goods (or bads) and, importantly, how their benefits (or costs) are produced and distributed.

2 An alternative strategy (see also Garland 1996) – that of dampening down demand for the collective security good – was also tried tentatively by British governments in the early 1980s, one example of which was the way property crime risks were interpreted from the findings of the first national crime victimisation survey in Great Britain (Hough and Mayhew 1983). Nevertheless, the concept of the 'statistically average victim' – with an apparently low level of actuarial risk – attracted criticism from those concerned to highlight inequalities in the distribution of victimisation risk (see Young 1986).

3 For example, the British government's recently announced anti-burglary programme – an expenditure programme of £50m in grants to local authorities and police in England and Wales for actions targeted on local communities – has as its goal a reduction of 5 per cent in the national rate of domestic burglary offences (Home Office 1999). More generally, the first stated aim of the Home Office is the reduction of crime, particularly youth crime, and in the fear of crime; and the maintenance of public safety and good order (Home Office 1998).

4 Property crime here includes offences of burglary, attempted burglary, break-in with damage, theft from inside and outside the dwelling (excluding milk bottles) and criminal damage to the property. Among individuals, the concentration of crime victimisation is even more stark – broadly around 4 per cent of people suffer about 40 per cent of crime victimisation (Farrell and Pease 1993).

5 Any *sufficient* explanation would also need to subsume the (rather plentiful) number of theories which account for individuals' incumbencies in the various criminogenic roles and the ways in which they interact in specific circumstances (see Wikstrom 1995; Bottoms and Wiles 1997).

6 For instance, Cohen and Felson (1979: 589) refer to 'the fundamental human ecological character of illegal acts as events which occur at specific locations in space and time, involving specific persons and/or objects'. As Bottoms and Wiles (1992) note,

the centrality of routine social interactions in accounting for structured patterns of victimisation over space and time (Cohen and Felson 1979) has close affinities with Giddens' (1984) general theory of structuration – particularly the reflexive relationship between social action and social structure.

7 In this view, all young people are attracted to and desire such commodities because they appeal to those things valued more in youth – i.e. short-term gratification and stimulation – which also relate to youth's greater propensity to crime (see Felson 1994; Gottfredson and Hirschi 1990).

8 The continuing low and stable crime rate of Japan throughout the post-war period also strains at least the 'consumption' side of the routine activity explanation.

9 Felson, for instance, sees crime as 'a study of accidents [requiring] ... a general science of surprise' (1987: 914).

10 The only exceptions, among renters, are the use of window bars or grilles and contributing towards organised security, including guards.

11 The indices were selected on the basis of a principal components analysis of Census variables pertaining to the areas as defined in the data (see Figure 5.1, note 1). Though simple additive variables, they reflect extracted principal components of variable sets which are collinear.

12 Similar disparities in risk also apply to the largest form of 'mobile' private property – people's cars: not only does the majority of autocrime occur while cars are parked outside people's homes at night, but car-owners in disadvantaged areas (who are far fewer than in more affluent areas) face the highest risk of such residential autocrime (Hope 1987).

13 Comparable estimates, to my knowledge, have not been made elsewhere, partly because, as with the United States, the data (such as that from the National Crime Victimisation Survey) cannot be, or have not been allowed to be, used in this way.

14 Thus, for example, Cohen *et al.* describe the principle of risk *homogamy* as: 'to the degree that persons share socio-demographic characteristics with potential offenders they are more likely to interact socially with such potential offenders, thus increasing the risk factor of exposure' (Cohen *et al.* 1981: 509).

15 The answer, reputedly common among dealers in residential property, to the question 'What are the three rules of valuation?'

16 For instance, detachment expresses the cultural value of *privacy* – i.e. distance and concealment from neighbouring property – coupled with *amenity* – i.e. external access to property, aesthetic and recreational (i.e. gardening, car-parking) facilities of private grounds. In densely populated countries like Britain, land values are high so that the production price of dwelling detachment is also high.

17 The one-way analysis of variance test reveals this trend to be highly significant (F=18.01, p<0.00001); observed differences between groups are significant according to the multiple range test at p<0.05.

18 This pattern of risk has been confirmed recently by multivariate logistic regression analysis of the combined 1996 and 1998 British Crime Survey data-sets (see Budd 1999, table B.1). In this latter model, 'end-terrace houses' now have a significantly lower risk than detached houses, with a risk similar to that of semi-detached dwellings, which they resemble structurally. While only using a standard geo-demographic classification system – ACORN – to typify area characteristics, the area types 'Thriving' and 'Expanding' have a similarly suppressant effect to that played by 'Affluence' in our model.

19 Although this measure may not capture all the qualities of 'area affluence' it reflects a residential concentration of key outcomes of consumption, and the variables were found to be collinear in the BCS/Census data set. The effect of this portmanteau variable in the model was highly significant (p<0.00001). Additionally, other 'suburban' features also seemed to reduce property crime risk, including low child-

densities, low rates of 'disrupted' families and high rates of home-ownership (Hope 1999). Nevertheless, probably as a consequence of colinearity, in other models of the 1992 BCS (e.g. Ellingworth *et al.* 1997) where the variables have been included separately, the effect of 'area affluence' was derived only from that part measuring the average number of cars per household.

20 The paucity of data, absence of theoretical models and lack of interest among economists has left an understanding of the security-value of dwellings and neighbourhoods relatively underdeveloped.

21 Multivariate analysis of property crime risk shows that households in 'owner-occupation' and 'non-manual employment' have higher risks, once area characteristics are taken into account (see e.g. Ellingworth *et al.* 1997). Yet as the latter invariable mirror the distribution of disadvantage (Hope 1997), it would seem that the highest risks are likely to be faced by better-off households in less well-off areas. Indeed, research by Hirschfield and Bowers (1997) in Merseyside finds class-mixed 'gentrifying' areas to have the highest rates in the metropolitan region of recorded crimes and calls for police service.

22 Of course, their poorer co-residents will also be given strong signals – either by not being offered insurance or by not being able to afford the premiums.

23 One might also add to this list the costs of other forms of private insurance or additional voluntary contributions taken out against other 'social risks' including 'poor' schooling and 'inadequate' medical care.

24 As Davis notes,

> homeowner politics have focused on defense of th[e] suburban dream against unwanted development ... as well as against unwanted persons ... the security-driven logic of urban enclavization finds its most popular expression in the frenetic efforts of Los Angeles's affluent neighbourhoods to insulate home values and lifestyles.
>
> (1990: 170, 244)

25 'Free-riding' is a technical term used to describe those who can enjoy the benefits of membership without contributing to the costs of their production and who cannot be excluded from doing so (Sandler 1992). It can be shown formally – in a game-theoretic context with standard rationality assumptions about individual action – that the conditions of non-excludability and voluntarism attaching to public goods leads to the strategy of free-riding for any participating individual. Even though greater collective benefit would be obtained if everyone contributed to the production of the public good, the individual incentive to free-ride which bears on every participant equally results in the underprovision of public goods which do not carry with them additional penalties, incentives or assurances to participate. That is the public goods dilemma.

26 These results were obtained from a factor analysis of the measures listed in Table 5.1 – for details see Lab and Hope (1998) and subsequent publications.

27 Interestingly, the other private property security factors identified by Lab and Hope (1998) all involved physical measures.

28 The modelling strategy, including variables used, is described in Lab and Hope (1998).

29 For an elaboration of this general process of normative development, see Coleman 1990.

30 Recent 'ecological' research in Merseyside suggests that as the spatial 'width' of relative disadvantage in the areas surrounding an affluent 'core' area increases, levels of assault and burglary to residents in the affluent core also increase, and levels of these

crimes decrease the greater the width of relative affluence in the surroundings (Hirschfield and Bowers 1997).

31 Although I have not pursued Jordan's argument in respect of the rise in crime among the poor, namely as a reflection of individuals' strategic adaptations to their exclusion from social and economic benefits (Jordan 1996: chapter 6).

6 NO MORE HAPPY ENDINGS? THE MEDIA AND POPULAR CONCERN ABOUT CRIME SINCE THE SECOND WORLD WAR

1 A recent example is Norman Dennis' assertion that

> In the 1960s the expanding media of television and magazines, and the recovering but culturally metamorphosed medium of film, were disseminating diluted but pervasive versions of the counter-cultural message. Within a few years, and almost across the board, the anti-law anti-hero, whether passive or active, replaced the model family and the heroic upholder of personal virtue and of community values in the cinema and television drama.

> (Dennis 1997: 25)

In Britain, the most celebrated example of this position is Mary Whitehouse's long-running campaign about the supposedly subversive effects of media permissiveness (see Newburn 1992: chapter 2 for a detailed account and critique; for an American example see Medved 1992).

2 The influential 'Cultural Indicators' Project developed by George Gerbner and his associates since the 1960s has monitored changes in media representations of violence, seeing these as a potential threat to democratic political institutions because of the public support for authoritarian control measures which they cultivate (e.g. Gerbner 1970, 1995; Signorielli 1990: 102). The power of the mass media to create moral panics and folk devils, and hence legitimise more repressive forms of policing and criminal justice, was a staple of radical criminology especially in the 1970s (e.g. Young 1971; Cohen 1972; Cohen and Young 1973; Hall *et al.* 1978; Hall 1979).

3 'Fear of crime' is a notoriously complex concept, which requires unpacking into such varying dimensions as perceptions of the risk of personal victimisation of different kinds, personal feelings of vulnerability to such victimisation and its impact, views about the prevalence of crime and the seriousness of its impact on others ranging from intimate associates and local areas to the wider society, and behavioural consequences of fear such as avoidance and prevention tactics (Box *et al.* 1988; Hale 1996; Zedner 1997: 586–93). There is also a subtle interaction between 'fear of crime' and more general and often amorphous senses of personal and social vulnerability and anxiety of a broader kind (Taylor 1995; Hollway and Jefferson 1997; Loader *et al.* 1998). Some of these dimensions are clearly much harder to capture and measure, and different studies use different indices of 'fear of crime', so that their results are incommensurable.

4 As Durkheim puts it, 'crime is reduced more and more to offences against persons alone, while religious forms of criminality decline' (Durkheim 1973: 303).

5 We defined a 'crime story' as one where (1) the central focus of the narrative was the commission and/or investigation of a crime, and/or (2) the principal protagonist was either an offender or a professional working in the criminal justice system.

6 The rise of police protagonists is structurally related to the representation of crime as more all-pervasive, and hence requiring a bureaucratic organisation of professionals to contend with it. The police are also subject to a process of normalisation. In demographic terms, the police are shown as becoming more like the population at large.

Whatever the reality, in films the old saw about police officers becoming younger is borne out. Not only are the police heroes becoming younger, they are becoming less middle-class, and there is an increasing representation of women and ethnic minority officers, although the overwhelming majority remain male WASPS.

7   The demographic characteristics of victims suggested by films is not unlike that implied by victim surveys, contrary to some previous research findings. Thus they are predominantly male and young, and although usually white, the proportion of ethnic minority victims is rising sharply. Newspaper stories are less in line with the survey evidence than fictional stories. Thus female and male victims roughly equal each other, and older victims are over-represented. The proportion of white victims in news stories is actually increasing.

7   PERSPECTIVES ON RISK AND PENAL POLITICS

1   Interestingly, some such regret seems discernible on both the 'hard science' and on the culturalist sides of risk debates. On the former, see briefly the views summarised in *The Times Higher Education Supplement* (14 March 1997; 18–21). On the latter, note Douglas's comment that 'our political discourse debases the word ... it has become a decorative flourish on the word "danger"' (Douglas 1992: 40).

2   Among social theorists of risk, Douglas's sensitivity to culture and attributions of blame and accountability make her uniquely aware of questions of justice and punishment (Douglas 1992). Beck has nothing expressly to say on the matter, although the formal structure of his argument attracts some of those who do (Beck 1992; see, for example, Ericson and Haggerty 1997). Giddens makes himself amenable to being read by those whose interests lie in changing 'projects of incarceration' (1991: 160) or in current responses to behaviour that is 'alien and discrete' (*ibid.*: 150). Bauman addresses himself directly to the fates of the 'strangers of the consumer era' (1997: 35–45).

3   This argument is further developed by Garland (1996) who argues that numerous routine non-penal measures (insurance, 'dataveillance', changes in architectural practice and so forth) similarly signify adjustments to the normality of high crime rates. In this respect there is no practical contradiction between the expanded scope of contemporary criminal justice systems on one hand and, on the other, the recognition of trends towards channelling out, diversion, 'no-criming' and otherwise 'defining deviance down' (1996: 12–13). Moreover, the bulk of everyday risk management and avoidance is not directly the responsibility of the state but is devolved to private (individual and corporate) actors or to novel public–private 'partnerships' (1996: 9–11). See also Ericson and Haggerty (1997: 12).

4   'Dangerousness' has long been regarded as posing both a moral obligation and a moral problem, primarily because of the intractably high level of 'false positive' predictions (which led some individuals – who would not have re-offended – to be held longer for precautionary reasons than is justified on grounds of retribution alone). This dilemma of 'old penology' has its own large literature (see, most recently, Walker 1996). In Britain its 'solution' has been the mixed constitution of the life sentence (which includes both a 'tariff' and a reviewable precautionary component). The questions raised by indeterminate sentencing on grounds of dangerousness are quite distinct from the version of incapacitation outlined above and require separate discussion. Note, however, (1) that life sentences have become newly controversial in Britain in part because the erstwhile Home Secretary, Michael Howard, took an activist view of his quasi-judicial powers *vis-à-vis* both tariffs and release decisions, in ways that brought him into direct conflict with the higher judiciary (see especially Windlesham 1996); (2) that even within the arena of dangerousness-proper actuarial techniques tend to supersede clinical judgement as a basis for pre-release risk-

assessment; and (3) life sentences are nevertheless not immune from the processes sketched above, especially where they come to include formulaic mandatory minima, as in so-called 'three strikes' legislation (Shichor and Sechrest 1996).

5   As such it owed much to perspectives inspired by the later Foucault on changing techniques of 'government' (e.g. Castel 1991; Pasquino 1991). Arguably, Simon and Feeley's subsequent and more open-textured interpretations go further in acknowledging the significance of all *three* 'points' of Foucault's proposed triangular relation between 'discipline–sovereignty–government' (Foucault 1991). See also O'Malley (1992), Garland (1997).

6   Simon argues that much contemporary criminal careers research largely eschews explanation in favour of prediction. Simon thus takes as a watershed the publication of Wolfgang *et al.*'s *Delinquency in a Birth Cohort* (1972) which urges the efficiency of intervention against the small minority of 'chronic offenders', conceived in effect as 'individual crime rates' (Simon 1996: 46). The latter view has, in Simon's analysis, 'helped legitimize a massive expansion of segregative strategies, mainly more use of incarceration' (*ibid.*). Simon acknowledges that this outcome has not in the main been consciously sought by criminologists, and certainly not in the blunderbuss form now embodied in many 'three strikes' laws. Rather, criminology has become a resource plundered by policy entrepreneurs. Greenwood responds by querying the rationality of 'three strikes' using different models of cost–benefit accounting (emphasising in particular the drain on state budgets engendered by policies of mass incarceration) (Greenwood *et al.* 1996).

7   Indeed, Simon and Feeley and Garland both make passing reference to Douglas's work. See e.g. Garland 1996: 17.

8   Moreover, Douglas's interest in 'pollution' readily calls to mind the many uses of metaphors of disease, miasma and so on in relation to crime. Conversely, Douglas's view of those professional risk analysts who wish to bracket off questions of culture and politics from the objective discussion of risk (and thereby to achieve 'innocence') is reminiscent of the 'technocratic rationalization' discerned by Feeley and Simon among practitioners of the new penology.

9   It is impossible here to undertake a more thorough mapping of the formal and substantive overlaps between social theories of risk generally and criminology, though I hope to do this in a subsequent chapter. The most obvious points of connection include: the role of criminology in the history of social statistics and 'moral science' (Hacking 1991) and the continuing refinement of procedures for prediction and control; the question for cultural theory of *which risks* are 'selected for attention' (Rayner 1992); the parallels between the 'amplification of risk' (Kasperson 1992) and deviancy amplification; the debates about the rationality respectively of risk-perception (Funtowicz and Ravetz 1992) and 'fear of crime' (Sparks 1992); the issue of social responses to risk and trust in authorities as applied to environmental controversies and to crime (sometimes, of course, these are one and the same) (cf. Wynne 1992 and Nelken 1994).

10   For analyses of recent US experience that seem consonant with this view see Zimring and Hawkins (1994); Krisberg (1994); Austin (1996).

8   SOCIAL CONFLICT AND THE MICROPHYSICS OF CRIME: THE EXPERIENCE OF THE EMILIA–ROMAGNA *CITTÀ SICURE* PROJECT

1   We would like to thank Richard Sparks for having read and commented a previous version of this chapter. The responsibility for the final result is of course only ours. Please send all inquiries to Dario Melossi. (melossi@giuri.unibo.it)

2 Attempts at revising Art. 117 of the Italian Constitution, which defines the respective roles and competencies of the central state and the regions, have until now failed. In the early 1990s this issue was muddled by the emergence of a political force, the Northern League, that demanded independence for northern Italy from the rest of the country.

3 That is, a system traditionally based on national centralisation.

4 See below, note 8.

5 As Garland (1996: 452) clearly stated, 'The responsibilization strategy involves a number of new techniques and methods whereby the State seeks to bring about actions on the part of 'private' agencies and individuals.' In Garland's words, this strategy focuses on the move of crime control – promoted by the public sector – from the public to the private. But, more generally, we see also a move from the state – as central government – towards different public authorities (the local ones), never before involved in crime control strategies.

6 The Italian constitution reserves these matters to the state, as does a recent law aiming to reform the distribution of competencies between central and local institutions.

7 ASL are the main local structures of the Italian national health system. They are managed by the regions and have many competencies related to 'safety' policies, e.g. in the fields of treatment of drug addicts, the mentally ill (also mentally ill offenders), and measures towards young people considered 'at risk'.

8 Basic assumptions of 'left realism' appeared for the first time in Italy in 1986, thanks to an essay by Jock Young (1986), published in *Dei delitti e delle pene* together with some critical remarks by Tamar Pitch (1986). The academic world, however, remained silent until the 1990s, when the issue was reintroduced by Massimo Pavarini (1994). On the contrary, the institutional and political world quickly assumed the main theoretical assumptions of this 'new' criminological trend.

9 This activity is well documented by the series *Quaderni di Città sicure*, especially in no. 10, July 1997, 'Il progetto, i riferimenti, le attività'.

10 See for instance the project 'Sicurezza urbana e qualità della vita' (Cardia 1998), in which there are many proposals for conservative urban renewal of neighbourhoods and parks. Many other cities have adopted similar programmes in recent years.

11 Note the emergence of a common European language of partnership (Crawford 1997), protocols, etc. – injecting a 'private' law language into a semantic world that until now had been solidly under the control of the bureaucratic language of an administrative type of law.

12 Following Wesley Skogan's classical distinction between 'insurgent' and 'preservationist' groups (Skogan 1988), we can identify two different forms of community organisations: the more traditional voluntary associations and the new active groups called *comitati di cittadini* (citizens' committees). This distinction recalls Skogan's differentiation, in the sense that voluntary associations work in the most conflictual and disorganised areas of the cities and do not exclusively address crime problems. By contrast, the new committees usually emerge in order to face a specific crime problem, and they work in neighbourhoods that were, once, quite cohesive. From other points of view, however, there are many differences from the two models described by Skogan with reference to North American community organisations.

13 See, for instance, this description of a leader of the *Comitato Spontaneo* (one of the most famous and active groups born in the district of San Salvario, Turin):

> the *responsible* of the committee is F.I. He comes from the Communist Party, he was an activist … He knows the system of political struggle, what works and what does not, the goals around which people are interested to join …

We could say that these committees are spontaneous, but, at the same time, they act in a well-known and established system of collective action.

(Belluati 1998: 99–100, note 21)

14 As in the Red Brigades's 1970s' slogan, 'Bring the attack at the heart of the state!' However, as the satirical magazine *Il male* wrote at the time, the Red Brigades were dismayed to find out that 'the state has no heart!'

15 Such is the title of a collection of Michel Foucault's essays in Italian, referring to Foucault's concept of 'micro-power' (Foucault 1977). Indeed, one could venture to suggest that Foucault's polemic against a state-centred concept of power was the way in which European culture started to question itself about the obsolescence of the old nineteenth-century European nation-states as well as about the introduction of the notion of political pluralism (Melossi 1990 and 1997).

10 THE PURSUIT OF SECURITY

1 This piece arises out of research carried out collaboratively with Nicola Lacey and funded by the Economic and Social Science Research Council (Crime, Social Order and the Appeal to Community in Britain and Germany ESRC Award no. L210 25 2021.) I am grateful to Niki for her customary generosity with time and ideas and to Isabella Moebius for excellent research assistance. Thanks are also due to the participants at research seminars at the Universities of Oxford, Cambridge and Frankfurt, in particular to Professors Richard Ericson, Klaus Günther, Cornelius Nestler and Andrew von Hirsch for their invaluable comments.

2 As Mike Davis has observed: 'the social perception of threat becomes a function of the security mobilization itself, not crime rates'; M. Davis (1998) *City of Quartz: Excavating the Future in Los Angeles,* London: Pimlico, 224.

3 Indeed, as Davis points out, many insurance companies now routinely review the security arrangements of their commercial clients and insist on upgraded security provision as a condition of policy renewal (*ibid.*: 243).

4 M. Feeley and J. Simon (1994) 'Actuarial justice: the emerging new criminal law', in D. Nelken (ed.) *The Futures of Criminology,* London: Sage, 181.

5 This is in striking contrast to Germany where the extension of surveillance has been the subject of intense debate, not least as to its constitutional implications, and has been much less widespread as a result.

6 D. Garland (1996) 'The limits of the sovereign state: strategies of crime control in contemporary society', *British Journal of Criminology,* 36(4): 445.

7 R.V. Ericson and K.D. Haggerty (1997) *Policing the Risk Society,* Oxford: Clarendon Press.

8 Although as we have observed elsewhere, it is questionable whether community safety can be pursued effectively when organic structures of social order are in decline or inadequate; N. Lacey and L. Zedner (1995) 'Discourses of community in criminal justice', *Journal of Law and Society,* 22.

9 Or even Germany or England during the terrorist campaigns of the Red Army Faction and the IRA respectively.

10 L. Freedman (1992) 'The concept of security', in M. Hawkesworth and M. Kogan (eds) *Encyclopedia of Government and Politics,* vol. 2, London: Routledge, 731.

11 R.N. Berki (1986) *Security and Society,* London: Dent, 5.

12 With obvious isolated exceptions such as the war in Kosovo.

13 The slipperiness of security is nicely illustrated by Davis's quote from the president of major US security firm Westec, who affirmed, 'We're not a security guard company. We sell a *concept* of security' (M. Davis (1998) *City of Quartz: Excavating the Future in Los*

Angeles, London: Pimlico, 250). See also H. Lisken (1994) ' "Sicherheit" durch "Kriminalitätsbekämpfung" ', *Zeitschrift für Rechtspolitik*, 2: 49–52.

14 Although the question as to which threats are subject to formal measuring may itself be the result of subjective judgements.

15 For a general discussion of research into fear of crime see C. Hale (1996) 'Fear of crime; a review of the literature', *International Review of Victimology*, 4: 79–150. On Germany, see W. Bilsky (1996) 'Diskussion – Die Bedeutung von Furcht vor Kriminalität in Ost und West', *Monatsschrift für Kriminologie und Strafrechtsreform*, 79: 357–72.

16 As A. Wolfers points out, in a rather different context, security connotes not only the objective absence of threats but also the subjective sense or absence of fear that acquired values will be attacked. A. Wolfers (1962) 'National security as an ambiguous signal', in A. Wolfers *Discord and Collaboration*, Baltimore: Johns Hopkins University Press, 150. See also J. Obergfell-Fuchs and H. Kury (1996) 'Sicherheitsgefühl und Persönlichkeit', *Monatsschrift für Kriminologie und Strafrechtsreform*, 79: 97–113.

17 C. Mirrlees-Black *et al.* (1996) *The 1996 British Crime Survey*, London: HMSO, 53.

18 J. Young, (1988) 'Risk of crime and fear of crime: a realist critique of survey-based assumptions', in M. Maguire and J. Pointing (eds) *Victims of Crime: A New Deal*, Milton Keynes: Open University Press.

19 For a revealing discussion of realist and other debates about fear of crime see R. Sparks (1992) *Television and the Drama of Crime*, Milton Keynes: Open University Press, 6–14.

20 See L. Zedner (1995) 'In pursuit of the vernacular: comparing law and order discourse in Britain and Germany', *Social and Legal Studies*, 4: 517–34.

21 L. Johnston (1996) 'What is vigilantism?', *British Journal of Criminology*, 36(2): 232.

22 M. Davis *City of Quartz*, 244.

23 N. Lacey and L. Zedner, 'Crime, social order and the appeal to community in Britain and Germany', ESRC project no. L210 25 2021. See also P.-A. Albrecht (1988) 'Das Strafrechet auf dem Weg vom liberalen Rechtsstaat zum sozialen Interventionsstaat', *KritV*: 182–209.

24 This faith has been severely challenged by the shock of unification and the expansion of the citizenry to include Eastern Germans who have good historical reasons to distrust the state and whose early optimism about the capacities of the Federal Republic to provide economic and personal prosperity proved short-lived.

25 For a discussion see L. Zedner, 'In pursuit of the vernacular', 520–21; also H. Kury (1992) *Opferfahrungen und Meinungen zur Inneren Sicherheit in Deutschland*, Wiebaden: Bundeskriminalamt; W.-D. Narr (1994) 'Das "System Innere Sicherheit" ', *Bürgerrechte und Polizei*, 48: 6–12.

26 Proposals to liberalise Germany's blood-based citizenship laws were attacked by the centre right CSU–CDU as a threat to the fundamental 'identity of the German nation'; 'German right fights citizenship plan', *Guardian*, 5 January 1999: 11. The president of Bavaria, Edmund Stoiber, described the threat to security as being greater than that posed by the Red Army Faction in the 1970s; 'Das Wohlfühlangebot', *Tageszeitung*, 11 January 1999: 12.

27 Proposals by the Metropolitan Police to replace police constables by private security guards have been described as 'turning back the clock 160 years. It was the failure of local patrols that led to the creation of the Metropolitan police in the first place'; 'Private guards may pound bobbies' beat', *Guardian*, 22 February 1999: 7.

28 D. Hay (1980) 'Crime in eighteenth- and nineteenth-century England', in N. Morris and M. Tonry (eds) *Crime and Justice*, vol. 2, 48.

29 K. Wrightson (1980) 'Two concepts of order: justices, constables and jurymen in seventeenth-century England', in J. Brewer and J. Styles (eds) *An Ungovernable People:*

The English and their Law in the Seventeenth and Eighteenth Centuries, London: Hutchinson, 24.

30 D. Downes and R. Morgan (1997) 'Dumping the "hostages to fortune"? The politics of law and order in post-war Britain' in M. Maguire *et al.* (eds) *The Oxford Handbook of Criminology*, Oxford: Oxford University Press, second edition, 92.

31 D. Garland (1996) 'The limits of the sovereign state: strategies of crime control in contemporary society', *British Journal of Criminology*, 36(4): 448.

32 D. Garland, 'The limits of the sovereign state', 449.

33 'Germans are staatsgläubig, they place their trust in government institutions and kow-tow to authority'; W. Glatzer *et al.* (1992) *Recent Social Trends in West Germany 1960–1990*, Frankfurt: Campus Verlag, 238.

34 Police chief Ian Blair observed of policing in Britain:

> The past fifty years have seen an accelerating loss of our share of the security market … This tide will continue. Within ten years it is possible that a substantial proportion of the police function may be absorbed by other local authorities and an unregulated private security sector.
>
> ('Off-beat solution', *Guardian* 17 July 1998: 20)

35 J. van Dijk (1991) 'More than a matter of security: trends in crime prevention in Europe', in F. Heidensohn and M. Farrell (eds) *Crime in Europe*, London: Routledge, 34.

36 P. Robert (1989) 'The privatisation of social control', in R. Hood (ed.) *Crime and Criminal Policy in Europe*, Oxford: Centre for Criminological Research, 104; D. Frehse, 'Zu den theoretischen Grundlage "Kommunaler Delinquenzprophylaxe"', *Kriminologische Journal*. 13: 64.

37 N. Lacey and L. Zedner (1998) 'Community in German criminal justice', *Socio-Legal Studies*, 7: 12.

38 A. Crawford (1997) *The Local Governance of Crime: Appeals to Community and Partnerships*, Oxford: Oxford University Press, chapter 2.

39 M. Brake and C. Hale (1992) *Public Order and Private Lives: The Politics of Law and Order*, London: Routledge, 11.

40 An interesting discussion of conservative interpretations of these developments can be found in P. Ireland (1995) 'Reflections on a rampage through the barriers of shame: law, community, and the new conservatism', *Journal of Law and Society*, 22(2): 206–7.

41 D. Garland, 'The limits of the sovereign state', 451–2.

42 A. Crawford (1997) *The Local Governance of Crime: Appeals to Community and Partnerships*, Oxford: Clarendon Press.

43 See H. Kury (ed.) (1997) *Konzepte Kommunaler Kriminalprävention*, Freiburg: Max Planck Institute.

44 L. Johnston (1996) 'What is vigilantism?', *British Journal of Criminology*, 36(2): 220–36.

45 L. Johnston, 'What is vigilantism?', 235.

46 D. Frehse (1998) 'Politische Funktionen Kommunaler Kriminalprävention', in H.-J. Albrecht *et al.* (eds) *Internationale Perspektiven in Kriminologie und Strafrecht*, vol. 1, Berlin: Duncker and Humblot, 757; N. Lacey and L. Zedner (1998) 'Community in German criminal justice' *Social and Legal Studies*, 7(1): 7–25.

47 See discussion in C. Messner and V. Ruggiero (1995) 'Germany: the penal system between past and future', in V. Ruggiero, M. Ryan and J. Sim (eds) *Western European Penal Systems: A Critical Anatomy*, London: Sage, 142–7.

48 I. Loader (1997) 'Thinking normatively about private security', *Journal of Law and Society*, 24(3): 383.

49 For a developed sociological analysis of the public–private dichotomy, see T. Jones and T. Newburn (1998) *Private Security and Public Policing*, Oxford: Oxford University Press, chapter 2.

50 Though note that Britain remains almost alone in Western Europe in failing to place the private security sector under statutory regulation; I. Loader, 'Thinking normatively about private security', 383.

51 N. Rose and P. Miller (1992) 'Political power beyond the state', *British Journal of Sociology*, 43(2): 176.

52 Police chief Ian Blair applauds police regulation of private security initiatives as 'a middle course between defending an indefensible monopoly over patrol, and the creeping unregulated privatisation of security in public places. This is the third way for the police service' ('Off-beat solution', *Guardian*, 17 July 1998: 20).

53 N. Lacey and L. Zedner, 'Community in German criminal justice'.

54 N. Lacey and L. Zedner (1995) 'Discourses of community in criminal justice', *Journal of Law and Society*, 22: 314. Crawford describes it as a 'decentring/recentring dialectic'; A. Crawford (1994) 'The partnership approach to community crime prevention: corporatism at the local level', *Social and Legal Studies*, 3: 497–518.

55 A. Crawford (1997) *The Local Governance of Crime: Appeals to Community and Partnerships*, Oxford: Oxford University Press.

56 Or indeed the suggestion by the Labour Home Secretary, Jack Straw, that individual citizens 'take on the criminals'. 'It is about all of us realising that we have a role to play in our everyday lives, in confronting the low-level disorder and disrespect that leads to more serious crime' ('Take on the criminals, Straw urges', *Guardian*, 19 February 1999: 6).

57 N. Lacey and L. Zedner, 'Community in German criminal justice', 15. The French have also regarded vigilantism with considerable suspicion; see P. Robert (1989) 'The privatisation of social control', in R. Hood (ed.) *Crime and Criminal Policy in Europe*, Oxford: Centre for Criminological Research, 111.

58 C. Messner and V. Ruggiero (1995) 'Germany: the penal system between past and future', in V. Ruggiero, M. Ryan and J. Sim (eds) *Western European Penal Systems: A Critical Anatomy*, London: Sage: 144–5.

59 U. Yanay (1994) 'Co-opting vigilantism: government response to community action for personal safety', *Journal of Public Policy*, 14(3): 383–96.

60 N. Christie (1994) *Crime Control as Industry*, London: Routledge, chapter 7; I. Loader (1999) 'Consumer culture and the commodification of policing and security', *Sociology*, 33: 373–92.

61 See the discussion in I. Loader (1997) 'Thinking normatively about private security', *Journal of Law and Society*, 24(3): 379–83.

62 For example, in the United States, business districts commonly pay for private patrols in order to make themselves more attractive to incoming investment.

63 L. Johnston (1992) *The Rebirth of Private Policing*, London: Routledge.

64 For a wider discussion of this phenomenon see A. Barron and C. Scott (1992) 'The Citizen's Charter programme', *Modern Law Review*, 55(4): 526–46.

65 D. Miller (1995) 'Citizenship and pluralism', *Political Studies*, 43: 443.

66 I. Loader, 'Thinking normatively about private security', 386. Given that insurance premiums, alarms, locks and the like are inherently commodified, the state should not seek to minimise the inequalities in distribution of protection that results.

67 M. Feeley and J. Simon (1992) 'The new penology: notes on the emerging strategy of corrections and its implications', *Criminology*, 30: 455.

68 J.W. Raine and M.J. Wilson (1993) *Managing Criminal Justice*, Hemel Hempstead: Harvester Wheatsheaf, though see also Raine and Wilson (1997) 'Beyond managerialism in criminal justice', *Howard Journal of Criminal Justice*, 36(1): 80–95.

69 N. Lacey (1994) 'Government as manager, citizen as consumer', *Modern Law Review*, 75: 534–54.

70 C. Jones (1993) 'Auditing criminal justice', *British Journal of Criminology*, 33: 187–202.

71 P. Robert, 'The privatization of social control', 111.

72 M. Feeley and J. Simon (1992) 'The new penology: notes on the emerging strategy of corrections and its implications', *Criminology*, 30: 467.

73 J. Young (1999) *The Exclusive Society*, London: Sage, chapter 1.

74 People of foreign descent commonly remain labelled as Ausländer however long they remain in the country, even into the second or third generation, and even if they gain formal citizenship; N. Lacey and L. Zedner, 'Community in German criminal justice', 19–21. See also M. Walter and M. Kubink (1993) 'Ausländerkriminalität – Phänomen oder Phantom der (Kriminal-) Politik?', *Monatsschrift für Kriminologie* 5: 306–19.

75 Franz Streng warns that *Nachbarschaftsbigotterie* (neighbourhood bigotry) is a necessary by-product of these strategies; F. Streng (1998) 'Wie weit trägt das broken windows-Paradigma?' in H-J. Albrecht *et al.* (eds) *Internationale Perspektiven in Kriminologie und Strafrecht*, vol. 2, Berlin: Duncker and Humblot, 937.

76 M. Davis, *City of Quartz*, 224.

77 Designed to alert potential intruders that armed security guards are contracted to protect the property; *ibid.*: 246–8.

78 A. Funk (1997) 'Ausgeschlossene und Bürger: Das ambivalente Verhältnis von Rechtsgleichheit und sozialen Ausschlus', *Kriminologisches Journal*, 4: 243–56; A. Scherr (1997) 'Sicherheitsbedürfnis, soziale Ausschliessung und Kriminalisierung', *Kriminologisches Journal*, 4: 256–66.

79 P. Ireland (1995) 'Reflections on a rampage through the barriers of shame: law, community, and the new conservatism', *Journal of Law and Society*, 22(2): 200; J. Young (1999) *The Exclusive Society*, London: Sage.

80 Professor Cornelius Nestler, University of Cologne, suggested to me that at a time when Germans are losing a clear sense of their cultural identity, fear of crime is an important point of commonality and cohesion.

11 SOME DAY OUR PRINCE WILL COME: ZERO-TOLERANCE POLICING AND LIBERAL GOVERNMENT

1 For debates about ZTP in the UK see Dennis (ed.) 1997; Crawford 1998; Hopkins Burke (ed.) 1998.; Leigh *et al.* (eds) 1998; Goldblatt and Lewis (eds) 1998; Johnston 1997.

12 WILLIAM HORTON'S LONG SHADOW: 'PUNITIVENESS' AND 'MANAGERIALISM' IN THE PENAL POLITICS OF MASSACHUSETTS, 1988–99

1 I would like to thank Katherine Beckett, Susan Silbey, Michael Tonry and Richard Sparks for advice on earlier drafts of the chapter. In addition, I gratefully acknowledge the support of the Ada Howe Kent fund, Middlebury College and the Center for Criminal Justice Policy Research at Northeastern University

2 Quotations are from the *Boston Globe*, 29 and 30 October. The House of Representatives' death penalty resolution differed from the Senate's in minor details so the two bills were sent to a joint conference committee for reconciliation. The differences were easily ironed out and the new 'joint' bill was returned to the two chambers for rubber-stamp approval. One week before the House was scheduled to take up the joint bill, however, the jury returned its 'guilty' verdict in the heavily publicised trial of au pair Louise Woodward for allegedly shaking to death a baby in her care. Many members of the press and public interpreted the Woodward verdict

as evidence of the justice system's fallibility and therefore of the possibility that the state, were it to adopt a death penalty law, might one day execute an innocent person. When the House of Representatives finally took up the joint death penalty bill, several members rose to the floor to draw this lesson from the Woodward trial. When one member announced that he had changed his mind and was prepared to vote against the joint bill, the death penalty died on the spot. For a full account, see Sasson 1998.

3   In this chapter, I focus narrowly on actions by the Massachusetts Legislature concerning the punishment of crime. I do not discuss 'responsibilisation strategies' aimed at dealing with crime in the community.

4   This chapter draws upon twenty in-depth interviews: twelve with law-makers, the rest with prosecutors, defence attorneys, legislative aides and others involved in shaping criminal justice policy-making in the 1990s.

5   Above-the-fold *Boston Herald* headlines in the weeks leading up to the vote included these: 'ENOUGH! Mom's murder, teen shooting latest shocks to the senses' (22 October); 'Date with Death' (23 October); 'Front Burner, Eager Lawmakers push for death penalty vote this week' (27 October). Later, following the refusal of the House of Representatives to enact the joint death penalty bill (see above, note 2), there was this: 'You'll Pay for This!' (8 November).

6   Interview with a member of the House of Representatives, October 1997.

7   As this excerpt illustrates, moreover, Feeley and Simon (1995) are largely correct in their contention that the public political rhetoric on crime is organised in the moralistic terms of 'old penology'. Notably, however, politicians' public pronouncements also occasionally foregrounded the issues of risk and dangerousness, thus blurring the lines between 'new' and 'old' penologies. This was especially the case with respect to discourse on the 'sex offender registry', an innovation that is as much about predicting and controlling future dangerousness in a 'high risk population' as it is about punishing offenders (on 'hybrid' discourses see Sparks, this volume; see also O'Malley 1992).

8   The state recorded roughly 150 homicides in 1990 but just 43 in 1997.

9   The case of Great Britain provides an interesting parallel. Downes and Morgan (1996) argue that law and order rhetoric in modern Great Britain originated in conservative efforts to discredit the tactics and aims of the militant labour movement.

10 This argument is developed in detail in Beckett 1997 and Beckett and Sasson 2000. Bottoms (1995) implies a similar interpretation when he argues that 'popular punitiveness' is less a reaction to public opinion than expression of a particular political project. Melossi (1993) offers an alternative (but kindred) interpretation: the crackdown on crime is part of a 'hegemonic strategy' to secure the domination of economic elites in a period of economic slow-down.

11 The ACLU has been a bogeyman of the political Right since the early 1960s, when it began litigating on behalf of civil liberties for criminal defendants and prisoners.

12 As noted in the Introduction, Horton's victim was the brother of Donna Cuomo, one of the state representatives who voted in favour of the death penalty in 1997.

13 Horton goes by the name William, not 'Willie'. The latter corruption is further evidence of the racist sub-text of the 'Willie Horton' saga. The quote 'a wonderful mix of liberalism' is from Karst, *Law's Promise, Law's Expression*.

14 Etched into a concrete sidewalk in the former governor's home town of Brookline is the phrase 'Dukakis Sucks' – a permanent reminder of those angry days.

15 This account is consistent with Savelsberg's (1992) theoretical argument concerning the inevitable substativisation of neo-classical initiatives that don't 'fit' modern society.

16 Being 'non-violent', for example, is one of the major bases for eligibility for intermediate sanctions.

17 For example, see the excerpt from the House Speaker's remarks on sentencing reform quoted further below. In everyday usage, 'violent offences' are treated not merely as violations of the moral or legal code that require retributive sanction (as in 'just deserts' theory, see essays in von Hirsch and Ashworth 1996, especially chapter 4) but also as indicators of future dangerousness. To the extent that 'new penology' emphasises the management of aggregates on the basis of actuarial assessments of dangerousness, 'violent offenders' is the most important group. In contrast, in the everyday policy and political discourse in Massachusetts, 'drug offenders' are treated as mostly 'non-violent' and hence less risky.

18 The term 'penal welfarism' refers to criminal justice practices that fit within the broader project of the welfare state. In the heyday of penal welfarism, from roughly the second decade of the twentieth century to the 1960s, these penal strategies emphasised rehabilitation as the central objective in punishment, and professional expertise as the bedrock for effective decision-making. For a thorough discussion, see Garland (1990).

19 Garland (1990), Feeley and Simon (1992) and Bottoms (1995) argue that managerialism is strictly a practitioners' discourse; that its concerns and rhetoric have yet to penetrate the public discourse. Although it is true that managerial concerns are less likely to capture newspaper headlines than calls for the death penalty, there is clearly a public discourse on managerial initiatives, including sentencing guidelines. Moreover, I argue in this chapter that managerialism has in fact become a political project for some penal reformers.

20 Most drug offences are currently governed by lengthy mandatory terms of incarceration. The proposed sentencing guidelines law would permit judges to choose between the statutory ('mandatory') penalties and the range of penalties specified in the new sentencing guidelines, the latter generally being less severe.

21 In this context it is significant that the Sentencing Commission ultimately established is comprised exclusively of lawyers (prosecutors, defence attorneys and judges) and administrators (the latter as non-voting members). Politicians were conspicuously excluded.

22 Doob (1995) argues that the US Sentencing Commission, while claiming agnosticism on the goals of sentencing, in practice used sentencing guidelines to pursue the utilitarian goals of incapacitation and deterrence thereby delivering on the demands of the US Congress for more punishment. In Massachusetts, sentencing guidelines were promoted with the opposite intentions in mind. Notably, in neither case was the neoclassical technology embraced for its ostensible purpose, namely to establish a system of 'just deserts' proportional retribution that is itself deaf to utilitarian appeals.

23 Struggles over issues such as these belie the notion that consensual 'bifurcation' (Bottoms 1995) – the practice of increasing penalties for more serious offenders while curtailing the same for less serious offenders – is at work in the Legislature.

24 Thus the story of Massachusetts sentencing guidelines will be told, perhaps, as yet another instalment in the saga of progressive initiatives co-opted. See Cohen (1985).

25 On restorative justice, see Beckett and Sasson (2000), chapter 10.

26 The punitive turn in Massachusetts penal policy was facilitated by the political defeat of Dukakis and subsequently much of the state's Democratic power structure. These political defeats were largely consequences of the politicisation of crime at the national level – thus we see the purposive nature of punitive rhetoric and its political and well as policy-specific rationality.

INDEX

INDEX

Haggerty, K. 3, 129, 134, 136, 139, 221, 258
Etzioni, A. 58
European Forum for Urban Safety 157, 158
Evans, K. *et al.* 53, 57, 60
Ewald, U. 167, 169, 183

Farrell, G. 18; *et al.* 18; and Pease, K. 254
Fattah, E. 166, 169, 171, 183, 186
fear of crime 219; analysis of 27–8; creating 21–4; as cultural preoccupation 1, 3; debates concerning 1–2; defined 33–4; empirical findings from Eastern Germany 173–5; experiences of 2; female 33, 44–6; in Germany 166–71, 190–4; ideological aspect 193; interpretation of 24; Italian research on 151–3; and lifestyle/victimisation 18–21, 24–7; location of 2–3; male 46–7; and mediaphobia 107–9; and middle class life *see* Prestbury; origins of 13–14; paradox of 176; as political discourse 1, 3, 22; private/public aspects 4; as proxy for social disadvantage 23; public responses to 4–6; questionable concepts 169–71; social meaning of 176–7; themes 8–9; theoretical confusion concerning 23–4; *see also* risk–fear of crime
Feeley, M. and Simon, J. 15, 122, 129, 131, 132–4, 168, 239, 240, 243, 248, 261, 265, 267
Felson, M. 89, 90, 98, 255
Ferracuti, F. 147
Ferraro, K.F. 166, 174, 252
Field, S. 90; and Hope, T. 88, 97, 100
Fitzgerald, M. and Hale, C. 21, 22
Foster, J. and Hope, T. 95
Foucault, M. 3, 192, 226, 258–9, 261
Franklin, J. 168
Fraser, P. 50
Freedman, L. 261
Frehse, D. 263
Fukuyama, F. 55
Funk, A. 265
Funtowicz, S. and Ravetz, J. 259

Garland, D. 3, 13, 25, 78, 83, 84, 86, 122, 129, 134–5, 138, 139, 141, 148, 149, 204, 205, 222, 233, 239, 240, 243, 249, 254, 258, 259, 261, 262, 263, 267
Gellner, E. 55
Genn, H. 51
Gensicke, T. 186
Gerbner, G. 257
Germany: empirical findings from Eastern sector 171–7; fear of crime/risk perception in 166–71, 190–4; individual behaviour/social control in 166–71, 190–4; victimological perspective in 177–90
Giddens, A. 2, 26, 51, 55, 62, 77, 84, 129, 135, 139, 168, 180, 181, 190, 194, 228, 255, 258
Girling, E. *et al.* 252, 253
Giuliani, R. 220, 227
Goldblatt, P. and Lewis, C. 265
Gordon, C. 224, 225
Gordon, M. and Riger, S. 21
Gottfredson, M.J. 20–1; and Hirschi, T. 255
Granovetter, M.S. 99
Gray, J. 140
Green, P. 149
Greenwood, P. and Abrahamse, A. 131; *et al.* 259
Greve, W. *et al.* 169
Griffiths, W. 217
Guardian Angels 206

Habich, R. *et al.* 170
Hacking, I. 259
Haeder, M. 183
Hale, C. 21, 23–4, 66, 90, 169, 252, 257, 261
Hall, S. *et al.* 135, 138, 257
Hanmer, J. and Saunders, S. 253
Hargreaves Heap, S. *et al.* 254
Hawkesworth, M. and Kogan, M. 261
Hay, C. 141
Hay, D. 262
Hay, W. 140
Hebberecht, P. and Sack, F. 156
Heidensohn, F. and Farrell, M. 263
Heitmeyer, W. 166
Hindelang, M. *et al.* 18–19
Hirsch, F. 98
Hirschfield, A. and Bowers, K.J. 257
Hobbes, Thomas 217–18
Hoffmeyer-Slotnik, J.H.P. 187

270